INTRODUCTION
TO
REVENUE LAW

AUSTRALIA
The Law Book Company Ltd.
Sydney : Melbourne : Brisbane

CANADA AND U.S.A.
The Carswell Company Ltd.
Agincourt, Ontario

INDIA
N.M. Tripathi Private Ltd.
Bombay
and
Eastern Law House Private Ltd.
Calcutta

M.P.P. House
Bangalore

ISRAEL
Steimatzky's Agency Ltd.
Jerusalem : Tel Aviv : Haifa

MALAYSIA : SINGAPORE : BRUNEI
Malayan Law Journal (Pte.) Ltd.
Singapore

NEW ZEALAND
Sweet & Maxwell (N.Z.) Ltd.
Auckland

PAKISTAN
Pakistan Law House
Karachi

INTRODUCTION
TO
REVENUE LAW

by

F. R. DAVIES, M.A.

of Gray's Inn, Barrister
Senior Lecturer in Law, Brunel University

LONDON
SWEET & MAXWELL
1980

Published in 1980 by
Sweet & Maxwell Limited of
11 New Fetter Lane, London
Computerset by
MFK Graphic Systems (Typesetting) Ltd., Saffron Walden, Essex
Printed in Great Britain by
Page Bros. (Norwich) Ltd.

British Library Cataloguing in Publication Data

Davies, Francis Ronald
  Introduction to revenue law
  1. Taxation – Law and legislation – Great
Britain
  I. Title
  343′.41′04   KD5359

  ISBN 0-421-25120-4
  ISBN 0-421-25130-1 Pbk

©
F. R. Davies

FOR MARGARET AGAIN

PREFACE

This book is in one sense a very ambitious project; I embarked on it with the ambition to prove that Aristotle was wrong when he said: "It is not possible to state simply that which in itself is not simple."

Well, of course, Aristotle is right and the trick cannot be done. But something can be done. As George Orwell nearly said: "All writers on revenue law are equal in obscurity, but some are more equal than others." I aim to be less equal. This book tries to take the mystique out of revenue law. It aims to provide a more relaxed exposition of the subject than is elsewhere available. Above all, the book aims to take the fear out of revenue law. Some people have a sort of mental or emotional blockage about tax. When I left the Bar and went into the Civil Service I was horrified to find myself posted to the Inland Revenue Solicitor's Office. But it turned out to be quite painless. I stayed there for 12 years. Then I went into university teaching.

What this book cannot do is to take the slog out of revenue law. It is not an easy subject: in fact it is mighty difficult. A good book helps; a good teacher helps; discussion with fellow-students helps; but what really counts is the *thinking* that you do "in the silence of your lonely room."

The book has very few footnotes. The point of this is to try to maintain (so far as the subject-matter allows) a narrative flow. In particular there are no footnotes for the citation of cases. After each case mentioned in the text there is the date of the case and, if it was decided in a court higher than the High Court, an abbreviation showing *what* court; "C.A." for Court of Appeal, "H.L." for House of Lords. A full citation for each case is given in the Table of Cases at the front of the book.

Writing a book on revenue law is like trying to take a photograph of a restless child—the blighter won't stand still for more than a moment. The moment I have tried to catch is September 30, 1979.

F.R.D.

CONTENTS

PART FIVE CAPITAL TRANSFER TAX

PART SIX DEVELOPMENT LAND TAX

PART SEVEN STAMP DUTIES

TABLE OF CASES

TABLE OF STATUTES

xv

PART ONE

INTRODUCTORY

CHAPTER 1

HOW TAX TICKS

The question "What is a tax?" is surprisingly difficult to answer. Even the well-known reply of the man who was asked to define an elephant does not work very well here. He said, "I can't define an elephant, but I know one when I see one." There are some imposts of which I would have to say "I'm not sure whether it is a tax or not." This would be so of, for example, national insurance contributions.

So, as the elephant man's approach does not seem to work, we had better try to define a tax. A tax has three characteristics. It is (1) a compulsory levy, (2) imposed by an organ of government, (3) for public purposes.

Next, we can make a list of many, many imposts which are, beyond doubt, taxes. It would be tedious to make a complete list of *all* the taxes in force in the United Kingdom at the present time, but here is a list of the principal taxes: income tax, capital gains tax, corporation tax, capital transfer tax, stamp duty, value added tax, development land tax, petroleum revenue tax, car tax, customs and excise duties. And I think one would have to say that the general rate is a tax. The so-called water rate is probably not a tax.

The two main government departments which administer taxes are the Inland Revenue and Customs and Excise. In this book we shall be dealing with six taxes: income tax, capital gains tax, corporation tax, capital transfer tax, development land tax, and stamp duties. All these taxes (and some others) are administered by the Inland Revenue. It is traditional to say that the Inland Revenue deals with direct taxes, and that indirect taxes are dealt with by other government departments. The distinction is said to be that a direct tax is a tax which is not passed on by the taxpayer, whereas an indirect tax is a tax which is passed on by the payer of the tax. This is only a formal distinction, concentrating on who hands over the cash to the tax authorities. If one looks behind this to see who really bears the burden of the tax, the distinction between direct and indirect taxes becomes blurred. For example, VAT is generally spoken of as being an indirect tax, but it seems pretty direct to the consumer who pays a bill for "£x plus VAT."

Let us look now at the tax system in the United Kingdom from the point of view of purposes, justice, efficiency and effects.

The primary purpose of taxation is to raise revenue for government expenditure. The government could raise revenue by borrowing or by "printing" money, but it is generally thought desirable that the bulk of the government's requirements should be raised by taxation. The government expends money partly on services which private enterprise cannot provide, such as defence and law and order and social security benefits, and partly on services which could be provided privately, such as education and health services. Attitudes to taxation depend to some extent on the views of taxpayers as to the merits of these items of government expenditure.

A possible purpose of taxation is to redistribute wealth. Certain aspects of this idea are generally agreed. Thus it is generally agreed that income tax should be "progressive," and that some of the government's revenue should be spent on social services. In this connection a new phrase has recently come into existence—"the social wage." Of course, in both these aspects the question of rate and amount is of immense importance. *How* progressive should income tax be? *How much* should be spent on social services?

A much more controversial view is that taxation should actually confiscate wealth. Thus the Labour Party is more or less committed to introducing a wealth tax. If this were imposed on top of the existing top rates of income tax on investment income it would impose on the rich taxation at more than 100 per cent. of income. That is the point at which confiscation begins.

Another possible purpose of the tax system is to control the economy. Changes in taxation can and do affect the economy, but control is probably more easily exercised by adjusting the money supply and credit.

It is possible, finally, to use taxation as a kind of moral control. We see this idea toyed with in connection with the taxing of alcohol and tobacco.

Let us look now at the tax system from the point of view of justice. The current thinking on this matter concentrates on "equity," which (I take it) means fairness. "Horizontal equity" is the idea that people in equal circumstances should pay an equal amount of tax. "Vertical equity" means that people in different circumstances should pay a different amount of tax. Horizontal equity commands almost universal support. Vertical equity is much more controversial. It is generally agreed that the richer should pay more tax than the poorer. But how much more? And on what principle? Even with a proportional tax the richer do pay more than the poorer. If there were an income tax at a flat rate of 50 per cent., a man with an income of £10,000 would pay £5,000 in tax, which is more than the £500 which a man with an income of £1,000 would pay. But it is fairly widely accepted[1] that that would not be equitable, and that the man with £10,000 should pay more tax than the man with £1,000, not merely absolutely but also proportionately. This is where a "progressive" tax comes in. Instead of paying at 50 per cent., the man with £10,000 income should pay (at least on part of his income) at 60 per cent., or 70 or 80 or 90. Again the "details" become as important as the principle. Precisely what percentage? And on precisely what part or parts of his income?

Inflation has played havoc with the justice of the tax system. This is particularly marked in the capital gains tax, but it is also true in very many aspects of the income tax. To take but one example, a taxpayer who invests £100 with a building society receives interest of, say, £8 a year, which is equivalent (when grossed-up at the basic rate) to about £11.50. If inflation is running at 15 per cent. he has in truth received a negative return on his investment of £3.50. But he is taxed on an "income" of £11.50.

Inflation is bad for taxpayers, but in a sense it is good for governments, because it leads to what is called "fiscal drag." This means the built-in tendency for the Revenue to get a bigger and bigger take, as a proportion of total personal income. This affects income tax particularly. Tax brackets are fixed in terms of money incomes. In an inflationary period money incomes rise (without any rise in real terms) and more and more people pass over the tax threshold and into higher tax rate brackets.

An important aspect of the justice or otherwise of the tax system is the "tax base." This means the precise boundary of what is taxed as distinct from what is not taxed. Let us take an example. Mr. Smith has £30,000 in hand. He spends it on buying a house in which he proceeds to live happily ever after, paying no rent. Mr. Brown has £30,000 in hand. He spends it on buying ordinary shares. He lives in a rented house. Mr. Smith pays no tax on the use he has made of his £30,000 (the occupation of his house). Mr. Brown does pay tax on the use he has made of his £30,000 (the dividends). Is this fair?

The tax base is intimately bound up with the rates of tax. If the tax base is widened the rates of tax can be reduced—and vice versa.

Another aspect of justice is certainty. The tax system should be certain. This involves two things. First, the tax law should be clear, so that a taxpayer can see in advance how much tax he will have to pay. Secondly, enforcement should be complete and universal. There is nothing more destructive of taxpayer morality than the suspicion that others are "getting away with it."

---

[1] See an article by Alan Lewis entitled "Perceptions of Tax Rates" in [1978] B.T.R. at p. 358.

The efficiency of the tax system is partly a matter of success in enforcement, and partly a matter of the cost. Enforcement, in the case of income tax, is not showing a very high success rate. There is growing up what is called the "black economy," meaning "moon-lighting" and other forms of tax evasion. In March 1979 the Chairman of the Board of Inland Revenue, giving evidence to a House of Commons sub-committee, said that the Revenue thought that un-declared income might amount to as much as $7\frac{1}{2}$ per cent. of the gross domestic product, about £10 billion a year.

As regards cost, in 1977–78 the cost of collecting the Inland Revenue taxes was 1.94 per cent. of the total net yield, and the cost of collecting the Customs and Excise duties was 1.63 per cent. But, of course, these figures deal only with the direct government costs. There are also hidden "compliance" costs, that is the costs incurred by taxpayers. Two notable examples of these compliance costs are the costs of an employer in terms of man-hours in acting as an unpaid collector of income tax for the Revenue under the P.A.Y.E. system, and the costs of a trader in complying with the VAT system.[2] And both may incur substantial costs for professional assistance and advice in connection with tax affairs. True, the cost of this assistance and advice is in practice deductible as an expense. But there is a point here which is not always kept clearly in mind: if tax is at say 60 per cent. and the taxpayer pays out £100 on professional assistance, the tax relief is £60, leaving £40 unrelieved which the taxpayer really does pay out of his own pocket.

There is also an even more deeply hidden cost, a kind of social cost, which the community as a whole pays as part of the price of taxation. What I have in mind is the expenditure (one might almost say waste) of brain-power. Some of the best brains in the country are exclusively devoted to tax matters; some on the Revenue side, some "against" the Revenue. This brain-power could be better employed in increasing the wealth, health or happiness of the community. This brain-drain is very closely linked to the immensity of the rates of tax. If income tax had a maximum rate of say 10 per cent. much less time and effort would be devoted to escaping the tax. With the rates of tax as high as they are, a great deal of effort goes into the endeavour to escape tax.

As regards the effects of taxation, I am afraid that in this area it is easier to ask questions than to answer them. Does a high rate of

---

[2] On the other hand, because of the time-lag between the employer's deducting income tax from his employees' wages (or the trader's collecting VAT from his customers) and his paying over the tax to the tax authorities, he does get a "cash-flow" benefit.

income tax encourage people to work harder or does it discourage them? Most people would say that it discourages them, that it is a "disincentive." But it is quite possible to argue that, on the contrary, it spurs people on to earn more, so that even when the tax-man has taken his cut they will have enough left to live on. Does a high rate of tax on businesses raise prices? Does a high rate of tax on individuals raise wages and salaries? No one seems to know the answers. It is probable that a high *average* rate of tax is an incentive to work, whereas high *marginal* rates are a disincentive.[3]

"Neutrality" is a principle of taxation much talked about. The modern doctrine of neutrality seems to mean, not that taxation should never distort the play of economic forces, but merely that it should not do so accidentally, only deliberately.

There is one point which it is very important to make at the outset of such a book as this, namely the distinction between "tax avoidance" and "tax evasion." Tax avoidance is so arranging one's affairs as to incur the smallest tax bill that is possible. This is perfectly lawful. Tax evasion is the escaping of tax by unlawful means. This usually involves some form of dishonesty, ranging from omitting to state some item of income in a tax return to forging a document so as to create untrue "facts." It is fairly easy to see (and keep to) the distinction between evasion and avoidance if one holds on to the idea that evasion involves some crime whereas avoidance involves no crime. But two factors tend to blur the distinction in practice. First, some quite honest and honourable people think that a tax crime is not really a crime at all. This is so for example of concealing at Dover a bottle or two of wine bought in Calais, or of omitting to mention in a tax return some jobbing gardening or book-reviewing done at weekends. We tend to think that what we do ourselves is not really criminal at all, but what others do is bigger and badder. The second factor is that crime versus no-crime is not the last word on the subject. Elaborate schemes of tax avoidance which have no other purpose may not be criminal, but they are distasteful to many taxpayers and to some judges.

Some taxes are more easily avoided than others. For example, income tax is more easily avoided than VAT. It is partly for this reason that the Conservative government made a big switch from income tax to VAT in the Finance (No. 2) Act 1979. Indeed an Expenditure Tax as such is strongly advocated in some quarters. The

---

[3] If X has an earned income of £100 and income tax begins at £50 and is at the rate of 30 per cent., X will pay £15 in tax. His average rate of tax is 15 per cent.; it is his whole tax bill viewed as a proportion of his whole income. His marginal rate of tax is 30 per cent., meaning that on every extra £ that he earns the rate will be 30 per cent.

merits of this are said to be that it would be less easily avoided or evaded, it would encourage saving, and it would be cheaper to administer. (Remember that the cost of collecting Customs and Excise duties is less than the cost of collecting Inland Revenue taxes.) But on the other hand it flies in the face of the progressive principle. An expenditure tax would hit the poor harder than it would hit the rich. So there are two strong ideas for the "reform" of taxation current at this time which are in direct conflict with each other—the idea of an expenditure tax and the idea of a wealth tax.[4]

Britain's entry into the European Economic Community limited the powers of the British parliament and government in respect of taxation. Certain articles of the Treaty of Rome prohibit rules of tax which would discriminate against persons in other Member States. Another article provides for Member States to work towards tax harmonisation. This movement has progressed furthest in the field of VAT. The Finance Act 1977, by section 14 and Schedule 6, enacts into United Kingdom law a uniform code for VAT. The EEC raises revenue by taking a share of certain taxes of the Member States. Section 77 of the Finance Act 1978 authorises the disclosure of information by Inland Revenue officers to the tax authorities in other Member States in accordance with the Council's Directive dated December 19, 1977, Dir. 77/799/EEC.

I want to end this chapter by referring again to the six taxes dealt with in this book. I want to try to state in a very few words what it is that each tax is taxing.

First, income tax. In a famous aphorism in *London County Council* v. *Attorney-General* (1901) (H.L.) Lord Macnaghten said: "Income tax, if I may be pardoned for saying so, is a tax on income." This is largely, but not absolutely, true. There are some items of income which are not taxed; for example, student grants. So income tax is not a tax on all income. On the other hand, there are some charges to income tax which are imposed on receipts which are not income receipts, but rather capital receipts. This is so, for example, of the taxing of premiums received on the leasing of land.

Second, capital gains tax. What is taxed here is the gain represented

---

[4] But see the Meade Committee Report (which is discussed at p. 17 below). The full name of this report is *The Structure and Reform of Direct Taxation*. The particular form of expenditure tax which the committee favours is a system of levying tax on *all income less all saving*. This system avoids the defect of a purchase tax type of tax in that it can be made as progressive as one likes. On the other hand it would have the same defects as an income tax, particularly as regards the scope for avoidance and evasion.

by the difference between the price at which an item was acquired and the price at which it is disposed of.

Third, corporation tax. This is simply the equivalent for companies of the taxing of individuals by income tax and capital gains tax.

Fourth, capital transfer tax. This taxes capital when, and to the extent that, it is transferred. A witty commentator has said: "If it moves, tax it." That is a neat summary, but it is not absolutely true. Sometimes capital can move without being taxed and sometimes capital can be taxed without moving.

(Of course, if a wealth tax came in that would tax capital without waiting for it to move; it would tax it while it was standing still.)

Fifth, development land tax. This taxes the "realised development value" which accrues as a consequence of the grant of planning permission to a land owner.

Sixth, stamp duties. These are taxes imposed upon certain specified documents, notably transfers of land (including houses and other buildings) and transfers of shares.

CHAPTER 2

PRACTISING TAX

As I pointed out in Chapter 1, an enormous amount of manpower and brain-power is devoted to tax matters. One could almost speak of there being a "tax industry." On the one hand, there is the Inland Revenue; on the other hand is the tax Bar, solicitors, accountants, and tax consultants.

First then, the Inland Revenue. This is headed by a small body of higher civil servants, called formally the Commissioners of Inland Revenue (less formally "the Board") of whom one is chairman with the rank of Permanent Secretary. The Commissioners are subject to the control of the Treasury, so the ultimate political head is the Chancellor of the Exchequer. In practice the Commissioners have considerable independence from the Treasury, whose directions are confined to matters of policy. The headquarters of the Inland Revenue (which I shall call from now on just "the Revenue") is at Somerset House, in the Strand. This is surely one of the most beautiful buildings in London. In Nelson's day, it housed the Admiralty. The room where Nelson worked is (not surprisingly) called "the Nelson Room." There is a contrivance there that shows which way the wind is blowing at Dover.[1] The Commissioners of Inland Revenue are referred to by the abbreviation C.I.R. or, more conveniently for indexing cases, I.R.C. The Commissioners are assisted by a substantial number of administrators. They receive specialist advice and assistance from valuers under the Chief Valuer and from lawyers under the Solicitor of Inland Revenue. In the Solicitor's Office there are some 50 or 60 qualified lawyers (barristers or solicitors without distinction) and two chartered accountants. The accountants advise the Board (and the lawyers) on accountancy matters and also appear as expert witnesses in tax cases when such matters arise.

The Inland Revenue is responsible for the care and management of income tax, corporation tax, capital gains tax, capital transfer tax,

---

[1] Since writing the above I have come across an official Revenue publication called *A Short History of Somerset House*, in which it is stated:

"... there is a legend that Nelson worked here for a time. It is almost certain that there is no foundation for this story although his elder brother Maurice was employed here. There is still a conference room known as the 'Nelson Room'; a graceful apartment which has a copy of the Probate of Nelson's will framed on the wall."

During the 12 years I worked in Somerset House I never heard anyone doubt the Nelson story. Why should a room be called after *Maurice* Nelson?

stamp duty, petroleum revenue tax and development land tax. The Department is also responsible for valuation for rating.

Under the control of the Board there are a large number of Inspectors, formally Her Majesty's Inspectors of Taxes. The whole United Kingdom is divided into "tax districts," and each district is headed by a District Inspector, who is assisted by other Inspectors and supporting staff. Inspectors obtain returns and other information, make assessments, negotiate settlements, appear at appeal hearings and generally conduct matters until the amount of tax due from any particular taxpayer is agreed or determined.

Spread over the whole country also are a large number of Collectors of Taxes, who actually get in the tax when it has been finalised.

If a taxpayer appeals against an assessment his appeal is heard by one or other of two bodies of appeal commissioners, namely the General Commissioners and the Special Commissioners. Some matters can only be heard by the generals, some matters can only be heard by the specials, and in some matters the taxpayer can elect which body to go to. The General Commissioners are laymen and unpaid. The Special Commissioners are professionals and are full-time, paid, civil servants. At the present time there are seven Special Commissioners. Four of them have been drawn from outside the Revenue; three from the Bar and one (the only woman Special Commissioner) from private practice as a solicitor. Three of them have been drawn from the Revenue; two were formerly in the Office of the Solicitor of Inland Revenue and one was an administrator. The Special Commissioners regard themselves as entirely independent of the Board of Inland Revenue.

In Northern Ireland there are no General Commissioners. Their functions are performed by the Special Commissioners or county court judges.

It is important to be clear that *the* Commissioners of Inland Revenue are "the Board," and are distinct from the "appeal commissioners," that is the Special Commissioners and the General Commissioners.

So much for the Revenue. Now let us see who, outside the Revenue, are, so to speak, engaged in the tax industry.

First, there is the "tax Bar," or the "Revenue Bar." That means those members of the Bar (barristers) who specialise in tax matters. These barristers are for the most part banded together in sets of chambers all the members of which so specialise. But this is not entirely true; there are some more general chancery barristers who have acquainted themselves with tax law in relation to their practice in trusts, say, or company law.

Amongst solicitors the situation is similar, but not identical. There

B

are very few firms which specialise exclusively in tax matters, but quite a number in which one or more partners so specialise. Solicitors were very slow to grasp the huge potentiality of tax work, but the importance of tax is now widely appreciated throughout the profession.

Much earlier into the field of tax were accountants. In recent years they have perhaps lost some of the jam to the lawyers, but they still enjoy the bread and (liberally spread) butter. After all, virtually all businesses, and quite a number of individuals, employ accountants to help them in their dealings with the Revenue.

There are now a substantial number of tax consultants. Many of them are barristers, solicitors or accountants, but they are not functioning as such. They are there to be consulted by reluctant taxpayers, and they offer advice and sometimes packaged tax-avoidance schemes.

There is a kind of running battle between the Revenue and the forces outside. When the outside forces get through a gap in the Revenue's defences, the breach is closed up by legislation in the next Finance Act. Someone then finds a way round, and the next Finance Act then extends the defences. Sometimes the government decides to legislate retrospectively, that is, to render ineffective for tax avoidance some course of action which at the time it was carried out did avoid tax successfully. Section 31 of the Finance Act 1978 denies loss relief in certain circumstances in respect of dealings in commodity futures. This measure was introduced to counter avoidance schemes which had been entered into on a very large scale in the previous two years. The Finance Bill back-dated the denial of relief to April 6, 1976, which was the date when the schemes had first been launched. At the Report stage in the House of Commons the Liberals with the support of the Ulster Unionists proposed an amendment that the provision should only take effect from April 11, 1978, which was the date when it had been announced in the budget. The Conservatives proposed a compromise amendment to have some back-dating but to limit it to November 25, 1977, which was the date when Treasury ministers first warned that legislation might be introduced. In the event both amendments were lost and the clause stood. It became section 31 of the Finance Act 1978, and that section applies to any scheme effected on or after April 6, 1976.

It is worth giving a brief account of how the commodity futures tax avoidance scheme worked. Suppose Mr. A was expecting to make huge profits in his principal business. He enters into a partnership (for a fee) with B Limited, a company dealing in commodity futures. "Commodity futures" are rights to buy (or sell) at a fixed time in the future a quantity of a commodity (*e.g.* cocoa) at a price fixed now.

These rights can be sold before the fixed time arrives. The partnership I am describing deals in futures. It can balance against a right to buy in the future a right to sell. Thus if the market goes up they will gain on one contract and lose on the other; if it goes down, vice versa. The gains and losses may occur at different times. At a point in time when the partnership has suffered a big loss, say on a contract to sell, Mr. A withdraws from the partnership. Mr. A can then claim to set his share of the loss against the profits of his principal business. Despite his loss, Mr. A can sell his share in the partnership without loss or with only a small loss, because the partnership is holding futures buying contracts which stand to yield a big profit and so Mr. A's share in the partnership remains valuable. The upshot is that Mr. A has a large loss for tax purposes, but only a much smaller loss in reality.

Let us use this commodity futures scheme to illustrate how the tax consultancy industry operates. You are, or your company is, about to make huge profits. You want to avoid some tax. You go to a consultancy and they offer to sell you an avoidance scheme. They will not tell you what the scheme is until you have bought it and they will not give you any guarantee. Also they will make you undertake not to disclose to other people how the scheme works. They will ask you how much tax you want to save or what amount of profit you desire should escape tax. They will charge you a substantial fee for the scheme. In the case of clients who are individuals the fee is usually a percentage (often 10 per cent.) of the expected tax saving. In the case of clients who are companies the fee is usually a percentage (often 8 per cent.) of the amount of profits which it is expected will escape tax. (The latter is, of course, a much higher fee than the former.) You are willing to buy the scheme on these terms because other businessmen have told you that this consultancy has saved them vast sums in tax. You hand over your money and buy the package containing the scheme.

The commodity futures scheme has effectively been knocked out by section 31 of the Finance Act 1978. That section may have an importance reaching far beyond commodity futures. It may (but it is too early yet to say) herald the end of this type of consultancy business. (Most tax consultancies offer other services as well as selling packaged schemes.) Section 31 is by far the most clear-cut instance yet of retrospective legislation against an avoidance scheme. Potential purchasers of any new scheme that comes along may feel that the risk of new retrospective legislation is so great that they will not buy it.

Of course there are very substantial arguments against retrospective legislation. This is widely accepted in the field of criminal law. To declare some act to be a crime which at the time it was done was not a crime outrages one's sense of justice and fair play. Some people, but (I think) much fewer people, feel the same about retrospective legislation against tax avoidance. Others feel that the social evil of utterly non-productive tax avoidance schemes is so great that stamping them out justifies a departure from the general principle of "no retrospection."

I want to end this chapter on a rather different note. Although there is a running battle between the Revenue and the tax forces outside, it would be incorrect to think of all these forces as being engaged all the time in warfare against the Revenue. Some of their work is collaborative with the Revenue. In the case of accountants, the *bulk* of their work is collaborative; indeed the tax system could hardly work at all without the accountancy profession.

CHAPTER 3

LEARNING THE TAX LAW

Let me emphasise at the outset of this chapter that I am writing about learning tax *law*, not learning tax. There are many aspects of tax (or taxation); there is the economic aspect, the accountancy aspect, the political aspect, the social aspect. I am dealing with the legal aspect.

The most difficult thing for lawyers and law students in approaching the study of tax law is to believe the unbelievable, namely that tax law is law, just as much as is, say, commercial law. The most difficult thing for non-lawyers is to become familiar with the way lawyers think. For them not a bad way to start would be to read *Learning the Law* by Glanville Williams.

The two leading students' textbooks are *Pinson on Revenue Law* (published by Sweet and Maxwell) and Tiley's *Revenue Law* (published by Butterworths). Both books deal with income tax, capital gains tax, development land tax, corporation tax and capital transfer tax. Pinson (but not Tiley) also deals with stamp duty and value added tax. There are students' books on particular taxes. There is a booklet issued by the College of Law called *Capital Transfer Tax and Development Land Tax*. I would also mention Hayton and Tiley's *Elements of Capital Transfer Tax* (published by Butterworths) and Coombes on *Capital Transfer Tax* (published by Professional Books). Both these books are intended for practitioners as well as for students. Hayton and Tiley's first edition was said to be for students first and practitioners second; the second edition reverses the order. Certainly, the distinction between students' books and practitioners' books is not clear-cut in tax law.

There are several major encyclopedias of tax law, each of which incorporates in effect one or more textbooks which a student could well consult with advantage. These include: the *British Tax Encyclopedia*, *Simon's Taxes*, the *Encyclopedia of Capital Taxation*, and the *Capital Taxes Encyclopaedia*.

The leading "learned journal" on tax law is the *British Tax Review*, which has the remarkable ability to be humorous as well as learned.

Statutes, of course, play an enormously important part in tax law, and as a great deal of tax legislation is made by amending existing statutes, it is very difficult to be sure how the legislation in force stands at a given moment. There are two very helpful publications which will tell you. These are *Butterworth's Yellow Tax Handbook* and *Butterworth's Orange Tax Handbook*. The *Yellow Book*, published every year, sets out the legislation in force on income tax, corporation tax and capital gains tax. The *Orange Book* does the same for capital transfer tax, development land tax, stamp duty and value added tax. Each book sets out the relevant enactments *as amended*. A companion volume called Rowland's *Tax Guide* is also very useful.

Another very helpful book is Potter and Monroe, *Tax Planning with Precedents* (published by Sweet and Maxwell). As is clear from the title, it is written from the point of view of tax planning and it is addressed to practitioners. But it contains a discussion of general principles as they apply to particular situations. There is much to be learned from it.

There is one publication which is *sui generis*. This is Simon's Weekly Tax Service. This is in two parts; Simon's Tax Intelligence and Simon's Tax Cases.

Reports of decided cases in the field of tax law sometimes appear in the actual Law Reports and/or the Weekly Law Reports and/or the All England Law Reports. But such appearances are rare. Most tax cases which get reported at all only appear in one or more of the specialised series dealing with tax. Simon's Tax Cases has already been mentioned. Another important series is Tax Cases. These reports are issued by the Revenue. A case is not reported here until the last appeal is over, so if a case goes to the House of Lords it may be several years after the case started that it appears in Tax Cases. In the meantime the Revenue issue Tax Leaflets dealing with each court hearing.

There is a collection of tax cases in Volume 28 of the English and Empire Digest. The volume is also sold separately under the title *Butterworth's Digest of Tax Cases*. There is a much cheaper collection of cases called *Tolley's Tax Cases*.

There is also a case book for tax law, similar to case books for other branches of law. This is *Cases and Materials in Revenue Law* by A. J. Easson.

In the titles of tax cases the Revenue side either appears as "Commissioners of Inland Revenue" or under the name of the relevant H.M. Inspector of Taxes. So one perk available to an Inspector is that he may get his name enshrined for ever in the law reports.

Statutes and decided cases are the two sources of tax law, but tax practice rests also on Revenue concessions. These arise where the strict law seems particularly unfair or where it creates serious administrative problems. In such circumstances the Revenue may by concession not enforce the full letter of the law. Some of these concessions are published by the Revenue in a booklet of "Extra-Statutory Concessions" ("IR1"). Others are published as answers to Parliamentary Questions. Others again are not published at all, except to some extent on the grapevine. Though in a sense taxpayers should be grateful for concessions, the Revenue practice of making concessions tends to perpetuate bad law. As Walton J. neatly put it in *Vestey* v. *I.R.C.* (1978): "One should be taxed by law, and not be untaxed by concession."

Quite apart from Revenue concessions are what one might call Revenue views. Sometimes the Revenue will publish their official view on a particular point of law in the form of a press statement. Sometimes again a Revenue official will write an open letter to a professional body expressing the official view on a specific question. Since July 1978 the Revenue have been re-issuing these materials in comprehensive "Statements of Practice." The Revenue's views can also be gleaned from the booklets and leaflets which they publish for the information of taxpayers. Some of these booklets and leaflets are extremely helpful and can really serve as, or instead of, a textbook. I would give as an example "CGT 8," entitled "Capital Gains Tax."

The Revenue also publish an annual report and an annual book of statistics.

A book of a wholly different character from any mentioned above is the Meade Committee Report. It is the report of a committee set up by the Institute for Fiscal Studies, chaired by Professor J. E. Meade, and published by George Allen & Unwin in 1978 as a 500-page book under the title *The Structure and Reform of Direct Taxation*. The committee was composed of economists, accountants, lawyers and tax administrators. The book makes very radical proposals for the reform of the tax system, notably a move from an income tax to an expenditure tax. The book's analysis of the existing tax system is very valuable, especially from the point of view of its social and economic effects.

There is also a book written by two economist members of the Meade Committee. This is *The British Tax System* by J. A. Kay and M. A. King (Oxford University Press, 1978). To a considerable extent this book adopts the same approach as the Meade Report. It is shorter and cheaper and it is a stimulating comment on the economic and social aspects of tax. These are aspects which a tax lawyer tends to lose sight of.

It is pleasing to a student of tax law to discover that quite a number of tax cases are leading authorities for some general point applicable in other branches of law. To take but one example, the tax case of *Baker* v. *Archer-Shee* (1927) (H.L.) illuminated the nature of a beneficiary's interest under a trust. But while it is good to know that tax cases sometimes contribute to other branches of law, the obverse must also be noted. It is this: many, perhaps most, tax cases contain a non-tax point which has to be solved before the tax point can be solved. Therefore the student of tax law should aim to be also a student of law in general, particularly of trust law, company law and commercial law.

PART TWO

INCOME TAX

CHAPTER 4

HISTORY AND ALL THAT

HISTORY

Income tax was first introduced in this country in 1799 by the Younger Pitt. Its purpose was to help finance the war against Napoleonic France. It was said to be "a temporary tax." In 1802, after the Peace of Amiens (a temporary peace) the tax was repealed. In 1803, when the war with France was renewed, Addington brought in a new income tax. Peace came again in 1815, and the 1803 Act automatically expired.

For the next 27 years there was no income tax, but in 1842 a new income tax was brought in by Peel. It was again described as "temporary" but it is with us still.

During its long history income tax has been chopped and changed and knocked about by succeeding parliaments, and that is one reason why the law of income tax is difficult to comprehend. It has not been written by one hand, not even by one committee: it is the patchwork product of almost innumerable parliaments. On three occasions (so far) the law of income tax has been consolidated; first in 1918, then in 1952, then in 1970.

The 1970 consolidation is contained in two Acts; the Taxes Management Act 1970 ("TMA 1970"), which can broadly be described as administrative, and the Income and Corporation Taxes Act 1970 ("the Taxes Act") which can broadly be described as substantive. But, of course, things have not stood still since 1970 and the current law in force consists of the 1970 consolidation Acts *and* all the Finance Acts passed since, including, by the way, the Finance Act 1970 which was passed after the consolidation Acts. Usually there is one Finance Act a year, but sometimes more than one. For instance, there was a Finance (No. 2) Act in 1975 and a Finance (Income Tax Reliefs) Act in 1977 and a Finance (No. 2) Act in 1979. In Finance Acts passed since the consolidation Acts, matters which are intended to be permanent are usually enacted in the form of amendments to the consolidation Acts, whereas matters (such as rates of tax) which are not expected to be permanent are not.

Despite all this change, some leading ideas in income tax have remained constant. For example, the idea of deduction of tax at source was present in the Act of 1803 and is with us still; the payer of an "annual payment" deducts from his payment the tax (or part of

21

the tax) for which the payee will be, or may be, liable, and so acts as a collector for the Revenue (see Chap. 11). Even some actual words have survived from the earliest times. Thus, it is pleasant to find in section 189 (1) of the Taxes Act that an employed person may deduct (only in certain circumstances, of course) the expenses "of keeping and maintaining a horse" (see Chap. 9).

A very leading idea indeed has survived from 1803 to the present day. This is what is called "the schedular system," the system by which income is classified, for the purposes of the tax, under different schedules. For example, income from land falls under one schedule, and income from a trade or profession falls under another schedule. The traditional belief is that the origin of this system was the strong dislike of the tax-paying classes of the possibility of one shabby clerk getting to know the total income of a taxpayer. The idea was hit upon of requiring each kind of income to be revealed to a different clerk. Be it true or false, it makes a good story. (There is more about the Schedules hereafter.)

Until 1911 income tax was proportional; since then it has been progressive. It was made progressive by means of a "super-tax" which was introduced by Lloyd George in his famous budget of 1909. The budget was finally enacted in a statute bearing the rather curious title "the Finance (1909–10) Act 1910." Super-tax later changed its name to surtax, and later still surtax was abolished but was (in effect) replaced by higher rate tax and additional rate tax from 1973–74. Those taxes, or rather those aspects of income tax, are still with us and are discussed in Chapter 7.

The war of 1914–18 revolutionised the rates of tax. In 1914 the maximum combined rate of income tax and super-tax was 12.5 per cent. In 1918 the maximum combined rate was 52.5 per cent. The 1939–45 war had its effect on income tax even before it began. That was because the war was preceded by re-armament. Thus in 1939 the maximum rate was 68.75 per cent. By 1941 the maximum rate had risen to 97.5 per cent. There have been some fluctuations since: *e.g.* for 1978–79 the maximum rate (on investment income) was 98 per cent.; for 1979–80 it was 75 per cent. Although I have given the tax rates above in percentages, the Finance Acts up to 1968 gave them in cash terms (old money at that). The Finance Act 1969, at section 7, enacted that "Income Tax for the year 1969–70 shall be charged at the standard rate of 41.25 per cent. (which is equivalent to 8s. 3d. in the pound). . . ." That was a very helpful conversion, but ironically such a conversion soon ceased to be necessary. Since decimal money came in (in February 1971) even the meanest arithmetician can see without help that, for example, a basic rate of 33 per cent. is the same as 33p in the pound.

Income tax is an annual tax. The tax year begins on April 6 but the Finance Act is not usually given Royal assent until towards the end of July. The Revenue used to administer the tax on the strength of the budget resolutions passed by the House of Commons. In the great case of *Bowles* v. *Bank of England* (1913) it was held that this practice was illegal, because resolutions of the House of Commons are not statutes. An Act was passed in 1913 to deal with the point, and that Act has since been replaced by the Provisional Collection of Taxes Act 1968. This Act gives temporary statutory effect to House of Commons resolutions. If such a resolution is passed in March or April it has statutory force until August 5; if passed in any other month it has effect for four months. The fact that a budget resolution is passed does not prevent the subsequent Finance Bill or the still more subsequent Finance Act from coming out differently, either because the Government changes its mind or because it is outvoted in the Commons. Thus, in 1978 the Liberals voted with the Labour Government on the budget resolutions (which passed), but against it on two amendments to the Bill, dealing with the amount of the basic rate and the threshold for higher rates. Those amendments were carried against the Government.

GEOGRAPHY

The Finance Acts apply to the United Kingdom. The United Kingdom is the United Kingdom of Great Britain and Northern Ireland. Great Britain comprises England and Wales, and Scotland. The Channel Islands and the Isle of Man are not within the United Kingdom for tax purposes. But, since the Finance Act 1973, the territorial sea and (as regards exploration and exploitation) the designated areas of the continental shelf are within the United Kingdom for tax purposes. ("There's gold in them there oils.") (And in 1975 a new tax, the petroleum revenue tax, was brought in by the Oil Taxation Act, but "PRT" is outside the scope of this book.)

Income tax is chargeable where one or other of two factors provides a link with the United Kingdom. As Lord Herschell put it in *Colquhoun* v. *Brooks* (1889) (H.L.): "either that from which the taxable income is derived must be situate in the United Kingdom or the person whose income is to be taxed must be resident there."

THE SIX SCHEDULES

We must now look in more detail at the schedular system. One expects to find a schedule at the end of a statute, but the six Schedules under which income tax is charged stand now in the body of the Taxes

Act. For example, Schedule D occurs at section 108 and Schedule E occurs at section 181.

The six Schedules are described by letters, A, B, C, D, E and F. Schedule A charges income derived from land. Schedule B charges income derived from woodlands. Schedule C charges certain government interest and dividends. Schedule D is divided into six "cases." The cases are described by Roman capital numbers. Cases I and II deal with the profits of trades and professions. Case III deals with what is engagingly called "pure profit income." Cases IV and V deal with income from abroad. Case VI has two aspects; it performs a sort of sweeping-up function and it is the head of charge for certain specific items of income. There was at one time a Case VII dealing with short-term capital gains and a Case VIII dealing with certain income derived from land. Cases VII and VIII do not now exist. Schedule E (this is where P.A.Y.E. comes in) charges income from offices, employments and pensions, and also certain other specific items of income. There are three cases of Schedule E: Case I applies where (normally) no foreign element is involved; Cases II and III are concerned where there is a foreign element. Schedule F charges dividends and other distributions made by companies resident in the United Kingdom. Under all the Schedules except Schedule D tax is charged on the profits of the current year. Under Schedule D tax is charged (normally) on the profits of the preceding year, except for Case VI profits.

The Schedules and Cases enumerated above produce 13 different heads under which income tax may be charged. There are some other heads of charge which stand apart from the system of Schedules and Cases. The most important of these heads are section 53 and section 54 of the Taxes Act (which deal with certain annual payments, royalties, etc.) and the charge to additional rate which occurs in each year's Finance Act on investment income.

CONSTRUING TAX STATUTES

Income tax (all tax, for that matter—we fought a civil war on the point) is the creature of statute. There is no income tax at common law. Judges do not make taxes, but of course they do make tax law. They do this by construing, or interpreting, tax statutes. Sometimes this interpretation is very fundamental, and it is not non-sensical to say that there is a common law of income tax. For instance, in Schedule D (Cases I and II) there is no statutory statement (as there is in Schedule E) of what expenses are allowable deductions. There is simply a list in section 130 of the Taxes Act of what expenses are not allowable. The judges have applied the principle that two negatives make an affirmative. Thus expenses which are not not allowable are allowable.

The rules governing the interpretation of taxing statutes are basically the same as the rules governing the interpretation of any statute. The general modern law on this matter can conveniently be found in the Report of the Law Commission and the Scottish Law Commission, June 9, 1969 (Law Com. No. 21; Scot. Law Com. No. 11). The three basic rules are the mischief rule, the golden rule and the literal rule. (It is fashionable nowadays to speak of the "purposive" or "functional" construction of a statute, but that seems only to be a modern restatement of the mischief rule.) There is no overriding rule laying down an order of priority for the three rules, and so judges have a pretty free hand in their task of interpretation.

There is one special rule which taxing statutes share with penal statutes, namely that the onus is on the Crown. A person is not to be taxed unless the words of the statute clearly impose the tax upon him. In colloquial language the taxpayer gets the benefit of the doubt. But in a famous passage Rowlatt J. said in *Cape Brandy Syndicate* v. *I.R.C.* (1921):

"Too wide and fanciful a construction is often sought to be given to that maxim, which does not mean that words are to be unduly restricted against the Crown, or that there is to be any discrimination against the Crown in those Acts. It simply means that in a taxing Act one has to look merely at what is clearly said. There is no room for any intendment. There is no equity about a tax. There is no presumption as to a tax. Nothing is to be read in. Nothing is to be implied. One can only look fairly at the language used. . . ."

Nearly 300 years ago, in a case called *City of London* v. *Wood* (1701) Holt C.J. said: "An Act of Parliament can do no wrong, though it may do several things that look pretty odd." Holt C.J. meant that it is not open to the judges to declare a statute void. But there is one tax case in which the House of Lords held that a particular subsection (now in the Taxes Act, s. 345) had no effect at all, because the state of the pre-existing common law (relating to mutual trading) was such that the enactment was meaningless. That case is *Ayrshire Employers Mutual Insurance Association Ltd.* v. *I.R.C.* (1946) (H.L.). And in *Vestey* v. *I.R.C.* (1978) Walton J., in order to avoid what he considered to be "rank, blatant injustice," robustly read into section 412 of the Income Tax Act 1952 (now section 478 of the Taxes Act) some words which are not there. More usually the judges, faced with an obscure and perhaps distasteful enactment, content themselves with the observation that it is "pretty odd." And notice that Rowlatt J. (speaking in 1921) referred to "what is clearly said." Much of what has been said in taxing statutes since 1921 has not been clearly said.

"FORM AND SUBSTANCE"

This is a perennial debate amongst tax lawyers. When a court is deciding whether or not a taxpayer is caught by a particular taxing enactment, should the court go by the *form* in which he has carried out a transaction, or should it go by the *substantial result* of the transaction?

In *I.R.C.* v. *Duke of Westminster* (1936) (H.L.) the Duke reduced the wages of his employees, and at the same time entered into deeds of covenant with them by which he bound himself for seven years to pay to them weekly sums equal to the reductions. There was nothing in the deeds to prevent the employees from claiming remuneration for the work which they did, but it was understood by each employee that he was expected to be content to receive no more than he had lately been receiving. The point was that as the law then stood (but not now), if the payments were annuities or other annual payments (and were not wages) the Duke could deduct the amount of the payments (grossed up) in arriving at his total income for the purposes of surtax. The Revenue contended that, although in form the payments were annuities, in substance they were wages. The Duke won. In the House of Lords it was said that the doctrine of the substance is correct if it only means that a court is not bound by the nomenclature used by the parties and is not bound by documents which are not bona fide; but the doctrine is incorrect if it means that a court can disregard the legal rights and liabilities of the parties.

But 1936 is a long time ago, and the courts show some signs of extending the doctrine of substance. An example of a changed attitude is to be found in *Sargaison* v. *Roberts* (1969), decided by Megarry J. A farmer had conveyed to trustees for his children the fee simple of his farm, and a settlement of even date between himself and the trustees provided for a "lease back" of the farm to himself for 40 years at a rack rent. He was now claiming an allowance for capital expenditure on agricultural land. He would be entitled to that allowance unless "the whole of his interest" in the land had been transferred to some other person, in which case that other person would be entitled to the allowance. Megarry J. held that the farmer had not transferred the whole of his interest. He said:

"Is the phrase 'whole of his interest ... is transferred ... to some other person' satisfied by a state of affairs in which the taxpayer had an interest in the land immediately before the transaction and also had an interest in the land (although a different interest) immediately after the transaction, but for one notional instant, while the change was being effected, had no interest at all? ... 'Substance' and 'form' are words which must no doubt be applied with caution in the field of statutory construction. Nevertheless, where the technicalities of English conveyancing and land law are brought into juxtaposition with a United Kingdom taxing statute, I am encouraged to look at the realities at the expense of the technicalities. The taxpayer's interest has, *uno icto* [at one stroke], been merely reduced from ownership of the freehold to ownership of a lease: the whole of his interest in the land has therefore not been transferred to another; and that is the end of the case."

There then follows a typical Megarryism: "I respectfully agree with the common-sense approach of the General Commissioners, and merely add that common sense is not a quality wholly to be abjured in the construction even of a taxing statute."

SCOTLAND AND TAX LAW

The judgment of Megarry J. in *Sargaison* v. *Roberts* (above) touches on an important point for tax law, namely that the legislation applies to the whole United Kingdom, that is, to three different jurisdictions. Where Megarry J. referred to the juxtaposition of the technicalities of English conveyancing and land law with a United Kingdom taxing statute, he was saying that because the statute must be made to work in Scotland (and in Northern Ireland) as well as in England, a court should not place too much emphasis on purely English technicalities.

Another aspect of this same point is that in tax cases English judges pay more than usual regard to Scots and Northern Irish decisions. Such decisions are not binding precedents, but they are (so to speak) super-persuasive.

CHAPTER 5

THE MECHANICS OF INCOME TAX

In this chapter I want to trace the steps in an income tax case. In practice the most litigated heads of income tax are Cases I and II of Schedule D, dealing with trades and professions. So let us look at a trader.

THE STEPS IN AN INCOME TAX CASE

Any person can be required (under section 8 of TMA 1970) to make a return of his income to an inspector. Of course, the Revenue may not know that a particular person is trading, and there is no doubt that some people get away with trading unknown to the Revenue for a long time. But since the introduction of Value Added Tax (on April 1, 1973) this has become less likely. It is advantageous to a trader to register for VAT. And then section 127 of the Finance Act 1972 enables the Commissioners of Customs and Excise to give information to the Commissioners of Inland Revenue. Once the Revenue know that a person is trading they can serve a notice on him requiring him to make a return.

In practice a trader usually submits a return which simply says "see accounts." And he (or his accountant) sends with the return a profit and loss account, a balance sheet and a "computation." This latter is simply an adjustment, bringing the commercial accounts into line with income tax requirements, the most common adjustment being that depreciation has to be added back for income tax purposes. The inspector can issue a notice requiring a person to deliver to him accounts and other relevant documents. This power is laid down in section 20 of TMA 1970, as substituted by the Finance Act 1976.

The next step is for the inspector to make an assessment on the trader. The normal time limit is six years.

If the trader does not appeal against the assessment and he does pay the amount charged by the assessment that is the end of the matter. If he does not pay up, the Revenue can sue him. Or, instead of suing, the collector can distrain on the lands or goods of the debtor. Such a distress can be levied without the Revenue having first to obtain a judgment against the debtor; all they need is a finalised assessment, and a warrant signed by the General Commissioners.

If the trader does appeal against the assessment, the inspector may enter into an agreement with the trader that the assessment should be upheld, or varied, or discharged or cancelled. Such an agreement has the same effect as a determination of the appeal by the Commissioners.

If there is no agreement between the trader and the inspector the appeal goes to the General (or Special) Commissioners. Some matters are reserved to the Special Commissioners and some to the General Commissioners but most matters can be taken to either the Specials or the Generals. There is provision (in TMA, s. 44 (3)) for transfer from one body to the other even after notice of appeal has been given. Putting it broadly a taxpayer would do well to go to the Generals if he has a good "sympathy" case and to go to the Specials if he has a good case in law.

In the past, appeals were often put in simply in order to delay the time at which the trader had to pay the tax. This tactic was virtually knocked out in 1975 when a new section 55 of the TMA 1970 was substituted. Now the tax cannot be left wholly unpaid pending the hearing of an appeal. Payment is postponed only on that part of the tax as to which the Commissioners decide (or the inspector agrees with the taxpayer) that there are reasonable grounds for believing that the appellant is overcharged. The rest of the tax is due as though there had been no appeal. Interest is payable on tax which is overdue. The rate of interest is 9 per cent., and there is no income tax relief for the interest payments, so there is a pretty hefty inducement to pay tax promptly.

At the hearing of the appeal the onus is on the taxpayer. Section 50 (6) of TMA 1970 says: "If, on an appeal, it appears to the majority of the Commissioners present at the hearing, by examination of the appellant on oath or affirmation, or by other lawful evidence, that the appellant is overcharged by any assessment, the assessment shall be reduced accordingly, but otherwise every such assessment shall stand good." This is an enormously important point. It provides the Revenue with a very strong lever indeed with which to extract from the taxpayer all necessary information. The assessment is right unless it is shown by the taxpayer to be wrong. And the Revenue has another lever, built on the same principle. By section 29 (1) (b) of TMA 1970 the inspector, if he is dissatisfied with any return, may make an assessment to tax to the best of his judgment. In Revenue circles this is called a BOJ assessment ("best of judgment"). Under this provision the inspector can make an assessment on an unforthcoming taxpayer in a nice large sum, and it is then for the taxpayer to show, if he can, that it is too high.

Once a taxpayer has given notice of appeal against an assessment he cannot withdraw his appeal. The reason for this judge-made rule is that on an appeal the assessment may actually be increased. But a taxpayer's appeal from the Commissioners to the court (see below) can be withdrawn in tax cases as in other branches of law.

Hearings before the appeal Commissioners are secret in the sense that they are not open to the public (nor to journalists) and in the sense that they are not reported. (In an appeal in 1978 by a woman theatre critic concerning her claim to deduct from her earnings the cost of a baby-sitter secrecy was waived at the express request of the appellant. So far as I know, this was a unique occurrence.) It is believed that the Special Commissioners circulate their decisions amongst themselves, and, though they are not as a matter of law bound to follow the decisions of their brethren, in practice they usually do. It may thus happen that the same point is taken by taxpayer after taxpayer. Unless and until the point is taken on appeal to the High Court taxpayer E has no means of knowing that his point has already been decided by the Special Commissioners against taxpayers A, B, C and D. For an example of this phenomenon see footnote 3 on page 51, below.

The Commissioners have no power to award costs (either way).

An appeal lies from the Commissioners to the court, but only on a point of law, not on fact.

There is a curiously worded subsection (1) in section 56 of TMA 1970 which says: "Immediately after the determination of an appeal by the Commissioners, the appellant or the inspector or other officer of the Board, if dissatisfied with the determination as being erroneous in point of law, may declare his dissatisfaction to the Commissioners who heard the appeal."[1] It used to be thought that to express dissatisfaction immediately was a necessary prerequisite to appealing to the court. This is not so now. In *R.* v. *H.M.I.T., ex p. Clarke* (1974) (C.A.) it was said by the Court of Appeal that the subsection is "directory" only, and not "mandatory." Even if a party does not express dissatisfaction immediately, he can still (by notice in writing within 30 days) require the Commissioners to "state and sign a case for the opinion of the High Court thereon," and the Commissioners must do so.

The "Case Stated" is a document prepared by the Commissioners setting out their findings of fact, the contentions of the parties, and the Commissioners' conclusions of law. It is by this procedure of Case Stated that an appeal is taken to the court. The appeal is heard by a judge of the Chancery Division of the High Court. The "Revenue Paper" (a list of Revenue cases) is allotted to a particular judge for a term or so. Until about 1950 the Revenue Paper was taken by a judge

---

[1] I once heard a burly Yorkshire taxpayer comply with this subsection by announcing in stentorian tones that he was "bloody disgusted."

of the King's Bench Division, often for a long period, almost for life. The most notable of these judges was Mr. Justice Rowlatt, who was on the bench from 1912 to 1932. Rowlatt J. is the great "folk-hero" of tax lawyers, in much the same way as Scrutton L.J. is the folk-hero of commercial lawyers.

Once a case gets to the High Court (or above) all secrecy is at an end.

Appeal lies from the Chancery Judge to the Court of Appeal, and thence to the House of Lords in just the same way as in other branches of law.

A very high proportion of the cases heard in the House of Lords are tax cases. The reason is that often there is a great deal of money at stake, and even where it is more a question of principle than of money one of the litigants has an almost bottomless purse.

It is very important to keep in mind the point made earlier that an appeal lies from the Commissioners to the court only on a point of law. The leading authority on this matter is *Edwards* v. *Bairstow and Harrison* (1956) (H.L.). The question at issue was whether certain transactions carried out by the respondents in relation to the buying and selling of textile machinery constituted an adventure in the nature of trade, in which case the profits were taxable, or whether they did not, in which case the profits were not taxable (though they would now be taxable as capital gains). The General Commissioners decided that there was no adventure in the nature of trade. The High Court and the Court of Appeal held that it was purely a question of fact and that the court could not interfere. But the House of Lords took a more robust stand. True, trade or no trade is a question of fact, but if the only reasonable conclusion to which the Commissioners could come on a consideration of all the facts contradicts the conclusion to which they did come, then their finding can be reversed by an appellate court. Naturally, this decision of the House of Lords greatly widened the scope for appealing from the commissioners to the courts. But it still quite often happens that the court holds that it has no power to interfere with a decision of commissioners because they are the sole judges of fact. It should be borne in mind that when this occurs the case is not much of an authority for the future. Where, on the other hand, the court does reverse a decision of commissioners the judgment is of much greater authority.

PENALTIES AND CRIMINAL PROCEEDINGS

So far the litigation that we have been considering has been purely civil litigation; the taxpayer and the Revenue have been arguing as to which of them is right on the facts or on the law. But there can be criminal proceedings by the Revenue and also quasi-criminal proceedings for penalties. Proceedings for penalties usually arise out of "back duty cases," that is, instances where the Revenue are investigating the possibility that a person has not paid all the tax in the past that he should have paid.

Penalties

The Revenue may take penalty proceedings against a person in a number of different circumstances. The main instances are where a person has failed to make a return at all or where a person has made an incorrect return. The latter is much the more important in practice. A penalty is incurred if there is negligence or fraud—not otherwise. The maximum penalty where there has been negligence is £50 plus the amount of tax lost to the Revenue. The maximum penalty where there has been fraud is £50 plus twice the amount of tax lost. The Board has a discretionary power to mitigate any penalty. At first sight it might seem that a penalty could be exacted without making any assessment. But on reflection it is obvious that an assessment is needed in order to establish how much tax has been lost, and therefore how much the penalty should be.

How far back can the Revenue go in making an assessment? The basic rule (in section 34 of TMA 1970) is that an assessment may be made at any time not later than six years after the end of the chargeable period to which the assessment relates. This is called the "ordinary time limit," and the six years are called "normal years."

In cases of fraud or wilful default there is no time limit for making an assessment but leave of a general or special commissioner is required (TMA, s. 36 and 41).

In cases of "neglect" there are time limits and they are rather complicated. There are two steps or stages. The first step is that an assessment can be made for any of the six years (called "earlier years") which precede a normal year, provided the assessment is made not later than one year from the end of the year when the assessment for the normal year is finally determined (meaning that no appeal is outstanding). Leave is required from a general or special commissioner. The second step is that the Revenue can go back again into a maximum of six years even earlier than the "earlier years." An assessment of this kind requires the leave of general or special commissioners (plural). (See sections 37 and 41 of TMA.)

Assessments on the personal representatives of a decreased taxpayer are, however, very much restricted. First, the time allowed for making an assessment shall in no case extend beyond the end of the third year next following the year of assessment in which the death occurred. Secondly, when the deceased had been guilty of neglect *or even fraud* the Revenue can only go back as far as the year of assessment which ended not earlier than six years before the death. (See section 40 of TMA.)

Criminal Proceedings

Making a false statement to the Revenue (for example, in a tax return) is an offence chargeable on indictment or summarily under section 2 (1) (*c*) of the Theft Act 1978: "where a person by any deception ... dishonestly obtains any exemption from or abatement of liability to make a payment ... he shall be guilty of an offence."

Making a false statement in a tax return with intent to defraud the Revenue is also an indictable offence at common law. The leading modern authority on this is *R.* v. *Hudson* (1956) (C.C.A.). This is the head under which the majority of Revenue prosecutions are brought.

Other heads under which criminal proceedings may be taken are forgery and perjury.

Sometimes the Revenue takes criminal proceedings not only against a taxpayer but also (or instead) against his accountant.[2] Such cases are very rare, and indeed the British tax system relies very heavily on accountants. The system would not work nearly as well as it does if there were no accountants or if there were more dishonest accountants.

DATES FOR PAYMENT OF TAX

The due dates for payments of income tax (after which interest begins to run on unpaid tax) are laid down in section 4 of the Taxes Act (as amended). The general rule (which applies, for example, to tax under Schedules A and B) is that tax becomes due on January 1 in the year of assessment or at the expiration of a period of 30 days beginning with the date of the issue of the notice of assessment, whichever is the later. But a special rule applies to tax charged on an individual or on a firm under Case I or Case II of Schedule D; here the tax is payable in two equal instalments on January 1 in the year of assessment (or at the expiration, if later, of the 30-day period mentioned above) and on the following July 1. There is a proviso to the effect that if the notice of assessment is not issued until after June 1 following the end of the

---

[2] A possible charge here is conspiracy. The abolition, by the Criminal Law Act 1977, of the offence of conspiracy at common law does not apply to conspiracy *to defraud* at common law (s. 5 (2)).

year of assessment the general rule applies and the tax is due after 30 days (all in one amount, not in instalments). Tax under Schedule E is treated as due when it is deducted by the employer. Tax at higher rates and at additional rates is due on July 6 following the end of the year for which it is assessed or at the end of the 30-day period mentioned above.

CHAPTER 6

CAPITAL AND INCOME

Income tax, as Lord Macnaghten wittily said, is a tax on income. But what is income? It is nowhere defined in the legislation. Presumably it can be contrasted with capital, which is not defined either. In other contexts capital is sometimes contrasted with labour. In a tax context labour is intertwined with income. Thus income may be derived from labour alone (*e.g.* Schedule E) or from capital alone (*e.g.* Case III of Schedule D), or from a combination of both (*e.g.* Case I of Schedule D). You see how we immediately start talking in terms of schedules and cases. That is because the legislation is framed in that way.

Income tax is a tax on income from various sources, measured according to rules which vary according to the source of the income. First one identifies the source, and then treats what flows from that source as income. If another metaphor is preferred, one can speak of identifying the tree and then treating its fruit as income. One striking result of this "source doctrine" (until it was struck down by legislation) was that the receipts coming in to a professional person (*e.g.* a barrister) after he had retired ("post-cessation receipts") were not taxable as income. There could be no income without an existing source. On retirement the barrister's source of income had ceased. Therefore subsequent receipts were not income. Simple. The source doctrine still remains important in that one must identify a source in order to determine what Schedule and Case applies to a particular item of income. If none applies the item is not taxable.

Some receipts which are of a capital nature are taxed as income. This is true, for example, of a premium taken on the granting of a lease of land.

On the other hand, some income receipts are not taxed. Thus, the first £70 of interest from ordinary deposits with the National Saving Bank or with a trustee savings bank is not taxed. Again, many social security benefits are not taxed: notably unemployment benefit, sickness benefit, supplementary benefits, and child benefit.

As a basic principle income, to be taxable, must be money or something capable of being turned into money, but there are a number of exceptions to this.

Another basic principle is that capital receipts are not taxable as income. It has been indicated above that there are some exceptions to this. And, anyway, what is a capital receipt, or what is capital? Some

35

of the cases make a distinction between fixed capital and circulating capital. There is some value in this distinction, but it must be borne in mind that an item which would be fixed capital in one person's hands may be circulating capital in another person's hands. To take an example, a factory owned by X, a manufacturer, is fixed capital. If X sells the factory (because he no longer needs it) at a profit, the profit is of a capital nature and is not chargeable to income tax. A factory owned by Y, who makes his living by buying and selling factories, is circulating capital. If Y sells a factory, the receipt is trading income and is an item in calculating his taxable profit.

The distinction between capital receipts and income receipts has its parallel in a distinction between two kinds of expenditure. But because "income expenditure" would be rather an absurd expression, it is usual in this context to speak of capital expenditure and revenue expenditure ("revenue" with a small "r," of course). If X (above) buys a new factory that is capital expenditure, and is not deductible in calculating X's income.[1] If Y (above) buys a factory, that is revenue expenditure and is deductible.

At first sight one might think that a payment must either be capital in the hands of the payer and in the hands of the recipient, or it must be revenue in the hands of the payer and in the hands of the recipient. But this is not necessarily so. Suppose X (above) buys a factory from Y (above): X's payment is a capital payment, but Y's receipt is an income receipt. (For another instance of the principle see the House of Lords case of *I.R.C.* v. *Church Commissioners for England* (1977).) And the converse may also occur: if Y buys a factory from X, Y's payment is revenue expenditure, but X's receipt is a capital receipt.

At one time, if a receipt were held not to be an income receipt but a capital receipt, it was not chargeable to any tax at all. Nowadays a capital receipt may be, though not chargeable to income tax, chargeable to capital gains tax. But the difference is still important, because capital gains tax is charged at a lesser rate than higher rate income tax.

As well as the distinction between income and capital, there is also a distinction between income (that is, taxable income) and casual receipts. Tips received by a taxi-driver are taxable; tips received by a nephew from an uncle are not. How does this difference arise? The explanation must lie in the source doctrine. The nephew has no source. The uncle is not a source, because a source must be a state of affairs which falls within one or other of the Schedules and Cases. The taxi-driver's tips have a source which falls either within Schedule E or

---

[1] But it may qualify for capital allowances; see Chap. 16.

within Schedule D, Case I, depending on whether he is an employee (of a taxi company) or self-employed.

Most casual receipts (such as uncles' tips) are gifts. Here again (as with capital receipts) at one time gifts were not taxable at all, but now they may be chargeable to capital transfer tax, and (if they are not in the form of money) to capital gains tax as well. For various reasons Uncle George's tip to little Bertie would almost certainly not be taxable, but in principle a gift is now capable of being taxed.

For over 70 years (since 1907) the law of income tax has made a distinction between two kinds of income, earned income and unearned income, and has taxed the latter more heavily than the former. Probably the moral or social basis on which this rests is the idea that the earning of income "takes it out of" the earner, whereas an investment can produce income without the investment itself or the investor being diminished in health or strength.

At one time the system was to have a "standard rate" of tax applicable to all income, but to have also a relief on earned income. The present system (since 1973–74) is to have a "basic rate" of tax applicable to all income, and also to have a further rate imposed (as well) on unearned income. This further rate is called in the legislation "additional rate," though it is usually called by commentators "investment income surcharge."

The legislation does not use the phrase "unearned income," but rather "investment income." And it does not define investment income except to say that investment income is any income other than earned income. Earned income is defined in section 530 of the Taxes Act. The definition is consonant with commonsense, but there are some difficult borderline cases. Some of these cases occur in connection with partnership income; (see Chapter 15, below).

CHAPTER 7

THE TAXATION OF INDIVIDUALS

With an arresting bluntness, the very first section of the Taxes Act (the Income and Corporation Taxes Act 1970) is entitled "The Charge." And that section announces that income tax shall be charged "in respect of all property, profits or gains respectively described or comprised in the Schedules contained in the following sections of this Act" [and it then lists the Schedules A to F] "and in accordance with the provisions of the Income Tax Acts respectively applicable to those Schedules." Before we get down (as we shall do in the following chapters) to the details of each Schedule, it will be interesting to look at the end-product, the tax bill of an individual taxpayer.

It maybe that some of the points in this chapter will not be entirely clear to the reader. Be of good heart; things will become clearer when you have read the later chapters on income tax. Undertstanding is cumulative; as you learn more about other aspects of income tax, things which now seem rather obscure will click into place. When you have read to the end of the income tax part of this book you may care to read this Chapter 7 again.

I have entitled this chapter, "The Taxation of Individuals." The word "individual" excludes companies (which, in tax law as in law generally, are "persons" but are not "individuals") and excludes also trustees and personal representatives, to whom special tax rules apply. There are special rules also for partners.

The process of working out an individuals's tax bill is quite complicated. I will try to state the process here in a series of steps. But it is not easy to reduce it to simplicity, because one has to accommodate "income" and "total income" (which are not the same) and one has to accommodate various kinds of deductions which operate at different stages of the process. But here goes.

1. Income is income under any particular Schedule. It is either (as for example in Schedule D, Case III) pure income or (as for example in Schedule D, Case I) the balance of income over expenditure.

2. Total income is the sum of the incomes under the Schedules minus what are called "charges on income," that is, such things as annuities and annual payments which the taxpayer pays out. Total income may include income which, for purposes other than tax, belongs to someone else. The most important example of this

phenomenon is that the income of a wife may (but see below) be deemed to be income of her husband.

3. Total income is not the same as taxable income. To arrive at taxable income one deducts from total income personal reliefs and also qualifying kinds of interest paid out.

4. To work out the tax bill of an individual one applies to his taxable income the various tax rates. One then deducts Double Taxation Relief (if any). One had now arrived at the "tax payable," being an actual sum in hard cash. One can call this the "tax bill."

Now let us look in more detail at the steps in the process.

1. INCOME

The amounts of income which an individual has under each Schedule are added together to make up his total income. Each Schedule has its own rules for computing that kind of income which falls within it. It is more convenient, therefore, to deal with those rules in separate chapters (following this chapter) dealing with the various Schedules. What does require to be stated here is a reminder of something which was said in Chapter 6, namely that some items of receipt are not subject to tax. Important examples are students' grants and scholarships, many social security benefits such as unemployment benefit and child benefit, and the first £70 of Post Office interest.

2. TOTAL INCOME

It is necessary to find a taxpayer's total income for two purposes: first to determine whether it is enough to entitle him to the personal reliefs which he claims; secondly, to determine his liability (if any) to higher rate tax and (indirectly) additional rate tax.

Kinds of Income

An individual's total income may include items of the following kinds.

Income not taxed by deduction before receipt

An important example of this kind of income is income from a trade under Case I of Schedule D. Another example is the state retirement pension (Old Age Pension). Another example is income from rents under Schedule A.

Income taxed by deduction before receipt

One example of this is income in the form of interest on Government stocks (gilt-edged securities) paid by the Bank of England. This income falls under Schedule C. Schedule C does not raise any particular problems, and it is not further discussed in this book. A more troublesome example is income in the form of an annuity or an annual payment. This kind of income will be dealt with more fully in Chapter 11. The point I want to make here is that income taxed by deduction before receipt has to be grossed-up, that is, converted into a gross sum, for the purpose of computing total income. I will explain grossing-up in a moment. The most important example of income taxed by deduction before receipt is salary or wage income. Tax is charged under Schedule E and is deducted by the employer under the P.A.Y.E. system. It is the gross amount which is included in total income, but of course the employee is credited with the tax deducted by his employer.

GROSSING-UP. An employee usually knows what his gross pay is, and so grossing-up does not present any problem. But the recipient of an annuity or of an annual payment under a covenant may not know the gross amount. The covenantor will deduct tax at the basic rate. If the covenantee receives £70 (net), the gross amount is £100. The gross amount is made up of the net payment (£70) plus tax deducted at the basic rate (at present 30 per cent.), £30. With less obvious figures, you gross-up by multiplying the net amount by 100 over 70. The explanation (for simple lawyers, not accountants) is that if basic rate is 30 per cent., net income is gross (which is 100 per cent.) less 30 per cent. of gross, so net income is 70 per cent. of gross. Putting it as an equation (or formula), and using N for net and G for gross,

$$N = \frac{70}{100} \times G$$

Conversely,
$$G = \frac{100}{70} \times N$$

One can play around a bit more by introducing T for tax.

$$T = \frac{30}{100} \times G,$$

and also
$$T = \frac{30}{70} \times N.$$

Summarising the above, three useful points emerge. If you know the net, you can find the gross by multiplying the net by $^{100}/_{70}$. If you know the gross, you can find the net by multiplying the gross by $^{70}/_{100}$. If you know the net, you can find the tax by multiplying the net by $^{30}/_{70}$.

I have dealt with the arithmetic of grossing-up at some length. The reason is that I want to say to law students that you need not be afraid of tax law because some arithmetic is involved. In fact very little is involved, and if I can do it (which I can, just) anyone can.

Going back to the annuitant, and emboldened by our arithmetical studies to give him a slightly less simple net income of say £280, we find that this when grossed-up amounts to £400. It is £400 which goes into the computation of his total income. But he gets credit for the £120 (tax at basic rate) which was deducted by the payer.

Building society interest

We are dealing here, of course, with interest received *from* a building society, not interest paid *to* a building society. Although it is, in effect, a form of income taxed by deduction before receipt it has some special features of its own and is best dealt with separately. Building societies may enter into arrangements with the Revenue under section 343 of the Taxes Act, and nearly all building societies do so. They then pay income tax at a special "composite" rate. Each investor is treated as having suffered deduction before receipt at the basic rate. The interest must be grossed-up at the basic rate for computing total income, but a credit is given equal to tax at the basic rate on the grossed-up amount. If an investor is not liable to higher rate tax or additional rate tax he has nothing to pay. But if he is not even liable to basic rate tax he cannot get a refund from the Revenue. So a building society is not a good place to invest for an individual who is below the basic rate threshold.

Dividends and similar payments from United Kingdom companies

These payments also have special features of their own. They fall under Schedule F. The amount to be included in total income is the net amount received (the "distribution") plus the "tax credit" that goes with it. (This is explained more fully in Chapter 20 below). But although it is the aggregate of distribution and tax credit which forms an item in the shareholder's total income, he gets credit in his tax bill equal to the amount of the "tax credit" (as one would expect from the phrase "tax credit"). Thus if a shareholder receives a "distribution" (that is a net expression) of £140 from a United Kingdom company, this carries with it a tax credit of $^{30}/_{70}$ of £140, which is £60. So as an item in his total income his receipt counts as £200, but in his tax bill he gets credit for £60. In the result he pays higher rate and additional rate tax on £200, but he does not pay basic rate tax because, in effect, the dividend suffered basic rate tax before it was paid to him. If he is not liable to higher rate or additional rate tax he has nothing more to pay. If he is a basic rate taxpayer he just stands still. If he is not even a basic rate taxpayer (because his overall income is below the threshold) he can get a repayment from the Revenue of the whole (or a part) of the amount of the tax credit. The ironical upshot is that a poor man should invest in, say, Imperial Chemical Industries Limited and not in, say, the Bradford and Bingley Building Society.

Trust income

A beneficiary under a trust has to include in his total income an amount equal to his share of the trust income, grossed up. He will have received his share after deduction of tax and he will be credited in his tax bill with the amount deducted.

Charges on Income

To arrive at total income one deducts what are called "charges on income." A charge on income arises when a taxpayer binds himself by a legally enforceable arrangement to make payments to another person on a regular basis. An example would be a covenant by A to pay to B £x a year. The basic theory is that if a person alienates part of his income it ceases to be his income, and so does not form part of his total income. The theory of alienation has been drastically cut down by tax legislation, but it still stands in a few circumstances. For example, if a former husband covenants to pay £x a year to his former wife, the payments are treated for all tax purposes as her income and not his. The man deducts tax at the basic rate from each payment and pays the woman the *net* amount. In calculating his own total income he can deduct the *gross* amount. (He is, however, required to pay to the Revenue the basic rate tax. This is fair, because if it were not so he would get relief twice over; he has had relief once by deducting basic rate tax from his payments to his former wife.)

In many circumstances this theory of alienation has been cut down by tax legislation. In some situations a payment out is treated as still being the payer's income for all tax purposes, *e.g.* a covenanted payment by a parent to his infant child. In other situations a payment out is treated as being the payee's income for purposes of basic rate tax and as being the payer's income for purposes of higher and additional rate tax, *e.g.* a covenanted payment by a taxpayer to his impoverished aunt. In both these situations the result is that the taxpayer cannot make any deduction in calculating his total income.

This whole matter is discussed much more fully in Chapter 14, below.

Wife's Income

The income of a married woman who is living with her husband is deemed, for tax purposes, to be part of her husband's total income from April 6 next after the marriage. This provision makes some women, and some men, very hot under the collar. The law may be changed in future, but even in the present state of the law two things can be done about it.

First, either the husband or the wife can apply for *separate assessment*. See the Taxes Act, ss. 37–42. This does not either reduce or increase the amount of the assessment; but it does split between them the couple's joint liability and reliefs, so that each spouse pays his or her respective share of the tax bill. Also, if a repayment falls to be made by the Revenue, the repayment is sent to the wife (if she is the one whose circumstances have led to the repayment). Where there has not been an application for separate assessment (or (see below) separate taxation), repayments are sent to the husband. That really is rather infuriating. A small gesture was made by the Finance Act 1978, s. 22. A repayment will be made to the wife if (a) it arises out of her Schedule E income, (b) she has no earned income assessed otherwise than under Schedule E, and (c) the husband is not liable to tax at more than the basic rate.

Second, an application can be made not merely for separate assessment, but for *separate taxation*. See F.A. 1971, s. 23 and Schedule 4. This application has to be made by the husband and the wife jointly. This is a much more far-reaching provision than separate assessment. It means what it says—separate taxation, but it is not complete. It only separates the wife's earnings, and it leaves the wife's investment income to be taxed as though it were her husband's income. Moreover, "wife's earnings" does not include all that, in other contexts, would count as earned income. In particular, a pension, etc., given in respect of the husband's past services is not "wife's earnings" and so it is no good the husband arranging to have his pension split between himself and his wife. Similarly, social security benefits including the retirement pension are not "wife's earnings" if they are payable otherwise than by virtue (wholly or partly) of her own contributions.

The level of earnings at which it becomes advantageous to apply for separate taxation varies according to the ratio between the husband's earnings and the wife's earnings, but the general principle is obvious, namely that a combined income when split in two will fall into lower bands of higher rate tax than would the combined income in its unsplit state. But it must be borne in mind that if the couple do elect for separate taxation the husband gets only the single person's relief instead of the married man's (higher) relief (see below) and also that he loses the "relief on wife's earned income" (see below).

Separate taxation is sometimes referred to as non-aggregation, to contrast it with the normal rule for husband and wife which is aggre-

c

gation. Another kind of aggregation was on the statute book from 1969–70 to 1971–72. That was aggregation with the parent's income of the *unearned* income of an infant (*i.e.* a person under 18) who was unmarried and not regularly working. It was aimed at covenants, etc., by grandparents and other relatives. This Labour government enactment was repealed by the Conservative government in 1971. But there still is a kind of aggregation where the infant's income is derived from a parent: see Chapter 14 below.

3. TAXABLE INCOME

Having arrived at an individual's total income, the next step is to convert it into taxable income. Two kinds of deduction may arise at this stage, namely personal reliefs and payments (outward) of interest.

Personal Reliefs

There are a considerable number of personal reliefs set out in Chapter II of Part I (sections 8 to 27) of the Taxes Act. They constitute an attempt at "vertical equity"—the idea that people in different circumstances should pay a different amount of tax.

I want to make three general points about personal reliefs.

First, if an individual's total income in any year is less than the reliefs to which his circumstances otherwise entitle him they are to that extent lost. There is no provision for carrying the balance forward into future years or back into past years.

Second, there is an inter-relation between personal reliefs and charges on income. The link is stated in section 25 of the Taxes Act, in words which I for one find rather difficult. Section 25 (1) says this:

"Where any of the claimant's income is income the income tax on which (at the basic rate) he is entitled to charge against any other person, or to deduct, retain or satisfy out of any payment, he shall not be entitled to relief under this Chapter in respect of that income, except to the extent, if any, that the relief would exceed tax at the basic rate on that income."

The reader may care to refer back to what was said about charges on income on page 42, above. Section 25 (1) is referring to what must surely be a very unusual circumstance, namely where a taxpayer has what one might call "income minus charges on income" which is less than the amount of his personal reliefs. Suppose a taxpayer, Albert, has income of £10,000 and he decides to live on his capital and make covenanted payments to his impoverished Aunt Beatrice amounting to £9,500 gross. It will be remembered that for the purpose of basic rate tax the law regards the amounts of these payments as being Aunt Beatrice's income whereas for purposes of higher and additional rate tax it regards them as being still Albert's income. In making the payments Albert deducts tax at the basic rate. Let us suppose that the only personal relief to which Albert is entitled is the single person's relief of £1,165. What section 25 (1) means is that Albert's personal relief for the purpose of basic rate tax is cut down to £500 so that consequently he must pay basic rate tax on £9,500. The point of this is so that the Revenue gets the basic rate tax which Albert deducted when he made his payments to Aunt Beatrice. But when it comes to higher rate and additional rate tax Albert can have his personal relief (£1,165) in full. For these purposes the law regards the covenanted payments as being Albert's income, and so he is entitled to the full extent of his personal relief.

Third, personal reliefs may be claimed only by individuals who are resident in the United Kingdom, except that certain non-residents listed in section 27 of the Taxes Act (notably British subjects) may claim reliefs in proportion to the ratio between their United Kingdom income and their world-wide income.

Let us now look at the personal reliefs in more detail. All of them (except life assurance relief: see p. 52, below) operate by way of deductions from total income. So if a relief is say £100, it does not mean £100 off the tax bill, but only £100 off the taxable income. In other words, the relief is whatever tax on £100 comes to according to the tax rate of a particular individual. So reliefs are worth more to the rich than to the poor.

1. The personal relief

It is slightly confusing that all these reliefs are called collectively "personal reliefs" and also one relief in particular is called "personal relief." The confusion can be avoided by speaking of this particular relief as either "the married man's relief" or "the single person's relief" as the case may be. The amounts of these reliefs are changed by almost every succeeding Finance Act. By the Finance (No. 2) Act 1979[1] they are: married £1,815, single £1,165. Notice that the married relief is about $1\frac{1}{2}$ times the single relief. A man who marries during the year gets (as well as the single relief) one-twelfth of the difference between the married and the single relief for each month (or part of a month) from the date of the marriage to the end of the

---

[1] The Finance Act 1979 was a very minor affair because the Labour Government had been defeated on a vote of confidence a few days before Budget day. The more normally-sized Finance Act for 1979 came later, after the Conservatives had won the election, and is entitled the Finance (No. 2) Act 1979.

tax year, and the wife gets the single relief in full. If a married man or his wife is aged 65 or over the relief is £2,455; if a single man or woman is aged 65 or over the relief is £1,540. This extra relief (sometimes called "age relief") is tapered if the total income exceeds £5,000. It is interesting to compare these tax thresholds with the retirement pensions which are (from November 1979): married couple £1,940 per annum (£37.30 per week); single person £1,212 per annum (£23.30 per week). The Finance Act 1977 introduced for the first time a kind of indexation, expressing, in section 22, an intent in future years to increase the reliefs "by not less than the same percentage as the increase in the retail price index for the previous calendar year." This intent has so far been kept to.

It is worth pointing out that an individual, *however young*, is entitled to the personal relief. A babe in arms is entitled. This is the basis of some fairly simple tax planning. If a grandparent covenants to pay £1,165 to a baby, the baby is not taxed on it because he can wave his personal relief in the taxman's face. But if the baby, or anyone else, does not have £1,165 in income the personal relief is wasted. The only individual who does not get a personal relief is a married woman living with her husband. But if she is earning, she does get another kind of relief, or rather her husband does.

2. Wife's earned income relief

This is what the husband gets. It is intended to encourage married women to go out to work. At present it is £1,165. Notice that it is the same in amount as the single person's relief.[2] £1,165 is the maximum; if a wife earns less, say £1,000, then the relief is £1,000; it serves to wipe out the wife's earnings, but the balance (£165) is wasted. As in the case of separate taxation so here, not all earned income attracts the relief. The wording is not quite the same, but the result is similar: pensions given in respect of the husband's services and most social security benefits do not qualify for the relief. The relief is not available until April 6 next following the marriage. This is to keep it in step with aggregation.

3. Child relief

It is important to keep distinct in one's mind "child relief" which is a deduction for tax purposes and "child benefit" which is an actual cash receipt collectable each week from the Post Office. Child benefit is not taxable. We have just passed through a period of transition in

---

[2] So a married couple where the wife goes out to work get altogether personal reliefs about equal to $2\frac{1}{2}$ times the single relief.

this matter, moving from a system of taxable benefits balanced (to some extent) by tax reliefs to a system of benefits free from tax and hence no reliefs. The only parents who still get any tax relief are parents of children living abroad and parents of certain students, and these cases are likely to be phased out soon.

4. Other reliefs

There are a number of other reliefs, but it is not proposed in this book to discuss them in detail, only to list them. They relate to: widower's or widow's housekeeper; additional relief for widows and others in respect of children; dependent relatives; claimant depending on the services of son or daughter; blind persons. At the end of this chapter there is a note on Life Assurance Relief. Although it is treated in the legislation as being one of the personal reliefs it is quite different in form from all the other personal reliefs.

Relief for Interest Paid

Besides the personal reliefs, the other kind of deduction that may be made from total income is relief for interest paid. I am not speaking here of interest paid out as one of the expenses of a business; that is deductible *in computing* the income of that business. I am speaking of payments of interest which are deductible *from* total income. The relevant section, section 75 of the Finance Act 1972, says that certain interest shall be deducted from "income," but my understanding is that it can be deducted from "total income."

The whole question of relief for interest has been very much a political football in recent years. At one time all interest was deductible, but now it is only in exceptional cases that interest is deductible. In the first place, interest is only deductible if it is of certain kinds; it must be annual interest chargeable to tax (on the recipient) under Case III of Schedule D or interest payable in the United Kingdom on an advance from a bank or a member of the Stock Exchange or a discount house. Interest on a bank overdraft (as distinct from a fixed loan by a bank) is not deductible, nor is interest under credit card arrangements nor under a hire-purchase contract. In the second place, the loan for which the interest is being paid must be for one of six specified purposes, discussed below. Here two general restrictions come into play: relief is only given up to the amount of a reasonable commercial rate of interest, F.A. 1972, s. 75 (2); and no relief at all is given if the sole or main benefit that might be expected to accrue to the claimant from the transaction under which the interest is paid was the obtaining of a reduction in tax liability by means of such relief; F.A. 1976, s. 38.

Leaving aside certain transitional provisions, the rules for the six specified purposes are as follows.

1. Loan for purchase or improvement of land

The loan must be for purchase or improvement. A person who owns a house on which he has paid off the mortgage can only qualify for relief if he raises a loan to improve the house. If he wants a mortgage otherwise than to improve the property he will have to move. He can then get relief on a mortgage of his new house. But see head 6 below.

The land in question must be either the claimant's main residence or property which he lets out. For a main residence the loan interest (including, for example, interest paid under a mortgage to a building society) is only relievable on a loan up to £25,000. Thus, if the loan is £50,000 only half the interest gets relief. The let property relief does not have the £25,000 (or any) limit. But there is a severe restriction which knocks out relief on a "second home." The property must be let at a commercial rent, in any period of 52 weeks, for more than 26 weeks, and when not so let be available for letting or used as the main residence of the claimant. This particular relief is not truly a deduction from total income, because it is only available against rental income derived from that or any other let property.

2. Loan applied in acquiring an interest in a close company

Putting it broadly, this relief applies to a claimant who uses the loan to invest in or lend money to a "close company" (for details see Chapter 22, below; for the moment let us say a small, private, family company) which is a trading company (not an investment company) and in which he actively works. This is one of the rare, but increasing, instances where tax law gives some encouragement to the development of small businesses.

3. Loan applied in acquiring an interest in a partnership

This relief is similar to number 2, and no doubt has the same socio-economic purpose.

4. Loan to purchase machinery or plant

This relief helps partners and employees. If a partner borrows money to acquire machinery or plant for use by the partnership he can get relief on the interest, and so can an employee who borrows money to acquire machinery or plant which he uses for the purposes of his employment. This relief (both for partners and employees) is limited to three years' interest.

5. Loan to pay capital transfer tax

This relief only operates where the capital transfer tax arises on a death, as distinct from a lifetime transfer. The relief is available to the personal representatives, and is some help to the estate in what is often the difficult task of getting together enough ready cash to pay the tax.

6. Loan to purchase a life annuity

This relief is designed to give some help in what has become a fairly common practice amongst retired people, namely borrowing money on the security of one's house and using the money to purchase an annuity. Interest on the loan (to the extent that the loan does not exceed £25,000) is entitled to relief if the borrower is aged 65 or more, if the loan is secured on land in the United Kingdom or in the Republic of Ireland, and if the land is his only or main residence.

4. THE TAX BILL

Having deducted from total income a taxpayer's personal reliefs and eligible interest (if any) we have arrived at his taxable income. We must now proceed to establish what amount of tax is payable. This is primarily determined by the rate or rates of tax applicable to an individual's taxable income.

The Rates of Tax

From 1973–74 a new method of charging income tax came into force. This is sometimes called the "unified system," the point of that epithet being that surtax was abolished. Under the new method income tax is all one tax, though it is levied at various rates. Until 1977–78 there were the basic rate, higher rates and additional rates. From 1978–79 onwards there has also been a lower rate. The introduction of a lower rate, although at first sight it seems a very simple point, has complicated the system, mainly because of the many cases in which income tax is "deducted at source" at the basic rate. It has also greatly complicated the P.A.Y.E. codes. On the other hand the introduction of a lower rate has achieved one very great social good; it has reduced the number of people caught in the "poverty trap." The poverty trap is the situation in which a family can actually be worse off if the bread-winner gets a rise than they were before. This absurdity arises from the interaction (at a certain low level of income) of income tax, national insurance contributions and means-tested social benefits. All the rates are subject to change from year to year. We must content ourselves with looking at the present position. Each rate applies to a stated band of income. Tax legislation applies each rate (other than the basic rate) to so much of an individual's "total income" but it would be more apposite if the reference were to "taxable income."

Lower rate

The lower rate is 25 per cent., and it applies to the first £750 of taxable income. In the case of a husband whose total income includes taxable *earned* income of his wife, the lower rate applies to £750 of his own income and to £750 of his wife's earned income.

Basic rate

The basic rate is 30 per cent., and it applies to taxable income of an individual above £750 up to £10,000. For non-individuals (*e.g.* trustees) the basic rate really is basic, because they do not have the benefit of the lower rate.

Higher rates

There are five different higher rates, each applying to a band of taxable income above £10,000. The rates are set out in a Table in the Finance (No. 2) Act 1979. They are as follows:

up to £12,000	40 per cent.
up to £15,000	45 per cent.
up to £20,000	50 per cent.
up to £25,000	55 per cent.
onwards and upwards	60 per cent.

Let me emphasise two points. First, the rates are levied on taxable income; so, for example, one begins to pay at 40 per cent. when one's income exceeds £10,000 clear of personal reliefs and interest relief. Secondly, the rates are, so to speak, inclusive of basic rate; so, if one has suffered basic rate deduction (30 per cent.), one only has another 10 per cent. to pay on the band of one's taxable income between £10,000 and £12,000.

Additional rate

Now we come to what commentators call the "investment income surcharge," but what the legislation calls the "additional rate." This rate truly is additional; it is not inclusive of basic rate. The additional rate is 15 per cent. on investment income over £5,000. Notice that one may be liable to additional rate without being liable to higher rate. Thus a taxpayer who has an income (after personal reliefs and interest relief) of £9,000, including an investment income of £6,000, will pay no higher rate tax, but will pay additional rate tax (at 15 per cent.) on £1,000 (tax = £150). And a very sinister point reveals itself at this stage. The Revenue takes the view that the wording of the legislation is such that if a person does not have enough earned income to absorb his personal reliefs they cannot be used to protect him from additional rate tax. Take the simple case of a married taxpayer who has no earned income at all, and has investment income of £6,000. The Revenue view is that he is liable to additional rate tax (at 15 per cent.) on £1,000. They say that his married man's relief is to be set against that part of his investment income which is not subject to the charge. This amounts to saying that he does not get any relief at all. I have argued elsewhere that this is not a correct reading of the legislation.[3] If this is the law, then the law is not merely an ass, but a vicious ass.

What is investment income?

Investment income is not defined in the legislation; it is merely said to be "any income other than earned income." The basic definition of earned income is in section 530 of the Taxes Act, though the list of items has been added to by other enactments. The following are the main items of earned income: (1) remuneration from an office or employment (2) pensions, including the national retirement pension (3) "golden handshakes" (4) any income charged under Schedule A, Schedule B or Schedule D which is "immediately derived" by the individual from the carrying on or exercise by him of his trade, profession or vocation (5) annuities payable under approved retirement annuity contracts (6) post-cessation receipts (7) income from patent rights where the invention was actually devised by the recipient. The words "immediately derived" in head (4) prevent the income of a sleeping partner from being earned income, and also the income of beneficiaries under a trust derived from a business carried on by the trustees. Also income charged under Case VI of Schedule D is not generally earned income. Maintenance payments are not investment income; see F.A. 1974, s. 15 and F.A. 1978, s. 21. This provision was no doubt intended to help separated and divorced women and their children, but its wording would seem to cover also annual payments by an ordinary dad in an ordinary unseparated, undivorced, family in favour of a child of his provided the child is 18 or over.

Investment income is what is left out from the list of items of

---

[3] See [1973] B.T.R. (*British Tax Review*) 194. For a contrary argument see [1974] B.T.R. 332 (Bowyer). I understand that the Special Commissioners have decided (five times) that the Revenue view is correct. So far as I know the point has never been taken to the High Court.

earned income. The main examples are dividends, interest, annuities (if not paid under approved retirement annuity contracts), rents, and income arising to a beneficiary under a trust.

Double Taxation Relief

We have still not quite arrived at an individual's tax bill. Having applied the appropriate rates of tax to his taxable income, one relief remains to be given at this stage (if it is applicable). I am referring to double taxation relief. The principal form of double taxation relief is relief by means of a credit for foreign tax paid. The credit is set against the United Kingdom tax payable.

We have at long last arrived at the individual's tax bill. We will leave him to write out a cheque in favour of "Inland Revenue."

Note on Life Assurance Relief

Before 1979–80 life assurance relief was given in the same way as credit for double taxation relief. It was given by way of deduction from the amount of tax chargeable. From 1979–80 onwards it has been given by permitting the policy holder to deduct a sum in respect of tax from the payment he makes by way of premium to his insurance company. The company is bound to accept the reduced payment, and it can recover the deficiency from the Revenue. This is the reverse of taxation at source; it is relief at source. The amount of the deduction is 17.5 per cent. of the premium.[4]

To be eligible for relief the policy must secure a capital sum on death. Also the relief is only given on premiums up to £1,500 or one-sixth of a person's total income, whichever is the greater.

In recent years a great deal of money has been put into life assurance because of the tax advantages. There is the advantage of life assurance relief, and also (more importantly) there is the advantage that the life funds of an insurance company enjoy very favourable tax treatment, thus enabling more favourable terms to be offered to policy holders than would otherwise be the case. Since 1968 there have been substantial anti-avoidance provisions which have been strengthened from time to time. Only a "qualifying policy" entitles the holder to life assurance relief. The main rules are that a policy must run for a minimum period of 10 years or until earlier death; there must be a reasonably even spread of premiums; and the policy must guarantee that the sum on death will be at least 75 per cent. of

---

[4] This system was enacted (in advance) in the Finance Act 1976. At that time the basic rate was 35 per cent., so 17.5 per cent. was half the basic rate. Despite changes in the basic rate since 1976 the figure of 17.5 per cent. has not been altered.

the total premiums that would be payable if the death occurred at age 75. (This last point is designed to strengthen the life element in the policy and cut down the endowment element.) In the case of a non-qualifying policy, not only is there no life assurance relief, but also there is a charge to tax (at the higher and additional rates but not at the basic rate) on the proceeds minus the premiums paid.

In their 121st Annual Report (for the year ended March 31, 1978) the Inland Revenue stated that they were considering the possibility of introducing a system for mortgage interest similar to the life assurance system of net payments. The borrower would make net payments to the building society, and the building society would receive the balance from the Revenue.

CHAPTER 8

INCOME FROM A TRADE OR PROFESSION
INTRODUCTORY

We now leave the more generalised aspects of income tax that we have been considering so far, and begin on a study of each particular kind of income. It is convenient to begin with income from a trade or profession.

The basic sections are sections 108 and 109 of the Taxes Act. Section 108 sets out the broad provisions of Schedule D as a whole. So far as concerns trades and professions it provides that: "Tax under this Schedule shall be charged in respect of—(a) the annual profits or gains arising or accruing— ... to any person residing in the United Kingdom from any trade, profession or vocation, whether carried on in the United Kingdom or elsewhere...." Section 109 sets out the various Cases of Schedule D and says that "The Cases are—Case I—tax in respect of any trade carried on in the United Kingdom or elsewhere; Case II—tax in respect of any profession or vocation not contained in any other Schedule...."

It has been held by the House of Lords in *Colquhoun* v. *Brooks* (1889) that, despite the words "or elsewhere," Case I does not apply to a trade carried on *wholly* outside the United Kingdom. See further on this in Chapter 18, below.

"Profits" and "gains" (in this context) mean the same thing. It is just a bit of legislative tautology. And the word "annual" carries very little weight. It only means that profits or gains, to be taxable, must be of an income nature; it does not mean that they must be recurrent.

What is the meaning of the curious word "vocation"? In ordinary speech it carries a rather starry-eyed idea. People talk about teachers or probation officers or such like having a vocation, which seems to mean that they should be prepared to pursue their good work without bothering about such mundane matters as rates of pay. It is somewhat ironic that the leading case as to what is meant by a vocation in tax law concerned a bookmaker. The case is *Partridge* v. *Mallandaine* (1886). It was held that the bookmaker was carrying on a vocation. That word, said the judge, means "the way a person passes his life." And he said that it was equivalent to a "calling." It is clearly a wider word than profession and brings within the scope of Case II callings which would not easily be described as professions. (It will be a relief to some people to know that it has been held that a person whose

54

means of livelihood is betting (as distinct from bookmaking) is not carrying on a vocation; see *Graham* v. *Green* (1925).)

Cases I and II are subject to the same principles, and can be considered together. But Case I raises one major problem and Case II raises a separate major problem.

The Case I problem is this: Is a given gain a trading gain or a capital gain? In the good old days a capital gain was entirely free of tax; since 1965 it has been subject to capital gains tax. But the maximum rate of capital gains tax is 30 per cent., whereas the maximum rate of (earned) income tax is 60 per cent., so the distinction is still important. In the vast majority of cases it will be the taxpayer who wants to say that his activity is not trading, but there are some exceptional circumstances (*e.g.* where there is a loss) where he will want to say that his activity is trading.

The Case II problem is this: Is a given person's exercise of his profession (or vocation) carried on within an office or employment, in which case he is to be taxed under Schedule E, or is it carried on outside any office or employment, in which case he is to be taxed under Schedule D? Remember that section 109 in reference to Case II says "tax in respect of any profession or vocation not contained in any other Schedule." The issue is between Schedule D and Schedule E. It is nowadays accepted that the distinction falls to be made on the same principles as in the law of tort. In tort the distinction is important in connection with vicarious liability, and it is generally described as the distinction between a servant (or employee) and an independent contractor. In tax law it is described as the distinction between an employed person (Schedule E) and a self-employed person (Schedule D). In both contexts it is the distinction between a contract of service and a contract for services. For example, a solicitor in private practice,[1] either as sole principal or as a partner, is self-employed and falls under Schedule D. A solicitor engaged in local government or in central government or in, say, Unilever Limited, is employed and falls under Schedule E, and so does an employed solicitor in private practice; that is a person qualified as a solicitor who works otherwise than as a partner in a firm of solicitors.

Is there any importance in this distinction? Yes, there is. The tax rules are very different as between Schedule D and Schedule E. The main differences are three: first, a Schedule E earner is subject to P.A.Y.E.; second, he is assessed on the current year's earnings, not on the earnings of the preceding year; third, the rules governing his expenses are less generous.

---

[1] A solicitor is said to be "in private practice" in the same circumstances in which an accountant would be said to be "in public practice." Curious.

Although the advantages are not all one way, most people would rather be taxed under Schedule D than under Schedule E. The argument has flared up in three main areas. The first area concerns what is called "The Lump." The Lump means the men in the construction industry who, though performing the functions of employed persons, claim the status of self-employed persons by means of "labour only" sub-contracting. The government has made several attempts at dealing with this situation. The latest attempt is in sections 68–71 of the Finance (No. 2) Act 1975. Except where a sub-contractor holds an "exemption certificate," the contractor must deduct from each payment that he makes to the sub-contractor a sum equal to the basic rate of tax, after allowing for the sub-contractor's expenditure on materials. So a sub-contractor, though nominally remaining under Schedule D, is to suffer deductions as though he were under Schedule E. That is the theory of the thing; in practice it does not work very well. Another group of workers to whom the government has turned its attention are "workers supplied by agencies." Section 38 of the Finance (No. 2) Act 1975 provides that these workers shall be taxed under Schedule E. Examples of workers caught by this provision are secretaries, typists and nurses. A third group of workers have been dealt with very differently indeed. These are "divers" and "diving supervisors." Section 29 of the Finance Act 1978 provides that "the Income Tax Acts shall have effect as if the performance by [a diver or a diving supervisor of his duties] constituted the carrying on by him of a trade within Case I of Schedule D; and accordingly Schedule E shall not apply. . . ." This is the reverse of the treatment meted out to "The Lump" and to agency workers; it is a case, not of treating self-employed persons as employed, but of treating employed persons as self-employed. One gathers that the reason for this generous treatment is the social, political or economic reason that if it were not done these divers and diving supervisors would leave the North Sea for sunnier places; sunnier fiscally speaking as well as climatically.

We shall return to the distinction between "employed" and "self-employed" when we come to deal with Schedule E in the next chapter. Now I want to discuss more fully what I called (above) the major Case I problem: Is a given gain a trading gain or a capital gain? Another way of putting the same question is, What is trading?

WHAT IS TRADING?

There is a kind of definition of "trade" in section 526 of the Taxes Act. I say a "kind of definition" because it is one of those so-called definitions, common in tax legislation, which merely expand a word without defining it. "Trade," we are told, "includes every trade, manufacture, adventure or concern in the nature of trade." Notice that the last few words are "nature of trade," not "nature of *a* trade."

The question whether a particular person is or is not trading is a question of fact. It was neatly described in one case as "a compound fact made up of a variety of things"; *Erichsen* v. *Last* (1881). We will look in a moment at the variety of things that may bear on the decision, but first I want to draw attention again (as I did in Chapter 5) to the point that an appeal lies from the General or Special Commissioners to the High Court only on a point of law. At first sight, therefore, it would seem that a finding by the Commissioners that a person is trading (or is not trading) can never be reversed by the court. But this is not so. Following the decision of the House of Lords in the great case of *Edwards* v. *Bairstow and Harrison* (1956), the court can and will reverse the Commissioners' decision if it is of the opinion that (*per* Lord Radcliffe) "the facts found are such that no person acting judicially and properly instructed as to the relevant law could have come to the determination under appeal."

The factors which bear on the question "Trade or No Trade" were graphically described by the 1954 Royal Commission on Taxation as "badges of trade." The Commission listed six badges of trade and though subsequent cases have indicated others those six are still the dominant factors. Quite a useful approach to the problem is to ask oneself, when considering a transaction or series of transactions, if it is not trading, what is it? The rival candidate is usually, though not always, investment. To purchase and subsequently realise an investment is not in itself trading.

The first point to consider is the subject-matter of the realisation. If the subject-matter is such that the purchaser cannot either use it himself or derive an income from it or derive pleasure from it that points towards trading. Thus in *Rutledge* v. *I.R.C.* (1929) the taxpayer, while in Berlin in connection with a cinema business, bought a million rolls of toilet paper for £1,000. Shortly after his return to England, he sold the whole lot to one purchaser at a profit of over £10,000. It was held that this was an adventure in the nature of trade. Notice that in this case, as in many others, the fact that there was only one transaction (a one-off job as the saying is) did not prevent its being held to be trading.[2]

---

[2] There is a rumour amongst tax lawyers that this case should really be called the case of the *imaginary* toilet rolls. It is said that the taxpayer invented the story of the toilet rolls to explain an increase in wealth, in the same way as many, many taxpayers claim that their wealth has arisen from betting-winnings (which are not taxable). It is said that this taxpayer thought that the toilet roll story would not be taxable. It is the tax law equivalent of the allegedly non-existent snail in the ginger beer bottle. Any student of tort law will be willing to explain this to the uninitiated.

The second point is length of ownership. This is not a very compelling consideration, but there is something in it. A quick re-sale points towards trading.

The third point is repetition. Although, as we have seen, a single transaction can amount to trading, there are situations where a single transaction would not be trading but that kind of transaction repeated several times would be trading. In *Pickford* v. *Quirke* (1927) a director of a spinning company formed a syndicate which bought the shares of a mill-owning company and then sold the assets of that company at a profit. He then took part in three similar transactions, although the members of the syndicate were not always the same people. The Court of Appeal held that he was carrying on a trade, even though each transaction considered by itself was not an adventure in the nature of trade.

The fourth point is supplementary work in connection with the realised property. In *Martin* v. *Lowry* (1927) (H.L.) the taxpayer (who had had nothing to do with the linen trade) purchased from the government its entire surplus stock of aeroplane linen, about 44 million yards. He found difficulty in selling it, and so he had to advertise extensively, rent offices and engage a manager and staff. He sold the linen to more than a thousand purchasers over a period of about 12 months and made a profit of between £1 and £2 million. It was held that the operations constituted trading. In *Martin* v. *Lowry* there was a very definite sales organisation, but there are cases where much more simple supplementary work has been held to make the transaction of buying and selling into trading. Thus in *I.R.C.* v. *Livingston* (1927) three individuals, a ship-repairer, a blacksmith and a fish salesman's employee, who had not previously been connected with each other in business, bought a cargo steamer, converted it (partly by their own labour) into a steam drifter, and sold it at a profit. The Court of Session overruled a finding of no-trade, and held that this transaction was the carrying-on of a trade.

The fifth point concerns the circumstances responsible for the realisation. There may be some explanation of why something is sold which negatives the idea of trading. In *West* v. *Phillips* (1958) a builder built some houses to hold as an investment and some for resale. Later on he decided to sell the investment houses, and he did so through the same organisation that sold his trading houses. The Special Commissioners held that there was trading, but the Court of Appeal reversed them, holding that the taxpayer decided to sell his investment houses because of rent control and the rising cost of repairs and higher taxation, and that in respect of the investment houses he was not trading.

The sixth point is motive. Although a trade may be held to exist even where there is no intention to make a profit, the absence of such an intention points against trading, whereas where there is such an intention that points towards trading. It is an important factor in a borderline case.

So much for the case law on trading. Some activities have been declared by statute to be trading. The most important are farming and market gardening. Section 110 of the Taxes Act states that "All farming and market gardening in the United Kingdom shall be treated as the carrying on of a trade...."

THE COMPUTATION OF PROFITS

The key to understanding the computation of profits is to visualise an account, because what is taxable is the excess of income over expenditure. It is an oversimplification to say that a receipt by a trader is taxable; the most one can say is that a receipt is a plus item in the computation of his taxable profit. A trader usually submits to the Revenue, with his return form, a copy of his accounts as prepared by his accountant.

There has been much debate in recent years as to the status in tax cases of accountancy practice and accountancy evidence. At one time it was thought in some quarters that if there was evidence in a case that the correct principles of commercial accountancy required, for example, that a particular item of expenditure be treated as of a revenue nature and not a capital nature, that that was binding on the judge. It has by now become perfectly plain that this is not so; such questions as whether an item of expenditure is of a revenue or a capital nature are questions of law for the court to decide. The judge is the boss, not the accountant. In *Heather* v. *P-E Consulting Group Ltd.* (1973) (C.A.) Lord Denning put it in this way: "The commissioners were entitled to give weight to the evidence of Mr. Bailey [an accountant witness], but the judge went further. He seems to have thought that ... the evidence of accountants should be treated as conclusive and that all the commissioners or the court would have to do would be to evaluate their evidence.... The courts have always been assisted greatly by the evidence of accountants. Their practice should be given due weight; but the courts have never regarded themselves as being bound by it. It would be wrong to do so. The question of what is capital and what is revenue is a question of law for the courts. They are not to be deflected from their true course by the evidence of accountants, however eminent." And in *ECC Quarries Ltd.* v. *Watkis* (1975) the court held a certain expenditure to be of a capital nature despite the unchallenged evidence of an independent and experienced accountant that such expenditure was correctly treated as revenue expenditure and that that treatment accorded with the general principles of commercial accounting.

We will deal first with trading receipts and then with trading expenses.

Trading Receipts

The first question to be asked about any receipt is, is it a trading receipt or is it a capital receipt? The reader may wish to refer back at this point to Chapter 6, above.

In some circumstances the answer to the question is perfectly plain. Thus if a manufacturer sells his factory because he has had a more up-to-date one built for him, it is clear that the proceeds of the sale constitute a capital receipt, which consequently does not enter into the computation of his profits for income tax purposes. It is equally plain that if the same manufacturer sells a widget[3] which has been made in his factory the proceeds of that sale constitute an income receipt which becomes an item in his income tax computation.

In other circumstances, however, the question "trading receipt or capital receipt?" is quite difficult to answer. This is particularly so where compensation is paid to a trader.

Compensation

There is a mass of decided cases on this matter. We will look at three of them. In *Van den Berghs Ltd.* v. *Clark* (1935) (H.L.) the appellant English company had entered into agreements with a competing Dutch company under which each company agreed to conduct its business on certain lines. After a dispute it was settled that the agreements should be terminated on condition that the Dutch company paid £450,000 to the English company. It was held that this was a capital receipt, and thus was not taxable. Lord Macmillan said that ". . . the cancelled agreements related to the whole structure of the appellant's profit-making apparatus."

In *Kelsall Parsons & Co.* v. *I.R.C.* (1938) the appellants were manufacturers' agents; they held contracts with several manufacturers under which they sold their products for a commission. One of these manufacturers wished to terminate its agency contract and it did so about 16 months before it was due to expire, paying Kelsall Parsons & Co. £1,500 as compensation. This sum was held to be an income receipt, and hence taxable. The loss of this one agency clearly

---

[3] "Widgets" are much beloved of American academic lawyers, but not many have crossed the Atlantic. They are simply unspecified units, where whether they are lollipops or lasers does not matter.

did not relate to the whole structure of the appellants' profit-making apparatus. Lord Normand said (in the Court of Session): "The agency agreements, so far from being a fixed framework, are rather to be regarded as temporary and variable elements of the profit-making enterprise."

In *London and Thames Haven Oil Wharves Ltd.* v. *Attwooll* (1967) (C.A.) the taxpayer company owned a jetty which was seriously damaged by a tanker when it was coming alongside. The owners of the tanker paid a sum of money to the taxpayer of which part was apportioned to physical damage to the jetty and part to consequential damage, namely loss of use of the jetty during the 380 days taken up in repairing it. The Revenue did not seek to tax that part of the payment which was apportioned to physical damage, but it did seek to tax the part apportioned to consequential damage. The assessment was upheld by the Court of Appeal. Diplock L.J. gave a limpidly clear judgment. He said:

> "Where, pursuant to a legal right, a trader receives from another person compensation for the trader's failure to receive a sum of money which, if it had been received, would have been credited to the amount of profits (if any) arising in any year from the trade carried on by him at the time when the compensation is so received, the compensation is to be treated for income tax purposes in the same way as that sum of money would have been treated if it had been received instead of the compensation."

The Lord Justice went on to say that two questions have to be asked. First, Was the compensation paid for the failure of the trader to receive a sum of money? If the answer to that is Yes, there arises a second question: If that sum of money had been received by the trader would it have been credited to the amount of profits of the trader? The same question can be put more shortly, namely, would it have been an income receipt of the trade (and not a capital receipt)? If the answer to that question is Yes, the compensation is taxable; if the answer is No, the compensation is not taxable. In the instant case that part of the compensation which had been apportioned to loss of use of the jetty (1) was paid for the failure of the trader to receive a sum of money, and (2) represented the profit (surplus of receipts over expenses) which would have followed from the use of the jetty during 380 days. So the assessment was correct.

Trading stock

It is very important to grasp that trading stock (stock-in-trade) is an essential item in a trader's account—for tax purposes no less than for commercial purposes. Let us take a simple trading account in the modern form in which it is usually presented nowadays.

	£	£
Sales for the year		27,000
Opening stock	2,000	
Purchases	21,000	
	23,000	
Less Closing stock	2,800	
Cost of goods sold		20,200
Trading profit		6,800

Notice that in the account I have used the phrase "trading profit." This account does not deal with expenses such as wages, rent, rates, heating, lighting, telephone, postage. Those matters would be dealt with in a further account, so reducing the trading profit to a taxable profit.

Trading profit is the amount by which the proceeds of the goods sold (£27,000) exceed the cost of those goods (£20,200).

If one omitted stock—both opening and closing—from the trading account one would get a different result. One would get sales £27,000, less purchases £21,000 = profit £6,000. But that would be unreal. This trader has not only made a profit of £6,000 on sales during the year compared with purchases during the year; he has also improved his position by having increased his stock during the year from £2,000 at the beginning of the year to £2,800 at the end of the year, an increase of £800.

The closing stock figure for one year becomes the opening stock figure for the next year.

As closing stock represents expenditure on goods not yet sold, that expenditure is credited to the current year and carried forward to be charged in the subsequent year—as opening stock—in which the stock is to be sold.

In *I.R.C.* v. *Cock, Russell & Co. Ltd.* (1949) the court gave its approval to the accountancy practice of permitting a trader to value stock at its cost price or its market price, whichever is the lower, and to treat each item of stock separately. So, when any item of stock is expected to fetch less than its cost, its market value (or "net realisable value") (instead of its cost) is included in the total of closing stock. The effect is to charge immediately, in the current year, that part of its cost which is considered to be irrecoverable.

In some of the reported cases on the matter closing stock has been described as being a receipt of the current year, and in other cases it has been described as a notional sale from one year to the next. And the use of a figure of less than cost has been described as an exception to the general income tax principle that an unrealised loss (or profit) cannot be brought into a tax computation. I venture to think that these views are based on a misapprehension as to the nature of the item of closing stock in a trading account, and that the correct view is that put forward by Russell L.J. in the Court of Appeal in *B.S.C. Footwear Ltd.* v. *Ridgway* (1971). Russell L.J. said:

"In my view the accepted practice of entering stock in hand at cost at the terminal date of the first period and the opening date of the second period arises from the fact that the expenditure has not contributed anything directly to the figures of gross profit in the first period. It is unused expenditure, to be carried forward into the second period, in which it is estimated that it will contribute on sale to the gross profit of that period. But if it is estimated that on sale it will not contribute to the gross profit of the second period—that is, if it is estimated that it will sell below cost—the shortfall is to be regarded in the course of stock valuation as irrecoverable and may properly be treated as a loss incurred in the first period. This I believe to be the basis of the principle that for tax purposes market value if below cost may be taken as the value of stock in hand."

WORK IN PROGRESS. "Work in progress" is the phrase used to cover such things as goods in the process of manufacture. A manufacturer, at the end of a particular accounting period, will have some items in his factory which are partially but not wholly constructed. Such items are brought into account in the same way (broadly) as is closing stock. And the same principle applies to many other things besides partially manufactured goods; it applies for example to partially performed contracts of a professional person.

RELIEF FOR INCREASE IN STOCK VALUES. In a period of inflation the inclusion of closing stock as a receipt of a trade leads to the taxation of profits which are only notional and not real. Some economists do not accept this view, but the view I have stated has been accepted by the government and acted upon, both for income tax and for corporation tax. The government view can be explained in this way: suppose a trader had as his opening stock 100 units which had cost £1,000. If at the end of the year he again has say 100 units they might not be the same units; he might have sold during the year the original 100 units and bought during the year 100 new units. Because of inflation during the year they might have cost say £1,300. On paper he has

made a profit (difference between opening stock and closing stock) of
£300. The argument is that this is not really a profit at all. Some relief
was first given in this respect by the Finance Act 1975. The relief was
extended by the Finance (No. 2) Act 1975. Then a new system of
relief was introduced by the Finance Act 1976. Under all these
enactments the relief was temporary only, in the sense that tax was
only deferred, not excused for ever. However, the then Chancellor in
his budget statement in April 1978 said that the amounts of tax
relieved would to a substantial extent be written-off by future legislation which would also introduce a permanent system of relief. The
present system is in section 37 and Schedule 5 of the Finance Act
1976, as amended by the Finance (No. 2) Act 1979. The relief takes
the form of a deduction (or, for companies, a deductible expense)
equal to the whole of the increase during the period of account in the
value of trading stock (including work in progress) *less* 10 per cent.
for individuals (15 per cent. for companies) of the trading income.
For this purpose trading income is trading income after deduction of
capital allowances. This is very important in practice as an encouragement to investment. The more investment (in *e.g.* new plant and
machinery) a taxpayer has made during the year the greater will be
his capital allowances and consequently the less will be the deduction
which falls to be made as 10 per cent. (or 15 per cent.) of trading
income and consequently the greater will be his stock relief. Individuals (or companies) may if they wish claim partial rather than total
relief. Above all, deferred relief is now written off after six years.

Let us see how this works out in the case of the account set out on
page 62, above. Let us suppose that expenses such as wages, rent,
rates, etc., amounted to £2,000. That gives a profit of £4,800. And let
us suppose that the trader was entitled to £1,200 capital allowances.
That reduces the trading income to £3,600. 10 per cent. of £3,600 is
£360. The increase in stock values was £800. The relief therefore is
£800 less £360 = £440.

The rule in Sharkey v. *Wernher.* This case established the rule that if
you transfer an asset from a taxable activity of yours to a non-taxable
activity, you must bring in to your accounts the market value of the
asset which you have transferred, just as though you had sold it.
Sharkey v. *Wernher* (1956) (H.L.) concerned Lady Zia Wernher, the
wife of Sir Harold Wernher, the owner of Luton Hoo and the
Wernher Collection.[4] Lady Zia carried on a stud farm, the profits of

---

[4] Someone ought to compile a "Who's Who in Tax Cases"; it would be like a tax case
itself—long and expensive.

which were assessable to income tax under Case I. She also owned horses and ran them at race meetings as a recreation, in respect of which activity no liability to tax arose. In one year she transferred five horses from the stud farm to her racing stables. The House of Lords held that the horses must be treated as having been disposed of by way of trade, and the sum which should be regarded as having been received on their disposal must be a sum equivalent to their market value. Lord Simonds neatly observed that the same point arises when "the owner of a stud farm diverts the produce of his farm to his own enjoyment or a diamond merchant, neglecting profitable sales, uses his choicest jewels for the adornment of his wife, or a caterer provides lavish entertainment for a daughter's wedding breakfast. Are the horses, the jewels, the cakes and ale to be treated for the purpose of income tax as disposed of for nothing or for their market value or for the cost of their production?" And the House of Lords (with one dissentient) answered "Market value."

Some years later the Revenue, very naturally, sought to apply the same rule to an author. In *Mason* v. *Innes* (1967) (C.A.) Hammond Innes (another celebrity) wrote a book called *The Doomed Oasis* and, before its publication, presented the copyright in it to his father as a gift. The Court of Appeal held that the rule in *Sharkey* v. *Wernher* did not apply. Their decision was apparently based on two points: first, that the taxpayer was carrying on a profession and not a trade, and that a professional person does not have stock-in-trade; second, that his accounts were not on an earnings basis but on a cash basis. (On this point see p. 73, below.) Neither of these points seems wholly convincing.[5]

SECTION 485 OF THE TAXES ACT. The rule in *Sharkey* v. *Wernher* is a common law rule, but there is a similar statutory rule in section 485 of the Taxes Act. The section applies to "bodies of persons" (including partnerships). Where the buyer and the seller are under common control ("associated") the Revenue may substitute in the accounts of either party the notional market price of the thing sold for the price in fact charged, thus counteracting a transaction at an over-value or an under-value. The section does not apply where the under-value or over-value will be reflected anyway in the accounts of the benefitted party, which is the case where he (or it) is taxable as a United Kingdom trader.[6] The section is clearly aimed at "transfer pricing"

---

[5] The book ought to have been renamed *The Lucky Oasis*.

[6] The Revenue will not lose any tax in this case, because an over-value will show an inflated plus item in the seller's profit computation and an under-value will show a deflated minus item (expense) in the buyer's computation.

between the United Kingdom and overseas. Bear in mind that where the section does not apply, the rule in *Sharkey* v. *Wernher* may apply.

Trading Expenses

The legislation relating to trading expenses is couched in very negative terms. There is no section stating what expenses are deductible under Cases I and II of Schedule D. This is very different from Schedule E, where there is a section (Section 189 of the Taxes Act) which states positively what expenses are deductible by the holder of an office or employment.

For Cases I and II of Schedule D there are two negative enactments. Section 519 (1) of the Taxes Act declares that "In arriving at the amount of profits or gains for tax purposes . . . no other deductions shall be made than such as are expressly enumerated in the Tax Acts." And section 130 of the Taxes Act declares: "Subject to the provisions of the Tax Acts, in computing the amount of the profits or gains to be charged under Case I or Case II of Schedule D, no sum shall be deducted in respect of " ———— and this preamble is followed by 15 lettered paragraphs ((a) to (o)) containing undeductible expenses. If these two enactments (s. 519 (1) and s. 130) had been taken absolutely literally the result would have been that no expenses at all would have been allowable under Cases I and II. A judge once said that the life of the law is not logic but commonsense. And in this case commonsense has triumphed over logic without much difficulty. After all, section 108 and section 109 (of the Taxes Act) state that tax is to be charged under Cases I and II in respect of the annual profits or gains arising or accruing from any trade, profession or vocation. If you keep a shop and sell goods in a year for £6,000 it would be absurd if you were assessed to tax on £6,000 if you had spent £3,000 on buying the goods in the first place and £1,000 on rent of the shop. Your profit or gain is not £6,000; it is £2,000. It is now absolutely settled law that some expenses are deductible under Cases I and II.

The only question is, *What* expenditure is deductible? The answer is, Such expenditure as fulfils three conditions: first, that it is revenue and not capital expenditure; second, that it is incurred wholly and exclusively for the purposes of the trade; third, that it is not caught by any of the prohibitions set out in section 130. Let us look at the three conditions in turn.

Revenue, not capital, expenditure

The same distinction falls to be made in regard to expenditure as in regard to receipts. It is not an easy distinction to make. In one case Lord Greene M.R. remarked: ". . . in many cases it is almost true to say that the spin of a coin would decide the matter almost as satisfactorily as an attempt to find reasons." (*British Salmson Aero Engines Ltd.* v. *I.R.C.* (1938) (C.A.).) But judges do not toss-up, at least not visibly. So we must look at some reasoning.

The first point to be clear about is that (as I pointed out in Chapter 6, above) a payment which is a revenue receipt in the hands of the payee is not necessarily an item of revenue expenditure by the payer. Equally a payment which in the hands of the recipient is a capital item may be a revenue expenditure on the part of the payer. The two things have to be looked at separately. The principles, however, are the same whether one is considering receipts or expenses.

In some cases of expenditure the matter is perfectly clear. If a manufacturer expends money on a new factory that is capital expenditure; if he spends money on raw materials that is revenue expenditure. Adam Smith's distinction between fixed capital and circulating capital is of some help here. But in the case of mines and quarries even this distinction gets blurred. The courts have held in a number of cases that an enterprise which spends money on buying a quarry, or on acquiring by contract the right to excavate gravel, or even on applying for planning permission to work a quarry, is making capital expenditure. The distinction was put in this way in *H. J. Rorke Ltd.* v. *I.R.C.* (1960), a case concerned with opencast mining: "They were not payments made for the purchase of coal but payments to put the company into the position to get coal."

One of the classic statements on this matter is to be found in the speech of Lord Cave in *British Insulated and Helsby Cables Ltd.* v. *Atherton* (1926) (H.L.): "When an expenditure is made, not only once and for all, but with a view to bringing into existence an asset or an advantage for the enduring benefit of a trade, I think that there is very good reason ... for treating such an expenditure as properly attributable not to revenue but to capital." There is no doubt that this is a helpful general statement, but it requires two qualifications. First, it is clear from later cases that "enduring benefit of a trade" must be taken as meaning "a thing which endures in the same way that fixed capital endures": see *per* Rowlatt J. in *Anglo-Persian Oil Co. Ltd.* v. *Dale* (1931), approved and adopted by Lord Wilberforce in *Tucker* v. *Granada Motorway Services Ltd.* (1979) (H.L.). Second, the word "enduring" must not be given too much weight. After all, in the *Rorke* case (above) the opencast coal mining company's lease was for only one year; the transience of the benefit was outweighed by the nature of the benefit acquired—the means of getting coal rather than coal itself.

Probably three main factors emerge from the welter of decided cases on the point: the nature of the benefit acquired in exchange for the payment; the manner in which that benefit is to be used; the means by which it is obtained (periodical payments or lump-sum payment). Different weights are to be attached to these three factors in different circumstances. In *Regent Oil Co. Ltd.* v. *Strick* (1966) (H.L.) Lord Reid said:

"Whether a particular outlay by a trader can be set against income, or must be regarded as a capital outlay, has proved to be a difficult question. It may be possible to reconcile all the decisions, but it is certainly not possible to reconcile all the reasons given for them. . . . The question is ultimately a question of law for the Court, but it is a question which must be answered in light of all the circumstances which it is reasonable to take into account, and the weight which must be given to a particular circumstance in a particular case must depend rather on commonsense than on a strict application of any single legal principle."

There is one particular kind of expenditure which deserves to be mentioned separately. This is the setting aside of a sum of money to cover depreciation. It is well settled that such expenditure is of a capital, not a revenue, nature. When a trader submits his accounts to the Inspector, depreciation (which appears in the commercial accounts as an expense) has to be added back. The trader (or his accountant) usually submits with his accounts a computation dealing with this matter. However, it must not be thought that income tax law gives no assistance in respect of depreciation; it does give such assistance, in some circumstances very generous assistance, but it gives it, not in the form of a deductible expense in computing profits, but in the form of allowances, called Capital Allowances, which are deductions *from* computed profits: see Chapter 16, below. Capital Allowances are of immense importance to industry.

Wholly and exclusively

The second test that an expense must pass if it is to be an allowable deduction arises from paragraph (a) of section 130, which states that "no sum shall be deducted in respect of . . . any disbursements or expenses, not being money wholly and exclusively laid out or expended for the purposes of the trade, profession or vocation." This paragraph differs from the other paragraphs in section 130 in that instead of referring to some specific item of expenditure it is a general test applicable to all expenditure.

It seems that the word "wholly" relates to *quantum*. The whole amount of the expenditure must be laid out for the purposes of the trade, or rather the expense is only allowable up to the amount of it which is laid out for the purposes of the trade. For example, if a company has paid over-generous remuneration to a director, a reasonable amount may be allowed, and the excess over what is reasonable disallowed.

The word "exclusively" has proved difficult to apply. The classic statement of the law is in the judgment of Romer L.J. in *Bentleys, Stokes & Lowless* v. *Beeson* (1952) (C.A.). This case was concerned with business entertainment expenditure. At the time of the case there was no special rule relating to such expenditure; there is such a rule now (in s. 411 of the Taxes Act) disallowing it, with an exception in favour of reasonable entertainment for an overseas customer. Romer L.J. said: "It is . . . a question of fact. And it is quite clear that the purpose must be the sole purpose. The paragraph says so in clear terms. If the activity be undertaken with the object both of promoting business and also with some other purpose, for example, with the object of indulging an independent wish of entertaining a friend or stranger or of supporting a charitable or benevolent object, then the paragraph is not satisfied though in the mind of the actor the business motive may predominate. For the statute so prescribes. *Per contra*, if in truth the sole object is business promotion, the expenditure is not disqualified because the nature of the activity necessarily involves some other result, or the attainment or furtherance of some other objective, since the latter result or objective is necessarily inherent in the act." And so the Court of Appeal allowed the expenditure which had been incurred in entertaining clients.

Lord Justice Romer made it all sound very easy, but in practice it has not proved easy to separate sole purpose cases from dual purpose cases, and one is left with the feeling that honesty is not the best policy. In *Bowden* v. *Russell & Russell* (1965) the sole principal of a firm of solicitors visited America and Canada with his wife to attend the annual meeting of the American Bar Association in Washington and the Commonwealth and Empire Law Conference in Ottawa. It was his intention to have also a holiday with his wife. The court held that the expenses incurred in connection with the conferences were not deductible, because they were incurred for a dual purpose, the advancement of his profession and the enjoyment of a holiday.

I want now to make special mention of certain types of expenditure.

TRAVEL FROM HOME TO WORK AND RETURN. There seems to be a lot of misunderstanding about expenditure on travel from home to work and from work to home. I have found that some people think that home to work (and return) travel is not allowable for Schedule E taxpayers but is allowable for Schedule D taxpayers. This is not correct. It is quite true that there is a big difference in the rules relating to expenditure under Schedule E and under Schedule D, and we shall be looking at the difference in the next chapter. But in practice the courts have reached, albeit by different routes, similar conclusions about the allowability or otherwise of travel expenses under both Schedules. This is because the phrase in Schedule E, "travelling in the performance of the duties," more or less balances the phrase in Schedule D, "wholly and exclusively for the purposes of the trade" (as applied to travel).

In *Newsom* v. *Robertson* (1953) (C.A.) a barrister who had chambers in Lincoln's Inn and lived at Whipsnade was held not entitled to deduct the expenses of travelling between the two places. This was so even though he had at his home a library of law books, and worked at home in the evenings and at weekends. On the other hand, in *Horton* v. *Young* (1972) (C.A.) a self-employed bricklayer was held entitled to deduct the expenses of travelling from his home to the various sites on which he worked. At first glance this may seem to be inconsistent with *Newsom's* case. But this is not so. Mr. Horton kept at his home his tools and account books and made his contracts there. It was held that his home was his base, whereas in Mr. Newsom's case it was held that his chambers were his base. If your home is your base, travel to work and back home is wholly and exclusively for the purposes of your trade or profession. If your home is not your base then such travel is not wholly and exclusively for the purposes of your trade or profession; it is partly because you choose to live at (*e.g.*) Whipsnade. A more recent case caused some consternation. This is *Sargent* v. *Barnes* (1978). A self-employed dental surgeon had a dental laboratory which was on the route between his home and his surgery. He called at the laboratory on his morning and evening journeys for the purpose of collecting dentures and discussing work with his technician. He claimed to deduct the expenses of travel between the laboratory and his surgery. His claim failed, the judge holding that the expenditure was not wholly and exclusively for the purposes of the taxpayer's profession. The journey did not "cease to be a journey for the purpose of getting to or from the place where the taxpayer chose to live."

VALUE ADDED TAX. Another point which deserves special mention is Value Added Tax. The Inland Revenue have stated in a Press Notice[7] that in the case of a person who is registered for VAT purposes his deductible expenditure for income tax purposes is cost exclusive of VAT. (This is because he will not ultimately bear the VAT.) Where the input tax is not deductible for VAT purposes (*e.g.* expenditure on motor cars) the deduction for income tax purposes

---

[7] The notice is dated May 7, 1973. It is printed (*e.g.*) in [1973] B.T.R. at p. 481.

will be the amount inclusive of VAT. A person who is not registered for VAT can claim, for income tax purposes, the full cost (inclusive of VAT) of trading expenses. A partially-exempt person for VAT purposes will (broadly speaking) be able to claim as a deduction any input tax that is not allowable for VAT purposes.

LEGAL AND ACCOUNTANCY CHARGES. The professional costs incurred in a tax appeal are not allowable. But as a matter of practice the fees paid to an accountant for agreeing tax computations with the Revenue are allowed, and so are fees paid for advice on tax liability.

PENSIONS AND PENSION CONTRIBUTIONS. A pension paid by an employer to a former employee will be held to be wholly and exclusively laid out for the purposes of the trade except in so far as it is excessive. And annual contributions by an employer to a fund to provide pensions for employees when they come to retire are deductible in most circumstances. An initial contribution to such a fund may be non-deductible as being a capital payment, but if the fund is that of an "exempt approved scheme" an initial contribution to it will be deductible: for details see F.A. 1970, s. 21.

INTEREST. Interest is quite capable of being wholly and exclusively laid out for the purposes of the trade and, if it is, it is a deductible expense. This is immensely important in practice.

Not prohibited
The third test than an expense must pass if it is to be deductible is that it must not be prohibited by any of the specific paragraphs of section 130. We will not deal with most of these paragraphs, but something must be said about paragraphs (d) and (g).

REPAIRS AND IMPROVEMENTS. Remember that the paragraphs are stating sums which are not to be deducted. Paragraph (d) says: "any sum expended for repairs of premises occupied . . . for the purpose of the trade, profession or vocation, beyond the sum actually expended for those purposes." And paragraph (g) says: "any capital employed in improvements of premises occupied for the purposes of the trade, profession or vocation." So the upshot is that expenditure on repair is allowable, whereas expenditure on improvements is not. In a famous passage Buckley L.J. (in *Lurcott* v. *Wakely & Wheeler* (1911) (C.A.) said: "Repair is restoration by renewal or replacement of subsidiary parts of a whole. Renewal, as distinguished from repair, is reconstruction of the entirety, meaning by the entirety not necessarily the whole but substantially the whole subject-matter under discussion." In subsequent cases the distinction made by Lord Justice Buckley between repair and renewal has been taken to be the same as the statutory distinction between repair and improvements. His idea of "the entirety" seems attractive, but of course it involves that everything depends on what the court regards, in any particular case, as the entirety. In *O'Grady* v. *Bullcroft Main Collieries Ltd.* (1932) the expense of replacing a chimney by another on a different site was held to be not deductible. But in *Samuel Jones & Co. (Devondale) Ltd.* v. *I.R.C.* (1951) the expense of replacing a factory chimney was held to be deductible. In the first case the court regarded the chimney itself as the entirety; in the second case the court regarded the chimney as part of a larger entirety, namely the factory.

The distinction between repair and improvements runs into (in some circumstances it is virtually the same as) the distinction between revenue and capital expenditure. In *Law Shipping Co. Ltd.* v. *I.R.C.* (1924) a trader bought a ship in a state of disrepair. The periodical survey of the ship was overdue, but she was ready to sail, with freight booked, and she did sail. When that voyage was over, the ship underwent survey, and the owners had to spend some £50,000 on repairs, of which some four-fifths was attributable to the disrepair of the ship at the time of purchase. It was held by the Court of Session that that latter expenditure was in the nature of capital expenditure and was therefore not deductible. In *Odeon Associated Theatres Ltd.* v. *Jones* (1973) (C.A.) the appellant company bought a large number of cinemas which had not been kept in repair. Some years later they carried out repairs which had been outstanding at the time of purchase. The cinemas were usable in their unrepaired state, but they were not up to the standard set by the new owners. The Special Commissioners made a finding of fact that on the principles of sound commercial accountancy these deferred repairs would be dealt with as a charge to revenue in the accounts of the company. The Court of Appeal held that the cost of the repairs was deductible as revenue expenditure. The *Law Shipping* case (above) was distinguished on three grounds: (1) in that case, but not in this case, the purchase price was less by reason of the disrepair, (2) in that case but not in this case the asset could not (except temporarily) earn profits until it had been repaired, and (3) in that case there was no evidence of accountancy practice, whereas in this case there was such evidence and it pointed towards deductibility. (But one must not put too much weight on this last point; see the comments at p. 59, above, under the heading "The Computation of Profits.")

THE BASIS OF ASSESSMENT

Under all the Schedules except Schedule D tax is charged on the profits of the current year. Within Schedule D this is also true of Case VI. But in the other cases of Schedule D (including Cases I and II) tax is charged on what is called "the preceding year basis." This means that in each year of assessment the assessment is based on the profits of the trader's accounting period which ended at any date in the preceding year of assessment. For example, a trader who prepares accounts each year up to September 30, will be assessed for the year 1979–80 on the basis of his accounting year to September 30, 1978. This accounting year is called the "basis period" for the year of assessment 1979–80.

Obviously a trader or professional person cannot be taxed in his first year of trade or practice on a preceding year basis, and so there are special rules for the opening year (and indeed the second year as well) by which the early profits are taxed on an actual basis.[8] There are also similar rules for the closing years (the last three years) of a trade or practice. Also there are rules dealing with changes in owner-ship. There is a certain amount of scope for tax planning or tax avoidance in these rules. This is especially so in relation to partner-ships, because by section 154 (1) of the Taxes Act a change in the partners (*e.g.* the retirement of a partner) amounts to the ending of one trade or profession and the setting up of a new one, and by section 154 (2) the partners can elect that that rule shall not apply and that, instead, the trade or profession shall be treated as continuing.

Mainly because of these tax avoidance possibilities, the idea is very much in the air at the present time that the preceding year basis should be abolished and that all sources of income should be taxed on a current year basis.

POST-CESSATION RECEIPTS

The phrase "post-cessation receipts" means sums which are received after the cessation of a trade, profession or vocation for items sold, or services rendered, before the cessation.

It is relevant to this matter to consider the distinction between what is called the "earnings basis" for computing profits and other bases. (And the distinction is relevant to other aspects of income tax as well; see, *e.g. Mason* v. *Innes* (1967) (C.A.) at p. 65, above.)

The earnings basis is described in section 151 (2) of the Taxes Act: "The profits or gains of a trade, profession or vocation in any period shall be treated as computed by reference to earnings where all credits and liabilities accruing during that period as a consequence of the carrying on of the trade, profession or vocation, are brought into

---

[8] And the taxpayer may elect to have the second *and* third years dealt with on an actual basis.

account in computing those profits or gains for tax purposes. . . ." So if a solicitor (to take an example) has, during a particular accounting period, got in, in hard cash, for services rendered during that period £10,000 and has rendered services which he has billed for a further £6,000, his incomings on an earnings basis are £16,000. On an earnings basis there will be brought into account—as well as his prospective incomings—the expenditure incurred for the period, whether paid or owing. The main basis other than the earnings basis is the "cash basis." This means that the taxpayer brings into account only payments actually received in the relevant period of account and outgoings actually paid. This basis is commonly used by barristers (possible because they cannot sue for their fees) and by authors (because it is impossible to estimate in advance how much they will make out of any particular book).

Any basis other than the earnings basis is called "a conventional basis" (*e.g.* in section 143 (2) of the Taxes Act). This is rather a curious phrase, especially as it is the earnings basis which is the most usual. One meaning of "convention," according to the dictionary, is "practice based on consent." So I take it that here the meaning is that the taxpayer and the Revenue have agreed to depart from the earnings basis.

The Revenue does not regard the cash basis as being satisfactory for traders, no doubt because of the extent to which trading stock, and trade debtors and creditors (none of which is reflected in a cash account) can fluctuate from month to month or even from day to day. But the Revenue will accede to the request of a professional practitioner to use a "conventional" basis of accounting, except for the three opening years of a practice, provided he gives an undertaking to render his bills to his clients frequently—and consequently collect his fees promptly.

Until 1960 the post-cessation receipts of a trade, profession or vocation escaped tax. A leading case concerned Leslie Howard, the famous film actor, who was killed in an air crash in 1943. His real name was Stainer and the case is called *Stainer's Executors* v. *Purchase* (1952) (H.L.). It was held by the House of Lords that royalties which were paid to his executors after his death were not taxable. This result stemmed from the source doctrine; income tax is a tax on what flows from a source; if the source has dried up there is nothing to tax. (See Chapter 6, above.) Another case concerned Peter Cheyney, the celebrated author. In *Carson* v. *Peter Cheyney's Executor* (1959) (H.L.) it was held that royalties received after Peter Cheyney's death were not taxable, again because of the source doctrine.

This happy state of affairs, which notably benefited retiring barristers, was ended by legislation in two bites, one in 1960 and the other in 1968. The enactments are now contained in sections 143–151 of the Taxes Act. Section 143 brings into charge to tax (under Case VI) all post-cessation receipts of a taxpayer who had been on the earnings basis and some post-cessation receipts of a taxpayer who had been on a conventional basis. Section 144 brings into charge (under Case VI) such post-cessation receipts of a taxpayer who had been on a conventional basis as are not caught by section 143. (Certain receipts are expressly excepted and are not caught by either section, *e.g.* a lump sum paid to the executors of an author for the assignment of a copyright.) There is some relief under section 144, but not under section 143. The relief is on a sliding scale according to age. An individual who was 50 or more on April 6, 1968 can benefit. For example if he was 65 or more on that date he would when he retired pay tax on $^5/_{20}$ of his post cessation receipts. The minimum age for relief is 51 on April 6, 1968; an individual of that age would pay tax on $^{19}/_{20}$ of his post-cessation receipts. For intermediate ages the relief varies by $^1/_{20}$ per year of age.

RETIREMENT ANNUITIES

A self-employed individual does not have an employer to pay him a pension when he retires; he must make his own provision for retirement. Until 1956 the income tax system did nothing to help him. The Finance Act 1956 introduced a measure of help. The point is now dealt with by the Taxes Act, ss. 226–229 as amended by the Finance Act 1971, s. 20 and Schedule 2. The relief takes the form of deducting from his earnings the amounts the taxpayer pays as premiums on any approved[9] retirement annuity contracts. In other words he does not pay tax on the amount of the premiums. The relief is limited; it cannot exceed £3,000 on all the annuity contracts of a taxpayer as a whole, nor can it exceed 15 per cent. of the taxpayer's earnings.

The relief described above is, of course, directed to the time when the taxpayer is still working, helping him to build up provision for when he comes to retire. And the provision is enormously increased by the fact that the fund itself into which he pays his premiums is exempt from income tax and also capital gains tax; Taxes Act, s. 226 (6). There is also a relief (in a sense) when he has retired, namely that when the annuity payments begin to come in they are treated as earned income and not as investment income (s. 226 (1)).

Both the reliefs I have mentioned, although mainly intended for self-employed individuals, are available for employed individuals in so far as their employment is not pensionable (s. 226 (9) (*a*)).

---

[9] "Approved" means approved by the Board of Inland Revenue.

D

INCOME FROM AN EMPLOYMENT

INTRODUCTORY

In the last chapter we considered the taxation, under Cases I and II of Schedule D, of self-employed individuals. Now we have to consider the taxation of employed individuals. Far more people are employed than are self-employed. Incomes from employment represent something like 70 per cent. of the gross national product, as against about 10 per cent. for incomes from self-employment. The income tax on employment incomes accounts for some three-quarters of the whole yield from direct taxes.

The Schedule we are concerned with is Schedule E. It is set out in section 181 of the Taxes Act. The Schedule contains three cases, Cases I, II and III. In this chapter I shall confine the discussion to situations where no foreign element is involved, leaving foreign elements to be dealt with in Chapter 18, below. Cases II and III necessarily involve a foreign element, and Case I can involve a foreign element, though it far more commonly does not. In this chapter therefore we shall be dealing solely with Case I, and with Case I only in so far as it does not involve any foreign element.

Section 181 (1) declares: "The Schedule referred to as Schedule E is as follows: . . . Tax under this Schedule shall be charged in respect of any office or employment on emoluments therefrom which fall under . . . Case I: where the person holding the office or employment is resident and ordinarily resident in the United Kingdom. . . ."

Two important points are contained in that passage, being the two factors which must be present if tax is to be charged under Schedule E: (1) there must be an office or employment; (2) there must be emoluments which are derived from that office or employment. (The beautiful symmetry of this proposition is broken by the fact that such social security benefits as are taxable at all are taxable under Schedule E, even although those benefits cannot be said to derive from an office or employment: Taxes Act, s. 219. Occupational pensions are also taxable under Schedule E, but that does not militate against the proposition because they *are* derived from an office or employment.)

OFFICE OR EMPLOYMENT

"Employment" is a much wider word than "office," but the word

76

"office" fulfils a useful function in that it catches some situations which might not be regarded as employments. An office was described by Rowlatt J. in *Great Western Railway Co.* v. *Bater* (1920) as "a subsisting, permanent, substantive position which has an existence independent of the person who fills it, and which is filled in succession by successive holders." A good example would be a judge, and that illustrates the point made above: a judge is taxed under Schedule E; it would be disrespectful (and, I think, inaccurate) to describe him as "employed," but he is undoubtedly the holder of an office. Another example is a company director. If he has a service agreement with his company he is probably employed; if he does not he is probably not employed. But in either case he is an office-holder, and he is taxed under Schedule E. This is so even if the company of which he is a director is what is called a "one man company" and he is the one man.

"Employment" is a very difficult word to define, and the tax legislation does not make the attempt. In one case Rowlatt J. said: "I thought of the expression 'posts.'" Perhaps the man on the Clapham omnibus puts his finger on the point when he says: "I used to be employed and work for a boss, but now I am self-employed and I'm my own boss." A very important case in this field is *Fall* v. *Hitchin* (1973). The taxpayer was a professional ballet dancer[1] engaged by Sadler's Wells. Under his contract he was paid £18 a week to rehearse, understudy and dance for a minimum period of rehearsals plus 22 weeks and thereafter until the contract was ended by a fortnight's notice on either side. He was permitted to accept outside work when not required by the Sadler's Wells manager. Pennycuick V.-C. held that he had been correctly assessed under Schedule E. The importance of the case is that it decides that the test of whether a person is an employed person is the same in a tax context as it is in a tort context: is he employed under a contract of service as distinct from a contract for services? The judge said:

"... unless some special limitation is to be put on the word 'employment' in any given context, the expression 'contract of service' appears to be coterminous with the expression 'employment.' I can find no such context in relation to Schedule E. I do not see how it could be said that emoluments arising from a contract of service are not emoluments arising from an employment within the meaning of the charging words in Schedule E."

Fall v. *Hitchin* cuts down the ambit of an earlier case, *Davies* v. *Braithwaite* (1931). In that case Lilian Braithwaite, an actress, contended that each one of her separate theatrical engagements was a

---

[1] It is a relief to find that the ballet dancer's name was not Fall, but Hitchin.

contract of employment, so that her earnings therefrom should be assessed under Schedule E. It was held that this was not so, and that she was correctly assessed under Case II of Schedule D.[2] The distinction between the two cases may depend on how numerous are the taxpayer's engagements. But I think also that in the 1970's it was clearer than it had been in the 1930's that a person may perfectly well be a professional person and yet be employed. This became clear in the case of doctors (and medicine is one of the traditional learned professions) after the establishment in 1948 of the National Health Service. A full-time hospital doctor is clearly employed. And in *Mitchell and Edon* v. *Ross* (1960) (C.A.) it was held by the Court of Appeal that a part-time consultant under the National Health Service was assessable under Schedule E in respect of that appointment and at the same time was assessable under Case II of Schedule D in respect of his private pratice. (The case went to the House of Lords but not on the above point. In the House of Lords it was held that expenses incurred (but disallowed) under the Schedule E office could not be allowed under the Schedule D profession.)

EMOLUMENTS THEREFROM

Section 183 (1) of the Taxes Act declares: "Tax under Case I . . . of Schedule E shall . . . be chargeable on the full amount of the emoluments falling under that Case, subject to such deductions only as may be authorised by the Tax Acts, and the expression 'emoluments' shall include all salaries, fees, wages, perquisites[3] and profits whatsoever." Notice that the subsection does not define 'emoluments,' it merely states what is included in that expression. The dictionary (Concise Oxford) definition of "emolument" is "profit from office or employment, salary." So the idea of the payment being *derived from* the office or employment is inherent in the word "emolument" itself. But the courts treat the matter as raising two questions: (1) has the employee received an emolument? and (2) is it an emolument *from* his office or employment?

In *Hochstrasser* v. *Mayes* (1960) (H.L.) I.C.I. set up a scheme to assist married male employees who had to move house on account of their employment with the company. If an employee sold his house at a loss the company paid him the amount of the loss. It was held that such a payment was not assessable under Schedule E. Lord Radcliffe said: ". . . it is not sufficient to render a payment assessable that an

---

[2] She wanted to show that she had employments, as distinct from a profession, because in that case she could (as the law then stood) have separated her U.S. earnings from her U.K. earnings.

[3] The common expression "perk" is an abbreviation of "perquisite."

employee would not have received it unless he had been an employee
... it is assessable if it has been paid to him in return for acting as or
being an employee." And Lord Simonds adopted the words of
Upjohn J. (at first instance): "... it must be something in the nature of
a reward for services, past, present or future."

In some circumstances the borderline between emoluments and
non-emoluments is a fine one. In *Tyrer* v. *Smart* (1979) (H.L.) a
company decided to "go public" and to offer for sale 5.6 million
ordinary shares. Ten per cent. of the shares were reserved at a price of
20 shillings[4] for employees who had been employed for five years or
more and who wished to accept the offer. One such employee was
Mr. Tyrer. He applied for 5,000 shares and paid £5,000 for them. On
the day he became the legal owner of the shares their value was
£6,000. He was assessed to income tax on the footing that the
difference (£1,000) was an emolument. The Special Commissioners
said that it was an emolument arising from his employment; Brightman J. and the Court of Appeal said that it was not; the House of
Lords said that it was a question of fact; that the Commissioners'
finding of fact did not fall within the principle of *Edwards* v. *Bairstow
and Harrison* (see pp. 31 and 57, above); and that the decision of the
Commissioners must be restored. The decisive finding of the Commissioners was to the effect that the offer was made to (*e.g.*) Mr.
Tyrer as a reward for past and future services. From that finding of
fact it followed that the offer was made "in return for acting as or
being an employee" within the meaning of that expression as used by
Lord Radcliffe in *Hochstrasser* v. *Mayes* (see this page, above).

Gifts

The most difficult area in which to draw the line between emoluments
and non-emoluments is in the field of gifts. There is a mass of decided
cases on this matter, and it is not easy to discern in them any clear-cut
principle. It is tempting to say that if a payment is made by an
employer it must be an emolument and if it is made by other persons
it is not an emolument. But the cases do not bear that out; the most
one can say is that a payment made by an employer is *likely* to be held
to be assessable. In *Ball* v. *Johnson* (1971) a bank clerk who was paid
£130 by the bank which employed him for having passed the examinations of the Institute of Bankers was held not to be assessable on
that amount. In *Calvert* v. *Wainwright* (1947) a taxi-driver was assessed on the tips paid to him by his "fares," who could not be con-

---

[4] The events in the case had occurred way back in 1969, before the decimalisation of
the currency.

sidered to be his employers. Again, it is tempting to say that if a payment is made in pursuance of a term of the contract of employment it must be assessable and if it is made without legal obligation it cannot be assessable. But that again is not borne out by the cases. In *Ball* v. *Johnson* (above) the £130 was as near as damn-it paid under a contractual obligation; a term of his employment required him to sit for the examinations, and it was stated in the bank's handbook that it was the usual practice to make such a payment. But perhaps *Ball* v. *Johnson* is rather an exceptional case. I think one can assert that a payment made in pursuance of the contract of employment is almost, but not quite, bound to be assessable. After all, because it is obligatory it is not a gift, so what is it? But the converse is definitely not true; it is not true to say that if a payment is not in pursuance of a contractual obligation it cannot be assessable. In *Wright* v. *Boyce* (1958) (C.A.) a huntsman was held to be rightly assessed on Christmas presents of cash received from followers of the hunt even though his contract of service conferred no right to the gifts. The payments were made in pursuance of a custom. Custom seems to be a very important factor in this area of the law.

The world of sport has produced some interesting cases in this field. In *Seymour* v. *Reed* (1927) (H.L.) where a benefit match was held for a professional cricketer on his retirement, the gate money was held not to be assessable. But in *Moorhouse* v. *Dooland* (1955) (C.A.) money collected from the crowd for a professional cricketer for outstanding performances was held to be taxable. A cynic might think that the distinction between these cases is the distinction between first-class county cricket and Lancashire League cricket, but the Court of Appeal were able to make more orthodox distinctions: in Dooland's case there was a contractual right to have a collection made whenever his performance was outstanding; and collections had been made for him not once but several times.

The case of *Moore* v. *Griffiths* (1972) arose out of England's winning of the World Cup in 1966. The Football Association paid £1,000 to each member of the squad. These payments were held not to be taxable. Brightman J. held that the payments had the quality of a testimonial or accolade rather than the quality of remuneration for services rendered, and he set out a number of factors which pointed to that conclusion. One factor was that "the payment had no foreseeable element of recurrence" (on which one might comment "You can say that again"). Another factor was that "each member of the team, regardless of the number of times that he played or whether he was a player or reserve, received precisely the same sum of £1,000. The sum therefore was not in any way linked with the quantum of any services rendered."

That last factor raises an important and constant theme in these cases. A payment may be unconnected with services rendered, either (as in the *Bobby Moore* case above) because it is given to more than one person without measuring their separate merits, or (more commonly) because it is given to one person precisely as an appreciation of his merits, but his merits as a human being rather than as an employee. There is a flavour of this latter idea in *Seymour* v. *Reed* (above) and in *Calvert* v. *Wainwright* (above), where Atkinson J. said: "Suppose somebody who has the same taxi every day, which comes in the morning as a matter of course to take him to his work, and then takes him home at night. The ordinary tip given in those circumstances would be something which would be assessable, but supposing at Christmas, or when the man is going for a holiday, the hirer says: "You have been very attentive to me, here is a 10-shilling note," he would be making a present, and I should say it would not be assessable because it has been given to the man because of his qualities, his faithfulness and the way he has stuck to the passenger."

Expenses Allowances

If an employee incurs an expense in such circumstances that it is deductible in calculating his tax liability under section 189 of the Taxes Act (on which see p. 88, below) and his employer re-imburses him, the amount paid to the employee by the employer does not form part of the employee's emoluments; so held by a majority of the House of Lords in *Owen* v. *Pook* (1970). If the employer, instead of reimbursing the employee's expenses after they have been incurred, makes round-sum payments to the employee as expenses allowances the practice of the Revenue is to treat such payments as not being emoluments, provided they are reasonable in amount. In strict law such payments probably are emoluments, but they would be offset by the deductibility of the expenditure in respect of which they are paid. It is important to be clear in one's mind that there is a distinction between an expense allowance that is not an emolument at all and an expense allowance that is an emolument but is balanced by the deductibility of the expense which it represents.

If an employer and his employee enter into arrangements about expenses which are a fraud on the Revenue the whole contract of employment is tainted with illegality and neither party can sue on it. Thus in *Napier* v. *National Business Agency* (1951) (C.A.) Napier was employed at a salary of £13 a week plus £6 a week for expenses. Both Napier and his employer knew that his real expenses could not exceed £1 a week. Napier was dismissed. He sued for arrears of salary confining his claim to £13 a week. It was held that the whole contract was illegal and unenforceable. Napier, therefore, could not even

x DAVIDSON V PILLAY '79
NEWLAND V SIMMONS + WILLER HAIR DRESSING '80.

recover his ordinary salary, never mind the bogus expenses allowances.

Benefits in Kind

So far we have been talking about payments made to an employee in actual money. But an emolument may take a form other than money. This is clear from the presence of the word "perquisites" in the definition (s. 183 (1)).

At this point it is necessary to distinguish between what one might call the common law principle and certain statutory modifications of that principle. Legislation has intervened in two ways: (1) it has declared that for *all* employees (and office-holders) certain things shall be regarded as emoluments which under the common law principle would not be emoluments; and (2) it has introduced a separate (harsher) code for directors and higher-paid employees (that is, employees earning £8,500 or more). Point (2) above must be constantly borne in mind in reading the following pages; you will not have the whole picture until you have read the section on directors and higher-paid employees beginning on page 90, below.

Let us look first at the common law.

Even the common law does not confine "emoluments" to money payments. It recognises that benefits in kind, and hence a number of fringe benefits, are emoluments. But it takes the view that benefits in kind are taxable only if they can be converted into money. In *Tennant* v. *Smith* (1892) (H.L.) Lord Halsbury said that the benefits which are taxable are "substantial things of money value ... capable of being turned into money." And in the same case Lord Watson used the expression: "that which can be turned to pecuniary account." The dividing line then is convertibility into money. If a thing can be turned into money it is assessable; if it cannot be turned into money it is not assessable. On this principle the following items (by way of examples) are not taxable; free travel, free board and lodging, free meals, free uniforms, free education. None of these can be turned into money. But if an employer, instead of providing, *e.g.* a free meal, gives his employee a cash payment with which to buy a meal, that payment is taxable.[5]

A clear example of a benefit convertible into money occurred in *Weight* v. *Salmon* (1935) (H.L.). The directors of a company by resolution each year gave Mr. Salmon the privilege of subscribing for unissued shares at par value, which was below market value. It was

---

[5] The customary free allowance of coal to miners has never in practice been treated as an emolument, even though they might sell it. This practice has been extended by Revenue Concession number A7 to cover cash payments in lieu of coal.

held that the difference between par and market value was assessable to tax.

Another good example of a "perquisite" convertible into money is to be found in the case of *Wilkins* v. *Rogerson* (1961) (C.A.). The employer decided to give certain of his employees a suit, overcoat or raincoat as a Christmas present. The employer made an arrangement with a tailor. The employee went to the tailor and got fitted out with a suit. The tailor sent the bill to the employer. It was held that there was here an emolument, and that its value was the amount for which the employee could turn the suit into money; that is, the second-hand value of the suit.

If the arrangement had been that the employee should himself contract with a tailor to get a suit made and that the employer should then discharge the employee's obligation to the tailor the value of the emolument would have been the contract price of the (new) suit. This is a general principle; if an employer discharges an obligation of the employee to a third party that constitutes an emolument, the value of which is the sum paid by the employer. For example, if an employer pays the rates, gardener's wages and other expenses of an employee's residence, thus discharging the employee's liabilities in those respects, the employee is taxable on the amounts so paid. This is called "the rule in *Nicoll* v. *Austin*" (1935).

One particular application of this principle is worth separate mention. Sometimes an employer agrees to pay his employee's income tax or agrees to pay a wage or salary "free of tax." In that case the amount of the tax is an emolument; the employer is discharging an obligation of the employee to a third party (the Revenue). The employer must gross-up the net salary and pay tax on that grossed-up amount. Thus (leaving aside personal reliefs, etc.), if the employer says: "I will pay you £2,000 a year and I will pay your income tax" the tax which the employer must pay to the Revenue is not 30 per cent. of £2,000 (= £600) but 30 per cent. of £2,000 grossed up at 30 per cent. The grossed up amount works out at £2,857 and the tax at £857.

We leave the common law now and turn to look at the statutory rules about benefits in kind. These rules apply to all employees: the additional rules for directors and higher paid employees are discussed later on, beginning on page 90.

Medical insurance

Where an employer provides insurance for an employee and for members of his family or household against the cost of medical treatment the cost of providing the insurance is treated by section 68 of the Finance Act 1976 as an emolument of the employment. There is a merciful exception for insurance against the cost of medical treatment outside the United Kingdom, "the need for which arises while the employee is outside the United Kingdom for the purpose of performing the duties of his employment."

Vouchers

The legislation distinguishes between cash vouchers and non-cash vouchers.

By section 37 of the Finance (No. 2) Act 1975 a cash voucher (which includes a stamp or similar document) is taxable and is subject to the P.A.Y.E. system. A cash voucher would have been taxable anyway under the common law principle stated above, and the real purpose of this enactment is to bring cash vouchers into the P.A.Y.E. system, and ensure that tax is deducted by the employer, thus avoiding the necessity of a separate assessment on each recipient employee.

A cash voucher is any voucher capable of being exchanged for a sum of money greater than, equal to or not substantially less than, the expense incurred in providing the voucher.

Non-cash vouchers are dealt with by section 36 of the Finance (No. 2) Act 1975. A non-cash voucher is a voucher which is not a cash voucher and which is capable of being exchanged for money, goods or services (or any combination of those things). The section has two effects. First, it treats the employee, if he or his spouse or family receives the voucher, as having received an emolument. Consequently certain things that were not previously taxable (because they were not convertible into money) become taxable, *e.g.* free holidays.[6] Second, it requires that the emolument be valued at the cost to the employer of providing the voucher and not at the value of the goods or services ultimately received by the employee. So if the employer in *Wilkins* v. *Rogerson* (above) were now to provide his employee with a voucher exchangeable for a suit, the emolument would be valued (in effect) at the contract price of the (new) suit, and not merely at the suit's second-hand value. But provided no voucher is used in the process of getting the suit, it would seem that the comparatively happy result in *Wilkins* v. *Rogerson* could still be achieved.

One particular kind of non-cash voucher is the subject of a (not very generous) Revenue concession. Concession A3 (in the booklet (I.R.1.) of "Extra-Statutory Concessions") says that luncheon-vouchers will not be taxed if they are non-transferable, used for meals

---

[6] But it seems that an employer can still give an employee a free (and tax free) holiday if he does so without recourse to a voucher.

only, available to lower-paid staff, and limited to a value of 15p for each working day.

Share option and incentive schemes

If an employee (or a director) is granted by his employing company an option to buy shares in the future at some specified price that right may of course turn out to be very valuable. Section 186 of the Taxes Act provides that when he comes to exercise the option tax will be charged (at earned income rates) on the difference between the price paid under the option and the market value of the shares acquired.

A share incentive scheme is a scheme whereby an employee can buy shares in his employing company or, indeed, in any other company, not in the future as is the case with an option, but immediately and in pursuance of a right conferred on him or an opportunity offered to him as an employee (or director) and not in pursuance of an offer to the public. The matter is dealt with by section 79 of the Finance Act 1972. If the shares come to have a value after seven years (or when the employee disposes of the shares if that is sooner) in excess of the price he paid for the shares, the excess is taxable under section 79 (4) (but as earned income, not investment income). Also, some share incentive schemes provide that the holders of incentive shares are to receive benefits which are not received by shareholders generally. In these circumstances the holder of incentive shares is taxed under section 79 (7) on an amount equal to the value of any benefit received (again at earned income rates).

Sections 53–61 of the Finance Act 1978 make elaborate provision for what are called Profit Sharing Schemes. These sections were put into the Bill at the instigation of the Liberals, with whom, in 1978, the Labour Government was in alliance. Shares held by a participant in an approved Profit Sharing Scheme are, at the time of appropriation, treated as not being income under the ordinary benefits-in-kind principle, and also they are not chargeable to income tax under section 79 (4) above nor under section 67 of the Finance Act 1976 (on which see p. 96, below) as being shares appropriated to him at an under-value.

Provision of accommodation

Section 33 of the Finance Act 1977 declares that where living accommodation is provided for a person (or for members of his family or household) by reason of his employment he is to be treated as being in receipt of emoluments of a value equal to the excess of the annual value of the premises over what he actually pays for the premises (if anything). Annual value is defined in section 531 of the Taxes Act, as being (in summary) the market rent on the footing that the tenant pays the rates and the landlord pays for repairs and insurance. This is, broadly speaking, the rateable value. That is the general rule, but if the employer (or other person providing the accommodation) is himself paying rent for the premises (*i.e.* he is not the freehold owner) and the rent which that person pays is greater than the annual value the employee's emolument is valued at the excess of the rent which that person pays over the rent which the employee pays. From any amount to be treated as emoluments the employee can deduct such expenses (if any) as would have been deductible if the employee had paid for the accommodation in full himself. The rules for what expenses are deductible are discussed in the next section.

There are three exceptional situations (section 33 (4)) in which the provision of accommodation does not count as an emolument and in which, also, the paying of the employee's rate bill does not count as an emolument (overriding the general common law principle that such discharge of a liability is an emolument; see p. 83, above). These exceptional situations are: (a) where it is necessary for the proper performance of the employee's duties that he should reside in the provided accommodation; (b) where the accommodation is provided for the better performance of the duties, and his is one of the kinds of employment in the case of which it is customary for employers to provide living accommodation; and (c) where, there being a special threat to his security, special security arrangements are in force and he resides in the accommodation as part of those arrangements. Exceptions (a) and (b) do not apply if the employee is a director of the providing company or an associated company unless he has no material interest in the company and either he is a full-time working director or the company is non-profit-making or is established for charitable purposes only. "Higher-paid employees" who are not directors have the benefit of the exceptions without any qualification.

DEDUCTIBLE EXPENSES

Tax is chargeable under Schedule E "on the full amount of the emoluments . . . subject to such deductions only as may be authorised by the Tax Acts" (section 183 (1) of the Taxes Act). There are three differences between the expenses which are deductible under Schedule E and those which are deductible under Schedule D, Cases I and II. The first is a practical difference, namely that whereas profits under Cases I and II do not begin to make sense until one visualises an account with expenses on one side and receipts on the other, expenses play a very much smaller part in Schedule E. Many employed people have no expenses (no deductible expenses, that is) at all. The second difference is that whereas the Schedule D legislation merely states what expenses are not deductible, Schedule E states in a positive form what expenses are deductible. And the third difference is that the rules are much more restrictively worded under Schedule E, so that many expenses which would be deductible under Schedule D are not deductible under Schedule E.

The expenses which are deductible under Schedule E are set out in section 189 (1) of the Taxes Act:

"If the holder of an office or employment is necessarily obliged to incur and defray out of the emoluments thereof the expenses of travelling in the performance of the duties of the office or employment, or of keeping and maintaining a horse[7] to enable him to perform the same, or otherwise to expend money wholly, exclusively and necessarily in the performance of the said duties, there may be deducted from the emoluments to be assessed the expenses so necessarily incurred and defrayed."

It is noticeable that the words "wholly" and "exclusively" are not applied to the expenses of travelling, but only to other expenditure. The words "in the performance of the duties" relate to both kinds of expenditure, as also does the word "necessarily." The presence of this word "necessarily" is one feature which makes the Schedule E rules more stringent than the rules of Schedule D, from which it is absent. Another feature which has that effect is the presence of the words "in the performance of the duties" which is a narrower phrase than the Schedule D words "for the purposes of the trade, profession or vocation."

We will look at travelling expenses first. The expense of travel from one's home to one's work is not deductible. This basic rule is established by *Ricketts* v. *Colquhoun* (1926) (H.L.). Mr. Ricketts was a barrister residing and practising in London. He was also the Recorder of Portsmouth (a part-time office). He claimed to deduct from the emoluments of his Recordership the expenses of travelling between London and Portsmouth and also his hotel expenses in Portsmouth. It was held by the House of Lords that neither the travelling expenses nor the hotel expenses were incurred in the performance of his duties, but rather before and after,[8] and, moreover, the expenses were

---

[7] They say you can tell the age of a horse by its teeth; you can tell the age of a section by its horses.

[8] Lord Cave rather sternly said that a person "does not eat or sleep in the course of performing his duties."

attributable to the Recorder's own choice of residence and were not necessary to the office as such. This latter, very objective point, was rather softened by a later decision of the House of Lords, *Taylor* v. *Provan* (1975) (see below).

The cost of travel from one place of work in an employment to another place of work in the same employment is deductible. In *Owen* v. *Pook* (1970) (H.L.) Dr. Owen was a G.P. at his residence in Fishguard, and he also held a part-time appointment at a hospital in Haverfordwest, 15 miles away. Under his appointment Dr. Owen was on stand-by duty to deal with emergency cases and he was required to be available by telephone. His responsibility for a patient began the moment he received a telephone call at home. It was held by a majority of the House of Lords that the duties of Dr. Owen's employment were performed in two places (where he received the telephone calls and the hospital) and that he could deduct the expenses of travel between those places.[9] This is akin to the Schedule D cases where a taxpayer is held to have his base at his home. But it is not identical, it is wider; sometimes Dr. Owen received telephone calls when he was not at home. It seems to have been regarded as more important when he received the calls than where. But undoubtedly the case does establish that if his home is one of the places at which a taxpayer works (and rightly works) under his contract of employment, then the cost of travel from home to another place of work under the contract is deductible.

In *Taylor* v. *Provan* (1975) (H.L.) Mr. Taylor lived and worked in Canada and the Bahamas. He was a world expert in arranging amalgamations and mergers in the brewing industry. He agreed to become a director of an English brewing company to carry forward such work. He did most of his work on English amalgamations in Canada and the Bahamas, but he paid frequent visits to England. The House of Lords, by a majority of 3 to 2, held that the expenses of travel to England were deductible. Two of the majority based their decision on the view that there were two or more places of work under the contract of employment. Lord Reid based his decision more on the view that "it was impossible for the companies which contracted with him to get the work done by anyone else." Lord Reid felt that this view reconciled the case with *Ricketts* v. *Colquhoun* (above), but there does seem to be a move away from *Ricketts* v. *Colquhoun* in that on this more recent view the expenditure does not need to be necessary to the office or employment as such provided it

---

[9] This related to that part of the expenses which was not reimbursed to him by the hospital. That part of the expenses which was reimbursed was held not to be an emolument at all (see p. 81, above).

is necessary to this particular contract with the only employee who can fulfil it.

The requirement of being "necessary" applies not only to the fact of the journey, but also to the *amount* of the expenditure. At one time the Revenue used to contend that hotel costs while travelling were not allowable at all. Then they adopted what was called the "home-saving" principle. In *Nolder* v. *Walters* (1930) it was held that an airline pilot could deduct hotel expenses in so far as they exceeded what his expenses would have been at home. Nowadays it is accepted that accommodation and meals while travelling, including hotel costs, are part of the cost of travel, and that if the travel costs themselves are allowable so also are the hotel costs (without any "home-saving" reduction). This is subject to reasonableness, because of the require-ment of being "necessary."

Let us now look at expenses other than travel expenses. These must be incurred wholly, exclusively and necessarily in the perfor-mance of the duties.

"Wholly" and "exclusively" are words which do not occur in relation to travelling expenses. In connection with non-travelling expenses the words proved to be of some importance in *Hillyer* v. *Leeke* (1976). Mr. Hillyer was required by his employer to wear a suit at work. So he bought a suit which he wore at work but on no other occasions. He claimed to deduct the cost of the suit. It was held that the expenditure had not been incurred wholly and exclusively in the performance of his duties. He wore the suit not merely for the purposes of the employment, but also to provide cover, warmth and comfort for himself. *MALLALIEU v DRUMMOND. CofA 1982 Nov*

The word "necessarily" has caused many a claim to founder. Stemming from *Ricketts* v. *Colquhoun* (above) the test is, as Dono-van L.J. put it in *Brown* v. *Bullock* (1961) (C.A.): ". . . not whether the employer imposes the expense . . . but whether the duties do." A bank manager was required by his employers (it was "virtually a condition of his employment") to be a member of a London club. It was held that the subscription fee was not a deductible expense. This is a harsh doctrine, and it may in time come to be softened as some of the ideas in *Taylor* v. *Provan* begin to percolate through. But it will still be the case that the expense must not be necessitated merely by the personal circumstances of the taxpayer as distinct from the neces-sities of the job. Thus in *Roskams* v. *Bennett* (1950) Mr. Bennett was the district manager of an insurance company. Because of bad eyesight he could not drive a car, and so he found it necessary to maintain an office at home. It was held that the expense occasioned thereby was not deductible.

The phrase "in the performance of the duties" has had similar effects on non-travel expenses as on travel expenses. In *Simpson* v. *Tate* (1925) a county medical officer of health joined certain medical and scientific societies so as to keep himself up-to-date on matters affecting public health. His claim to deduct these subscriptions was rejected, the court holding that the expense was incurred, not in the performance of the duties, but so that the taxpayer might keep himself fit to perform them. This seems a very restrictive doctrine, and indeed this particular point has been altered by statute. Section 192 of the Taxes Act now permits deduction of (I quote the marginal note to the section) "fees and subscriptions to professional bodies, learned societies, etc." But the doctrine still stands where it has not been changed by statute. In *Humbles* v. *Brooks* (1962) the headmaster of a school attended a course in history at week-ends. He claimed to deduct the expenditure. The court refused the claim on the ground that he was only qualifying himself to teach, not teaching; hence the expenditure was not incurred in the performance of his duties. The rule surely tends to discourage employees from making themselves better employees.

DIRECTORS AND HIGHER-PAID EMPLOYEES

We must now study the special rules which apply to directors and higher paid employees. The rules apply to directors[10] however much or however little they earn, and they apply to non-director employees who earn £8,500 or more. The rules are statutory and one can think of the relevant enactments as setting up a kind of code and I shall speak of people who are affected by the legislation as being "within the code."

The question whether a person has earnings of £8,500 or more has to be tested on the assumption that the code applies and also that benefits in respect of living accommodation and medical insurance and vouchers are included, and without (at this stage) making any deduction for allowable expenses. So if an employee has a salary of £8,000 and reimbursed expenses of £1,000 he is in the code, even though the bulk of the £1,000 is tax deductible. Also, separate employments with the same employer are treated as one employment, and so are employments with employers who are under a common control.

---

[10] A director is not caught as such if he does not have a material interest (= 5 per cent. or more) in the company and either he is a full-time working director or the company is non-profit-making (or charitable). But, of course, he may be caught as being higher-paid.

The code is now set out in sections 60–72[11] of the Finance Act 1976 (as amended by the Finance Act 1977).[12]

The Principles of the Code

Before going into the details of the code, I want to try to state the main differences in the taxing of people who are within the code as compared with people outside the code. There are three such differences.

First, any sums paid to a person within the code in respect of expenses are to be treated as emoluments; see section 60 of the Finance Act 1976. For a person outside the code that is not so. We have seen (at p. 81) that for him a reimbursement of deductible expenses is not an emolument, and in practice a round-sum payment for expenses, if reasonable in amount, is not treated as an emolument. For a person within the code not only a round-sum payment for expenses but even a reimbursement of expenses is an emolument. Mind you, this is not fatal; if he expends, or has expended, the payment in such circumstances that his expenditure is deductible under the ordinary principles, the potential taxability of the allowance is balanced by the deductibility of the expense, so no tax becomes due. But there is an important point here; the onus of proving that a receipt is an emolument lies on the Revenue, whereas the onus of proving that an expenditure is deductible lies on the taxpayer. So for a person within the code the Revenue is relieved of its onus, because the payment in respect of expenses is treated by statute as being an emolument, and the only onus left standing is the onus on the taxpayer to prove that the emolument is balanced by deductibility. This point is illustrated by *Owen* v. *Pook* and *Taylor* v. *Provan*. In *Owen* v. *Pook* the taxpayer was not within the code, and it was held that the reimbursement of his travel expenses was not an emolument at all. In *Taylor* v. *Provan* the taxpayer was within the code, and it was held that the reimbursement was an emolument. It so happened that Mr. Taylor was held to be entitled to an equalising deductibility, but it was a near thing; three Law Lords said Yes, two said No. There is an element of absurd circuity about an emolument which is reduced to nil by deductibility, and section 70 of the Finance Act 1976 recognises this by permitting an Inspector to grant a dispensation to an employer (and hence to his employees) where he is satisfied that the arrangements for paying expenses are such that no

---

[11] s. 68 (medical insurance) applies to *all* employees. It is rather odd to find this enactment in a group of sections which otherwise deals only with people within the code.

[12] There is a useful guide issued by the Revenue (no. 480) called "Notes on Expenses Payments and Benefits for Directors and Certain Employees."

tax will be involved. A dispensation carries the great advantage that the dispensed expenses are left out of account in calculating whether a particular employee is within the code.

Second, for people outside the code benefits which are not convertible into money are not (in principle) emoluments. (There are a few statutory exceptions which we have looked at above.) For people within the code the principle of convertibility is irrelevant, with the result that *all* benefits (with a few statutory exceptions and a few extra-statutory concessionary exceptions) whether convertible into money or not are emoluments: section 61 of the Finance Act 1976. But here again all is not lost; the ordinary principles of deductibility are available to off-set the emoluments where the facts warrant such deduction.

Third, for a person not within the code a benefit in kind is valued (with certain statutory exceptions such as medical insurance and non-cash vouchers) at the value which it has to the employee, and not at the expense to the employer of providing the benefit. For a person within the code a benefit in kind is valued by reference to the expense of the employer in providing it (called the "cash equivalent").[13] This point can be clearly seen by comparing *Wilkins* v. *Rogerson* (1961) (see p. 83, above) and *Rendell* v. *Went* (1964) (H.L.). It will be recalled that in *Wilkins* v. *Rogerson* the employee (who was outside the code) was taxed on the second-hand value of the suit which his employer bought for him. In *Rendell* v. *Went* the taxpayer (who was a director and so within the code) was charged with causing death by dangerous driving, for which he would be liable, if convicted, to imprisonment for a term up to five years. The employing company had special need of Mr. Rendell's services at that time, and they were most anxious that his services should not be lost to them by reason of his imprisonment. Mr. Rendell at first arranged for the Automobile Association (AA) to conduct his defence, but the company arranged for their own solicitors to defend him (with counsel) at the company's expense. The company paid out £641 in costs. If the AA had conducted the defence Mr. Rendell would only have had to pay £50 or £60. It was held by the House of Lords that Mr. Rendell was taxable on the sum of £641, because that was the cost to his employers of providing the benefit. But even though people within the code are charged to tax on benefits in kind by reference to the cost to the employer of providing each benefit, there is still a tax-saving element

---

[13] s. 63 (1) of the Finance Act 1976 lays down that the "cash equivalent" is "an amount equal to the cost of the benefit, less so much (if any) of it as is made good by the employee...."

in benefits in kind. If an employer buys for £250 a hand-made suit and gives it to one of his higher-paid employees, the employee pays tax on £250, so if he is (say) in the 60 per cent. band he pays £150 in tax and that is the total of his outlay. If he had bought the suit himself he would have had to use £625 (before tax) of his income. When an asset is provided, not by way of outright gift, but by being placed at the employee's disposal (without any transfer of ownership) the taxable amount is the annual value (or, if more, the rent or hire-charge which the employer is paying). In the case of land the annual value is as defined by section 531 of the Taxes Act; in the case of cars special rules apply which are discussed below; in the case of other items section 63 (5) (c) provides that the annual value is to be taken as 10 per cent. of the market value of the asset at the time it was first provided. So the annual value of the hand-made suit mentioned above is £25. The employer may decide to charge his employee say 2.5 per cent. of the capital value of the suit for a year's use; that would be £6.25. The employee would be taxed on the balance of the ten per cent., *i.e.* 7.5 per cent. = £18.75. The actual tax bill (at 60 per cent.) would be £11.25.[14]

I have tried to state the three basic principles of the code. Now let us look at some specific rules of the code.

Living Accommodation Expenses

The first point concerns certain expenses connected with living accommodation, and it is dealt with in section 63A of the Finance Act 1976. This section is a beneficial section because it cuts down (or at least limits) what would otherwise be the tax charge. The section applies where the provided living accommodation comes within the three exceptions stated in section 33 (4) of the Finance Act 1977 (see p. 86, above; necessary for proper performance of duties, customary for better performance of duties or part of special security arrangements). In those premises, the provision to the employee of the following things, though it is an emolument, is subject to a tax limit; heating, lighting, cleaning, repairs, maintenance, decoration, furniture, and normal appurtenances and effects. The limit is that the taxable amount of the emolument shall not exceed 10 per cent. of the employee's emoluments for the year (less capital allowances and certain pension contributions). So, if a person within the code, with an income of £9,000, enjoyed such benefits to an amount of, say,

---

[14] I have taken the hand-made suit example from an article in the *Sunday Times* of September 17, 1978. The article suggests that such arrangements are quite common with business executives.

£1,500 in a particular year, he would only be taxable (in this respect) on an emolument of £900.

Cars

The legislation taxes a person within the code on the private benefit he gets from being given the use of a car. The provisions apply where there is not any transfer to him of the property in the car. (Where there is a transfer of the property in (ownership of) the car its value is taxable on ordinary "common law" principles, and, being convertible into money, it is taxable in the hands of all employees, not only directors and higher-paid employees.) There are three separate situations.

The first situation is where a car is used wholly for private purposes or where its use for business purposes is insubstantial. (The Revenue have said in a Press Release[15] that the business use of a car will not be regarded as insubstantial if it exceeds 10 per cent. of its total use in a tax year.) Tax is levied on the annual value of the use of the car, which is declared by section 63 (5) (b) to be 20 per cent. of its original market value or 10 per cent. if at the end of the year its age exceeds four years. (See sections 61 and 62 of the Finance Act 1976.)

The second situation is where a car is made available for private use but is also used to a substantial extent for business travel. The taxation is less severe here than in the first situation. Here section 64 of the Finance Act 1976 applies, and Schedule 7. The cash equivalent of the private benefit is laid down in Tables, which can be altered by statutory instrument. The amount varies according to the cost of the car, its cylinder capacity and age. The amount which would otherwise be the taxable amount is halved if the employee travels 25,000 miles or more on business in a year.

The third situation is where there is a "car pool." If a car is included in a car pool no charge to tax arises in respect of the use of that car. The conditions are that the car was used by more than one employee, that it was not normally kept overnight at an employee's house, and that any private use of it was merely incidental to its business use. (Finance Act 1976, s. 65.)

(To a person outside the code the use of a "company car" for private purposes will not normally be taxable because it is not convertible into money, at least if the employer imposes the (very reasonable) condition that the car may not be hired out. In some circumstances the benefit of the car could be taxable, as it was, for

---

[15] November 11, 1976; printed, *e.g.* in [1976] B.T.R. at p. 462.

example, in *Heaton* v. *Bell* (1970) (H.L.), a case which turned on the particular arrangements of a voluntary car loan scheme.)

Beneficial Loan Arrangements

Where a person within the code has the benefit of a loan which is obtained by reason of his employment and the loan is either without interest or at a rate of interest less than the "official rate" (*i.e.* the rate prescribed from time to time by the Treasury; at present 9 per cent.) the cash equivalent of the benefit is treated under section 66 of the Finance Act 1976 as an emolument. The cash equivalent is the difference between the amount of interest actually paid in the year and the amount of interest which would have been payable at the official rate. The tax charge does not arise where the cash equivalent does not exceed £50 in a year. So this means that an interest-free loan of £550 or less is not caught. Also the tax charge does not arise where the loan interest is eligible for relief under section 75 of the Finance Act 1972. (See p. 47 *et seq.*, above.) One very important practical aspect of this is that the popular "perk" of low-rate housing loans for employees is still tax free even for employees within the code.

Where in any year there is released or written off the whole or part of a loan which was obtained by reason of a person's employment, an amount equal to that which is released or written off is treated as an emolument.

Employee Shareholdings

Section 67 of the Finance Act 1976 applies where a person employed or about to be employed in director's or higher-paid employment (or a person connected with him) acquires shares in a company at an under-value in pursuance of a right or opportunity available by reason of the employment. The employee is treated as having an interest-free loan ("the notional loan"), so bringing him within section 66. The section only applies in so far as the transaction is not caught for tax under the principle of *Weight* v. *Salmon* (on which see p. 82, above). The loan is treated as outstanding until (a) the whole amount outstanding is made good, or (b) the debt is released, or (c) the shares are disposed of, or (d) the employee dies. In case (a) the tax charge comes to an end; in cases (b) and (c) the employee is taxed as if the notional loan had been written off; in case (d) there is no income tax charge.

Section 67 also imposes a charge to tax where shares are acquired by a person employed or about to be employed in director's or higher-paid employment in pursuance of a right or opportunity available by reason of the employment, whether or not they were acquired at an under-value, and the shares are disposed of for a consideration which exceeds their then market value. The amount of the excess is treated as an emolument.

When shares are held in an approved Profit Sharing Scheme (on which see p. 85, above) a participant is not chargeable to tax under section 67 in any case where the shares are appropriated to him at an under-value.

That concludes what I want to say about directors and higher-paid employees. The rest of this chapter applies to all employees, whether within or outside the code.

GOLDEN HANDSHAKES

One of the pleasures of studying tax law is that it is bedecked with vivid phrases which start as slang and are then taken into the dictionary, if not into the statute book. One such phrase is "Golden Handshakes." These can, more prosaically, be called "terminal payments."

It is necessary to distinguish three different kinds of payment on the termination of an office or employment.

First, where there is a contractual provision that a certain sum will become payable if the contract is determined early, that sum is treated as remuneration for past services and is taxed under Schedule E.

Second, if employer and employee agree that the employee will stay on at a reduced salary and the employer makes a payment to an employee in connection with this agreement, that payment is treated as being in anticipation of future services and is taxed under Schedule E.

Third, where a payment is made which is not related to services rendered or to be rendered but is paid as consideration for the release of the employer's obligation under the contract of employment, it is not taxable under the ordinary principles of Schedule E, but is taxable under special statutory provisions which were first enacted in 1960. The provisions are now contained in sections 187 and 188 of the Taxes Act.

Section 187 applies to:

"any payment (not otherwise chargeable to tax) which is made, whether in pursuance of any legal obligation or not, either directly or indirectly in consideration or in consequence of, or otherwise in connection with, the termination of the holding of the office or employment or any change in its functions or emoluments, including any payment in commutation of annual or periodical payments (whether chargeable to tax or not) which would otherwise have been made as aforesaid."

(The words from "including" onwards catch a payment in commutation of pension rights.) The section is clearly very wide in its scope. One important kind of payment which it catches is a redundancy payment. (This point is confirmed by section 412 (8) of the Taxes Act.) Some payments (listed in section 188) are exempted from section 187, such as: (a) any payment made in connection with the termination of an office or employment by the death of the holder, or made on account of injury to or disability of the holder; (b) any sum chargeable to tax under section 34 of the Taxes Act (which charges to higher rate tax (but not to basic rate tax)) any sum paid to an employee for a restrictive covenant; (c) payments under retirement benefit schemes.

Payments which are caught by section 187 are treated as earned income received on the following date: (a) in the case of a commutation payment, the date of commutation; (b) in the case of any other payment, the date of the termination or change in respect of which the payment is made.

Tax is not charged under section 187 on the first £10,000 of any payment. This (new) figure was laid down by section 24 of the Finance Act 1978. (Because of this threshold this is one of the rare circumstances where it is advantageous to be a Schedule E taxpayer rather than a Schedule D taxpayer. A similar sort of payment made to a Schedule D taxpayer would in most situations be taxable, and taxable in full without any exemption for the first £10,000. See *I.R.C. v. Brander & Cruickshank* (1971) (H.L.).

Apart from this threshold, there are two possible reliefs. The first relief relates to payments which are not by way of compensation for loss of office; an example would be a retirement gratuity. Where an employee's "standard capital superannuation benefit" is in excess of £10,000 the excess is exempt from tax. "Standard capital superannuation benefit" means the average annual emoluments during the last three years of the employment, (say, for example, £12,000) divided by 20 and multiplied by the number of years of service (say, for example, 40) minus any non-taxable lump sum received or receivable under a retirement benefit scheme (say, for example, £8,000). In this example the standard superannuation benefit is $(£12,000 \times {}^{40}/_{20}) - £8,000 = £16,000$. If the employee in the example received a retirement gratuity of £18,000, he would get the ordinary £10,000 exemption and he would get this further relief of £6,000 (excess of £16,000 over £10,000), and so he would only be taxable on £2,000. The other relief applies to all payments chargeable under section 187. It is directed to the point mentioned above that the payments are treated as income (earned income) received on one date. This brings the whole amount of the payment or payments into one year of assessment. Relief is available in a form which is generally called "top-slicing" A very similar form of relief is available in connection with lease premiums, and it is described in Chapter 12, below.

The £10,000 exemption raises a point stemming from what is called "the Gourley principle." That principle was laid down by the House of Lords in *British Transport Commission* v. *Gourley* (1956). Mr. Gourley was injured in a railway accident, and was unable to work again. He sued in tort for damages for (amongst other things) loss of earnings. It was estimated that if the plaintiff had not been injured his earnings over the rest of his working life would have come to £37,000. The defendants argued that since the plaintiff's earnings would have been taxed, the damages should be reduced to take account of that factor. It was estimated that Mr. Gourley's earnings *after tax* would have been only £6,000. So the issue was whether his damages should be £37,000 or £6,000. The House of Lords decided for £6,000. *Gourley's* case was brought in tort, but the same principle applies to breach of contract. The reasoning of the principle is that the plaintiff ought not to make a profit out of the tort or breach of contract. The principle only applies where two factors are present: (1) what the award represents is lost receipts which, if they had been received, would have been taxed, and (2) the award itself is not taxable. The principle has been applied to an award of damages for wrongful dismissal which fell within what is now section 187. In *Bold* v. *Brough, Nicholson & Hall Ltd.* (1964) the judge awarded damages well over the then limit of exemption (£5,000). He applied the *Gourley* principle to the first £5,000 and reduced the damages by £800, that being the figure of estimated tax. He did not apply the principle to that part of his award which was in excess of £5,000. His reasoning was that below £5,000 the award would not be taxable and yet it represented lost earnings which if they had been received (and not lost) would have been taxable. Both of the essential *Gourley* factors were therefore present. As for the part of his award above £5,000, the second *Gourley* factor was not present because this part of the award was itself taxable. Thus, to this part of the award he did not apply the *Gourley* principle.

PENSIONS

Many employees, when they come to retire, do not receive any occupational pension. They do get the national retirement pension ("old age pension").[16] Payments received under this state system are taxable under Schedule E and count as earned income.

An increasing number of employees do enjoy an occupational pension. When such an employee retires, and begins to receive periodical pension payments, he is taxed on those payments under Schedule E and they count as earned income.

During his employment such an employee will probably have been subject to some kind of pension scheme, under which he paid contributions and his employer also paid contributions. Two questions arise: are the employee's contributions deductible in computing his emoluments? and are the employer's contributions treated as emoluments of the employee?

The answer to the first question is that the employee's contributions are not deductible unless the pension scheme is what is called an "exempt approved scheme" under section 21 of the Finance Act 1970 or it is a "statutory scheme" (s. 22). In some employments where the employee's contributions are not deductible a lesser relief, namely life assurance relief, is available in respect of the contributions. A very important further advantage of an "exempt approved scheme" is that the fund of the scheme is itself exempt from income tax and also capital gains tax (F.A. 1970, s. 21).

The answer to the second question is that the employer's contributions are treated as emoluments of the employee unless the scheme is an "approved scheme" (not necessarily an "exempt approved scheme") or a statutory scheme (see s. 24 of the Finance Act 1970).

THE MECHANICS OF SCHEDULE E

All income taxed under Schedule E counts as earned income. It is collected by means of the Pay-As-You-Earn system (P.A.Y.E.). That name indicates two things: first, that the tax is on a current year (not a preceding year) basis, and, second, that the tax is collected bit by bit as the year goes on. It is collected by the employer by means of deducting the appropriate amount for tax from each weekly or monthly payment that he makes to his employees. The employer is then under a duty to hand over the tax to the Revenue. Every employed person earning over a certain amount (the amount being varied from time to time by statutory instrument in line with variations in the tax threshold) is given a code number by the Inspector. This code number tells the employer the amount of allowances and reliefs that any particular employee is entitled to. By applying the code number to the cumulative tax tables with which he is supplied by

---

[16] The basic retirement pension (from November 1979) is for a married couple £37.30, for a single person £23.30, per week.

the Revenue, the employer can know how much tax to deduct from the pay of a particular employee in any particular week (or month) of the tax year.

It is obvious from this (very brief) account that the employer is acting as a collector of tax (unpaid) for the Revenue.

The present system is based on the emoluments that an employee is expected to earn over the whole year. Consequently if an employee's earnings drop below the expectation he becomes entitled at once to a repayment. One important application of this is that an employee who goes on strike gets a repayment forthwith. In the early 1970s the idea was in the air that the system might be re-cast on a weekly basis instead of a yearly basis, so that no repayment would arise if an employee went on strike. At the present time the idea is either dead or slumbering.

In theory the P.A.Y.E. system should produce the result that at the end of the tax year an individual employee has paid (by deduction) exactly the correct amount of tax. In many, many cases it does so in practice. Consequently the law (very sensibly) provides that no assessment needs to be made. However, the Inspector may make an assessment if he feels it necessary. Also (and this is worth emphasising because many people seem unaware of it) an employee can require an assessment to be made if (for example) he thinks that too much tax has been deducted in a year (Taxes Act, s. 205). If it turns out, when the assessment is made, that too much tax has been deducted, the taxpayer can either get a repayment from the Revenue or have the credit taken into account in determining his code number for a subsequent year.

TAILPIECE

Before ending this chapter it is perhaps worth pointing out that payments or benefits in kind which are receipts in the hands of the employee are, looked at from the point of view of the employer, payments out. But the point is this: the question whether a particular receipt in the hands of an employee is taxable under Schedule E is quite independent of the question whether, in calculating the employer's tax liability (under Schedule D) a particular payment out by him is a deductible expense.

CHAPTER 10

CASE SIX

This chapter is about Case VI of Schedule D. Case VI is a residuary case or, less politely, a rag-bag. Section 109 of the Taxes Act charges under Case VI "tax in respect of any annual profits or gains not falling under any other case of Schedule D, and not charged by virtue of Schedule A, B, C or E." The section does not refer to Schedule F (dividends and similar distributions by companies), but presumably if a receipt does fall within Schedule F it is not assessable under Case VI.

Case VI has two aspects, which one might call the "general aspect" and the "particular aspect." By the "particular aspect" I mean that certain kinds of income are specifically directed by other sections to be charged under Case VI. These items include post-cessation receipts, certain balancing charges (see Chapter 16), some lease premiums and other anti-avoidance tax charges such as loss relief withdrawn retrospectively under section 31 (dealings in commodity futures) of the Finance Act 1978. But perhaps the commonest example of a Case VI income is income from furnished lettings.

Turning to the "general aspect" of Case VI, the ambit of this aspect is not as wide as it might at first seem to be. "Annual profits or gains" is the same phrase as that which governs Cases I and II. Indeed the phrase covers the whole of Schedule D. It follows that profits, to be taxable under Case VI, must be of the same kind (*ejusdem generis*) as profits which are taxable under Cases I, II, III, IV or V. Let us remind ourselves of three points about the phrase "annual profits or gains." First, "profits" and "gains" mean the same thing. Second, since what is taxable is profits, expenses incurred in earning the profits are deductible. Third, "annual" does not mean that the profits must be recurring, but it does mean that the profits must be income profits and not capital profits. It follows that a profit from buying something and then re-selling it is not assessable under Case VI. If the buying and re-selling is done in the course of trading, the profit is assessable under Case I. If the buying and re-selling is not done in the course of trading, the profit is assessable (if at all) to capital gains tax. In *Jones* v. *Leeming* (1930) (H.L.) Leeming and three other people obtained options to buy two rubber estates in the Malay Peninsula which they subsequently sold at a profit. The Commissioners found that the transaction was not a concern in the nature of trade. The House of

Lords held that on that finding the profits could not be assessed under Case VI.

So what *is* caught by the general aspect of Case VI? In *Scott* v. *Ricketts* (1967) (C.A.) Lord Denning said that what is caught includes "remuneration for work done, services rendered, or facilities provided." A good example of a Case VI profit is in *Leader* v. *Counsell* (1942). A group of racehorse owners purchased a stallion. If any member of the group did not have a mare which required the services of the stallion he could sell his nomination to anyone else. It was held that there was not a trade, but that these receipts from the user[1] of property were income receipts and were taxable under Case VI.

Gifts, betting winnings and "winnings" by finding are not assessable under Case VI any more than they are under Case I or Case II.

There are four points to be made about assessment under Case VI.

First, assessment is on a "current year basis unless otherwise directed." The phrase I have used is taken from the marginal note to section 125 of the Taxes Act. The text of the section is rather curiously worded. It says' this: "Income tax under Case VI of Schedule D shall be computed either on the full amount of the profits or gains arising in the year of assessment or according to an average of such period, not being greater than one year, as the case may require and as may be directed by the inspector."

Second, "arising" has been held to mean "received": *Grey* v. *Tiley* (1932) (C.A.). So assessment is on the cash basis rather than the earnings basis.

Third, losses under Case VI are not so favourably treated as losses under Cases I and II, because a Case VI loss can only be set off against Case VI profits, not against other kinds of income.

Fourth, income falling within the general aspect of Case VI is, except in rare circumstances, investment income and not earned income: see the definition section, section 530 (1) (c) of the Taxes Act. Income falling within some particular aspect of Case VI may or may not be earned income depending on the circumstances. For example, post-cessation receipts are earned income if the profits of the trade which has ceased would have been earned income, but, if not, not: Taxes Act, s. 148.

---

[1] "User" is a lawyers' word meaning "use."

Chapter 11

PURE PROFIT INCOME

THE SCOPE OF CASE III

The meaning of this phrase "pure profit income" is best understood by contrasting it with other kinds of income. Trading income is the best contrast. A sum of money received by a trader in the course of carrying on his trade is a credit item in calculating his profits but it is not in itself in full a profit. Against it there have to be set various expenses; the cost of buying the thing which he has now sold and the overhead expenses of the selling organisation. In short, the receipt is not pure profit. On the other hand (to take an example) if a will provides for the payment of an annuity to the deceased's aunt, each annuity payment in the hands of the aunt is pure income, or pure profit income, because there are no expenses to set against it.

Most, but not all, pure profit income is taxed under Case III of Schedule D. An important exception is dividends, which are taxed under Schedule F. The governing section for Case III of Schedule D is section 109 of the Taxes Act. The most important items are interest, annuities and other annual payments.

Interest has been defined as "payment by time for the use of money." Interest on a judgment is taxable. At one time there seemed to be a doubt as to whether interest awarded by a judge as an addition to damages was truly income and so taxable. Now it is well settled that such interest is taxable. There is one exception, by statute. Section 375A of the Taxes Act declares that interest on damages for personal injuries or death under the Law Reform (Miscellaneous Provisions) Act 1934 is "not to be regarded as income for any income tax purpose."

An annuity is an income which is paid year by year.

An annual payment is much more difficult to define. We can reduce the difficulty if we confine ourselves to defining such an annual payment *as falls within Case III of Schedule D*. Before we embark on a definition, it is perhaps worth pointing out why it matters whether a sum is an annual payment (within Case III) or not. The payee may want to show that a payment is an annual payment; for example, a charity is exempt from tax on annual payments. And there are circumstances where a payer would want to show that a payment is an annual payment. This is because an annual payment (such as a payment under a covenant) is, *unless statute provides otherwise*,

103

deductible in computing, for higher rate tax purposes, the total income of the payer. Remember, from Chapter 4, the Duke of Westminster. Since his day, statute *has* provided otherwise more and more, and today most annual payments do not qualify as deductions from total income, but some still do. Towards defining an annual payment one can state five principles.

First, the *ejuisdem generis* rule applies. The context is highly important. Section 109 says: "Case III—tax in respect of— ... any interest of money, whether yearly or otherwise, or any annuity or other annual payment...." A payment, to be an "other annual payment," must be the same kind of payment as is interest and an annuity.

Second, the payment must be made under a binding legal obligation. A gift, even if it be in money and even if it be one of a series, is not an annual payment. But it is important to appreciate that a payment under a covenant is an annual payment. How can this be, since a covenanted payment is (most commonly) given for no consideration? The answer is that a covenant is a promise under seal, and the seal creates a legal obligation.

Third, the payment must have the quality of recurrence. But this requirement is not very exacting. Payments which are variable or contingent are not thereby prevented from being recurrent. Also a payment does not need to be made only once a year; weekly or monthly payments can be annual payments provided they may continue for more than a year.

Fourth, the payment must be, in the hands of the recipient, pure profit income and not merely a receipt which enters into the computation of profit. In *I.R.C.* v. *National Book League* (1957) (C.A.) the League (which was a charity) decided to raise the membership subscription except that those members who entered into seven-year covenants could continue to pay their subscriptions at the existing rate. Over 2,000 members executed such deeds of covenant, and deducted tax in making the covenanted payments. The League claimed repayment of the tax from the Revenue, arguing that the payments were annual payments within Case III. The argument was not upheld. The subscriptions were not pure income profit (or pure profit income) of the League, because the League had to provide benefits, such as the amenities of a club, in return for the subscriptions.

Fifth, the payment must be of the nature of income, and not capital, in the hands of the recipient. This is an immensely difficult field in which there is a huge number of decided cases. The point arises when A sells property to B in return for instalment payments. Are the instalments income or capital? A payment may be of a revenue nature from the point of view of the payer and yet may be of a capital nature in the hands of the payee. Conversely, a payment may be of a capital nature from the point of view of the payer and yet be of an income nature in the hands of the payee. If it is of a capital nature in the hands of the payee it cannot be an "annual payment" even from the point of view of the payer. If it is of an income nature in the hands of the payee it may or may not be of a revenue nature from the point of view of the payer. In *I.R.C.* v. *Ramsay* (1935) (C.A.) Mr. Ramsay agreed to buy a dental practice. A primary price of £15,000 was agreed, but it was further agreed that Mr. Ramsay should pay £5,000 at once and then pay each year for 10 years a sum equal to one-quarter of the net profit of the practice for that year. No interest was payable It was held that the yearly payments were capital from the point of view of the payer. In *Vestey* v. *I.R.C.* (1962) Lord Vestey sold a block of shares valued at £2 million for the sum of £5.5 million payable without interest by 125 yearly instalments of £44,000. It was held that the instalments should be dissected into capital and interest, and that the interest element was taxable income of the payee. In *I.R.C.* v. *Church Commissioners for England* (1977) (H.L.) the Church Commissioners sold to their tenant the reversion on a lease in consideration of rent-charges payable annually for 10 years and totalling £96,000 a year. The tenant was not willing to buy for a single lump sum. The House of Lords held that these payments were pure income in the hands of the payee and were not to be dissected into capital and interest elements. The Church Commissioners, being a charity, were entitled to repayment of the tax which had been deducted by the payer from each payment. (The same rent-charges had previously been held—also by the House of Lords—to be capital payments from the point of view of the payer: *I.R.C.* v. *Land Securities Investment Trust Ltd*. (1969) (H.L.).

SECTIONS 52 AND 53

As we have seen interest, annuities and other annual payments fall within Case III of Schedule D. Where they are assessed under Case III the basis of assessment is normally the preceding year basis, except in the opening and closing years of a particular source of income, when the current year basis applies.

But often such payments are not assessed under Case III because they are subjected to deduction of tax at source under section 52 or section 53 of the Taxes Act. Interest used to be dealt with under those sections but is now dealt with separately under section 54.[1] Sections 52 and 53 now apply to annuities and other annual payments and also

---

[1] But see below at the end of this chapter.

(with slightly different rules) to patent royalties and certain mining royalties.

The distinction between section 52 and section 53 is as follows. Section 52 deals with payments which are made wholly out of profits or gains brought into charge to income tax, whereas section 53 deals with payments which are not made, or not wholly made, out of profits or gains brought into charge to income tax. Notice that the phrase is "income tax," not just "tax": so a payment made by a United Kingdom company cannot fall within section 52 because a United Kingdom company pays corporation tax, not income tax.

The basic idea behind section 52 is that the payer has alienated part of his income. If Albert covenants to pay his aged and impecunious Aunt Beatrice £100 a year, the law regards that £100 as being Aunt Beatrice's income and not Albert's. So Aunt Beatrice should pay the tax on it and not Albert. The section empowers Albert to deduct tax (at the basic rate: section 36 of the Finance Act 1971) from the £100 and pay Aunt Beatrice the net amount, which at the present basic rate would be £70. The amount deducted is treated as tax paid by Aunt Beatrice. As he is paying out of his taxable income, Albert keeps the amount deducted to recoup himself for the tax which he has paid (or will pay) on the £100. This is a classic example, indeed *the* classic example (it has been in the tax system since 1803) of deduction of tax at source. The payer is acting as a collector (unpaid) for the Revenue. The *machinery* of section 52 is that the payer pays the tax on the amount of the payment and recoups himself by deducting tax from the payment. The *effect* is that the payee in reality bears the tax and the payer does not. One can state the point in a table as follows (ignoring personal reliefs).

Machinery		*Effect*	
Payer's income	*£1,000*	Payer's income	£1,000
Annual payment		*less*	
gross £100. Deduct		alienated income £100	————
tax at 30 per cent.			£900
Therefore, actual			
payment	70	Payee pays tax on £100	30
Payer pays tax on		Payer pays tax on	
£1,000 at 30 per cent.	300	£900 at 30 per cent.	270
Payer has in pocket	630	Payer has in pocket	630
Payee has in pocket	70	Payee has in pocket	70

I just want to refer to two rather "olde worlde" phrases in section 52 (1) (*b*). That paragraph says: "the whole of the profits or gains shall be assessed and charged with income tax on the person liable to the annuity or other annual payment, without distinguishing the annuity or other annual payment." The "person liable to the annuity or other annual payment" means the person who is under a legal obligation to pay the annuity. "Without distinguishing the annuity or other annual payment" means without making any deduction for it.

If, on the other hand, Albert pays Aunt Beatrice, not out of taxable income but, *e.g.* out of capital, then a new income springs up in the hands of Aunt Beatrice which has not been taxed. So Albert deducts tax (at basic rate) from his payment to Aunt Beatrice, but this time section 53 applies and he must hand over to the Revenue the amount which he has deducted. This time Albert is doing an even better collecting job for the Revenue because in this situation the Revenue are really interested; they want the tax on what is a new source of income. So Albert *must* deduct tax in making payment to Aunt Beatrice and he *must* hand over the amount deducted, through an assessment, to the Revenue, though the Revenue has an alternative power to assess the payee. In the section 52 situation, by contrast, the Revenue are not so interested because they have got (or will get) the tax from Albert just as though he had not alienated any of his income. Consequently Albert *need not* deduct tax from his payment to Aunt Beatrice; but he may, and if he has any sense he will, in order to recoup himself for the tax he has to pay. If Albert does not make a deduction from his payment to Aunt Beatrice and if, for extraneous reasons, the Revenue cannot get the tax out of Albert they can (since 1971) make an assessment on Aunt Beatrice.

Another difference between the sections is that under section 52 (out of taxable income) tax is to be deducted at the basic rate applicable to the year of assessment when the payment is due, whereas under section 53 (not out of taxable income) tax is to be deducted at the basic rate applicable to the year of assessment when the payment is actually made.

The payee must accept the net amount as discharging the payer's obligation. This is expressly stated in section 52 and is taken as implied in section 53.

If the payee is not liable to tax at the basic rate he can reclaim from the Revenue the whole or part of the amount deducted. The system of deduction of tax at source could be seen in all its beautiful symmetry if the basic rate were the only rate of tax. The introduction of lower rate, higher rate and additional rate tax has spoilt the picture a bit. If the payee is not liable to tax at all he can get from the Revenue a full repayment. If he is liable at lower rate only he can get a repayment of the difference between lower rate and basic rate tax on the gross amount of the payment (section 32 (1C) of the Finance Act 1971, as inserted by section 14 (2) of the Finance Act 1978). If the payee is liable to higher rate and/or additional rate tax, then the

E

annual payment counts as part of his total income and for this purpose the net amount received must be grossed up (as described at p. 40, above). The ability of the payee to make a repayment claim means that annual payments (*e.g.* under a covenant) are a useful bit of tax planning. A covenant to a charity enables the charity to get from the Revenue the whole of the tax deducted. Thus if our friend Albert covenants to pay Oxfam each year (for say seven years) £100 gross, he pays Oxfam £70 and Oxfam gets £30 from the Revenue. Oxfam thus gets altogether £100. If Albert is paying out of taxable income it has only cost him £70, because he would have had to pay tax on the £100 anyway. In regard to Albert's covenant to Aunt Beatrice let us suppose that Aunt Beatrice is liable to tax only at the lower rate (25 per cent.). Albert deducts £30 and pays Aunt Beatrice £70. Beatrice gets from the Revenue the difference between £30 and £25, namely £5. So Beatrice gets altogether £75. Again (if Albert is paying out of taxable income) it has really only cost him £70. The key to this is that Aunt Beatrice has a lower rate of tax than Albert. If she was not liable to tax at all she would get repayment in full (£30) like Oxfam (a charity). The key to this is that an individual is not liable to tax if his income is less than his personal reliefs. It has recently dawned on the National Union of Students that this is so of most students, and they have begun to publicise the idea of parents covenanting with their student offspring. Everyone has a personal allowance however young, even a babe in arms. In principle, a father can covenant to make an annual payment (for say seven years) in favour of his student son or daughter at a cost to him of £70 for every £100 in the student's hands. So it is obviously better than simply making ad hoc gifts of £70. The scheme does not work if the "child" is below the age of 18 (and unmarried), though even at that age the scheme would work alright if the covenantor was a grandparent, not a parent, of the covenantee. (You will not have a complete picture of this matter until you have read Chapter 14, on settlements.)

Which Section?

It is obviously a matter of great importance to the payer that section 52 should apply to his payment, because if it does he can keep the tax deducted whereas if section 53 applies he must hand it over to the Revenue. It may also be of some importance to the payee, because if section 52 applies the payment is part of his total income for the year in which it was due, whereas if section 53 applies it is part of his total income for the year in which it was paid, and the rates of tax may vary between those years. Many, many cases have been fought out on this issue. In *Chancery Lane Safe Deposit and Offices Co. Ltd.* v. *I.R.C.* (1966) (H.L.) the taxpayer company borrowed money to finance the rebuilding of its premises, a fixed capital asset. The interest payable on the borrowings was "capitalised," *i.e.* treated as part of the cost of the asset and not charged to the profit and loss account. Consequently the interest did not reduce the amount of profit available for dividend. It was held by the House of Lords that the company could not subsequently make an inconsistent attribution to revenue account, and so its payments of interest fell outside what is now section 52 and inside what is now section 53. The company must hand over to the Revenue the tax deducted from the interest payments. It is interesting that in 1977 a similar point arose in *Fitzleet Estates* v. *Cherry* (1977) (H.L.) and the House of Lords declined to reverse the majority decision which the House had reached in the *Chancery Lane* case. The *Fitzleet Estate* case is of more general importance than the narrow issue between section 52 and section 53, because in it their Lordships made observations about the circumstances in which the House of Lords would act on the famous Practice Statement of 1966 in which the Lord Chancellor had stated that the Lords of Appeal would henceforth feel free to depart from a previous decision of the House "when it appears right to do so." In the *Fitzleet Estate* case their Lordships said that the Practice Statement did not permit an appellant to argue that an earlier decision of the House should not be followed *merely because it was wrong*. It was immaterial that the earlier decision had been by a narrow majority. Before the House would depart from an earlier decision, some other ground, such as material change of circumstances, had to be shown which would justify the House adopting such a course.

TAX FREE PAYMENTS AND "THE FORMULA"

If A makes an annual payment to B, he either may (if he pays out of taxable income) or must (if he pays otherwise than out of taxable income) deduct tax at basic rate in making the payment. In undertaking to make these payments it is important (and difficult) to use words which make it absolutely clear what is to be the position with regard to tax. For many years now a conventional formula has been in use, whereby the payer's undertaking to pay is couched in the following (or similar) words: "Such a sum as after deduction of income tax at the basic rate for the time being in force will amount to the sum of (£100)." The effect of this form of words is that the payer undertakes to pay £100 net to the payee and to notionally gross up £100 at the current basic rate and notionally deduct tax at the current rate. At the present basic rate, 30 per cent., the gross of £100 net is £142.86, and basic rate tax on £142.86 is £42.86, leaving £100 net.

If the parties use some form of words radically different from "the formula," difficulties may arise. One difficulty stems from section 106 (2) of the Taxes Management Act 1970, which says: "Every agreement for payment of interest, rent or other annual payment in full without allowing any such deduction shall be void."[2] The question has arisen, What is the effect of this subsection on an agreement to pay £100 "free of tax"? In *Blount* v. *Blount* (1916) Scrutton J. held that the then equivalent of section 106 (2) rendered void the words "free of tax" but did not render void the rest of the agreement. Consequently the agreement was to be read as though the words "free of tax" had simply been crossed out and it was construed to mean a payment of £100 gross. This was pretty certainly not the intention of the parties; they meant the £100 to be a net sum. *Blount* v. *Blount* stood for over 50 years. Then in *Ferguson* v. *I.R.C.* (1970) (H.L.) *Blount* v. *Blount* was overruled by the House of Lords. Lord Diplock said that in that case "a Homer nodded." The true effect of an agreement to pay £100 "free of tax" is that it obliges the payer to pay such a sum as after the deduction of tax equals £100. The £100, in other words, is a net sum. Section 106 (2) is confined to cases where the agreement uses some such phrase as "without deducting tax," making it plain that the parties really are attempting to state a gross sum and not a net sum. Section 106 (2) never applied to wills or voluntary settlements or court orders. This is because the subsection uses the word "agreement." So the effect of *Ferguson's* case is to bring agreements in which the words used are "free of tax" into line with these other obligations.

However, the expression "free of tax" raises another difficulty which may occur in a will, or a voluntary settlement or (since *Ferguson's* case) an agreement. It does not arise in court orders. If "the formula" is used, the payer fulfils his duty to the Revenue by deducting tax at the basic rate (and, if he pays not out of taxable income, by accounting to the Revenue) and by so doing he also fulfils his duty to the payee. What happens after that between the payee and the Revenue does not concern the payer; if the payee gets a repayment it does not concern the payer, and if, on the contrary, the payee has to pay higher or additional rate tax that does not concern the payer either. But if the expression "free of tax" is used the position is different. At first sight it might seem (after *Ferguson's* case) that "free of tax" has the same effect as the formula. This is so as regards deducting basic rate tax, but it is not so thereafter. "Free of tax" may mean that if the payee gets a repayment from the Revenue he must hand it over to the payer because if he does not he will have obtained

---

[2] The point of this enactment (which goes back to 1803) is to protect the payer against an irate payee who demands his money in full without deduction.

in total more than £100 net. "Free of tax" may also mean that if the payee has to pay higher and/or additional rate tax the payer must reimburse him, because if he does not the payee will have received in the end less than £100 net. In *Ferguson's* case the House of Lords left open these two points. The matter is complicated, but the position can be broadly stated by reference to two cases.

In *Re Pettit* (1922) an annuity was given in a will free of income tax. The annuitant was repaid by the Revenue part of the tax which had been deducted. It was held that he was not entitled to retain the whole of the repayment but must pay a proportion of it to the trustees of the will. The proportion is the proportion which the gross amount of the annuity bears to the annuitant's total income. This is sometimes called "the rule in *Re Pettit*." The rule applies not only to wills but also to voluntary settlements and agreements. It does not apply to any of those obligations if "the formula" is used for the reason stated above, namely that the formula is fulfilled as soon as the payer has paid to the payee the net sum. The rule in *Re Pettit* does not apply to court orders.

In *Re Reckitt* (1932) (C.A.) an annuity had been given by a will. The annuitant was liable to tax in excess of the standard rate (broadly equivalent to the basic rate), and it was held that the trustees of the will must reimburse the annuitant for the amount which he had had to pay in tax over and above the standard rate. It is thought that the principle of this case applies, like the rule in *Re Pettit*, to wills, voluntary settlements and agreements but not to orders of a court. It does not apply where "the formula" is used for the same reason that *Re Pettit* does not apply.

These difficulties do not arise in connection with a sum of money ordered by a court to be paid periodically, *e.g.* maintenance payments. Section 106 (2) of the Taxes Management Act 1970 does not apply, and *Re Pettit* (and presumably *Re Reckitt*) does not apply. If a court orders a party to pay to the other party periodically (say every month) £100 "tax free" the payer must pay such sum (£142.86 at the present basic rate, 30 per cent.) as after deduction of income tax at the basic rate amounts to £100. £100 is a net sum. In practice it is more common for a court order to reach the same result by using the following form of words: "£142.86 less tax."

Small Maintenance Payments

There is one particular kind of court order to which different rules apply. This is an order for what is called a Small Maintenance Payment. This is a payment ordered by a court in the United Kingdom either (a) by one party to a marriage (including a marriage which has been dissolved or annulled) to the other party for maintenance, or

(b) to any person for the maintenance or education of a person under 21, where the amount ordered to be paid does not exceed in case (a), £21 a week or £91 a month, or, in case (b), £12 a week or £52 a month. The amounts are varied from time to time by statutory instrument. The figures stated were set by S.I. 1977 No. 662. A small maintenance payment order usually does not mention tax at all. Its effects are well known and are laid down in section 65 of the Taxes Act. First, payment is made without deduction of tax; although the payments are "annual payments," sections 52 and 53 are expressly stated not to apply. Second, if the payee is liable to tax he or she is assessed under Case III of Schedule D, treating the payment as a gross sum and treating it as earned income. But assessment is unlikely to happen, because the whole point of a small maintenance order is that it is designed to save all the palaver of deduction followed by repayment in a case where it is known that the payee is not in receipt of sufficient income for the payment to attract any tax at all. Third, the payer is entitled to deduct the amounts of the payments he has made in the year in computing his total income. No question of grossing-up arises because the payments are, in effect, gross sums.

PURCHASED LIFE ANNUITIES

Many annuities arise under a will or similar instrument of gift. But it is perfectly possible to buy an annuity "in the market." These purchased life annuities, or some of them, have a special rule applying to them. Until 1956 purchased life annuities were taxed as though the annuity payments were wholly income, whereas the commercial reality is that each payment contains a capital element; that is to say, in each payment there is an element which, in effect, goes towards repaying the capital sum for which the annuity was bought. In 1956 the law was changed and the relevant section is now section 230 of the Taxes Act. The capital content of each periodic payment to the annuitant is exempt from income tax. The capital is found (putting it broadly) by dividing the purchase price of the annuity by the normal expectation of life of the annuitant, calculated at the date when the annuity begins. Once the calculation has been made the figure remains constant for every year. Income tax is charged each year on the amount by which the annuity payment exceeds this capital content, whether or not the annuitant survives for the period of normal expectation. Let us take an example. Suppose a widow buys an annuity for £24,000. Her age is 60, and the government mortality tables show that a female at age 60 has a normal life expectation of (say) 20 years. The capital content is £24,000 divided by 20 = £1,200. The annuity brings in say 14 per cent.; on £24,000 that is

£3,360. Tax is payable on £3,360 less £1,200 = £2,160. The taxable amount counts as unearned (investment) income. There are some important exceptions where section 230 does not apply. In particular, it does not apply where an annuity is purchased as a retirement annuity under section 226 of the Taxes Act. It will be remembered (from the end of Chapter 8, above) that retirement annuities do have other tax advantages (relief on premiums; payments counted as earned income) so it is not altogether surprising that they do not also qualify for this relief under section 230.

INTEREST

We saw in Chapter 7 how relief is given in some circumstances to the payer of interest. Here we are concerned with interest from the point of view of the payee. We saw at the beginning of this chapter that interest is taxable under Case III of Schedule D. And later on we saw that interest used to be collected at source under what is now section 52 or section 53. That was so until 1969, but now interest is not within section 52 or section 53. There is a somewhat similar provision now in section 54. But I want to emphasise that section 54 only applies to certain kinds of interest and that most interest does not come within section 54 and is not collected at source at all but is paid by the payer to the payee in full and then taxed in the hands of the payee. All interest is in principle chargeable under Case III, but it may be assessed under Case I where interest is an income item in the computation of the profits of a trade, or it may be collected at source under section 54.

Section 54 applies only to "yearly" interest, not to "short" interest, meaning interest where the obligation to pay it is to continue for less than a year. Short interest is always payable in full without deduction of tax. And section 54 only applies to certain kinds even of yearly interest, as follows: (a) interest paid by a company or local authority (in each case, otherwise than in a fiduciary or representative capacity; that is, where the payer is a trustee or is paying on behalf of someone else), (b) interest paid by or on behalf of a partnership of which a company is a member, (c) interest paid by any person to another person whose usual place of abode is outside the United Kingdom. The reason for (a) and (b) is that companies are under a special system of taxation, and the reason for (c) is that the government wants to be sure of getting the tax before the money goes outside its grasp. There are two exceptions whereby section 54 does not apply even though the interest falls within (a), (b) or (c). These are: interest payable in the United Kingdom on an advance from a bank carrying on a bona fide banking business in the United Kingdom; and interest paid by such a bank in the ordinary course of that business.

It follows from all this that interest paid to a bank (*e.g.* on a loan or on an overdraft) or by a bank (*e.g.* on a deposit account) and interest paid to a building society is always payable in full without deduction of tax. The latter point is reinforced by section 343 (4) of the Taxes Act. The special rules relating to interest paid *by* a building society were discussed at p. 41, above.

CHAPTER 12

INCOME FROM LAND[1]

"Land," observed Anthony Trollope, "is about the only thing that can't fly away."[2] This is a thought that has occurred to landowners, would-be landowners and the Revenue. The taxation of land has a long and tangled history. Income from land is now taxed under Schedule A, which is dealt with in sections 67 to 90 of the Taxes Act. For reasons which will appear in a moment one can call this "the new Schedule A." Before studying it, we should look briefly at some history.

HISTORY

"The old Schedule A" was a tax on the *ownership* of land. From that it followed that it caught not only landowners who let out their land but also owner-occupiers. It was based on annual values. These annual values were supposed to be revised every five years, but in fact the last revision was made in 1935–36, and after that year they became hopelessly out-of-date and absurdly low. The Finance Act 1940 then introduced a system of taxing landlords (under Case VI of Schedule D) on what were called "excess rents," that is on rents received to the extent that they exceeded the annual values fixed under Schedule A.

Then the Finance Act 1963 re-modelled the whole system. Tax on owner-occupiers was abolished and does not now exist. They had, after all, only been subjected to income tax on the basis of a notional income (equal to the annual value) not a real income. And in practice many owner-occupiers had been able to eliminate any tax charge by making a "maintenance claim" in respect of repairs, insurance, etc. This is still a fairly hot political potato, many people taking the view that since owner-occupiers are spared the burden of paying rent the notional income from their property should be taxed.[3] So far as non-occupiers were concerned the Finance Act 1963 combined the

---

[1] "Land" in tax law, as in law generally, includes buildings (except where the context requires otherwise).
[2] See *The Last Chronicle of Barset*, Chap. 58.
[3] The amount of "tax relief" (or "subsidy" as critics call it) is enormous. On November 24, 1978 the Chief Secretary to the Treasury estimated that for 1978–79 it would be £1,110 million.

115

old Schedule A and the excess rents provisions into a new taxing code which was labelled Case VIII of Schedule D.

For the next six years there was no Schedule A; that label was vacant. Then by the Finance Act 1969 Case VIII was re-named "Schedule A." It can be seen that this new Schedule A was (and is) very different from the old Schedule A.

There was also a Schedule B tax. This was a tax on the *occupiers* of land. It was in addition to Schedule A. So an owner-occupier paid both, with the important exception that dwelling-houses and trade premises were exempted from Schedule B. Farms used to fall under Schedule B, until farming was transferred by statute to Case I of Schedule D. Schedule B tax was based on one-third of gross annual value.

THE PRESENT SCHEDULE B

Schedule B still exists, but it is confined (since 1963–64) to the occupation of woodlands "managed on a commercial basis and with a view to the realisation of profits" (Taxes Act, s. 91). The assessable value is one-third of the annual value. The annual value is no longer a fixed amount with formal re-valuations every five years. It is determined ad hoc by the Inspector, but as if the land, instead of being woodlands, were let in its natural and unimproved state. The occupier of woodlands can elect for assessment under Case I of Schedule D. He might well do so in the early years of a plantation when the profits are nil or low. When the plantation is mature, Schedule B will almost certainly be more advantageous. This seems to open up a means of tax avoidance. But the Revenue have thought of that, and an election for Schedule D once made cannot be reversed by the same occupier. But a new occupier automatically starts on Schedule B, so by means of, *e.g.* a lease to a relative, there is still scope for minimising tax. Indeed, it is pretty clear that lenient taxation of woodlands is part of government policy—the wooden walls of old England and all that.

THE MODERN SCHEDULE A AND ASSOCIATED CHARGES

The reason for this rather clumsy heading is that some income from land is taxed under Schedule A and some under Case VI of Schedule D. We have to distinguish between on the one hand rents (and similar receipts such as rent charges, ground annuals and feu duties) and on the other hand premiums.

Rents

Section 67 of the Taxes Act charges tax under Schedule A on the annual profits or gains arising in respect of rents (etc.). The phrase "profits or gains" shows that it is not the rents themselves which are charged to tax, but the excess of the rents over deductible expenses. One has to envisage, as with Case I of Schedule D, an account containing income items and expenditure items. The word "annual" preceding "profits or gains" serves to show that capital profits are not subject to Schedule A tax (though they may incur capital gains tax or development land tax). The tax is imposed by direct assessment and not by deduction of tax at source; that is, not by deduction of the tax by the tenant from his payments of rent. The tax is on a current year basis, not on a preceding year basis. And the tax is charged by reference to the rents to which a person becomes "entitled" in the chargeable period. Since the chargeable period is the current year this entitlement rule sometimes creates a difficulty, because a taxpayer may be entitled to rent and yet not receive it. If this happens an adjustment can be made (under section 87) in two cases: (1) where the landlord has taken any reasonable steps available to him to enforce payment, or (2) where the landlord has waived the rent and the waiver was without consideration and was reasonably made in order to avoid hardship.

If a landlord defaults in payment of tax, the Revenue can require the tenant to pay the tax, but the tax demanded of the tenant in any period cannot exceed the amount of the rent due in that period. A tenant from whom tax has been collected is empowered to deduct an amount equal to the tax which he has paid from any subsequent payment of rent.

Furnished lettings

Where premises are let furnished, that part of the rent which is attributable to use of the furniture is assessable under Case VI of Schedule D. Section 67 (1) of the Taxes Act provides that the rest of the rent (the true rent, the rent for the land) is to be charged also under Case VI, unless the landlord elects for Schedule A for this part of the rent. A landlord of furnished premises may be held to be carrying on a trade, in which case he will be charged to tax under Case I, but even if he is not carrying on a trade the income will count as earned income (not investment income) if he does more than merely provide accommodation and furniture, *e.g.* if he provides meals or cleaning.

Premiums

Premiums, to the extent we shall discuss in a moment, are taxable. If premiums were not taxable there would be an obvious and simple tax-avoidance device—don't charge a rent, just take a premium, which, being a capital sum, would not be subject to income tax because it is not an *annual* profit or gain.

The normal meaning of premium in relation to land is a lump sum paid for the granting of a lease. But for income tax purposes "premium" has an extended meaning, as we shall see.

The broad principle is that premiums are charged to income tax. The detailed provisions in sections 80 to 85 are concerned to stop up various tax-avoidance devices which would otherwise be open. This is an excellent field in which to observe the battle between tax avoiders and the Revenue.

A premium (or part of a premium) which is not caught for income tax may be caught for capital gains tax. Conversely, that part of a premium which is caught for income tax is not chargeable to capital gains tax.

There are three main heads of charge on premium income: (1) under section 80, premiums and like sums are chargeable; (2) under section 81, where a lease is granted at an undervalue the "amount foregone" may be chargeable on a subsequent assignment of the lease; (3) under section 82, where land is sold with a right to reconveyance the difference between the selling price and the reconveyance price may be chargeable to tax.

Let us look first at section 80. Subsection (1) is the provision which catches a "premium" in its normal meaning. It says: "Where the payment of any premium is required under a lease, or otherwise under the terms subject to which a lease is granted, and the duration of the lease does not exceed 50 years, the landlord shall be treated for the purposes of the Tax Acts as becoming entitled when the lease is granted to an amount by way of rent (in addition to any actual rent) equal to the amount of the premium reduced by one-fiftieth of that amount for each complete period of 12 months (other than the first) comprised in the duration of the lease."

Notice that the way the subsection taxes a premium is to treat the landlord as being in receipt of rent. Notice also that a lease for more than 50 years is not caught, and that the nearer a lease gets to being for 50 years the less tax is payable. Thus a premium on a lease for 49 years is reduced by forty-eight-fiftieths, or 96 per cent., leaving only 4 per cent. taxable. A lease for nine years is reduced by eight-fiftieths (or 16 per cent.), leaving 84 per cent. taxable. A lease for one year enjoys no reduction at all. Because of this sliding scale there are detailed rules (in section 84) for ascertaining the duration of leases.

We now come to some extended meanings of the word "premium." Section 80 (2) treats as a premium a requirement on the tenant to carry out works on the premises (beyond mere maintenance and repairs). The deemed premium is of an amount equal to the increase that the requirement makes in the value of the landlord's reversionary interest. So the premium provisions cannot be avoided by requiring works rather than a cash payment.

Section 80 also deals with other kinds of disguised premium. Subsection (3) deems a sum to be a premium if it becomes payable by the tenant in lieu of rent or as consideration for the surrender of the lease. Subsection (4) deems a sum to be a premium if it becomes payable by the tenant as consideration for the variation or waiver of any of the terms of the lease.

Where a premium (or a deemed premium, as above) is payable by instalments the tax may be paid in corresponding instalments spread over a maximum of eight years, but only if the recipient satisfies the Revenue that he would otherwise suffer undue hardship. This undue hardship test (and the eight-year limit) was introduced in 1972. Before that no such test was required and there was no time-limit, and ingenious leases appeared under which a premium was to be paid over a period of, say, 250 years, with the bulk becoming payable in the 250th year.

Section 81 deals with another possible avoidance device. A premium paid on the *grant* of a lease is taxable (as we have seen), but a premium paid on the *assignment* of a lease is not taxable under the provisions we have so far looked at. Therefore, if it were not for this section 81, a simple avoidance device would be for A to grant a lease to B (a relative, say, or a friendly company) at a very small premium or without any premium at all and then for B to assign the lease to C (a stranger) at a premium. Section 81 catches this situation. Suppose the market is such that A could have required a premium of £1,000 on the grant of the lease to B, whereas in fact he took a premium of only £200, then £800 is said to be "the amount foregone." If B later assigns the premises for £1,400 he is charged to tax (under Case VI of Schedule D) on the excess of £1,400 over the amount of the original premium (£200), except that the chargeable amount cannot exceed the amount foregone. So on these figures the chargeable amount would have been £1,400 less £200 (= £1,200), but the upper limit is £800, and so the chargeable amount is £800. If B had assigned the premises to C for a premium of £500 the chargeable amount would have been £300. In that circumstance the Revenue would not have collected tax on the whole of the amount foregone, but they would be able to pick up the balance on subsequent assignments by C, D, E, etc.

Section 82 deals with yet another avoidance device, namely selling land subject to a right of reconveyance. If A, a landowner, is minded to take a premium of, say, £7,000, on granting a lease to B, he could, instead, sell the land to B on terms that he, A, could buy back the land from B for the sale price minus £7,000. Section 82 ensures that on such a transaction A is charged to tax (under Case VI) on £7,000. If the sale contains a right for A to take a lease back of the premises from B, the lease back counts as a reconveyance. This lease back procedure is very common in practice, because it is a neat way of solving a liquidity problem or a cash-flow problem, and, as it is not very wicked, section 82 contains a proviso excepting such a transaction from the tax charge if the lease back is granted, and begins to run, within one month after the sale. That seems a very arbitrary way of marking out the exception, but it does enable (as it is intended to do) a genuine lease back arrangement to be free of the tax charge under section 82. But capital gains tax may be chargeable on the transaction; also if the lease back is at more than a commercial rent, only the commercial rent will be an allowable business expense (section 491 of the Taxes Act); also in certain circumstances a proportion of the sale price may be taxed as though it were income (section 80 of the Finance Act 1972).

Top-slicing relief

Because premiums and the similar receipts mentioned above are treated as receipts for a single year of assessment they would push the recipient up into an unduly high tax rate band if some relief were not offered. Relief is offered, but only to *individuals* (and so not, *e.g.* to companies). The relief is called "top-slicing" relief, and it is set out in Schedule 3 of the Taxes Act. It is similar, but not identical, to top-slicing relief on golden handshakes. The terms of the relief are complex, but the broad effect of it can be explained fairly simply by an example. Suppose A grants to B a lease for six years at a premium of £4,000. After reduction at 2 per cent. for each year of the lease other than the first the "chargeable sum" is £3,600. The "relevant period" is six years. To apply top-slicing relief one divides the chargeable sum (£3,600) by the relevant period (6), giving a "yearly equivalent" of £600, and one then determines A's top rate of tax by adding to his other income not the whole £3,600 but only £600. One then applies that top rate to the whole £3,600. So A still has to pay tax on the whole £3,600 in one year *but* he pays it at a lower *rate* than would otherwise be the case.

Deductions

The rules about deductible expenses are of mind-boggling complexity. First one has to distinguish between (a) deductions from rent payable under a lease and (b) deductions from receipts other than rent under a lease (such as a payment for a licence to use land). It is not entirely clear under which category expenses connected with a premium come. One thing is clear, namely that it is only receipts falling under Schedule A which attract the Schedule A expenses rules; expenses connected with receipts falling under Case VI of Schedule D (those under section 81 and section 82) go by the Case VI expenses rules. Beyond that it is not clear whether Schedule A premiums (and deemed premiums) go into category (a) or category (b) above. My view is that reading together sections 71 (1), 72 (1) and 80 (1) they go into category (a).

Let us now look at category (a) (sections 71 and 72). One has to distinguish between three kinds of lease. First, in a lease not at a full rent (meaning a rent which is likely to leave the landlord out of pocket) payments out are only deductible from rent paid in respect of the very premises on which the expenses are incurred. Also the payments must relate to expenditure during the currency of the lease or, in the case of maintenance and repairs, must relate to dilapidations occurring during the currency of the lease. Second, in a lease at a full rent which is a tenant's repairing lease expenditure for a previous period is also allowed if it is what is called a "previous qualifying period," meaning a period during which there is a full-rent lease by the same landlord or a "void period" (unlet). Third, in a lease at a full rent which is not a tenant's repairing lease, expenditure for a previous period is allowed and also there may be set off against the rent of such a lease any surplus expenditure on another full-rent lease (of other premises) the rent of which is insufficient to absorb the expenditure.

Category (b) comprises deductions from receipts other than rent. The relevant sections are 71 and 74. The payments out are only deductible if they relate to the very premises and the very transaction from which the receipt is derived. An excess of expenditure can be set off against income from any like transaction in the same period or in a later period.

In all these cases the expenses which are allowable include maintenance, repairs, insurance and management. A land-owning *company* can also deduct further management expenses under section 304 of the Taxes Act.

"ARTIFICIAL TRANSACTIONS IN LAND"

This is the title of section 488 of the Taxes Act. It derives from a section first enacted in 1960. Subsection (1) of section 488 states the reason for the section: "This section is enacted to prevent the avoidance of tax by persons concerned with land or the development of land." One must bear in mind that the section dates from 1960, that is before there was a capital gains tax. In those days an owner of land who sold the land could make a tax-free profit, unless he was a dealer in land. If he was a dealer in land he was taxed on the gain as an item in his trading profit. He could avoid this tax by forming a company to hold the land, and then selling the shares rather than selling the land as such. That transaction would be tax-free unless he was a dealer in shares.

Section 488 seeks to block this device. It is not so important since capital gains tax came in in 1965, but it is still of some importance because the rate of that tax is much lower than the higher rates of income tax. Where the section applies the gain is taxed as income (unearned) under Case VI of Schedule D. The gain which is taxed is the gain on the disposal of land where the land was (a) acquired with the main object of realising a gain or (b) was held as trading stock or (c) was developed with the main object of realising a gain. "Disposal of land" for the purposes of this section includes disposal of "control over the land." This is the phrase that brings within the tax-net the selling of shares in a land-holding company.

It is not entirely clear what the word "artificial" means in the title of the section; possibly it refers to the selling of the shares instead of the land.

END-PIECE

In considering the taxation of receipts from land, one should bear in mind that as well as income tax (in connection with rents and premiums and section 488 gains) a transaction in land may attract capital gains tax or development land tax.

CHAPTER 13

TRUSTS[1] AND ESTATES

We need to look now at the way in which the income tax system works in relation to trusts and in relation to the estates of deceased individuals.

There is a similarity between income which arises during the administration of the estate of a deceased individual and income which arises under a trust, but there are also differences. It is quite common (though not so common as in the old days of estate duty) for a "dad" to leave his property by will to his wife for her life and then to his children absolutely. On his death there is first a period during which his estate is being administered (or wound up) and then a period during which there is a trust in operation. In both periods the widow will be entitled to all the income, but the tax rules are somewhat different in the two periods. The executors and the trustees may well be the same people; they are executors during the administration period and then become trustees.

In the general law—quite apart from tax law—there is a fundamental difference between the position of a person entitled to income of a residuary estate and a person entitled to income arising under a trust. The former is not entitled to anything until it is paid to him or at least appropriated to him: see *Corbett* v. *I.R.C.* (1938) (C.A.). The latter is entitled to his share of the income of the trust from its inception, or, more strictly, to his share of the income of the investments which constitute the trust fund: see *Baker* v. *Archer-Shee* (1927) (H.L.).

We will look at the two situations in turn.

TRUST INCOME[2]

The existence of trusts causes great difficulties for tax legislators and for everyone else connected with tax, including students of tax law. Tax law would be very much simpler if there were no trusts. But there are trusts, and we must face the difficulties. For income tax the difficulties are considerable; for capital gains tax and, above all, capital transfer tax they are even greater.

For income tax there is a kind of two-tier system: to some extent

---

[1] Authorised unit trusts are taxed not as trusts but much as though they were investment companies.

[2] For income tax purposes a trust is one kind of settlement, and consequently the reader is advised to look at Chap. 14 along with this chapter.

income tax is charged on the trustees; to some extent it is charged on the beneficiary.

The Charge on the Trustees

Trustees are not "individuals" for the purposes of income tax, but they are "persons." Consequently they are liable to basic rate tax and on the other hand they are not entitled to any lower rate band nor to any personal reliefs. (It would be clearer if the so-called "personal reliefs" were called "individual reliefs" since they only apply to individuals.) Trustees are not liable to higher rate tax, again because they are not individuals and higher rate tax is charged only on individuals. Logically one would expect trustees not to be liable to additional rate tax, and at one time this was so, but it is not wholly so now.

By section 16 of the Finance Act 1973 additional rate tax (as well as basic rate tax) is charged on income arising to trustees if it is income which is to be accumulated or which is payable at discretion (whether or not the trustees have power to accumulate income). So, putting it broadly, additional rate tax is payable by accumulation trusts and discretionary trusts and by trusts which are subject to section 31 of the Trustee Act 1925. (That is the section which gives trustees power to apply income for the maintenance, education or benefit of an infant). In years when there is more than one additional rate it is the higher or highest of the rates which applies to trusts, and they do not have the surcharge-free band of income which an individual has. Not the whole of the income is charged, but only the income net after expenses.

The trustees of a discretionary trust may be subject to a further charge to tax when they come to make a distribution of income to a beneficiary. Such a charge will arise if the rate of tax is higher in the year of distribution than it was in the year in which the income arose to the trustees. This matter is dealt with by section 17 of the Finance Act 1973.

The Charge on the Beneficiary

A beneficiary's income from a trust forms part of his total income for determining his reliefs and his rate of tax. It would be nice and neat if one could say that one works out the beneficiary's tax bill and then gives him a straight credit for the tax (basic rate and, if applicable, additional rate) already paid by the trustees. Unfortunately this is not precisely so. There is a case called *Macfarlane* v. *I.R.C.* (1929) (C. Sess.) which held that although trust expenses are not deductible in computing the trustees' income, they are deductible in computing the beneficiary's income. The position now is even more complicated, because although trust expenses are not deductible in computing the trust's liability to basic rate tax, they are deductible in computing the trust's liability to additional rate tax. However, one can say this: the tax charge on the beneficiary *takes into account* the tax already charged on the trustees.

Income to which a beneficiary is *entitled* forms part of his total income whether or not he receives it. This follows from the general principle stated above, namely that a beneficiary who is entitled at all is entitled from the very inception of the trust. Of course this principle does not apply to a discretionary trust; if there is a discretion whether to pay any particular beneficiary he has no entitlement until the discretion is exercised in his favour. When a sum is actually paid to such a beneficiary that sum forms part of his total income. Whether one is talking of a fixed trust or a discretionary trust, payments in kind may, just as much as money payments, constitute income. This would be so, for example, of a right to occupy a house rent free.

A payment may perfectly well be income in the hands of a beneficiary, even although it is made out of the capital (and not the income) of the trust.

An important tax point arises in connection with income which is accumulated by a trust. One has to make a distinction here between a vested interest and a contingent interest. This is a matter of general law rather than tax law and it involves some fairly complicated points. But broadly the distinction is that a vested interest is one which (generally) cannot be upset, whereas a contingent interest is one which is dependent on some contingency happening. The clearest example is where a trust provides that X is to have a certain interest under the trust when he attains a certain age. As he may never attain that age his interest is until then contingent. When he has attained that age his interest becomes vested. (A person may attain a vested interest in income before he attains, or without ever attaining, a vested interest in the capital of the fund.) For a person who has a vested interest in the income of a trust, that income (as has been said above) forms part of his total income, and that is so even if it is not in fact received by him. But for a person who has only a contingent interest, until that contingency occurs the income of the trust is not his income. It follows that if the trust's income is accumulated for him it is not his income. And it does not become his income even if the contingency occurs (*e.g.* he attains the age of 18) and the accumulations are paid to him. The payments reach him as capital. The leading authority on this point is *Stanley* v. *I.R.C.* (1944) (C.A.). True, the trust will have borne basic rate tax (at present 30 per cent.) and additional rate tax (at present 15 per cent.) (45 per cent. in all), but higher rate tax is avoided. The beneficiary cannot claim repayment of basic rate or additional rate tax from the Revenue, because the sum he receives is not income in his hands but capital, so he cannot complain that tax has been deducted from *his income*.

ESTATE INCOME

What we are considering here is income arising during the period of administration of the estate of a deceased individual. When an individual dies his estate is administered by executors or administrators. The generic name for these is personal representatives; for tax purposes there is no need to distinguish between the two species.

As with trusts, so with estates, there is a kind of two-tier system of income tax. Personal representatives are like trustees in that they are chargeable to basic rate tax, are not chargeable to higher rate tax, and do not qualify for the lower rate band nor for personal reliefs. In another respect, however, personal representatives differ from trustees; they are not chargeable to additional rate tax.

How is the beneficiary taxed? That depends on the nature of his benefit. If the will gives him an annuity, the annuity payments are part of his total income from the date of death. So far as legatees are concerned it is perhaps worth stating the fairly elementary point that a legacy as such is not subject to income tax because it is not income; it is capital. But a legatee may be entitled to interest or (in the case of a specific legacy) to income from the date of death. In those cases the legatee is chargeable to income tax on the interest or income.

What we have to look at in more detail is the position of a residuary beneficiary. One has to distinguish between a beneficiary who has a limited interest in the residue of the estate and a beneficiary who has an absolute interest in the residue. A person has an absolute interest if he has an interest in the capital, and a person has a limited interest if he does not have an absolute interest. An example of a person with a limited interest is a person who gets a life tenancy. Everything that is paid to him by the personal representatives must be income for the simple reason that he is not entitled to any capital. Therefore very little complication arises in his case. Each sum that is paid to him during the administration counts (grossed-up) as part of his total income when it is paid. At the end of the administration period the final payment that is made to him and all sums paid to him during its currency are aggregated, and then that aggregate sum is re-allocated on a day-by-day basis. The income is thus allotted into correct years of assessment, which is important because the beneficiary's tax rate may differ from one year to another. This process may require new computations and assessments.

A beneficiary who has an absolute interest has, by definition, an entitlement to capital. Therefore it is by no means certain that every-thing paid to him during the administration of the estate is income. To get at his tax liability the income element must be sorted out from the capital element. The first step is to calculate the "residuary income" of the estate for each year of assessment during the administration period. To arrive at residuary income the personal representatives (unlike trustees) are permitted to deduct certain management expenses. The residuary income of the estate is divided into a residuary income for each beneficiary according to his share. For example, if there are three absolute beneficiaries each with an equal share the residuary income of each is one-third of the residuary income of the estate. Then any sums which are paid to a beneficiary are treated as income in so far as (grossed-up) they do not exceed his residuary income. In so far as they do exceed it they are treated as capital. Finally, at the end of the administration period adjustments may be necessary similar to those which are made for limited interests.

CHAPTER 14

SETTLEMENTS: ANTI-AVOIDANCE RULES

In reading this chapter the reader should bear in mind the method by which trustees and beneficiaries are taxed (see Chapter 13) and the system of deducting tax at source from annuities and annual payments (see Chapter 11).

In Chapter 13 we saw that trustees are liable to tax at the basic rate, and sometimes also at additional rate, and that beneficiaries may be liable to higher rate tax and may be entitled to personal reliefs.

In this chapter we are going to look at detailed rules relating to settlements, by which in some circumstances the settlor and not the beneficiary is liable to higher rate tax and in some circumstances the beneficiary is not entitled to reliefs.

The rules are contained in Part XVI of the Taxes Act (sections 434 to 459). A "settlement" for this purpose includes any disposition, trust, covenant, agreement or arrangement and also includes, in the case of a settlement on children, any transfer of assets. Those are very wide words, but it has been established by case law that each one of the words is subject to an overriding idea, namely that a transaction only amounts to a settlement if it contains an element of bounty. To put the same point the other way round, a bona fide commercial transaction is not a settlement. Two leading cases on this point are *Bulmer* v. *I.R.C.* (1967) and *I.R.C.* v. *Plummer* (1978) (C.A.). It is very important to bear this exception in mind.

The background to Part XVI is that settlements have long been a favourite means of tax avoidance, and so the government has from time to time introduced restrictions to cut down the amount of tax avoidance which can be achieved by means of settlements. If there were no restrictions, any settlement would enable a payer with a high rate of tax to unload some of his income on to a comparatively poor member of his family to the great advantage of the family viewed as a whole, because the poor member has a lower rate of tax or may not be liable to tax at all. For example, if a high-rate taxpayer covenanted with trustees to pay £1,100 a year to his infant child, he would pay £770 net per year under the covenant. He would then claim to have alienated £1,100 gross of his income, so that upon that £1,100 he would not have to pay higher rate (or additional rate) tax. The child would claim from the Revenue the amount deducted for tax by "daddy" and the child would get a repayment of £330 as the covenant payment would be covered by his personal relief.

So a number of restrictions have been introduced by the government to limit the tax-saving effects of settlements in certain circumstances. The legislation provides that settlements which have certain specified characteristics shall have no tax-saving effects at all, and that settlements which have certain other specified characteristics shall have only a limited tax-saving effect. Although these restrictions are all now collected together in one Part of the Taxes Act, they were originally enacted piece-meal at different times, and consequently they are somewhat lacking in coherence.

This is not a very easy branch of the law to get hold of, but it is less difficult if one considers separately income settlements and capital settlements. An income settlement is a settlement which involves the transfer of income only. A covenant is a typical form of income settlement. A capital settlement is a settlement which involves the transfer of income-producing property. An income settlement is the handing-over of fruits; a capital settlement is the handing-over of a fruit tree. An income settlement may provide for payment to trustees or for payment direct to the beneficiary; a capital settlement necessarily involves trustees.

INCOME SETTLEMENTS

I am going to deal with the statutory restrictions under numbered heads.

Head 1: Settlements which cannot exceed Six Years

This matter is dealt with by section 434. The section could in theory apply to a capital settlement as well as to an income settlement, but in practice is must be very rare indeed for a capital settlement to fall foul of this section, and if it does it would be caught under some other head as well. The section catches a "disposition" (including any trust, covenant, agreement or arrangement) for a period which cannot exceed six years. It is this rule which has led to the popularity of what are called "seven-year covenants," because a seven-year covenant is not caught by the rule. The effect on a covenant which is caught is that the income is deemed for *all* tax purposes to be the income of the covenantor and not to be the income of any other person. This has two aspects. First, the covenantor is not excused from higher rate or additional rate tax; it is just as though he had not alienated the income. Second, the covenantee (the recipient, the beneficiary) cannot get a tax repayment even if he has no other income. This follows from the point that the income from the covenant is deemed not to be the covenantee's income.

The idea which lies behind the rule in section 434 seems to be that a person should not be allowed to get a tax advantage out of an obligation which is only going to be binding on him for a short period. The rule, by the way, ceases to apply if the covenantor dies during the currency of the covenant. (This raises an important (non-tax) point for covenantors to bear in mind: if the covenant is for a fixed period then, in the absence of words to the contrary, it will bind his estate even after his death, until the fixed period expires.)

Section 435 provides for certain adjustments between the "disponor" (the covenantor) and the trustees (or, in a direct covenant, the covenantee). The covenantor can recover from the trustees (or from the covenantee) the tax which he has had to pay on the amount of the covenant. (Also, if the covenantor gets a repayment of tax for a relief more than he otherwise would have got, he must pay it to the trustees (or to the covenantee). This is very unlikely to arise in practice; it could only arise where the covenantor's income is so small that without the deeming brought about by section 434 his income would not have been enough to absorb all his reliefs.) This adjustment (section 435) may seem at first sight to restore the tax advantages that section 434 took away. But this is not so. Although, by virtue of section 435, the tax is to be *borne* by the covenantee, the tax is *measured* by the circumstances of the covenantor and for this purpose the covenanted income is deemed to be the highest part of the covenantor's income. In any case, the tax point of a covenant is not to shift the tax burden from the covenantor on to the covenantee but (so to speak) on to the Revenue.

Head 2: Covenants for the Covenantor's Own Children

A covenant is caught by section 437 if it is in favour of a child of the covenantor (or other "settlor") and that child is under 18 and unmarried. The section ceases to apply if the settlor dies during the currency of the covenant. The section does not apply at all if the settlor is not resident in the United Kingdom. Consequently such a covenant remains a useful bit of tax-saving for a parent resident abroad. Even a parent resident in the United Kingdom can tax-save to the magnificent extent of £5 a year, because a covenant under which the yearly payment does not exceed that princely sum is not caught by section 437.

Where the section does apply the effect is that the covenanted income is treated for *all* tax purposes as the income of the settlor and not as the income of any other person. So, as with section 434, there is no saving in respect of higher rate or additional rate tax and no repayment from the Revenue to the (infant) covenantee. The section does not apply to covenants by persons other than parents of the beneficiary. So grandparents can covenant in favour of their grandchildren without falling foul of the section. And anyone can covenant in favour of someone else's children. But the Revenue have foreseen the possibility of X covenanting in favour of Y's children in return for Y covenanting in favour of X's children, and such reciprocal arrangements are (by section 442 (2) brought within section 437.

Section 441 contains adjustment provisions similar to those in section 435.

The idea behind section 437 is that a person should not be able to get a tax advantage out of a transfer of income to his young children. After all, a parent could see to it that the covenanted income was used to maintain the child and consequently he would not have to provide for the child's maintenance out of his unalienated income, with the overall result that the parent would be fulfilling his legal duty of maintaining his child at the expense (partly) of the Revenue.

Head 3: Revocable Settlements

A covenant (or other income settlement) which is revocable is caught by section 445. The idea behind this section is similar to the idea behind section 434 (Head 1); a person should not be enabled to get a tax advantage out of an obligation which he can end at will. An income settlement is revocable if it provides that any person has or may have power to revoke the settlement or otherwise determine it or to diminish the amount of payments thereunder.

The effect of the section is that the covenanted payments (or the amounts by which they can be diminished) are to be treated for *all* tax purposes as the income of the settlor and not as the income of any other person. There is a proviso which excepts a power which is not exercisable for six years from the time when the first annual payment is payable. But that proviso only suspends the operation of the section; the section will apply as soon (after the six years) as the power is exercisable.

Where the section applies, there is no saving of higher or additional rate tax and no possibility of the covenantee getting a repayment.

Section 449 contains adjustment provisions similar to those mentioned under Heads 1 and 2.

Head 4: Discretionary Power for Settlor or Spouse

An income settlement is caught by section 448 if under its terms there is discretionary power to apply the income for the benefit of the settlor or his spouse, *e.g.* as an alternative beneficiary under a covenant. The effect of the section is to treat the covenanted income, even if neither the settlor nor his spouse does in fact benefit, as the income for *all* tax purposes of the settlor and not as the income of any other person. If the power cannot be exercised within six years, the application of the section is suspended. The section does not apply if the discretion can only be exercised in certain specified circumstances, such as the death under the age of 25 or some lower age of some person who would become beneficially entitled on attaining that age. And the section does not apply to the extent that income would be treated as the settlor's income under some other section Where the section does apply there can be no saving of higher rate or additional rate tax, and no repayment of basic rate tax. The adjustment provisions of section 449 apply. Clearly the idea behind the section is that a person should not be able to get a tax advantage where he has not made an out-and-out gift.

Head 5: Undistributed Income
Undistributed income is of course income which is not distributed. Putting it broadly, that means income which is so dealt with that it does not fall to be treated as the income of the persons who are entitled to it. For example, income is undistributed to the extent that the trustees of a discretionary settlement do not exercise their discretion.

There are two enactments that deal with undistributed income; one dealing with the position where the settlor retains an interest and one dealing with the position where the settlor does not retain an interest.

(a) Where settlor retains an interest
Section 447 applies to an income settlement in which the settlor has an interest and in which the income in any year while the settlor is alive is not wholly distributed. The settlor is deemed to have an interest if any income or property arising under or comprised in the settlement is or will or may become payable to the settlor or his spouse. By the proviso to section 447 (2) the settlor is not deemed to have an interest if his interest arises only in certain specified events, notably the death under the age of 25 or some lower age of some person who would be beneficially entitled on attaining that age. Where the section applies the effect is that any undistributed income is treated for *all* tax purposes as the income of the settlor and not as the income of any other person. So there is no higher rate or additional rate saving and there is no possibility of a repayment for the beneficiary. Adjustments are provided for by section 449. Section

447 does not apply to the extent that section 445 (or section 446—see below under capital settlements) does apply.

The idea behind section 447 is that a person should not be enabled to gain a tax advantage from a transaction whereby he has not made an out and out gift. If it were not for the presence of this section, a taxpayer could make a covenant for payments to trustees, with a power for them to accumulate the income and indicating himself or his spouse as beneficiary. He would thus be able to set up his own investment fund free of higher rate tax.

(b) Where settlor does not retain an interest

Where the settlor does not retain an interest section 447 does not apply, but to the extent that some income remains undistributed section 450 does apply. The effect of section 450 is that sums paid by the settlor (covenantor) will not be allowed as deductions in computing his total income. The section does not apply to so much of any income arising under the settlement as has already been caught by sections 445, 448 or 447. The importance of this is that those sections provide for adjustments of tax; this section (450) does not. Notice that section 450 does not treat the income as being the income of the settlor for *all* tax purposes. In this it differs from the sections considered under Heads 1, 2, 3, 4 and 5 (a) above. But the difference turns out not to be very great. Subsection (1) expressly removes any possibility of the covenantor escaping higher rate or additional rate tax. Also, subsection (3) expressly forbids any relief by way of repayment to the trustees or the beneficiary.

What section 450 is hitting at is the possibility of paying out sums to trustees (for example, under a covenant) and having the trustees pile up those sums as capital. The section attacks income settlements only. However, as we shall see, capital settlements are dealt with (by section 451) in a similar though not identical way.

Head 6: "Excess Liability"

We now come to section 457, which is very general in its scope. It applies to all income settlements (with certain specified exceptions which we will come to in a moment) even if they have successfully jumped all the hurdles set up by Heads 1, 2, 3, 4 and 5.

Section 457 provides that (apart from the exceptions) the income of all income settlements (*e.g.* covenants) shall be treated during the life of the settlor for the purposes of "excess liability" as the income of the settlor. "Excess liability" means "the excess of liability to income tax over what it would be if all income tax not charged at a lower rate were charged at the basic rate to the exclusion of any higher or additional rate." So it means liability to higher rate or additional rate tax.

The three exceptions are as follows:

(1) Annual payments made under a partnership agreement for the benefit of a former partner or the widow or dependants of a deceased former partner.

(2) Annual payments made in connection with the acquisition by an individual of a business, provided the payments are for the benefit of (broadly speaking) the individual from whom the business was acquired or, if he is dead, his widow or dependants.

(3) Annual payments made in connection with divorce, nullity or separation. The payments must be by one party to the marriage by way of provision for the other party. The payments may be by agreement or under a court order. Payments for the children do not fall within this exception, but in practice the Revenue treat payments to children *under a court order* as not being a settlement at all and so not caught by section 457 or (see Head 2) section 437.

Where none of the above exceptions applies all income settlements are caught by section 457, except that the section does not apply where the income is deemed to be that of the settlor under some other section. The importance of this point is that section 457 does not contain any provisions for the settlor to recover the relevant tax from the trustees, and so he has to bear the excess liability himself, whereas (as we have seen) in the other sections (except 450) there are provisions for adjustment.

Notice that section 457 does not say that the income is to be treated as the income of the settlor (and not as the income of any other person) for *all* tax purposes. It simply says that it shall be treated as the income of the settlor (and not as the income of any other person) for the purposes of excess liability. This is very important. It means that a covenant to an individual, although it will not save any higher rate or additional rate tax, will enable the covenantee to get a repayment of tax from the Revenue if his personal reliefs leave him below the basic rate threshold on the whole or any part of the covenanted payment.

Similarly with a covenant to a charity. A charity is not taxable on annual payments. So Mr. X can covenant to pay £1,000 (gross) to the Y charity. Mr. X actually pays to Y £700, and Y then gets a repayment from the Revenue of £300.

A covenant which uses the conventional formula ("such sum as after deduction of tax at the basic rate for the time being in force will amount to £700") alters its gross value to the recipient if the basic rate of tax changes. Ironically, if the basic rate goes down (which one might think was a matter for universal rejoicing) the gross receipt of the recipient goes down.

The principle mentioned at p. 128, above, namely that a transaction which contains no element of bounty is not a settlement has been used as the basis of a tax avoidance device. The device is called a "reverse annuity." In *I.R.C.* v. *Plummer* (1978) (C.A.) Mr. Plummer, a surtax payer,[1] covenanted to pay an annuity to a company which was a charity, in consideration of a capital sum paid by the company to Mr. Plummer. It was held that the transaction was not caught by section 457 because there was no element of bounty.[2] Therefore Mr. Plummer was able to avoid surtax on the payments which he made to the company. (And, of course, the capital sum paid to Mr. Plummer was not taxable.) This device was stopped by section 48 of the Finance Act 1977. The section is to some extent retrospective, in that it applies to any payment made after March 29, 1977, even though the obligation to make the payments was entered into before that date.

For Heads 1, 2, 3, 4 and 5 I have tried to state the legislative purpose. It is not easy to be sure of the purpose behind section 457. I would say that the purpose is to cut out avoidance of excess liability (save in the three excepted cases) but to leave standing the more modest advantage of basic rate repayment where the objectionable circumstances covered by Heads 1 to 5 do not exist.

Summary

One must not get so mesmerised by the anti-avoidance provisions that one comes to believe that there are no advantages in income settlements. There are. First, a covenant which clears all the hurdles brings the advantage of freedom from higher rate and additional rate tax *and* the advantage of repayment of basic rate tax deducted. This is true, for example, of a covenant by Mr. X in favour of his divorced wife. Second, a covenant which clears all the hurdles except section 457, although it does not bring any advantage in respect of higher rate or additional rate tax, does bring the advantage of repayment of basic rate tax. It is quite easy to clear all the hurdles other than section 457. This is achieved by an irrevocable seven-year covenant for any charity or any individual other than a child of the covenantor who is under 18 (and unmarried) provided that there is no discretionary power to benefit the settlor or his spouse and that all the covenanted income is distributed. An example of this would be a covenant by an

---

[1] The years in question were before the abolition of surtax.

[2] Nor was it caught by s. 434 because that section is expressed not to apply to a "disposition made for valuable and sufficient consideration."

ordinary dad in an ordinary undivorced and unseparated family in favour of his adult child. The National Union of Students publicises this point; see page 108, above. If Dad covenants to pay his student offspring £100 (gross) he actually pays £70 and the Revenue pays £30.

CAPITAL SETTLEMENTS

A capital settlement involves the transfer of income-producing property rather than (as in an income settlement) the transfer merely of income. The transfer must necessarily be to trustees. As we saw in Chapter 13 trustees do not pay higher rate tax. Clearly therefore there is some possibility of tax-saving by setting up a capital settlement (trust) in favour of (say) a less well-to-do member of the settlor's family. Not surprisingly there are a number of anti-avoidance enactments similar to those relating to income settlements. We will look at the rules under numbered heads, and the heads will broadly correspond to the heads applying to income settlements.

Head 1: Six Years

Section 434 which we looked at under Head 1 of income settlements could in theory apply to a capital settlement. A person could transfer capital to trustees on trust to pay the income to someone else for, say, five years, with a provision that at the end of the five years the property was to be reconveyed to the settlor.

There is no need to add anything to what was said under Head 1 of income settlements.

Head 2: Settlements for the Settlor's Own Children

We have already considered section 437 under Head 2 of income settlements. That section applies equally to capital settlements.

But here we come to a very important difference between capital and income settlements. Section 438 (2) provides an exception to section 437, which exception by reason of its wording can only apply to a capital settlement. Moreover, it applies only to an irrevocable capital settlement, and the word "irrevocable" is given a restricted meaning by section 439. The exception is to the effect that to the extent that income arising under the settlement is *accumulated* such income is not to be treated under section 437 as income of the settlor. And, though the point is rather obscure, it seems that income derived from the accumulations is also not to be treated as income of the settlor. Section 438 (2) constitutes the only means by which a high-rate taxpayer can provide for his infant unmarried children and avoid higher rate income tax; the vehicle is an irrevocable capital accumulation settlement.[3] The trustees will be liable to basic rate and additional rate tax, but not higher rate tax. The ultimate liability of the beneficiary will depend on whether his interest is vested or contingent: see page 125, above. If his interest is contingent he will not be liable to any tax. If his interest is vested he may be liable to basic rate tax (but this will, broadly speaking, have been borne already by the trustees) and he may be liable to higher rate tax, but even so it is likely to be at a less high rate than the settlor's rate would have been. In any event there will have been a tax-saving, viewing the family as a whole.

Income which is not accumulated but distributed is caught by section 437. This will be so, for example, of income which is applied for the child's maintenance, education or benefit under section 31 of the Trustee Act 1925. And it is no good the trustees thinking that they can avoid section 437 by accumulating income and using capital for the maintenance, etc., of the infant beneficiary. This device has been stopped up by section 438 (2) (b), which provides that any sum whatsoever paid out for the benefit of an infant beneficiary shall be deemed to be income (and not capital) up to the amount of the whole income of the trust.

The legislative purpose behind section 438 is difficult to fathom. It is clear that the idea of section 437 is to stop parents from maintaining their infant children at the expense (partly) of the Revenue. It seems that in section 438 the legislature is saying: "But we don't mind parents building up a nest-egg for the child's future."

Head 3: Revocable Settlements

A capital settlement which is revocable is caught by section 446. This section corresponds very closely to section 445 which deals with income settlements. The reader is referred to what has been said under Head 3 of income settlements. It is perhaps worth emphasising that the sections apply even although there has in fact been no revocation; it is the *power to revoke* which attracts the sections. The effect of section 446 (as of section 445) is that there can be no advantage concerning higher rate or additional rate tax nor any advantage concerning repayment of basic rate tax. The adjustment provisions of section 449 apply to section 446 (as to section 445).

Head 4: Discretionary Power for Settlor or Spouse

Section 448 applies to capital settlements as well as to income settlements. It applies where the terms of the settlement are such that there is a discretionary power to benefit the settlor or his spouse by the

---

[3] The vehicle must avoid the pitfalls mentioned under Head 5, below.

application of any part of the income or property of the settlement. As under Head 3, so here, it is the presence of the power that attracts the section, regardless of whether or not the power has in fact been exercised.

The effect of section 448 is as stated under Head 4 of income settlements.

Head 5: Undistributed Income

It is necessary to sub-divide this Head (as was the case also with Head 5 of income settlements) according as the settlor does or does not retain an interest in any income or property of the settlement.

(a) Where settlor retains an interest

Section 447 applies as well to capital settlements as to income settlements. The reader is referred to what was said under Head 5 (a) of income settlements. Let me emphasise that it is the existence of the interest which attracts the section, and the settlor shall be deemed to have an interest if any income or property of the settlement "is, or will or may become, payable to or applicable for the benefit of the settlor or the wife or husband of the settlor in any circumstances whatsoever." The section may apply, therefore, even although in fact no income or property has been so paid or applied. The section treats as the settlor's income, for all tax purposes, any income arising during the life of the settlor to the extent to which it is not distributed.

The proviso to section 447 (2) is particularly important in connection with a capital settlement. Under it the settlor is not deemed to have an interest if his interest can only take effect in certain specified events. An important such event is the death under the age of 25 or some lower age of some person who would be beneficially entitled on attaining that age. The settlor of a family settlement often wishes to benefit primarily his child but he wishes also to ensure that the persons to be benefited, if the child shall die under the age of 25, shall be himself or his wife. Such a provision does not bring down section 447 on his head.

(b) Where settlor does not retain an interest

Section 450, which we looked at under Head 5 (b) of income settlements, does not apply to capital settlements. But section 451 does apply. Whereas section 450 attacks sums paid *by* the settlor into the settlement, section 451 attacks sums paid *to* the settlor out of the settlement. It does not attack sums paid by way of income; they are sufficiently dealt with by other sections. It attacks capital sums. "Capital sum" is defined to include "any sum paid by way of loan or repayment of a loan." This is the key to the understanding of what the section is primarily aimed at. It is designed to stop a settlor (a high-rate taxpayer) making a settlement, causing the trustees not to distribute the income, and causing them to let him (or his spouse) have the income in the form of a loan.

Where a capital sum is paid by the trustees to the settlor (or his spouse) such sum (grossed up at basic rate plus additional rate) is to be treated for all tax purposes as the income of the settlor to the extent that such sum falls within the amount of "income available." "Income available" means, broadly speaking, the aggregate of all income arising to the settlement since its inception which has not been distributed and not deemed to be income of the settlor under some other provision. The point of this is that what the section is attacking is the payment out as capital of money which came into the settlement as income.

There is no provision for adjustments of tax between the settlor and the trustees.

Head 6: "Excess Liability"

Section 457, which deals with the "excess liability" of settlors in certain cases, applies primarily to income settlements, and we discussed it under Head 6 of income settlements. The section can apply to a capital settlement, and it will apply unless the income is "income from property of which the settlor has divested himself absolutely by the settlement." The settlor will not be deemed to have divested himself absolutely if that property or income therefrom "is, or will or may become, payable to or applicable for the benefit of the settlor or the wife or husband of the settlor in any circumstances whatsoever." Then there is a proviso to the effect that the settlor shall not be deemed not to have divested himself absolutely if property or income may become payable to him only in certain specified events. This proviso is similar to that contained in section 447 (see under Head 5 (a), above). In particular section 457 does not apply merely because the settlor or his spouse may benefit in the event of a child beneficiary dying before the age of 25 (or some lower age).

If the settlor has divested himself absolutely section 457 does not apply. If the settlor has not divested himself absolutely, then prima facie he is caught by the section. But he will not be caught if the settlement falls within the exception in favour of settlements for a divorced (etc.) spouse. (The other exceptions, which we discussed under Head 6 of income settlements are so worded that they cannot apply to a capital settlement.) Also, the section does not apply to income which is treated as the settlor's income under some other section.

Where the section does apply, the effect is that income is treated, for the purposes of excess liability, as the income of the settlor and not as the income of any other person. So there is no advantage as regards higher rate or additional rate tax, but the advantage as regards repayment of basic rate tax is left unimpaired.

Summary

It is perfectly possible for a capital settlement to clear all the hurdles. It can, and almost invariably will, be capable of lasting for more than six years. It need not be revocable. It need not contain any discretionary power to benefit the settlor or his spouse. There need not be any undistributed income; and even if there is some, that will not matter provided the settlor has not retained an interest and provided no capital sums are paid to him or his spouse. A capital settlement can even surmount the hurdle which has been set up against settlements on infant children; that hurdle is jumped by an irrevocable capital accumulation settlement in which the settlor has not retained an interest and from which no capital sums are paid to him or his spouse.

CHAPTER 15

PARTNERSHIP INCOME

A partnership, unlike a registered company, is not, in English law,[1] a legal entity separate from its members, but for purposes of income tax it is to some extent treated as though it were a separate legal entity. But this treatment really only concerns the machinery of assessment and collection.

A partnership is defined in the Partnership Act 1890 as the relation which subsists between persons carrying on business in common with a view of profit. There is no definition of partnership in the tax legislation; but section 152 of the Taxes Act speaks of the situation "where a trade or profession is carried on by two or more persons jointly." It is thought that this is equivalent to saying "where a trade or profession is carried on by a partnership."

I want to make three non-tax points at the outset. All of them are extremely elementary, but I have found that they come as a surprise to some students. First, a partnership is quite different from a company registered under the Companies Acts, of which the main species is a limited company, e.g. Imperial Chemical Industries Limited. Nevertheless the name of a partnership may contain the word "Company," or "Co.," e.g. Price Waterhouse & Co. This does not make it a company in law; it is a partnership. The word "firm" is equivalent to the word "partnership," and should not be used in reference to a company. Second, there is no requirement of law or practice that the shares of each partner in the profits (or losses) of the partnership should be equal. Third, a company can be a partner in a partnership.

Section 152 of the Taxes Act states that: "Where a trade or profession is carried on by two or more persons jointly, income tax in respect thereof shall be computed and stated jointly, and in one sum, and shall be separate and distinct from any other tax chargeable on those persons or any ot them, and a joint assessment shall be made in the partnership name."

The "precedent partner" (usually the one first named in the partnership agreement) must make a return of the profits or gains of the trade or profession of the partnership. The partnership income is computed as for individuals. Thus a trading partnership has its

---

[1] In Scotland, a partnership *is* a separate entity, a legal *persona*.

141

income computed in the same way as a sole trader, under Case I of Schedule D and on the preceding year basis. (But there are special provisions where one of the partners is a company; this is because corporation tax is on a current basis.) The taxable income of the partnership is allocated to each partner according to the share of the profits to which he is entitled in the year of assessment. The share of partner A may be different in the year of assessment from what it was in the basis year and also the profits of the partnership may be widely different in those two years. So it is obvious that some very odd tax results may be thrown up. There is added to each partner's share any salary and/or interest on capital to which he may be entitled. Personal reliefs are allowed against each partner's share to the extent that they have not been exhausted against his non-partnership income. The tax liability of each partner is thus calculated including both basic rate and (where a partner's share exceeds the threshold) higher rates and (where loan interest (above the threshold) is involved) additional rate. The aggregate is then assessed in the partnership name. The tax is payable by the partnership as such. In other words the liability is the joint liability of all the partners. The partners will then make their own arrangements amongst themselves to recoup the tax from the individual partners. In practice this will usually be done by debiting to each partner's current account with the firm the amount appropriate to his share of the tax bill. A partner's income from a partnership also forms part of his total income. But of course he gets credit for his part of the partnership assessment.

Where there is a change in the partners, *e.g.* by death or retirement or the introduction of a new partner, section 154 (1) brings in the normal discontinuance provisions; it is as though a new trade had been set up. But if at least one person was in the partnership both before and after the change, there can be an election that section 154 (1) shall not apply, that is, an election for continuation. Whether an election will be advantageous depends on the pattern of profits in the relevant years.

EARNED AND UNEARNED INCOME

For an active partner not only his share of the profits (and salary, if any) but also any interest on partnership capital counts as earned income. But interest on loan capital is unearned income. The distinction is this: partnership capital is what the partners have agreed to contribute as working capital; loan capital is any sum lent by a partner beyond that agreement.

For a sleeping partner, none of his partnership income is earned income. Thus his share of profits as well as all interest on capital is investment income. This follows from section 530 (1) (*c*) of the Taxes Act wherein it is stated that earned income includes any income which is charged under Schedule D "and is immediately derived by the individual from the carrying on or exercise by him of his trade . . . either as an individual or, in the case of a partnership, as a partner personally acting therein."

Annual payments by way of pension paid to a retired active partner or to his widow or to a dependant of his count as earned income (and so not investment income) up to an amount equal to one-half of the average of his share of the partnership profits in the best three of the last seven years before he retired: F.A. 1974, s. 16.

CHAPTER 16

CAPITAL ALLOWANCES

When we were considering in Chapter 8 the computation of profits under Schedule D, Cases I and II we saw that the cost and depreciation of capital assets are not allowable deductions, because they are not of a revenue character. But this does not mean that no relief is given for tax purposes in respect of capital expenditure. Instead of being given by way of deduction in the computation of profits, it is given by a separate system of "capital allowances."

Capital expenditure is allowable in respect of the following items:
Machinery and plant;
Industrial buildings and structures;
Agricultural land and buildings;
Mines, oil wells, etc.;
Dredging;
Scientific research;
Patents;
Know-how;
Cemeteries.

It can be seen from the list that many items of capital expenditure do not attract any allowance. Also, all the allowances, with one exception, are confined to income taxable under Schedule D, Case I, that is, the profits of a trade. The exception is the allowances for machinery and plant, which are available to persons carrying on a profession (or vocation) or to persons in employment, as well as to traders.

The law relating to capital allowances was not consolidated in the Taxes Act 1970 because it had already been consolidated in the Capital Allowances Act 1968. That Act has since been supplemented by subsequent Acts, notably the Finance Act 1971. Capital allowances must not be confused with regional development grants under the Industry Act 1972; the former are allowances against tax; the latter are cash hand-outs.

We will look first at allowances on machinery and plant, and then (much more briefly) at some of the other allowances.

ALLOWANCES ON MACHINERY AND PLANT

Neither machinery nor plant is defined in the tax legislation, and it is often a matter of some difficulty to decide whether a particular item is

144

entitled to an allowance. It is an interesting fact that the case most often cited as a starting point is not a tax case at all, but a tort case. The case is *Yarmouth* v. *France* (1887) (D.C.). A workman brought a claim under the Employers Liability Act 1880 for damages for injuries caused by a defect in his employer's "plant," namely a vicious horse. Lindley L. J. (in holding that the horse was plant) said: ". . . in its ordinary sense [plant] includes whatever apparatus is used by a business man for carrying on his business—not his stock-in-trade, which he buys or makes for sale; but all goods and chattels, fixed or movable, live or dead, which he keeps for permanent employment in his business."

From that beginning a huge structure of case law has been built-up as to what constitutes machinery or plant. They must be goods or chattels; they must have some degree of durability; they must be items *with* which a trade (or profession) is carried on as distinct from the setting *in* which it is carried on.

It is obviously easier to apply these ideas to a trade than to a profession, and in *Daphne* v. *Shaw* (1926) it was held that law books bought by a solicitor and used in his practice were not plant. However, 50 years later, in *Munby* v. *Furlong* (1977) (C.A.), *Daphne* v. *Shaw* was overruled by the Court of Appeal. Mr. Munby, a barrister, won his claim for capital allowances in respect of law reports and textbooks bought in his first year of practice. Lord Denning said:

"Counsel for the Crown . . . would confine a professional man's 'plant' to things used physically like a dentist's chair or an architect's table or, I suppose, the typewriter in a barrister's chambers; but, for myself, I do not think 'plant' should be confined to things which are used physically. It seems to me that on principle it extends to the intellectual storehouse which a barrister or a solicitor or any other professional man has in the course of carrying on his profession."

Lord Denning divided what he called "a lawyer's library" into three parts: first, a set of law reports; second, textbooks; third, periodicals, including current issues of law reports. Expenditure on this last group was, said Lord Denning, revenue expenditure (and so deductible in computing the profits of the profession); expenditure on the first two groups was capital expenditure, and qualified for capital allowances.

An individual (who is, of couse, subject to income tax) has to make a claim if he wants a capital allowance, whereas a company (which is subject to corporation tax) does not need to make a claim. The reason is that for income tax capital allowances are *deductions from* profits, whereas for corporation tax capital allowances come into the *computation of* profits; the amount of any capital allowance is treated as a trading expense. It is considered not appropriate to treat the capital allowances of an individual trader as trading *expenses* because of the complications arising from the fact that trading profits are taxed on a preceding year basis. These complications do not arise with corporation tax because that tax is computed on a current basis.

We must now look to see how the allowances work. There are two allowances; first year allowances and writing-down allowances.

First Year Allowances

Where a person carrying on a trade incurs capital expenditure on the provision of machinery or plant for the purposes of the trade he may claim what is called a "first year allowance." This, and ancillary provisions, apply (as well as to trades) to professions, employments, vocations and offices and to the occupation of woodlands assessed under Schedule D. The first year allowance is, at the moment, of an amount equal to the whole of the expenditure (in other words, 100 per cent.). First year allowances do not apply to capital expenditure on mechanically propelled road vehicles other than commercial vehicles, vehicles used for public transport and vehicles provided for hire to the public (as distinct from long-term hire to one client). (But "writing-down allowances" (see below) may be claimed.) An individual may prefer to claim (and a trading company may prefer to disclaim) *part* of the first year allowance in order to have higher writing-down allowances in subsequent periods. This is permitted. It might be advantageous, depending on the pattern of profits year by year.

A first year allowance of 100 per cent. is obviously immensely important. It means that although in principle capital expenditure is not a deductible expense for income tax (as revenue expenditure is), in practice it is almost as good as deductible, since it can be written off in one year. It is not quite as good because, unlike an expense, it can be brought back into charge to tax. This happens (in effect) when the item of machinery or plant is sold: see p. 147, below under the heading "Pooling."

Writing-down Allowances

If a 100 per cent. first year allowance has been given, no question of writing-down allowances arises. But if a trader (or professional person, etc.) has claimed only (say) 60 per cent. as a first year allowance, he can claim a writing-down allowance (at present, 25 per cent.) year by year. Suppose X buys a machine in year one for £800. He receives a first year allowance of 60 per cent. of £800 = £480. This leaves a balance of £320. In year two he can have an allowance of 25 per cent. of £320 = £80. In year three he can have an allowance of 25 per cent. of (£320 − £80) £240 = £60. And so on. The £60 at the end of year three is commonly called the "written-down value" of the machine. The legislation calls it the "qualifying expenditure." It is equal to the original expenditure *less* the allowances already given, so it is the amount which "qualifies" for further allowances in the future.

Pooling

All the items of machinery and plant belonging to a trader are treated as being in one "pool." (There is one exception to this; each car costing more than £8,000 is treated as being in a separate pool.) The 25 per cent. is calculated on the qualifying expenditure of the pool as a whole. Each new expenditure increases the qualifying expenditure in the pool. Each disposal of an item of machinery or plant reduces the qualifying expenditure in the pool by an amount equal to the disposal value of the item. If the price obtained for the sale of an item exceeds the amount of qualifying expenditure in the pool, a "balancing charge" is made on the taxpayer. Let us continue our example of Mr. X (above) to see how the pooling system works. During the period described above X only had one machine. Suppose that later on he acquires several more machines, and that at the end of year six he has qualifying expenditure in the pool amounting to £6,000. In year seven he gets a writing-down allowance of 25 per cent. of £6,000 = £1,500, leaving £4,500. In year eight he buys a new machine for £3,500. His qualifying expenditure becomes £8,000. In year nine he sells a machine for £8,400. A "balancing charge" is made on him in the sum of £400. A balancing charge is (notionally) income, and X may be charged to tax on it, including higher-rate tax if appropriate. If X were to sell the machine, not for £8,400 but for £7,600, he would not get a balancing allowance; all that would happen would be that the qualifying expenditure in the pool would go down from £8,000 to £400. When X permanently discontinues the trade there will be a balancing charge or a balancing allowance depending on whether the proceeds of sale of all the machinery and plant in the pool amount to more than or less than the qualifying expenditure.

Just as a taxpayer may if he wishes claim part only of a first-year allowance, so he may claim part only of a writing-down allowance. He would want to do this, for example, if his income in a particular year was so low that if he received the whole 25 per cent. allowance his tax bill would not be big enough to absorb his personal reliefs.

Anti-avoidance

Tax avoidance schemes were invented to exploit the 100 per cent. first year allowances. If you expend £5,000 on a machine and have no profits, you have in effect a loss of £5,000. So, a high-rate taxpayer could join with a company in a partnership quite separate from his ordinary business to buy such a machine and lease it out. In the first year there could be a substantial loss, and "our friend" could set off his share of this loss against the profits of his ordinary business. He could then retire from the partnership leaving the company to collect the leasing income, its profits being taxable at the corporation tax rate which was (and still is) less than the top rates of income tax. The trick depends on there being a loss for tax purposes without there being a real loss; after all, the machine is worth £5,000. This device (and some others) was stopped up by section 41 of the Finance Act 1976. That section declares that such a loss cannot be set off against profits of any other trade than the leasing trade itself; relief under section 168 of the Taxes Act is denied. This point will be better understood when Chapter 17 has been studied.

There are a number of other (less dramatic) avoidance possibilities, and these have been largely blocked by the legislation, particularly the Finance Act 1971 and 1972. Many of these points turn on transactions between "connected persons" as defined in section 533 of the Taxes Act.[1] There is also a beneficent provision (in the Finance Act 1971, Sched. 8, para. 13). Where a person succeeds to a trade carried on by another person, and they are connected persons, those persons may make an election to the effect that (a) for capital allowance purposes the trade will not be treated as discontinued; and (b) the successor takes over the qualifying expenditure of the predecessor, no account being taken of any sale of machinery or plant by the predecessor to the successor.

Extensions

The provisions about allowances for machinery and plant have been extended to expenditure on fire safety and on thermal insulation and on safety at sports grounds.

INDUSTRIAL BUILDINGS

Expenditure on the construction of an industrial building or structure enjoys what is called an "initial allowance" of 50 per cent., and writing-down allowances of 4 per cent. per year. The taxpayer can in the first year have the 50 per cent. allowance *and* the 4 per cent. allowance. That, no doubt, is why the 50 per cent. allowance is called an "initial allowance" and not a "first year allowance." The 4 per

---

[1] The concept of "connected persons" is of pretty general importance in tax legislation (and not only income tax); it is clearly a useful weapon in the anti-avoidance armoury.

cent. allowance is 4 per cent. of the original expenditure, not 4 per cent. of a written-down value. Notice that it is only *industrial* buildings and structures which qualify for the allowance so that, for example, dwelling-houses, shops, showrooms and offices do not qualify. But, by section 38 of the Finance Act 1978, certain hotels do qualify (with modifications).

AGRICULTURAL LAND AND BUILDINGS

The expenditure concerned here is expenditure on the construction of farmhouses, farm or forestry buildings, cottages, fences "or other works." In the case of a farmhouse only a maximum of one-third of the expenditure qualifies for the allowances. By section 39 of the Finance Act 1978 the allowances are (a) an initial allowance of 20 per cent. of the expenditure and (b) writing-down allowances over a period of eight years (including the first year) of an aggregate amount equal to 80 per cent. of that expenditure.

OTHER CAPITAL EXPENDITURE

The other items of capital expenditure listed at the beginning of this chapter are not discussed in this book.

CHAPTER 17

LOSSES

This chapter is concerned with losses arising in a trade, profession or vocation. The tax position of a trade, profession or vocation is calculated by subtracting from the income the relevant expenses. If that calculation leaves a credit balance there is a taxable profit. But if it leaves a minus quantity there is a loss. Thus far, a loss is calculated in just the same way as a profit is calculated. In particular a trader cannot claim for tax purposes to have made a loss merely because on one transaction he has made a loss. For example, if a builder undertakes to build a house for £25,000 and in the event it costs him £27,000 to build the house, he cannot claim to have made a loss of £2,000. What matters is the overall relationship of trading income and expenses throughout a whole year's operation of his trade.

But now we come to a very important difference between a profit and a loss. Profits are computed (except at the beginning and end of a trade) on a preceding year basis; losses are computed on a current year basis. In other words, a loss is treated as accruing in the year of assessment in which it is incurred and not by reference to some (different) basis period. It is very important to grasp this point at the outset; without it the law about losses will not make sense. From this principle two results follow where a trader's accounts for a particular accounting period show a loss: first, there is no profit for the year of assessment for which that period is the basis period; secondly, there is a loss for the year of assessment in which the accounting period falls. The odd effect of this latter point is that there can be both a profit and a loss for the same year of assessment from the same trade; the profit being based on a preceding period and the loss being based on the actual period.

If the accounting period extends into more than one year of assessment the loss should, according to strict law, be apportioned between them, but by practice the Revenue allow a loss to be treated as a loss of the year of assessment in which the accounting period ends. (This concession is not usually given in the opening or closing years of a trade.)

There are four main ways in which relief for losses may be given: set-off against general income; carry-forward against subsequent profits; carry-back of terminal losses; and (since 1978) a special

150

mode of relief for losses in the early years of a trade. We will look at these in turn.

SET-OFF AGAINST GENERAL INCOME

By section 168 of the Taxes Act a person who sustains a loss in any trade, profession or vocation carried on by him either solely or in partnership may make a claim for relief. The relief works by way of setting off the loss in the trade (etc.) against profits in some other trade or indeed against any income of the claimant in the same year. If the claimant's income of that same year is not sufficient to absorb the whole of the loss then the balance may be set off against the claimant's income of the next year (but no further than that).

Section 169 provides that a claim under section 168 may be created or augmented by capital allowances. This may seem at first sight to be rather mysterious. The key to the understanding of the point is that a capital allowance is not part of the computation of profits or losses; it is something that falls to be deducted *from* profits. Thus, if a trader has a profit of £15,000 and a capital allowance of £9,000, his profit is still £15,000 though he will only have to pay tax on £6,000. If he has a profit of £15,000 and a capital allowance of £19,000 he still, technically, has a profit of £15,000 and this is where section 169 comes in. He can make a claim under section 168 *as though* he had a loss of £4,000. So he can claim to set off £4,000 against his other income.

By section 170 a loss is not available for relief under section 168 unless it is shown that the trade was being carried on on a commercial basis and with a view to the realisation of profits. And by section 180 an even more stringent rule applies to farming and market gardening, namely that a loss cannot be relieved under section 168 if in each of the prior five years a loss was incurred. The point of these two sections (170 and 180) is to exclude from loss relief against other income "hobby-trading" and particularly "hobby-farming." In each section "loss" includes the quasi-loss arising from capital allowances. Hobby-farming is a pretty popular activity. It arises in this way: a person with a substantial income (say a stockbroker) buys a farm and spends a great deal of money on building it up as a capital asset. If he could contrive to have no farming profits because of vast capital expenditure and set the farming losses against his stockbroking profits he could lay a gigantic nest-egg largely at the expense of the Revenue. The Revenue has disobliged.[1]

---

[1] On the other hand, the Revenue has always taken a benevolent view of genuine farming. The latest instance of this is s. 28 of the Finance Act 1978, which provides for the "ironing out" of severe fluctuations in a farmer's profit between one year and another.

CARRY-FORWARD AGAINST SUBSEQUENT PROFITS

Section 171 provides for the carrying forward of a loss in one year against the profits in a subsequent year of the same trade, profession or vocation. Notice that it must be the *same* trade, etc. In that respect this relief is totally different from the relief under section 168. A loss can be carried forward under section 171 indefinitely, but it must be set off against the first subsequent assessment and then, so far as it remains not fully relieved, against the next assessment, and so on. If a loss has been partially relieved under some other provision (*e.g.* section 168) the unrelieved amount may be carried forward. Or, if he chooses, a trader can ignore section 168 and go straight for section 171 relief.

It may happen that the profits of a particular year are not big enough to absorb a loss which is being carried forward into that year. In that case, interest or dividends (if there are any) arising to the trader will be treated as though they were trading profits. This point needs a bit of explanation. If interest or dividends which have borne tax by deduction are received by a trader they are not included in the computation of his profits under Case I. The present point (in section 171 (3)) is that those receipts can nevertheless be *treated as* profits, and a carried-forward loss can be relieved against them by means of a repayment of tax.

Another point which may arise under section 171 relates to payments out by the trader under section 53. (See Chapter 11, above.) Section 53 applies where an annual payment is made otherwise than wholly out of profits brought into charge to income tax. This would be so, for example, where the payer had no profits in the year in which he made the payment. So under section 53 he would have to pay over to the Revenue the tax which he deducted in making the annual payment. The point here is that section 173 says that in such a case, provided the payment was made wholly and exclusively for the purposes of the trade (or profession or vocation) the grossed-up amount of the payment can be treated as a loss and given relief under section 171. (I say "grossed-up" because the section (173) says "the amount on which tax has been paid.")

Another point on section 171 concerns interest, meaning payments of interest outwards. If a trader makes a payment of interest that will, prima facie, be an expense of his trading. But if he has an overall loss the interest will not get relieved. And if he has insufficient other income, the interest will not get relieved under section 75 of the Finance Act 1972 either. The present point is that by section 175 (of the Taxes Act) the amount of the interest payment may be carried forward under section 171 "as if it were a loss."

The general rules for section 171 relief are that not only must the prior loss and the subsequent profit be incurred in the same trade, but also the claimant must be the person who incurred the loss. This latter rule has two exceptions. First, when there is a change in a partnership causing a discontinuance (under section 154) a person who is a partner both before and after the change may carry forward his share of a previous loss against his share of future profits despite the discontinuance. Secondly, section 172 provides that where a business carried on by an individual (or individuals) is transferred to a company, the individual may claim to set off under section 171 any losses which he incurred before the transfer against income derived by him from the company after the transfer. The consideration for the transfer of the business must consist solely or mainly of the allotment of shares in the company. The income from the company may take the form of director's remuneration or salary or dividends.

CARRY-BACK OF TERMINAL LOSSES

By section 174 terminal losses (meaning losses outstanding at the termination of a business) may be set off against the profits of a trade, profession or vocation for the three years of assessment preceding the year in which the discontinuance occurs. Where the business was carried on by a partnership, this relief is available on a real discontinuance of the partnership and also on what one might call a statutory discontinuance caused by a change of partners. In the latter case the retiring partner can have relief under this section (174) but the continuing partners cannot. This is fair, because (as we have just seen) they can, despite the discontinuance, have relief against subsequent profits. If an election is made (under section 154 (2)) for continuance the retiring partner can still have relief, but (of course) the continuing partners cannot, because for them there is no discontinuance; that is, no termination, and hence no terminal losses.

LOSSES IN THE EARLY YEARS

Section 30 of the Finance Act 1978 introduced a new head of loss relief. The three heads we have so far looked at provide for relief for losses by set-off against any income of the same or the following year; against profits of the same trade, etc., in any following year; and (for terminal losses) against profits of the same trade for three previous years. This new relief works by way of a set-off of losses in the year of commencement of a trade, profession or vocation and/or in the next three years of assessment against any income of the taxpayer for the three years of assessment preceding that in which the loss is sustained. The relief applies to sole individuals and to partners. It does not apply to companies. Of course, a new company would not have any previous income, so the possibility of this relief could not arise. But an existing company sometimes sets up a new trade; it will not qualify for this relief. There is a provision to exclude hobby-trading from the relief. This seems a wise precaution on the part of the Revenue.

CHAPTER 18

A FOREIGN ELEMENT

For a charge to British income tax to be made one or other (or both) of two factors must exist; either the income in question must arise from a source in the United Kingdom or the recipient of the income must be resident in the United Kingdom.[1] It follows from that statement of principle that a foreign element can be present in a taxing situation in one or other of two ways. First, the person to be charged with the tax may be not resident in the United Kingdom; one may broadly call this person a foreign taxpayer. Second, the income to be taxed may have its source outside the United Kingdom; one may call this income foreign income. We will discuss these two kinds of foreign element in turn, and then we will discuss Schedule E income separately, because in that Schedule the elements of foreign residence and foreign income are intertwined.

A FOREIGN TAXPAYER

A foreign taxpayer is chargeable to British income tax if he has income from a source situated in the United Kingdom. There are some exceptions, a notable one being that tax is not charged on interest on $3\frac{1}{2}$ per cent. War Loan while it is in the beneficial ownership of a person not ordinarily resident in the United Kingdom. (The difference between residence and ordinary residence is discussed below at pp. 160–161.)

It is usually not difficult to decide whether a source is or is not situate in the United Kingdom. This is true, for example, of land, woodlands, other property (for Case III of Schedule D), and dividends.

One problem does however arise. That is in connection with Cases I and II of Schedule D. Section 108 (1) (*a*) (iii) of the Taxes Act declares that tax shall be charged on the annual profits or gains arising or accruing "to any person ... although not resident in the United Kingdom ... from any trade, profession or vocation exercised within the United Kingdom." So one has to distinguish trade *within* the United Kingdom from trade *with* the United Kingdom. The basic principle is that a trade is carried on where the contract (particularly a contract of sale) is made. In English law a contract is made where the

---

[1] But see Case II of Schedule E, below.

acceptance of an offer is made. See the whole matter of acceptance by post, by telegram, by telex, and face to face discussed in *Entores Ltd.* v. *Miles Far East Corporation* (1955) (C.A.). But the place where the contracts (*e.g.* of sale) are made is not decisive. It seems from the case of *Firestone Tyre and Rubber Co. Ltd.* v. *Llewellin* (1957) (H.L.) that the test is whether in substance the trading operations giving rise to the profit in question take place in the United Kingdom, and that within that test the place where the contracts are made is an important though not decisive factor.

Though a foreign resident may be *liable* to tax, it by no means follows that the tax can be successfully collected from him. There is a principle generally accepted in private international law that a country will not allow its courts to be used for the enforcement of another country's revenue laws. Sections 78 and 79 of T.M.A. 1970 provide for assessment of a non-resident in the name of any trustee, guardian, tutor, curator or committee and also any branch or agent. It is the last two words, "branch" and "agent," which are important for trading profits. Where there is no branch or agent in this country an assessment can of course be made on the non-resident himself, but it will not usually produce any actual cash. As Mrs. Beeton might have said: "First catch your foreign resident."

FOREIGN INCOME

A person resident in the United Kingdom can be taxed on income which arises from a source situated abroad. Such income can be taxed under Schedule C (securities of foreign states) or under Schedule D, Cases IV and V. We will not deal further with Schedule C.

Case IV of Schedule D charges tax in respect of income arising from *securities* out of the United Kingdom (except income charged under Schedule C).

Case V of Schedule D charges tax in respect of income arising from *possessions* out of the United Kingdom. The word "possessions" has been given a very wide meaning. It includes virtually all sources of income other than securities.

Before we come on to see how tax is charged under Cases IV and V we need to look to see what is the territorial extent of Cases I and II of Schedule D. At first sight it would seem that a trade or profession carried on abroad is within Case I or Case II. Section 108 (1) (*a*) (ii) of the Taxes Act declares that tax shall be charged on the annual profits or gains arising or accruing to "any person residing in the United Kingdom from any trade, profession or vocation, whether carried on in the United Kingdom or elsewhere." Despite the words "or elsewhere" it is quite clear from case law that if a trade or profession is carried on *wholly* outside the United Kingdom it is not within Case I or Case II, but it is caught by Case V. The trade or profession is a foreign "possession." A leading authority on this point is *Colquhoun v. Brooks* (1889) (H.L.). On the other hand, if a trade or profession is carried on partly within the United Kingdom (even though it is also carried on partly outside the United Kingdom) Case I or Case II applies. There is a qualification to this. Where a trade or business is carried on by a partnership and the partnership is controlled and managed abroad, the United Kingdom profits are charged under Case I and the share of the foreign profits attributable to a partner resident in the United Kingdom is charged under Case V. (See section 153 of the Taxes Act.)

Where Case I or Case II does apply, a deduction from the profits to be assessed is permitted by section 27 and Schedule 4 of the Finance Act 1978. If an individual (including a partner) is abroad on business for 30 or more days in a year (called "qualifying days") he is entitled to a deduction from his profits equal to one-quarter of the profits for that proportion of a year which is made up of qualifying days. So if X's profits for a year are £12,000 (including both foreign and United Kingdom profits) and X is abroad on business for 35 days he is assessed on £12,000 minus $\frac{1}{4}$ of $\frac{35}{365}$ of £12,000.

Let us now see how tax is charged under Cases IV and V of Schedule D. The basic principle is that tax is charged on the full amount of the income arising in the year preceding the year of assessment, whether the income has been or will be received in the United Kingdom or not. This is called the arising basis. In one set of circumstances, however, what is called the "remittance basis" applies instead. This is much more favourable because it only charges income *received in* the United Kingdom. The remittance basis only applies to a person "who satisfies the Board that he is not domiciled in the United Kingdom, or that, being a British subject or a citizen of the Republic of Ireland, he is not ordinarily resident in the United Kingdom." See section 122 of the Taxes Act. A person who does not qualify for the remittance basis and is therefore on the arising basis may, however, be entitled to a deduction. If he has foreign income immediately derived from the carrying on by him of any trade, profession or vocation, either solely or in partnership, he is allowed a deduction of one-quarter of the amount of that income; if it is pension income he is allowed a deduction of $\frac{1}{10}$ of its amount. (See sections 23 and 22 of the Finance Act 1974.)

THE FOREIGN ASPECTS OF SCHEDULE E

Schedule E is divided into three Cases which are set out in section 181 of the Taxes Act. That section uses the phrase "foreign emoluments" and that phrase is relevant to all three Cases. "Foreign emoluments" are "emoluments of a person not domiciled in the United Kingdom from an office or employment under or with any person, body of persons or partnership resident outside and not resident in, the United Kingdom." Notice that there are two factors here, one turning on the domicile of the employee and one on the residence of the employer. (The meaning of domicile, residence and ordinary residence is discussed below at pp. 160–161.

Case I

Case I applies where the person holding the office or employment is resident and ordinarily resident in the United Kingdom. The charge to tax is on the *whole* of the emoluments. That is the basic position, but there are four possible deductions. The first three stem from section 31 and Schedule 7 of the Finance Act 1977. The fourth rests on section 21 and Schedule 2 of the Finance Act 1974.

First, there is a deduction in respect of earnings from work done abroad during an absence from the United Kingdom of 365 days or more. The deduction is the whole of the amount of the emoluments attributable to that period.

Second, there is a deduction for work done abroad during an absence of less than 365 days but more than 29 days. Here the deduction is one-quarter of the emoluments attributable to duties performed outside the United Kingdom.

Third, there is a deduction for "foreign employments." This deduction is allowed where two factors are present: (a) the duties of an employment are performed wholly outside the United Kingdom, and (b) the employment is with a person, body of persons or partnership resident outside, and not resident in, the United Kingdom. Notice that "foreign employments" are not the same as "foreign emoluments"; the status of the employer is the same, but the status of the employee is different. Foreign employments are not concerned with the domicile of the employee; they are concerned with where his duties are performed. And the duties must be performed *wholly* outside the United Kingdom, whereas for the first and second deductions (above) the duties may be performed wholly or partly outside the United Kingdom. For this, third, deduction there is no need to accumulate 30 days of absence. The deduction is one-quarter of the amount of the total emoluments.

Deduction is not allowed in respect of the same emoluments under more than one of the three heads above.

Fourth, there is a deduction for foreign emoluments. The deduction is one-half of the amount of the foreign emoluments, except that if the employee has been resident in the United Kingdom for nine out of the previous 10 years and is now resident the deduction is only one-quarter.

Where the duties of an office or employment are performed wholly outside the United Kingdom and the emoluments are foreign emoluments the emoluments shall be excepted from Case I. (See Finance Act 1974, Sched. 2, para. 4.)

Case II

Case II applies where the person holding the office or employment is not resident, or if resident, is not ordinarily resident, in the United Kingdom. Tax is charged only on emoluments for the year of assessment in respect of duties performed in the United Kingdom. So this case can only apply to a person who performs duties here but does not become resident or alternatively does not become ordinarily resident here. There is the like deduction from foreign emoluments as in Case I (*i.e.* the fourth head above). Case II is not strictly consonant with the principle that a non-resident can only be taxed on a United Kingdom source of income, unless one regards the United Kingdom duties as a "source."

Case III

Case III applies to a person who is resident in the United Kingdom (whether ordinarily resident here or not) in one or other of two situations. The first situation is where the emoluments are from an employment whose duties are performed wholly outside the United Kingdom and the emoluments are foreign emoluments. Because the duties are performed wholly outside the United Kingdom, this situation is not caught by Case II, and because of this fact coupled with the further fact that the emoluments are foreign emoluments the situation is not caught by Case I (see Finance Act 1974, Sched. 2, para. 4). The second situation is where the emoluments are for duties performed outside the United Kingdom and the employee is resident but not ordinarily resident in the United Kingdom. Because the duties are performed outside the United Kingdom Case II does not apply, and because the taxpayer is not ordinarily resident here Case I does not apply. Case III is designed to apply, and does apply, only where Cases I and II do not apply. The charge to tax under Case III is only on emoluments received in the United Kingdom (the remittance basis).

Expenses in Connection with Work done Abroad

In Chapter 9 we discussed what expenses are deductible under Schedule E. There we were considering work done in the United Kingdom. In connection with work done abroad, section 32 of the

Finance Act 1977 provides that certain extra expenses involved in such work shall be allowable. For example, expenses incurred in travelling to take up the overseas employment (and returning on its termination) are allowable.

DOMICILE, RESIDENCE AND ORDINARY RESIDENCE

Three terms, "domicile," "residence" and "ordinary residence" have come into our discussion in this chapter. It is now necessary to look a little more closely at them.

Domicile

Domicile, in tax law, means what it means in any other branch of law. Every individual is born with a domicile; in whatever country he is born that country is his domicile of origin. That domicile can be changed to a domicile of choice. Such a change requires two factors; a physical presence in the country of choice and an intention to reside there indefinitely. An individual cannot have more than one domicile at a time.

Domicile is important in determining whether a person is entitled to the remittance basis under Cases IV and V of Schedule D and in determining whether an emolument is a foreign emolument under Schedule E.

Residence

Residence is of pervasive importance in every tax situation in which there is a foreign element. A person not resident in the United Kingdom is not taxable on any income which does not arise here.[2]

The law on the matter of residence is a mixture of a few (a very few) statutory pronouncements and a considerable body of case law. And, apart from law, the *practice* of the Revenue is very important in this field.[3]

Section 51 of the Taxes Act declares that a person who is in the United Kingdom for some temporary purpose only and not with a view or intent of establishing his residence here, and who has not actually resided in the United Kingdom at one time or several times for a period equal in the whole to six months in any year of assessment shall not be chargeable as a United Kingdom resident, but that a person who has so actually resided shall be so chargeable for that year.

---

[2] With the exception or quasi-exception of Case II of Schedule E (see p. 159, above).
[3] See pamphlet IR 20 ("Residents and Non-residents") and IR 1 ("Extra-statutory Concessions").

It is implicit in section 51 that a person may be held to be resident here even though he has been present for less than six months provided his presence has what is called a "residential quality." There are three main factors that may enter into this concept.

First, if a person has a place of abode here he will be treated as resident in any year of assessment in which he visits the United Kingdom, however short his stay. But there is a statutory qualification to this rule. It is declared by section 50 of the Taxes Act that if a person works full time abroad the question whether or not he is resident in the United Kingdom must be determined without regard to any place of abode maintained here. And also (in regard to Schedule E) where the employment is in substance one of which the duties fall to be performed outside the United Kingdom, merely incidental duties performed in the United Kingdom are treated as performed abroad.

Second, even if a person does not maintain any place of abode here, he may be held to be resident if he pays regular visits to the United Kingdom and these visits form part of his habit of life.

Third, section 49 of the Taxes Act declares that where a British subject or citizen of the Republic of Ireland, whose ordinary residence has been in the United Kingdom, leaves the country for the purpose only of occasional residence abroad, he will be treated during his absence as actually residing in the United Kingdom.

A person may be resident in the United Kingdom and elsewhere at the same time.

Ordinary Residence

In a Canadian case, *Thomson* v. *Minister of National Revenue* (1946), Rand J. said that ordinary residence means "residence in the course of the customary mode of life of the person concerned and it is contrasted with special or occasional or casual residence."

A person may be resident here without being ordinarily resident. Conversely a person may be ordinarily resident here without being resident.

A person may be ordinarily resident in the United Kingdom and elsewhere at the same time.

Ordinary residence is important in connection with interest on $3\frac{1}{2}$ per cent. War Loan (see p. 155, above); in connection with the remittance basis for Cases IV and V; in connection with Cases I and II of Schedule E; and in connection with the transfer of assets abroad (see p. 162, below).

DOUBLE TAXATION RELIEF

Where income arises in one country and belongs to a person in another country it may be subject to tax in both countries. British tax law may provide relief from this double burden in one of the following ways.

First, section 497 of the Taxes Act provides for the making of "arrangements" with other countries. These arrangements are nowadays generally called Conventions. The word Treaty is sometimes used and this gives the true flavour. Each Convention is different, but the relief which it provides generally falls in to one or other of two forms. Certain kinds of income are made taxable in only one of the two countries, usually in the country where the taxpayer is resident. Other income is taxable in both countries but the foreign tax is allowed as a credit.

Second, section 498 of the Taxes Act provides for unilateral relief by way of credit for foreign tax where there is no Convention in force.

Third, section 516 of the Taxes Act provides for unilateral relief by way of deduction (from the foreign income in question) of any sum paid in respect of tax in the foreign country. This relief is not available where income is charged on the remittance basis.

Relief by deduction is usually less beneficial than relief by credit. This is best shown by an example. Suppose X has overseas income of £100, and that the foreign tax is at 25 per cent., and that X is a United Kingdom basic rate taxpayer at 30 per cent. Relief by deduction would work like this: X's foreign tax is £25; his United Kingdom tax is 30 per cent. of (£100 − 25) = £22.50. So X's total tax bill (on this income) is £47.50. Relief by credit would work like this: his foreign tax is £25; his United Kingdom tax is £30 less £25 credit = £5. So his total tax bill is £30. But there are circumstances where relief by deduction would be more advantageous than relief by credit. This is because relief by credit only does any good if there is some United Kingdom tax against which to set it, whereas relief by deduction may produce a loss which can be carried forward.

TRANSFER OF ASSETS ABROAD

If income arises outside the United Kingdom to a person not resident in the United Kingdom that income is not liable to United Kingdom income tax. So if the device were not stopped, an individual resident in the United Kingdom could transfer income-producing property to a company resident abroad and enjoy the income abroad. This device is stopped by sections 478–481 of the Taxes Act. Where in consequence of a transfer of assets an individual who is ordinarily resident in the United Kingdom has power to enjoy income of a person (including a company) resident or domiciled abroad, that income is treated as that individual's income for all the purposes of income tax.

PART THREE

CAPITAL GAINS TAX

CHAPTER 19

CAPITAL GAINS TAX

GENERAL

Capital Gains Tax is, not surprisingly, a tax on capital gains. It is not a tax on income and it is not a tax on capital as such (as a wealth tax would be) but only on gains. It is in this latter point (gains) that it differs from capital transfer tax. Both capital transfer tax and capital gains tax are concerned, broadly speaking, with the movement of capital from one person to another, but whereas on such a movement capital transfer tax charges tax on the whole amount of capital which moves, capital gains tax charges tax only on the gain as between the value it has at the time of this movement (*e.g.* sale by A) compared with the value it had on the occasion of its last previous movement (*e.g.* purchase by A).

The social idea behind capital gains tax is that it is too arbitrary, and therefore unfair, to tax a person on his income (*e.g.* dividends) and not to tax a person on his capital gains (*e.g.* buying shares on the stock exchange and selling them at a higher price). The latter is thought of as being as much a taxable resource as the former.

But the theory has been spoiled by inflation. If you bought something in 1974 for £400 and sold it in 1978 the probability is that you would get around £800 for it. On paper you have made a gain of £400; in real terms you have not made any gain at all. But theory prevails over practice and you pay tax on the paper gain. The point has been tested in court, and in *Secretan* v. *Hart* (1969) it was held that no adjustment for inflation (or to put it in another way, for the fall in the value of money) is allowable.

This is a grave injustice, widely acknowledged, but so far not acted upon by any government. The Revenue have responded to pleas for "indexation" or other forms of relief such as "tapering" by stressing the immense administrative problems that would arise.

Capital gains tax was introduced in the United Kingdom in 1965 by a Labour government. It had been preceded by a less rigorous measure introduced by a Conservative government in 1962 whereby gains which were "short-term" gains[1] were taxed as though they were income. That system no longer exists.

---

[1] In its final form this meant gains which accrued where there was an acquisition of an asset and a disposal of it within 12 months.

The enactments relating to capital gains tax were consolidated in the Capital Gains Tax Act 1979.[2] So we now have a reasonably coherent code, more homogeneous than the code (if one can call it that) of income tax.

The administration of capital gains tax is similar to that of income tax. The tax is under the "care and management" of the Inland Revenue. Assessments are made by HM Inspectors of Taxes. Appeals lie to the general or special commissioners. The Taxes Management Act 1970 applies to this tax as it does to income tax. Section 57 of that Act empowers the Board (the Commissioners of Inland Revenue) to make regulations concerning capital gains tax appeals. The Board have made such regulations by Statutory Instrument 1967 No. 149, dealing with matters (such as market value) which do not arise in income tax appeals but do arise in capital gains tax appeals.

The tax is due and payable three months after the end of the year of assessment or 30 days after the making of the assessment, whichever is the later.[3] Interest (at 9 per cent.) is payable on overdue tax.

Section 1 (1) of the Capital Gains Tax Act 1979 declares: "Tax shall be charged in accordance with this Act in respect of capital gains, that is to say chargeable gains computed in accordance with this Act and accruing to a person on the disposal of assets."

This subsection contains in summary form the whole of the law relating to capital gains tax. We shall know that law when we know what a chargeable gain is, how the Act requires computation to be made, what a person is, what an asset is, and what a disposal is. Two of those matters, namely computation and the meaning of "disposal" will be discussed at length later on. But "chargeable gain," "person" and "asset" can be discussed now.

Chargeable Gains

All gains other than exempted gains are chargeable gains (section 28 (2)), but (by Schedule 5) the amount of chargeable gains accruing on the disposal of assets which were owned on April 6, 1965 is restricted. A gain accrues on the disposal of an asset. So a disposal after April 6, 1965 may attract the tax even though the asset was acquired before that date. But where the acquisition *was* before that date then, broadly speaking, only that part of the gain is charged to tax which has taken place between April 6, 1965 and the later disposal. The

---

[2] From here onwards in this chapter references are, unless otherwise stated, to this Act.

[3] In the case of gifts and also certain disposals by trustees, the tax can be paid by instalments over eight years if the asset concerned is land, controlling shares, unquoted shares or certain business assets.

chargeable gain is, broadly speaking, the difference between the cost of the asset and the consideration received on its disposal. The cost is usually referred to as the "base cost." If a person acquired some quoted shares before April 6, 1965 and disposed of them after that date he is deemed to have sold and re-acquired them on April 6, 1965 at their then market value. Thus their market value on that date is their base cost. One must get used to this idea of a deemed sale and re-acquisition on the same day. It crops up in many circumstances. The point of the deeming is that it uplifts the base cost. It looks to a future disposal.

Although each asset disposed of in a year of assessment has to be considered separately, the tax is charged on the total amount of chargeable gains in the year after deducting allowable losses (section 4 (1)).

Persons

"Person" has the same meaning as in income tax law. So not only individuals are persons but so also are companies and trustees and personal representatives.

Partners

A partnership (or firm) is not a "person" in the law of England. In Scottish law a partnership is a "person." For capital gains tax purposes in all parts of the United Kingdom partners are treated separately as individuals for their share of the gains or losses arising from the disposal of partnership assets or other partnership dealings; section 60. This, of course, is in marked contrast to the income tax regime in which the partnership itself is the assessable unit; see Chapter 15, above. The Board of Inland Revenue have issued a Statement of Practice about partnerships, which is printed in, e.g. [1975] B.T.R. at pp. 408–412. When an asset is disposed of by the partnership each partner is treated as making a disposal of his fractional share of that asset. In computing gains or losses the proceeds of disposal will be allocated between the partners in the ratio of their shares in asset surpluses. Where this is not specifically laid down the allocation will follow the actual destination of the surplus as shown in the partnership accounts. If a lump sum is paid to a partner on his leaving the firm that represents consideration for the disposal of his share in the partnership assets. But where a retiring partner receives annual payments instead of a lump sum the capital value of this annuity will not be treated as consideration for a disposal of his share of the partnership assets if it is no more than can be regarded as a reasonable recognition of his past work and effort. The Statement of Practice contains many other detailed rules as well as the above.

Companies

Companies are not assessed to capital gains tax as such, but their chargeable gains are assessed to corporation tax, and the computation is broadly the same as with capital gains tax assessed on individuals. Part XI of the Taxes Act deals with "Company Taxation" and Chapter II thereof (sections 265–281) deals with "Companies' Capital Gains."

Residence, etc.

A person is only chargeable to capital gains tax in respect of chargeable gains accruing to him in a year of assessment during any part of which he is resident in the United Kingdom, or during which he is ordinarily resident in the United Kingdom (section 2 (1)). The reference to ordinary residence as an alternative to residence prevents a person normally resident here from escaping the tax by going abroad temporarily and disposing of assets whilst so abroad. It will be recalled that the dual principle of income tax is that it is charged where the recipient of income is resident in the United Kingdom *or* the source of the income is situated in the United Kingdom. For capital gains tax the first part of the principle is strengthened by the addition of the ordinary residence test, but the second part of the principle (the source point) does not in general exist. The disposal of an asset which is situated in the United Kingdom only imposes tax on a person who is not resident and not ordinarily resident here if he is carrying on a trade through a branch or agency in the United Kingdom and the asset is connected with the trade (section 12 (1)). An individual who is resident or ordinarily resident but not domiciled in the United Kingdom is taxed on a remittance basis on gains from the disposal of assets outside the United Kingdom (section 14 (1)), and losses on the disposal of such assets are not allowable losses (section 29 (4)).

Assets

All forms of property are assets, and this is so whether they are situated in the United Kingdom or not. (Section 18 (4) contains rules for determining where certain kinds of assets are situated.) Section 19 (1) declares that the following items are included amongst assets: (a) options, debts and incorporeal property generally; (b) any currency other than sterling; and (c) any form of property created by the person disposing of it, or otherwise coming to be owned without being acquired. Notice that head (c) brings into charge things which never were acquired but were on the contrary created by the tax-payer, such as a building, a chattel, the copyright of a book, and (very importantly) the goodwill of a business (which of course may have been built up from nothing). Some items, as we shall see later, are expressly stated not to be chargeable assets.

THE RATE OF TAX

The highest rate of capital gains tax is, and always has been, 30 per cent. During the life of the tax there have been various schemes for tempering the wind to the shorn lamb. The present scheme is contained in section 5 and Schedule 1. One has to bear in mind here that there is a distinction between on the one hand, individuals and, on the other hand, personal representatives, trustees and companies.

An individual shall not be chargeable to capital gains tax for a year of assessment if his "taxable amount" for that year does not exceed £1,000. His taxable amount is the total of his gains less allowable losses. If his taxable amount exceeds £1,000 but does not exceed £5,000 he is taxed at 15 per cent. on the excess over £1,000. If his taxable amount exceeds £5,000, the amount of his tax shall not exceed £600 plus one-half of the excess over £5,000. These three cryptic points are set out in section 5. It is clear that up to £1,000 the tax is nil. Beyond that one needs to do a bit of arithmetic to put flesh on the bones. Here are some examples:

Taxable amount, £	Tax, £	Overall average rate of tax
2,000	150	7.50 per cent.
3,000	300	10.00 per cent.
4,000	450	11.25 per cent.
5,000	600	12.00 per cent.

Notice that the £600 (which is 12 per cent. of £5,000) is carried on into the next phase. Thus an individual with a taxable amount of £6,000 pays in tax £600 plus one-half of £1,000. That amounts to £1,100 tax, which is an overall *average* of 18.33 per cent. The *marginal* rate in this phase is, of course, 50 per cent. Our table goes on like this:

Taxable amount, £	Tax, £	Overall average rate of tax
6,000	1,100	18.33 per cent.
7,000	1,600	22.86 per cent.
8,000	2,100	26.25 per cent.
9,000	2,600	28.89 per cent.
9,500	2,850	30.00 per cent.

At £9,500 the relief ceases and the flat rate of 30 per cent. begins. At this stage the basic section (section 3) takes over: "The rate of capital gains tax shall be 30 per cent." That means 30 per cent. of the whole taxable amount, not 30 per cent. of the taxable amount in excess of £1,000. At this stage the marginal rate and the average overall rate are both 30 per cent.

For married individuals the basic rule in Schedule 1 is that husband and wife count as one and so only get one relief if they are living together but (as for income tax) not in the first year of marriage—unless the wedding-day happens to be on April 6. If a married couple separate they count as one until the separation and thereafter as two. Either husband or wife can apply for separate assessment (section 45 (2)). This is similar to the income tax provision for separate assessment, but there is no provision in the capital gains tax corresponding to the income tax provison for separate *taxation*.

For personal representatives Schedule 1 provides that the above relief applies to them in the year in which an individual dies and for the next two following years. After that they pay the tax at 30 per cent.

As regards trustees the above relief applies to the trustees of a settlement created for a mentally disabled person or a person in receipt of an attendance allowance. For other trustees there is no relief at all if the settlement was made on or after June 7, 1978, and the whole taxable amount is charged at 30 per cent. For settlements made before June 7, 1978, trustees have a nil rate up to a taxable amount of £500 and then tapering relief up to a taxable amount of £1,250.

Companies, as mentioned previously, do not pay capital gains tax *as such* but they do pay corporation tax on their capital gains. But they pay it not at the normal rate of corporation tax (which at present is 52 per cent.) but, in effect, at the normal (unrelieved) rate for capital gains tax, namely 30 per cent. I say "in effect" because that result is achieved in the following way. A company's net gains (gains less allowable losses) are reduced by such fraction as Parliament may from time to time determine. The present fraction, enacted in F.A. 1974, s. 10 (1), is $^{11}/_{26}$. If you reduce the net gains (say £100) by $^{11}/_{26}$ that leaves $^{15}/_{26}$. If you apply corporation tax at 52 per cent. to $^{15}/_{26}$ of say £100 that makes 30 per cent. ($^{15}/_{26} \times 52 = 30$). For authorised unit trusts and investment trusts the fraction is $^{21}/_{26}$, making in effect 10 per cent.: see F.A. 1978, s. 17.

The present structure of the tax rates has led to a greatly increased use by stock exchange investors of what is called "bed and breakfasting." Towards the end of a tax year an individual taxpayer sells a block of shares at a gain and buys them back the next day. He can thus contrive to end the tax year with a "taxable amount" of £1,000 (which will not involve any tax) or £5,000 (which will enjoy the 15 per cent. rate), and at the same time get a new, higher base cost for when he comes to sell the shares out-and-out in a future year. This advantage is only open to individuals; it was stopped for companies by the Finance (No. 2) Act 1975, s. 58.

DISPOSALS

The basic event on which capital gains tax depends is the disposal of an asset. Whenever a disposal takes place a calculation must be made to see whether there has been a gain or a loss or neither.

The word "disposal" has first of all to be given its ordinary meaning before going on to consider the extended meaning given to it by the Act. In its ordinary meaning a disposal occurs whenever the owner of an asset (which, remember, may be an abstract entity such as a right) divests himself of his entitlement to the asset. Thus the ordinary meaning includes sale, exchange and gift.

It is very important to grasp that the making of a gift is a chargeable event. At first sight this may seem very odd. Clearly the giver of a gift has made a disposal, but how on earth can he be said to have made a gain? The point was challenged in court in *Turner* v. *Follett* (1973) (C.A.). It was inevitably held that a gift is a chargeable event, because in section 19 (3) (*a*) it is enacted that where a person acquires an asset by way of gift the disposal of it to him (as well as the acquisition of it by him) shall be deemed to be for a consideration equal to its market value. So if a dad gives to his son an asset which he bought for £10,000 and at the time of the gift its market value is £14,000, dad has made a chargeable (albeit notional) gain of £4,000. But notice that if the gift is a gift of British money there is no charge to *this* tax (though there may be to capital *transfer* tax) because sterling is not an asset; section 19 (1) (*b*).

The market value rule stated in section 19 (3) (*a*) applies not only to a disposal by way of gift but also to a disposal "otherwise than by way of a bargain made at arm's length." It may seem surprising that so dignified a document as an Act of Parliament should use the phrase "at arm's length " but that is a phrase well-known to lawyers. The idea is that if two people are closer than arm's length away from each other their dealings may be not wholly governed by commercial considerations, with the result that a deal may be done at less than market value. This might be so, for example, where a young man sells his sailing dinghy to his girl-friend. In such a case the disposal is deemed for the purpose of capital gains tax to be at market value. So

G

if Fred bought a boat for £150 and later sold it to Freda for £180 when its value was really £200, Fred has a chargeable gain of £50 and Freda gets a base cost of £200.

Where the parties to a transaction are "connected persons" the transaction is automatically treated as a transaction otherwise than by way of a bargain at arm's length; section 62 (2). "Connected person" is defined in section 63 (2) as follows: "A person is connected with an individual if that person is the individual's husband or wife, or is a relative, or the husband or wife of a relative, of the individual or of the individual's husband or wife." And by section 63 (8) "relative" means "brother, sister, ancestor or lineal descendant." There are also definitions in section 63 of "connected persons" in relation to trusts, partnerships and companies.

Where there is a gift or a sale at an undervalue the donor or vendor is primarily liable for the tax, but if he does not pay it the donee or purchaser can in certain circumstances be required to pay it.

Now we come on to the extended meanings of "disposal" for the purposes of the tax.

First, "disposal" includes a part disposal (section 19 (2)). Thus where a person disposes of less than the whole of an asset (or disposes of less than his whole interest in an asset) that counts as a disposal. For example, a person's holding of shares of the same class in the same company is treated as a single asset. If some of those shares (but not all of them) are sold, the sale is a part disposal of the holding. Generally speaking, the gain accruing on the sale is calculated by reference to an appropriate part of the cost of the entire holding. A part disposal also includes the disposal of an interest in an asset, which interest is created by the disposal and did not exist before the disposal. If the owner of freehold land grants a lease (for a premium) over the land the granting of the lease is a part disposal notwithstanding that the lease only comes into existence at the moment when the part disposal takes place. The freeholder has disposed of part of his interest in the land. While we are talking of leases let me point out that a premium for a lease is only chargeable to capital gains tax in so far as it is not chargeable to income tax (Schedule 3, paragraph 5 (1). This is part of a wider principle, namely that any sum charged to income tax is not to count as part of the consideration for a disposal for the purposes of capital gains tax (see section 31 (1)).

The second extended meaning of "disposal" is this: if a capital sum is derived from assets by their owner there is assumed to be a disposal of those assets notwithstanding that no asset is acquired by the person paying the capital sum (section 20 (1)). The clearest example of this is where a shareholder receives a capital distribution in respect of his shares. Section 20 (1) then goes on to say that the principle applies in particular to four defined circumstances. (a) Capital sums received by way of compensation for any kind of damage or injury to assets or for the loss, destruction or dissipation of assets or for any depreciation or risk of depreciation of an asset. An example would be compensation for infringement of copyright; another example would be damages paid by a tortfeasor for physical damage done to an asset. (b) Capital sums received under a policy of insurance covering the risk of any kind of damage, etc., to assets. This hardly needs examples. (c) Capital sums received in return for forfeiture or surrender of rights, or for refraining from exercising rights. An example would be a payment received by A for releasing B from his obligation under a contract. (d) Capital sums received as consideration for use or exploitation of assets. This seems to point towards such transactions as the grant of a right to use a copyright. But such a transaction would be caught anyway under section 19 (2) as a part disposal, so it is a bit of a mystery why this head (d) exists.

The third extended meaning of "disposal" is set out in section 22 (1): ". . . the occasion of the entire loss, destruction, dissipation or extinction of an asset shall . . . constitute a disposal of the asset whether or not any capital sum by way of compensation or otherwise is received in respect of the destruction, dissipation or extinction of the asset." The *entire* loss, destruction, etc., of an asset would normally mean that it had become valueless, so the deemed disposal is a disposal for a nil consideration. The next subsection—section 22 (2)—deals with a situation where there has not been entire loss, destruction, etc., but where the value of an asset has become "negligible." The effect here is that the owner is deemed to have sold and immediately re-acquired the asset at its then market value. The deemed disposal, being at a negligible value, may well give the owner a loss (compared with the price for which he had acquired the asset); the point of the deemed re-acquisition is that if the value of the asset picks up so that there is a gain on its subsequent disposal, that gain is calculated by reference to this new, low, acquisition value.

Whether the asset becomes entirely lost, destroyed, etc. or whether it merely becomes of negligible value, if the asset is a building it is treated as an asset separate from the land on which it stands. But the owner is deemed to have disposed of the land (as well as of the building) and also to have immediately re-acquired the land at its then market value. The effect of this is that any loss relief that the owner gets in respect of the building will be reduced by the amount of any appreciation in the value of the land itself since he acquired it.

Let us look now at the inter-relation between the destruction, etc., of an asset and the receipt of a capital sum. If an asset is totally destroyed that will produce a loss, because the deemed disposal is for a nil consideration. If the destroyer pays a sum in damages or an insurer pays insurance money that may reduce or wipe out the loss. Suppose A bought an asset for £6,000. Subsequently it was totally destroyed. A is deemed to have disposed of the asset for nothing. That produces a loss of £6,000. A few weeks later an insurance company pays A £6,000. That produces a gain of £6,000. The one balances the other, so all in all there is no loss or gain. Of course, the insurance company may pay A less than £6,000, say £5,500, in which case there is an overall loss of £500. Or the insurance company may pay A more than £6,000, say £7,000, in which case there is an overall gain of £1,000. There are provisions in section 21 whereby in some situations tax on such a gain may be deferred until there is a disposal in the future. This is a kind of "roll-over" relief. For example, if our friend A spends the insurance money within one year of receipt on buying a replacement asset for £7,000 the £1,000 gain is dealt with by deducting £1,000 from the acquisition cost of the replacement asset. This will have the effect of increasing by £1,000 the gain to A when he comes to dispose of the replacement asset in the future. So A will be in exactly the same position as he would have been in if the asset had never been destroyed. Suppose A sells the asset (the replacement asset) eventually for £9,000. When he sells the asset, he deducts £1,000 from the replacement cost (which was £7,000) so his gain is £9,000 minus £6,000 = £3,000. If the original asset (which cost £6,000) had never been destroyed his gain would equally have been £3,000. These provisions apply not only to insurance money received but also to damages received. A somewhat similar system operates where an asset is not destroyed but only damaged.

We have now dealt with the extended meanings of "disposal," except for some which occur in connection with settled property (on which see below at p. 183 *et seq.*).

What we must do now is to look at some particular disposal situations.

Appropriations to and from Stock in Trade

It will be remembered that under the principle of *Sharkey* v. *Wernher* (1956) (H.L.) where a trader disposes of part of his stock in trade not by sale but for his own use he must, for the purposes of income tax, bring into his accounts as a receipt the market value of the asset at that time. And of course the converse applies—where a trader transfers an item from his own recreational enjoyment into his trade he can show in his accounts the market value of that item as an expense of the trade.

Now, how does capital gains tax bear on these events? Where a person who is a trader transfers a personal asset to his trade that appropriation is treated as a disposal, thus involving a gain or a loss compared with its earlier acquisition cost. But he can, if he wishes, avoid payment of capital gains tax by electing to bring the asset into trading stock not at its then market value simply, but at its then market value reduced by the amount of the chargeable gain or increased by the amount of the allowable loss (section 122 (3)). (A partner can only make this election if the other partners concur.) Take the case of a gain; the effect is that the item appears in his trading account amongst "purchases" at a figure below its true value by the amount of the gain, thus swelling his trading profits for that year by that amount.

In the converse case, where a trader transfers an item of trading stock to his personal enjoyment he is treated as having acquired it for a consideration equal to the amount then brought into the accounts of the trade in respect of that item for income tax purposes. Thus the closing figure for the item for income tax purposes is taken as the base cost for capital gains tax purposes. For income tax purposes no doubt the trader would like to put a low figure on the item, thus reducing his trade receipts and so his profits. But a low figure for income tax means a low base cost, which will in the end involve him in more capital gains tax.

The practical importance of the provisions we have been discussing is reduced by the presence of an exemption from capital gains tax in the case of a disposal of an asset which is tangible movable property and which is a wasting asset: see below at p. 197. But of course not all stock in trade is tangible movable property. It may be tangible without being movable (*e.g.* land) or movable without being tangible (*e.g.* stocks and shares).

Capital Distributions by Companies

Where a person receives a capital distribution (other than a new holding, on which see the next heading) in respect of shares in a company, he is treated as if in consideration of that distribution he had disposed of an interest in the shares (section 72). This applies for example when a company makes a "rights" issue of shares and a shareholder sells his rights. Another example of its application is when a liquidator makes a payment to shareholders in the course of a winding-up. If, however, the Inspector is satisfied that the amount of any capital distribution is "small" as compared with the value of the shares he may direct that the occurrence shall not be treated as a disposal, but that instead the amount of the distribution shall be deducted from the expenditure allowable as a deduction in computing a gain when the shareholder comes to dispose of the shares in the future. This of course has the effect of increasing the gain and hence the tax. It is a kind of roll-over relief.

Company Adjustments

There are detailed provisions (in sections 77–91) as to the bearing of capital gains tax on the re-organisation of a company's share capital, the conversion of securities and the amalgamation of companies. We will not go into all the details here. One example is this: where a company makes a "bonus" issue or a "rights" issue of shares and a shareholder takes up the shares (a "new holding") the new shares are treated as acquired when the original shares were acquired, and the acquisition cost of the total holding is the cost of the original shares plus the sum (if any) which the shareholder pays for the new holding. In the case of a company amalgamation (or take-over) then, subject to certain conditions, the exchange of shares in one company for shares in another company does not count as a disposal. This rule led to a great deal of tax avoidance and the relief has been subjected to two conditions, namely that the change must be effected for bona fide commercial reasons and it must not form part of a scheme or arrangements of which the main purpose or one of the main purposes is avoidance of tax liability: see section 87.

Transfer of Business to a Company

Where a person (other than a company) transfers a business as a going concern (and with its assets) to a company wholly or partly in exchange for shares, the gain on the transferred assets is computed but not charged to tax. The gain is apportioned between the shares received and any other consideration received. That part of the gain attributed to the shares is not assessed but is deducted from the allowable cost of the shares when the transferor of the business comes to dispose of them in the future. So it is a form of roll-over relief. The part of the gain attributed to the consideration other than shares (*e.g.* cash) is assessed at once in the normal way. This matter is dealt with in section 123.

Debts

The "satisfaction" of a debt is a disposal by the creditor. "Satisfaction" of a debt includes payment-off of the debt, and it also includes assignment of the debt. It may be worth discussing what the creditor whose debtor pays him a debt is disposing of. The answer is that he is disposing of the debt itself, which is a chose in action—a species of right. There are many circumstances in the law of capital gains tax where it is more obvious that a person is acquiring something (*e.g.* money in satisfaction of a debt) than that he is disposing of something. If one looks closely one sees that he is disposing of the right to obtain that which he acquires. Where does the capital gain come in in connection with a debt? The answer to that is that the capital gain is the difference between what the creditor lent and what he gets back as a capital sum.

Although, in general, satisfaction of a debt is a disposal (section 134), so far as concerns the original creditor no chargeable gain accrues on the disposal. And the same is true of the original creditor's personal representative or legatee. At first sight this seems very nice of the Revenue, but the point is really directed against losses. It is a general principle of capital gains tax law that a loss cannot be claimed from a transaction upon which, if there had been a gain, it would not have been a chargeable gain. This principle was to some extent modified for debts which prove to be bad debts by section 49 of the Finance Act 1978. That section was enacted because huge losses had been incurred during the slump of the mid-seventies. The section provides that where a loan or part of a loan *to a trader* becomes irrecoverable the original creditor or a guarantor can claim the loss as an allowable loss. The section only applies where the loan was made (or the guarantee was given) after April 11, 1978 (which was budget day). It is notable that the government which insisted on retrospection in respect of the anti-avoidance section 31 (see p. 12, above) was not willing to make this relieving section (section 49) retrospective. They agreed to lock the stable door but the horse had already bolted. The provision is now at section 136 of the Capital Gains Tax Act 1979.

The rule that no chargeable gain (and hence—subject to section 136—no allowable loss) can arise to the original creditor (or his personal representative or legatee) does not apply to a "debt on a security." The exact boundaries of a debt on a security are a matter of judicial controversy, but it is clear from section 82 (3) (*b*) that an example is loan stock of a company. And, paradoxically, a security is still a security if it is unsecured. So the (very common) unsecured Loan Stock of a company is a debt on a security. Thus an ordinary investor who buys and subsequently sells such stock makes a chargeable gain or an allowable loss—as the case may be.

The assignee of a debt (as distinct from the original creditor) does make a chargeable gain (or an allowable loss) when the debt is satisfied, whether it be a debt on a security or not. This rule (if it stood alone) would open the way to a great deal of tax avoidance, because it is very easy to contrive a loss on a debt. So there are provisions to stop up these possibilities. A loss made by a person on the disposal of a debt is disallowed if he acquired the debt from a "connected person": section 134 (4). So if A sells a debt to B for £120 and later X (the debtor) pays up £100 to B, B cannot claim a loss of £20 if A and B are connected persons. If this were not so, and B *could* claim a loss, it would be a way of B making a gift of £20 to A, to which gift the Revenue would be contributing.

Sometimes a creditor takes property instead of money in satisfaction of a debt. In that case the base cost of the property is its then market value and no more. This looks as though it is going to prejudice the creditor when he comes to sell the property. And so it does in the case of a creditor who is not the original creditor, but is a person who has acquired the debt by assignment. So if A assigns to B a debt of £500 for £500 and then X (the debtor) hands over to B in satisfaction of the debt property worth £450, the base cost of the property is £450. So if, later, B sells the property for £520 he has made a gain of £70. But if the *original* creditor (A) (not having assigned the debt) accepts from the debtor in satisfaction of the debt property worth £450, the chargeable gain to A, when he comes to sell the property, is not to exceed the chargeable gain which would have accrued to him if he had acquired the property for a consideration equal to the amount of the debt. So if the debt was £500, the property was worth £450 and A later sells it for £520, A's chargeable gain is £20 (not £70). These matters are dealt with in section 134 (3).

Options

An option is an asset. The grant of an option is treated as a disposal. Where the option is exercised the grant and the exercise are treated as all one transaction. So if A grants to B an option to buy certain property and B subsequently exercises the option and buys the property, the sum paid for the option and the sum paid for the property are added together to ascertain the disposal cost (for A) and the acquisition cost (for B). Supposing, on the other hand, that an option is granted and then abandoned (*i.e.* not exercised): A is left with the gain on the grant of the option; for B the abandonment of the option does not (generally) count as a disposal—with the result that, although he has lost money, he does not get any loss relief. These and other rules are set out in sections 137–139.

Value Shifting

This is the dramatic and cryptic marginal note given to sections 25 and 26. Section 25 begins with a general introduction, and it then proceeds to deal with four specific situations.

First, if a person having control of a company exercises his control so that value passes out of his shares (or other rights) or out of the shares (or rights) of a person with whom he is connected into other shares (or rights) that is a disposal of the shares (or rights). An example would be if A, who holds the only shares which carry voting rights in a company, were to pass a resolution to transfer the voting rights to the shares held by other shareholders. It is, after all, a kind of gift. For a more sophisticated example, see *Floor* v. *Davis* (1979) (H.L.).

Second, if there has been a shift of value as above, and subsequently the transferor disposes at a loss of some other asset which has depreciated in value by reason of the shift, that loss is not an allowable loss.

Third, if there is a sale and lease back of land or other property and then subsequently there is an adjustment of the rights and liabilities under the lease which is favourable to the lessor, that counts as a disposal by the lessee of an interest in the property. The idea behind this rule is that the seller has really sold the property for less than its true value. Suppose A, the owner of a factory, sells the freehold of it to B for £100,000 and B immediately leases it back to A at a rent of £5,000 a year. Later an adjustment is made in the terms of the lease in favour of B, so that in effect B is to get £6,000 a year from the property. On this footing the price that A received for the freehold turns out to be less than what he could have got for it, with the result that A paid less capital gains tax on the disposal of the freehold than he "should" have done. This present provision, by treating the adjustment in the lease as a disposal by A, enables the Revenue to pick up the lost tax.

Fourth, if an asset is subject to some right or restriction and then the person entitled to enforce the right or restriction abrogates it, that abrogation counts as a disposal by that person of the right or restriction. An example of this would be if A, who had chartered a ship from B, were to release B from his obligations under the charterparty. That would be a disposal by A of his rights under the charterparty.

Section 26 was enacted (originally in 1977) to strike at some tax avoidance schemes which were based on transferring some of the value of a chargeable asset into a non-chargeable asset. The section is in very wide terms and has the potentiality to become a general anti-avoidance weapon.

Husband and Wife

As for income tax so far capital gains tax a husband is assessable and chargeable with the gains made by his wife if they are living together, unless they have elected to be assessed separately. There is no provision (as there is for income tax) for separate *taxation*. The spouses can set off the gains of either of them against the losses of either of them. But either of them can elect that this set-off shall not apply.

As regards disposals *between* spouses who are living together, both spouses are treated (by section 44) "as if the asset was acquired from the one making the disposal for a consideration of such amount as would secure that on the disposal neither a gain nor a loss would accrue to the one making the disposal."[4] Broadly the effect of this is that the transferee takes the asset at the base cost which it had in the hands of the transferor. But it is a little better than that, because the words of the paragraph seem to involve that if there are some incidental costs of the inter-spousal transfer the base cost for the transferee is to include those costs. Thus if H bought an item for £100 and subsequently transferred it to W and the costs of the transfer were £5, the base cost for W (looking to a future disposal by her) would be £105. Schedule 5, paragraph 17 provides that where an asset is transferred from spouse A to spouse B and is later disposed of by spouse B, spouse B is treated as if he (or she) had acquired the asset at the time when spouse A in fact acquired it. This rule will be important if spouse A's acquisition was before April 6, 1965. (See below under "Computation.")

DEATH

Until 1971 death was in itself a chargeable event for capital gains tax. The Finance Act 1971 abolished the charge. But a person's death still has important consequences—for his survivors. The subject of death is now dealt with in section 49 of the Capital Gains Tax Act 1979. Section 49 (1) provides:

"... the assets of which a deceased person was competent to dispose—

(a) shall be deemed to be acquired on his death by the personal representatives or other person on whom they devolve for a consideration equal to their market value at the date of death; but

(b) shall not be deemed to be disposed of by him on his death. ..."

The main point of the phrase "assets of which a deceased person was competent to dispose" is to exclude settled property in which the deceased had an interest. Settled property is governed by different rules which are discussed under the next heading. To take an example, if, when A dies, he is the life tenant under a settlement, he is not "competent to dispose" of the settled property. One can speak of property of which a deceased person was competent to dispose as being his "free estate."

---

[4] This rule does not apply if (a) the asset is trading stock of the transferor or is acquired as trading stock of the transferee, or (b) the disposal is by way of donatio mortis causa.

The effect of section 49 (1) is that so far as concerns the deceased's free estate, the death does not give rise to a charge to capital gains tax, but it does give rise to an "uplift" in the base cost of his assets. This, of course, is advantageous for the future. If A bought an asset for £50,000 and later died when its market value was £60,000, the base cost becomes £60,000. On a future disposal of the asset for £65,000, the gain is £5,000 and not £15,000. It must be borne in mind, however, that capital *transfer* tax will (or may) be payable on the death of A. Indeed the idea behind the exemption from capital *gains* tax on death is that death should not be an occasion of charge to both taxes. But it goes a bit further than that, because there is no charge to capital gains tax on death even if there is no charge to capital transfer tax either, as for instance where assets are left to a surviving spouse. (See p. 246, below.)

The next question which arises is this: when the personal representatives come to dispose of the assets in the course of the administration of the deceased's estate, is that disposal a chargeable event? The answer is that if the disposal is to a legatee that is not a chargeable event, but if the disposal is to anyone else it is a chargeable event.

A legatee gets as his base cost the market value of the asset at the time of the deceased's death; section 49 (4). "Legatee" is given by section 47 (2) and (3) an extended meaning. It includes any person taking under a testamentary disposition (a will) or under an intestacy or partial intestacy, whether he takes beneficially or as trustee. And where the personal representatives appropriate assets to satisfy a legacy, the person taking under the appropriation is deemed to be a legatee. Also, by section 49, subsections (6) to (9), if the deceased's dispositions are varied by an instrument in writing made by the persons entitled within two years of the death, the variations do not count as disposals, except such variations as are made for a consideration (other than a consideration consisting of some other variation).

A disposal by personal representatives otherwise than to a legatee *does* involve a chargeable gain or allowable loss. This is so, for example, if they sell an asset in order to pay capital transfer tax, or if they simply re-arrange the investment portfolio. There is no provision for personal representatives to offset their losses against gains of the deceased. If the deceased had, in the year of assessment in which he died, an excess of losses over gains these may be "rolled backwards" for the preceding three years.

SETTLED PROPERTY

"Settled property" is defined in section 51 as "... any property held in trust[5] other than property to which section 46 . . . applies." So the first thing to do is to find out what section 46 is all about. It deals with the situation where one person is nominee for another person, or is a bare trustee for another person. Neither a nominee nor a bare trustee counts as a trustee, and the property they hold is not settled property. The property is treated as though it were vested in the person for whom the nominee or bare trustee is holding it, *i.e.* the beneficiary. Unfortunately (from the point of view of clarity) section 46 itself does not use the phrase "bare trustee," but that is an illuminating translation of the phrase used in the section, namely "trustee for another person absolutely entitled as against the trustee, or for any person who would be so entitled but for being an infant or other person under disability (or for two or more persons who are or would be jointly so entitled) . . ." The phrase "bare trustee" does occur in the marginal note to section 46. And section 46 (2) says this:

> "It is hereby declared that references in this Act to any asset held by a person as trustee for another person absolutely entitled as against the trustee are references to a case where that other person has the exclusive right, subject only to satisfying any outstanding charge, lien or other right of the trustee to resort to the asset for payment of duty, taxes, costs or other outgoings, to direct how that asset shall be dealt with."

This form of words does not fit very well with normal principles of trust law, and there are still some unsolved mysteries. But some points at least are clear. The words "jointly so entitled" in section 46 do not refer only to persons who are technically joint tenants; they cover also persons who are tenants in common. So *concurrent interests* can exist (whether in the form of a joint tenancy or a tenancy in common) without the property in which the interests subsist being settled property, provided the "tenants" can direct the trustee how the asset shall be dealt with: see *Kidson* v. *MacDonald* (1974). This point is not confined to real property; the word "jointly" refers to "persons who are, as it were, in the same interest," whatever the subject-matter of the trust (*per* Walton J. in *Stephenson* v. *Barclays Bank Trust Co. Ltd*. (1975)). On the other hand it was held in both those cases that where there are *interests in succession* (*e.g.* where there is a trust for A for life with remainder to B) the trustees can never be bare trustees and the property must be settled property. This is because, although A and B are *together* entitled absolutely as

---

[5] A unit trust scheme does not count as a trust (nor does an investment trust company). Both count as companies, though with some special rules of their own.

against the trustee, they are not entitled *"jointly"* and so section 46 can never be satisfied.[6]

If the trustees are not bare trustees then "any property held in trust" is settled property.

We must now consider the events connected with settled property which count as disposals.

Putting Property into Settlement

A gift in settlement is a disposal of the *entire property* thereby becoming settled property; section 53. This is so even if the donor takes some interest as a beneficiary under the settlement or is a trustee or the sole trustee of the settlement. This is a pretty harsh rule. Suppose Mr. Smith wishes to give his house to his nephew, but to retain for himself the right to occupy the house for the rest of his life, so that the nephew will only come into occupation when S dies (S for Smith and also for "settlor"). S can only carry out this transaction by putting the house into settlement. It is a "gift in settlement," and so it is treated as a disposal of the entire property. That involves that the deemed consideration for the disposal is the whole capital value of the house. This does not accord with the reality, because in reality all that S has given away is the remainder interest. The same point can occur the other way round: S may want to allow his aged aunt to live in the house for her life. He makes a settlement under which the aunt gets a life interest and he retains the remainder interest. There is a charge to tax based on the value of "the entire property" when this "gift in settlement" is made. In reality all that S has given away is a tiny fraction of the value of the entire property.

So far I have been dwelling on the harshness of the rule. But the rule can be turned on its head and made the instrument for tax avoidance. This happened in *Berry* v. *Warnett* (1978). It was held in that case that if the settlor takes so great an interest under the settlement that the putting of property into the settlement is no longer a gift (in settlement), section 53 does not apply. Instead there is simply a part-disposal of the property. It may make a colossal difference (as that case shows) according as the disposal (the putting of the property into settlement) is treated as a disposal of the entire property or as merely a part-disposal.

Disposals by Trustees

Trustees, though they are not "individuals," are "persons," and they

---

[6] These two cases were followed in *Booth* v. *Ellard* (1978) where, incidentally, Goulding J. did not altogether approve of the use of the phrase "bare trustee" in this context. He was quite happy to state the distinction as being between "settled property" and "nominee property."

are chargeable to capital gains tax. They are chargeable, for example, on gains made in the course of switching investments in the trust's portfolio.

There are also two situations (special to trustees) where they are *deemed* to dispose of assets comprised in the settled property. These situations are: (1) where a person becomes absolutely entitled to settled property (s. 54 (1)); (2) where a life interest in possession terminates (section 55 (1)). We will look at these situations in turn.

(1) A person becoming absolutely entitled

Suppose assets are held in trust for A contingently on his attaining the age of 25. When A becomes 25 that is an occasion of charge under section 54 (1). The assets are deemed to have been disposed of by the trustee and immediately re-acquired by him in his capacity as a bare trustee within section 46 (1), for a consideration equal to their market value. After that it makes no difference whether the trustee hands over the property to A at once or keeps it as bare trustee for him. The actual handing over of the property to A is not a chargeable event because it is deemed to be A's already by virtue of section 46 (1). The upshot is that the trustees pay tax on the gain represented by the increase in value of the assets between the time when they were put into trust and the time when A became 25, and A takes as his base cost the market value on the day when he attained 25.

Where the event which causes a person to become absolutely entitled is the termination of a life interest by the *death* of the person entitled to that interest no chargeable gain accrues on that disposal (section 56 (1) (*a*)). All that happens is that the trustee is deemed to dispose of the settled property and immediately re-acquire it as a bare trustee. The effect is that there is an uplift of the base cost to the market value at the time of the death. The person who becomes absolutely entitled acquires the property at the up-to-date value. This, of course, is advantageous to him when he comes to dispose of the property in the future. Suppose property is settled on A for life, with remainder to B absolutely. On A's death B becomes absolutely entitled. There is no charge to capital gains tax (even if there is no charge to capital transfer tax either) but there is an uplift.

There is a special exception to this advantageous rule where there arises what is called "reverter to the disponer." The background to this point is that no capital *transfer* tax is payable on the death of X where X has been given a life interest by S (settlor) in such terms that the property reverts, on X's death, to S. If in this situation S could also get, on the death of X, an uplift in the base cost for purposes of capital *gains* tax that would be too favourable to S. So he cannot; see section 56 (1) (*b*). If, on the life tenant's death, property reverts to the disponer (settlor), the disposal and re-acquisition shall be deemed to be for such consideration as to secure that neither a gain nor a loss accrues to the trustee. Thus, suppose S grants a life interest to X in property which at the time of the grant is worth £10,000. X dies at a time when the market value of the property is £14,000. The property reverts to S. The trustee is treated as re-acquiring the asset for £10,000 (not £14,000) and that figure (£10,000) becomes S's base cost.

(2) Termination of a life interest in possession

This situation is dealt with by section 55 (1). Naturally, the termination of a life interest and the absolute entitlement of some person often happen on the same event. If property is held in trust for A for life with remainder to B, the event of A's death brings about the termination of a life interest (A's) *and* the absolute entitlement of some person (B). In this situation it is section 54 (1) which applies. Section 55 (1) only applies where there is a termination of a life interest but still no one becomes absolutely entitled. This would be so, for example, where property is settled on A for life, remainder to B for life, remainder to C absolutely, and A dies. On A's death (or to take another example, A's surrender of his life interest) there is the termination of a life interest but no one becomes absolutely entitled; B becomes entitled for life; section 55 (1) applies. On B's death (or surrender) section 54 (1) applies, because C does become absolutely entitled.

Where section 55 (1) applies, the result is the same as where section 54 (1) applies. (Until 1971 the results were different—or, at least, were thought to be different—now they are the same.) If the event causing the termination of a life interest in possession is something other than the death of the person entitled to the life interest there is a charge to tax on the trustees and an uplift in base cost for the future. If the event which causes the termination is the death of the person entitled to the life interest there is not any charge to tax, but there is an uplift in the base cost: section 56 (2). There is still an uplift (and no charge to tax) even if the property is exempt from capital *transfer* tax (*e.g.* because the property passes from a deceased husband to his widow).

The expression "life interest" includes (*per* section 55 (4)) a right under the settlement for the life of a person other than the person entitled to the right. Thus, if A (who is a life tenant) assigns his interest to X, X has an interest during the continued life of A, and X's interest is a "life interest." (The technical description of X's interest is that it is an interest *pur autre vie*.)

This raises an important point. The exemptions from charge given by section 56 (1) (*a*) and (2) (which we have just been speaking about) only apply where the event causing a person to become absolutely entitled or causing the termination of a life interest is the death of the person *entitled* to the life interest. If A is life tenant (with remainder to B) and A dies still holding the life tenancy, there is no charge to capital gains tax, only an uplift. But if A (life tenant) assigns his interest to X, there is a charge when A dies. B becomes absolutely entitled, and section 54 (1) imposes a charge to tax. The charge is not relieved by section 56 (1) (*a*) for the reason that B's becoming absolutely entitled is not caused by the death of the person *entitled* to the life interest because A was not (at death) *entitled* to it. Similarly if A is life tenant under a settlement for A for life, then for B for life, then for C absolutely. If A is still holding the life tenancy when he dies there is the termination of a life interest but no charge to tax, because the termination arises on the death of the person entitled. But if A had assigned his life interest to X there is a charge on A's death; section 55 (1) applies and it is not relieved by section 56 (2).

The charge to tax under section 54 (1) or 55 (1) which arises on the death of a former life tenant who has assigned his interest will be in addition to a charge to capital *transfer* tax (under F.A. 1975, Sched. 5, para. 4 (2)).

Conversely (as explained earlier) where a life tenant dies without having assigned his interest there will be no charge to capital *gains* tax and there may be no charge to capital *transfer* tax either. This will be so, for example, where the property passes from a husband to his widow.

Just let me re-state where the relevant charging provisions and relieving provisions are to be found. The charging provisions are in sections 54 (1) and 55 (1); the relieving provisions are in section 56 (1) (*a*) and (2).

Tax Position of the Beneficiaries

The legislation is not notably generous to trustees or beneficiaries, but beneficiaries do have one crumb of comfort. It is to be found in section 58 (1). If a person is holding an interest under a settlement and that interest was created for his benefit, no chargeable gain arises if he disposes of his interest. Thus, suppose property is held in trust for A for life with remainder to B absolutely. If A assigns (*e.g.* sells) his life interest that is not a chargeable event. The same is true if B sells his remainder interest. And if it happens that B dies while A is still alive, B's personal representatives can sell B's remainder interest without tax arising. But a person who acquired an interest for consideration in money or money's worth (other than consideration consisting of another interest under the settlement) and then sold the interest is liable to tax on any gain involved. So if X bought A's life interest (or B's remainder interest) and then sold it at a gain he would be liable to tax. And if X bought B's remainder interest and was still holding it when A died, X would be treated as disposing of the remainder interest in consideration of obtaining the settled property itself and so a charge to tax would arise: section 58 (2).

This legislation permits adjustments of the interests of several beneficiaries amongst themselves without a charge to tax arising. "Partition" of settled property is quite a common occurrence. A, a life tenant, may surrender his life interest in part of the trust property in return for an interest in the capital. A is not treated as acquiring his interest in capital for money or money's worth because he has acquired it in exchange for "another interest" (*i.e.* his life interest) "under the settlement" and that does not count as money or money's worth. Consequently if A were to carry out the above transaction and then sell his interest in capital (a remainder interest) at a gain he would not be liable to tax.

Payment of the Tax

A beneficiary may become liable to pay tax which has been assessed on the trustees. This will be so where the tax is not paid within six months of its due date and the asset concerned or a part of it or the proceeds of it are transferred by the trustees to the beneficiary. He can be assessed at any time within two years from the due date on the chargeable gain or, in the case of a transfer of a part, on a proportionate part of the chargeable gain; section 52 (4).

Non-resident Trusts

We saw at page 168, above that a person is only liable to capital gains tax in respect of chargeable gains accruing to him in a year of assessment during any part of which he is resident in the United Kingdom, or during which he is ordinarily resident in the United Kingdom. If one adds this point to the point that it is the trustees who are primarily liable for tax on gains in respect of settled property, one can see that there would be scope for tax avoidance by vesting property in non-resident trustees. To meet this it is provided that if the settlor is (or was at the time of the settlement) domiciled and resident or ordinarily resident in the United Kingdom *and* there is a beneficiary who is domiciled and resident or ordinarily resident here, the beneficiary will be chargeable in respect of a proportion of the gains accruing to non-resident trustees, the proportion being such as is "just and reasonable." This matter is dealt with in section 17.

COMPUTATION OF GAINS AND LOSSES

Putting it very broadly the amount of a chargeable gain or of an allowable loss is arrived at by comparing the consideration received on the disposal of an asset with the cost of its acquisition. What we must now do is to look in more detail at the way in which the computation is done.

It is provided by section 29 (1) that a loss is to be computed in the same way as a gain is computed.

We will look first at the general rules of computation laid down in Part II, Chapter II (sections 28–43), and then at the special rules which apply when the asset in question was already held by the taxpayer on April 6, 1965: see Schedule 5.

General Rules

First, there is to be excluded from the consideration for a disposal any sum which is taken into account for income tax. An example would be the whole of the consideration for the sale of an asset by a dealer in such assets. Another example would be that part of a lease premium which was chargeable to income tax. Special rules apply to assets which have enjoyed capital allowances.

Second, there may be deducted from the disposal consideration the following amounts:

(a) the cost of acquisition of the asset (together with the incidental costs) or, if the asset was not acquired, the expenditure incurred in producing it (*e.g.* the expenditure incurred in writing a book and thereby creating a copyright);

(b) the expenditure incurred for the purpose of enhancing the value of the asset (*e.g.* extensions to a building) and expenditure incurred in establishing, preserving or defending one's title to, or right over, the asset (*e.g.* the costs involved in taking out probate);

(c) the incidental costs of making the disposal.

It will be recalled that there are many instances where there is deemed to be a disposal (and re-acquisition). Can there be incidental costs of such a notional disposal? Section 32 (4) says (rather laconically): "Any provision . . . introducing the assumption that assets are sold and immediately re-acquired shall not imply that any expenditure is incurred as incidental to the sale or re-acquisition." It has been held in the courts that real expenditure on a notional disposal is allowable (*e.g.* legal costs), but that notional expenditure is not. Real lawyers' fees could arise, for example, in respect of a deemed disposal and re-acquisition by trustees on the death of a life tenant. Such real fees are deductible. But where the deemed disposal and re-acquisition arises because the asset in question was held by the taxpayer on April 6, 1965 (see p. 191, below) the taxpayer cannot say: "If I had really sold and re-bought the shares on the stock exchange on that day I would have incurred brokers' fees and stamp duty, and I claim to deduct those notional expenses."

Certain kinds of expenditure are not deductible, notably expenditure on insuring an asset in respect of damage, injury, loss or depreciation. Another notable non-allowable expenditure is the payment of interest (except as provided by the Taxes Act, s. 269 in relation to companies).

A word must be said about Value Added Tax. If VAT has been suffered on the purchase of an asset but that VAT is available for set-off in the purchaser's VAT account, the cost of the asset for the purposes of capital gains tax will be the cost exclusive of VAT. Where no VAT set-off is available, the cost will be inclusive of the VAT which has been borne. Where an asset is disposed of, any VAT chargeable will be disregarded in computing the capital gain (because the disponer will have to pay over the VAT to Customs and Excise). If the disponer is not selling in the course of a business VAT is not chargeable. VAT which is payable for services (such as stockbrokers' services) is deductible as part of the incidental costs. The Revenue issued a press notice on VAT and capital gains tax on May 7, 1973; see, *e.g.* [1973] B.T.R. 417.

It is perhaps worth saying again at this point something that was said at the beginning of this chapter, namely that no "allowance" is permissible for the fall in the value of money between the date of acquisition and the date of disposal.

Part disposals

Where there is a part disposal the amounts of acquisition or production expenditure (see (a) above) and subsequent expenditure (see (b) above) have to be apportioned between the part disposed of and the part retained. The apportionment is done by applying to the total of expenditure the fraction $\dfrac{A}{A + B}$ where A is the consideration for the part disposal and B is the market value of the property retained. To take an example, suppose Mr. Smith owns an asset which has a base cost of £10,000 and he sells part of that asset for £7,000 and the market value of the part he retains is £21,000. The "attributable" expenditure is

$$£10,000 \times \frac{£7,000}{£7,000 + £21,000} = £2,500$$

So the gain on this part disposal is £4,500 (*i.e.* the difference between

the sale consideration (£7,000) and the attributable expenditure
(£2,500)). The balance of expenditure (£7,500) which was not
allowed on this part disposal is carried forward for use on any future
disposal of the part of the asset which was retained.

Wasting assets

There is a restriction on the amount of expenditure that may be
deducted in respect of what are called "wasting assets." A wasting
asset means (*per* section 37 (1)) an asset which has a predictable life
not exceeding 50 years. Plant and machinery are expressly regarded
as having a life not exceeding 50 years. The residual or scrap value of
the asset is deducted from the acquisition cost and the resulting sum is
written-off on a straight line basis over the life of the asset. Let us take
an example. Suppose Mr. Jones bought an asset which had a predictable life of 30 years. He paid £10,000 for it. Ten years later Mr. Jones
sold the asset for £8,000. It has a scrap value of £1,000. The computation for capital gains tax on the occasion of the sale goes like this:

Proceeds of sale		£8,000
Less: cost	£10,000	
Deduct scrap value	£1,000	
	£9,000	
Deduct amount written-off		
$\frac{10}{30} \times £9,000$	£3,000	
	£6,000	£6,000
Chargeable gain		£2,000

Notice that this procedure, on the above facts, converts what at first
sight looked like a loss (cost price £10,000; sale price £8,000) into a
gain. The idea behind this is that if you buy a wasting asset and use it
for a number of years and then sell it you have had the enjoyment of
part of its useful life and you have sold it when its prospective useful
life is diminished. So the Act deals with this situation by providing
that the buying price must be notionally reduced to take account of
the enjoyment of the asset which you have used up.

Amongst other things, a life interest in settled property is a wasting
asset when the predictable expectation of life of the life tenant is 50
years or less. The legislation is somewhat inconsistent in that it
counteracts by these artificial means the inherent depreciation of a
wasting asset, such as a life interest, but it charges in full as an
ordinary chargeable gain the inherent appreciation in a naturally
appreciating asset such as, for example, a remainder interest.

A lease is a wasting asset when its future duration is 50 years or less. But for leases the straight line basis of writing-off is not used. What is used is a fixed Table set out in Schedule 3. On this Table the line of wastage is curved and it accelerates as the lease approaches its end.

Assets held on April 6, 1965

It will be recalled that capital gains tax is only charged on gains which accrue after April 6, 1965. It is obvious therefore that rules must be laid down as to how a gain (or loss) is to be computed where the asset in question was in the ownership of the taxpayer on April 6, 1965. The rules are set out in Schedule 5.

A distinction is made between, on the one hand, quoted securities and land which has a development value, and on the other hand all other assets (including unquoted securities and land which does not have a development value).

Quoted securities

Let us look first at quoted securities. These are shares and securities which have quoted market values on a recognised stock exchange and also units in unit trusts whose prices are published regularly by the managers.

The basic point is that a person who owned a quoted security on April 6, 1965 is deemed to have sold and re-acquired the security at its market price on that day. His base cost when he comes to sell that asset is thus established. To compute his gain or loss one compares the price that he gets on the sale with that base cost. By this technique any gain that had taken place between the time when the asset was acquired and April 6, 1965, is eliminated.

But sometimes this elimination is unfair to the Revenue or unfair to the taxpayer, so there are further rules to deal with such situations. If there would be a smaller gain by taking the original cost then that original cost is taken. Suppose Mr. Robinson bought some shares in 1960 for £100 and at April 6, 1965, they were worth £80 and when he sold them in 1978 they fetched £130. If you take the 1965 price he has made a gain of £50. But you do not; you take instead the 1960 price, because that shows a smaller gain, a gain of £30. The same principle applies to losses; you take the smaller loss.

In one circumstance there is deemed to be no gain or loss. This is so where the 1965 value shows a gain whereas the original cost shows a loss—or vice versa. Suppose Mr. Smith bought some shares in 1960 for £150 and at April 6, 1965, they stood at £100 and in 1978 he sold them for £130. The 1965 value throws up a gain; the 1960 value throws up a loss. The rule then is that there is deemed to be no gain or loss on the 1978 disposal. Now take the converse case: Mr. Jones acquired some shares in 1960 for £100 and in 1965 (April 6) they were worth £150 and he sold them in 1978 for £130. The 1965 value shows a loss; the 1960 value shows a gain. So the rule applies that there is deemed to be no gain or loss. You can draw a diagram of this. Put the sale price on a horizontal line (in our examples at £130). If the acquisition price and the 1965 price are on opposite sides of this line the "no gain—no loss" rule applies.

Sometimes it is necessary in order to determine which of the above rules applies to identify shares bought at different times. The rule for this is "first in—first out"; shares acquired at an earlier time are deemed to be disposed of before shares acquired at a later time.

A taxpayer may elect (see Schedule 5, paragraph 4) to take the value on April 6, 1965 instead of going through all the palaver of the above rules. The election may be for all his fixed interest securities or for all his ordinary shares (including units in a unit trust) or for both classes. The effect of an election (which is irrevocable) is that *all* the disposals of that taxpayer (in the elected class) are calculated on the April 6, 1965 basis. The original cost thus never comes into the matter. The "first in—first out" rule does not apply; instead all the taxpayer's shares of the same class in the same company are treated as a "pool."

Land with development value

This is dealt with by paragraph 9 of Schedule 5. The paragraph applies to a disposal of land situated in the United Kingdom if the consideration on the disposal exceeds the current use value *or* if any material development of the land has been carried out (after December 17, 1973) since the person making the disposal acquired the land. Where the paragraph applies the rules are similar to those discussed above for quoted securities. The primary rule is that the market value on April 6, 1965 must be taken, but that rule can be ousted (as for quoted securities).

Other assets

Notice that these other assets include securities which are not quoted securities and also land which does not have a development value. The technique used here is quite different. It is set out in paragraphs 11 to 14 of Schedule 5. The heading to paragraph 11 is: "Apportionment by reference to straightline growth of gain or loss over period of ownership." That gives the idea. Instead of taking the April 6, 1965 value, you assume that the gain (or loss) has accrued at a uniform rate over the whole period of ownership. So if Mr. Brown acquired an asset on April 6, 1960 for £100 and sold it on April 6,

1978 for £460 the amount of the chargeable gain is £260. That is arrived at in this way. The total period of ownership was 18 years, of which 13 came after April 6, 1965. It is only the gain during those 13 years which is chargeable. So $^{13}/_{18}$ of £360 (*i.e.* the whole gain) is chargeable. And $^{13}/_{18}$ of £360 is £260. There is a cut-off date for expenditure, namely April 6, 1945. Thus if Mr. Brown had acquired his asset in 1940 and sold it in 1978 he could not claim that the fraction to be applied to £360 (the whole gain) was $^{13}/_{18}$; it is deemed to be $^{13}/_{33}$.

A taxpayer can elect (if he wishes) to have his gain or loss computed by reference to market value on April 6, 1965 instead of by reference to the uniform rate method. He would be more likely to make this election if there is a loss than if there is a gain (see below). So paragraph 12 (2) of Schedule 5 provides that he cannot by means of this election get relief for a larger loss than the uniform rate method would throw up. But where the uniform rate method would show a gain and the 1965 method would show a loss there is deemed to be neither a gain nor a loss.

It is pretty obvious that because of the much increased rate of inflation since 1965 the uniform rate method is likely to be more advantageous to the taxpayer than the 1965 method. This is particularly true of land, because the value of land has increased much more rapidly since 1965 than it did between 1945 and 1965. Suppose a taxpayer bought some land in 1951 and sold it in 1979. The whole period of ownership is 28 years, of which 14 years fall after 1965. On the uniform rate method he will only be charged on half the total gain. It is virtually certain that far more than half the total gain accrued after 1965. So if the 1965 method applies he will be charged on far more than half the total gain. This is the commonsense justification for the legislation to apply the 1965 method to land with a development value.

LOSSES

I want to collect together under this heading certain leading points about losses. Some of the points have been mentioned before; some are new.

Losses are computed in the same way as gains are computed; section 29 (1).

If a transaction is such that a gain (if there had been one) would not be a chargeable gain, then if a loss occurs (instead of a gain) that loss is not an allowable loss; section 29 (2). This provision has some very important consequences. A good example arises in connection with the disposal of gilt-edged securities which have been owned for 12 months or more (see p. 195, below).

Capital gains tax is charged on the total amount of chargeable gains in a year of assessment after deducting any allowable losses. Any surplus of losses over gains in a year of assessment may be carried forward to future years. Both these points are to be found in section 4 (1). If in any year a person has a taxable amount (chargeable gains minus allowable losses) (see p. 169, above) not exceeding £1,000 the accumulated losses of earlier years are not required to be used in eliminating that taxable amount. For example if at the end of year 1 a person has accumulated losses of £2,234, and in year 2 his taxable amount is £934, no part of the £2,234 needs to be used in knocking down the £934 to nil. He goes forward into year 3 with his accumulation of losses (£2,234) intact: section 5 (4) (*a*). Similarly, if his taxable amount in year 2 had been £1,234, he need only use so much of his accumulated losses as is needed to reduce that taxable amount to £1,000. So he goes into year 3 with an accumulation of losses of £2,000: section 5 (4) (*b*). The same principle applies to losses carried *back* from the year in which an individual dies. (See p. 181, above.)

Losses incurred in a disposal to a "connected person" are only allowable against gains made on subsequent disposals to the same connected person: section 62 (3).

A loss only becomes allowable when it is realised. On the stock exchange one way of realising a loss is by means of the practice called "bed and breakfasting." We looked at this process on p. 170, above in relation to gains. We now see that it has a part to play in relation to losses; indeed this was its original use. If an investor has made substantial gains in a particular tax year he can neutralise the gains by selling some shares at a loss near the end of the tax year and buying them back the next day. But this process only works for individual investors and only in relation to shares. It was robbed of its tax advantage for corporate investors in respect of shares by the Finance (No. 2) Act 1975, s. 58. As regards gilt-edged stocks, bed and breakfast deals were struck at for both individual and corporate investors in 1971 and again in 1975. See now section 70 of the Capital Gains Tax Act 1979.

EXEMPTIONS AND RELIEFS

An exemption arises where either some asset is expressed to be not a chargeable asset or some gain is expressed to be not a chargeable gain. A relief arises where although there is a chargeable asset and a chargeable gain the full amount of tax is not exacted. (We have already looked at some reliefs at page 169 and this page above.)

Some Miscellaneous Exemptions

Private motor cars are not chargeable assets. Nor are savings certificates, nor betting winnings.

There is no chargeable gain when a person disposes of foreign currency which he had acquired for personal expenditure abroad.

Sums obtained by way of compensation or damages for any wrong or injury suffered by an individual in his person or in his profession are not chargeable gains.

Gifts totalling not more than £100 in value in any one year of assessment do not constitute a chargeable gain. This is an exception from the general principle that a gift is a chargeable event.

Gilt-edged Securities

A gain is not a chargeable gain if it accrues on the disposal of certain specified gilt-edged securities which have been held by the taxpayer for 12 months or more: see sections 64 and 67 and Schedule 2. The list of specified securities has been added to from time to time by statutory instrument and now comprises virtually all government stocks. At first sight this seems a generous gesture on the part of the Revenue, and it was probably introduced to give a boost to the gilt-edged market, but as things have turned out losses have been much commoner than gains in dealings on the gilt-edged market, and the rule that where no chargeable gain (if there had been a gain) would have arisen there can be no allowable loss has meant that this exemption has mainly operated to prohibit losses rather than to exempt gains.

Life Assurance and Deferred Annuities

In principle the receipt of policy monies under a policy of life assurance, or the receipt of the first instalment of a deferred annuity, is a disposal (a disposal of the right in return for the money). But no chargeable gain arises where the money is paid to the original holder of the policy or his personal representatives or trustees. Nor is there a chargeable gain if he surrenders (or they surrender) the policy. But if the policy is assigned for money or money's worth (*e.g.* sold) and then the policy money is paid to the assignee (or the policy is surrendered) that is a chargeable event. This matter is dealt with by section 143.

Private Residences

This point is dealt with in sections 101–105. A gain on the disposal by an individual of a dwelling-house is not a chargeable gain if the house was the individual's only or main residence. This exemption is another instance (remember Schedule A income tax) of the government's benevolent view of owner-occupiers. But the benevolence does not extend (as we shall see) to capital *transfer* tax; for that tax a private residence is no different from other property. The capital gains tax exemption does not apply if the house was acquired wholly or partly for the purpose of realising a gain from its disposal: section 103 (3).

To get the full capital gains tax exemption the house must have been the individual's only or main residence throughout his period of ownership except that it does not matter if it has not been such for all or any part of the last 12 months of his ownership. The point of this exception is (I take it) to meet the case where an individual has moved to a new house before he has been able to sell his old one. If the house has not been the taxpayer's only or main residence throughout his period of ownership (disregarding the last 12 months) a fraction of the gain is exempted corresponding to the period of occupation. In certain circumstances a period of absence can be disregarded.

If the gain accrues from a disposal of a dwelling-house part of which is used exclusively for the purposes of a trade or business or of a profession or vocation the exemption applies only to that part of the gain which falls to be apportioned to the "private" part of the house. (This is a point to be weighed against the income tax advantage of claiming that a part of one's house is being used exclusively for business, etc., purposes.)

A married couple can only have one residence or main residence. If they are not separated it is no good claiming that Mon Repos is the man's main residence and Dunromin is the wife's main residence.

If a marriage breaks down an important Revenue concession comes into play (Concession No. D6). The effect of the concession can be stated in this way. If the husband leaves the matrimonial home while still owning it, capital gains tax exemption will be given in respect of the husband's subsequent transfer of it to the wife, provided that she had continued to live in the house and the husband had not elected that some other house should be treated as his main residence during the period between his leaving the matrimonial home and his transfer of it to her.

Chattels disposed of for £2,000 or Less

Section 128 provides that "a gain accruing on a disposal of an asset which is tangible movable property [*i.e.* a chattel] shall not be a chargeable gain if the amount or value of the consideration for the disposal does not exceed £2,000." Section 128 does not apply to a disposal of currency of any description, nor to a disposal of commodities by a person dealing on a terminal market. A terminal market is not defined but it means a market in which you can buy or sell, *e.g.* cocoa, for a price fixed now but for delivery at some future date (*e.g.* three months hence). It is sometimes called a futures market. Notice that the figure of £2,000 refers to the amount of the consideration, not to the amount of the gain.

Where the amount of the consideration exceeds £2,000 there shall be excluded from any chargeable gain so much of it as exceeds five-thirds of the difference between the consideration and £2,000.

These provisions are very generous to such inflation hedges as stamp collecting. It is nice to be able to sell a stamp from your collection for £2,000, making a gain of say £600, without attracting tax.

But the section is far from generous as regards losses. If there is a disposal at a loss, and the consideration for the disposal is less than £2,000, the consideration is deemed to be £2,000. Thus if a chattel was bought for £2,200 and sold for £1,800 the actual loss (£400) is not allowable; the loss relief is limited to £200.

If two or more assets forming part of a set of articles (say a set of Chippendale chairs) are disposed of by the same seller to the same buyer (or to different buyers who are acting in concert or who are connected persons) whether on the same or different occasions, the two or more transactions are treated as a single transaction.

The disposals of two (or more) quite separate articles qualify separately for the relief. It is no bar to getting the relief that you have (in the same year) sold a table for £2,000 and a stamp for £2,000, or even for that matter two unconnected stamps for £2,000 each.

Works of Art, etc.

Section 147 lays down the rather complicated and limited circumstances in which a gain on the disposal of a work of art or similar object is not a chargeable gain. Putting it very broadly the exemption applies where the disposal is such that the work of art is likely to be accessible to the public.

Tangible Movables which are Wasting Assets

No chargeable gain shall accrue on the disposal of an asset which is tangible movable property [*i.e.* a chattel] and which is a wasting asset: section 127. It will be recalled that a wasting asset is an asset which has a predictable life not exceeding 50 years. This exemption applies (unlike the exemption mentioned next-but-one above) irrespective of the amount of the disposal consideration. The exemption does not apply to disposal of commodities on a terminal market, nor does it apply to assets used solely in respect of a trade, profession or vocation and in respect of which capital allowances have been, or could have been, claimed.

Replacement of Business Assets

Section 115 to 121 are the operative sections here. They provide not a complete exemption from tax but a relief in the "roll-over" form. The relief arises when a trader disposes of business assets (of certain types) at a gain, and uses the disposal consideration to acquire replacement assets. The relief is given by allowing the trader to defer payment of tax on the disposal gain and (instead) to deduct the gain which he makes on the disposal of the old assets from the acquisition cost of the new assets. This will have the effect of increasing the tax payable when he comes (if he does) to dispose of the new assets in the future.

To get the relief the trader must acquire the new assets within three years after the disposal (or within 12 months before the disposal).

The relief applies only to the following classes of assets: (1) any building or structure in the nature of a building occupied and used only for the purposes of the trade, and any land so occupied and used, and fixed plant or machinery; (2) ships, aircraft and hovercraft; (3) goodwill.

The relief is not available if the new assets were acquired wholly or partly for the purpose of realising a gain from their disposal.

The relief applies (as well as to trades) to a profession, vocation, office or employment, and to the occupation of woodlands on a commercial basis. It also applies to certain other activities, such as the discharge of the functions of a public authority.

Disposal of a Business by an Individual aged Sixty or More

This relief is set out in sections 124 and 125. The heading to these sections is "transfer of business on retirement." But nowhere in the text of the sections is the word "retirement" used, and consequently it can confidently be asserted that retirement is not essential to attract the relief. The relief depends on there being a disposal by an individual who has attained the age of 60.

The relief applies to an individual who is 60 or more years of age and who disposes by way of sale or gift of the whole or part of a business which he has owned throughout a period of at least one year ending with the disposal. The relief is on a sliding scale depending on the individual's age and the period of his ownership. He gets a relief of the "relevant percentage" of £10,000 for every year by which his age exceeds 60 and a corresponding part of the relevant percentage of £10,000 for "any odd part of a year" (*sic*). The "relevant percentage" rises from 10 per cent. for one year's ownership to 100 per cent. for 10 years' ownership. So an individual who is 65 or more and has owned the business for 10 years or more gets relief of £50,000, which is the maximum. To take another example, an individual who is 63 and has owned the business for two years gets relief of £6,000. The relief is only given in respect of " chargeable business assets"; that is, assets used for the purposes of the trade. So, if Mr. Smith disposes of his business when he is aged 63, having owned the business for two years and he makes a gain on the disposal of £10,000, of which £9,000 is attributable to the chargeable business assets, the chargeable gain on the chargeable business assets is £3,000. The chargeable gain on the other assets of the business stays at £1,000.

The relief is also available where the business is owned by a company which is a trading company and is the individual's family company and he is a full-time working director of it. And it also applies where the sale or gift is not of the business as such but is of shares in the company. The relief applies to a trade, profession, vocation, office or employment.

Gifts of Business Assets

There is a relief for gifts of business assets which is now enacted in section 126. The relief arises where an individual makes a disposal otherwise than under a bargain at arm's length to a person resident or ordinarily resident in the United Kingdom of an asset used for the purposes of a trade, profession or vocation (or the occupation of woodlands managed on a commercial basis) carried on by the transferor or by his family company. The relief also applies to a similar transfer of shares of a trading company which is the transferor's family company. This relief is additional to the relief provided by section 124 (above), but it only applies to the extent that the transfer was not relieved by section 124. Notice that whereas in section 124 the thing transferred is a *business* or shares, in section 126 the thing transferred is an *asset* or shares. And the relief takes a quite different form. The relief here is a kind of "roll-over" relief, though the phrase used is "held over." What happens is that the gain on the transfer is held over in the sense that the transferor is not charged to tax and the transferee takes the asset (or shares) at the base cost which it had in the hands of the transferor. So if Alec gives a business asset to his son Barry, there is no tax now on Alec, but when Barry comes to dispose of the asset in the future the gain will be calculated on the difference between Barry's disposal consideration and Alec's base cost. So there is no uplift. The scheme is subject to modifications in respect of agricultural property. The relief is available, in certain circumstances, to trustees of settled property.

Charities

A gain which accrues to a charity and is applicable and applied for charitable purposes is not a chargeable gain; section 145 (1). But if property is held on charitable trusts and then ceases to be so held there is a deemed disposal at market value and any gain so accruing is chargeable: section 145 (2).

Turning now to a disposal *to* a charity, such a disposal if by way of gift is exempt from capital gains tax in the sense that neither a gain nor a loss is treated as accruing on the disposal. If the charity subsequently disposes of the property which was given to it, and disposes of it at a gain, the gain will not be a chargeable gain if the gain is applicable and applied for charitable purposes. If the gain is not so dealt with, the disposal will be charged to tax on the footing that the charity is deemed to have acquired the property when (and at the price that) the donor in fact acquired it. (See s. 146.)

Double Taxation Relief

Section 10 provides for double taxation relief in respect of capital gains tax on the same lines as relief in respect of income tax.

CHARGEABLE GAINS OF COMPANIES

We have seen above (at pp. 168 and 170) that companies do not pay capital gains tax as such but that they do pay corporation tax on chargeable gains, at the rate (in effect) of 30 per cent. And we shall be dealing in detail in the next three chapters with the taxation of companies generally. It is, however, convenient to make two points here.

Groups of Companies

There are special provisions relating to disposals between companies which are in the same group of companies. The matter is dealt with in sections 272–279 of the Taxes Act. Putting it broadly, the disposal of an asset from one member company of the group to another member company does not give rise to a chargeable gain or an allowable loss. A gain or loss arises only when an asset is disposed of outside the group or when a company ceases to be a member of the group.

Gains of Non-resident Companies

In general the rules for a non-resident company are the same as for other non-resident persons; see page 168, above. But special rules are laid down by section 15 relating to a non-resident company which "would be a close company if it were resident in the United Kingdom." (For a discussion of close companies see Chapter 22, below.) Every person who at the time when the chargeable gain accrues to the company is resident or ordinarily resident in the United Kingdom and who, if an individual, is domiciled in the United Kingdom and who holds shares in the company shall be treated as if part of the chargeable gain had accrued to him. That part shall be equal to the proportion of the assets to which that person would be entitled on a liquidation of the company. If the attributable part of the gain is less than one-twentieth it is disregarded. Any amount which is distributed to the shareholder within two years of the accrual of the gain is excepted from the charge. Certain other matters are excepted, including gains on the disposal of certain trading assets.

The meaning of this section (15) is rather mysterious. It is expressed not to apply to the gains of a non-resident company which is carrying on business through a branch or agency in the United Kingdom. (This, no doubt is because such gains can be charged on the company direct.) So it would seem that it only applies to gains which accrue to a company which does not have such a branch or agency. But such gains are not chargeable gains. To make sense of the section one has to read into it that the gains are such that they would be chargeable gains if the company were resident in the United Kingdom. Whether a court would uphold such a reading-in seems doubtful.

s.79 of F.A. 1980 General hold over relief for gifts.

PART FOUR

CORPORATION TAX

CHAPTER 20

THE TAXATION OF COMPANIES AND SHAREHOLDERS: GENERAL INTRODUCTION

A company does not pay income tax or capital gains tax as such; the tax which it pays is corporation tax. Corporation tax is charged on the "profits" of the company, and "profits" means income and chargeable gains; Taxes Act, s. 238. The amount of any income shall be computed in accordance with income tax principles (Taxes Act, s. 250 (1)), and the total amount of chargeable gains shall be computed in accordance with the principles of capital gains tax (Taxes Act, s. 265 (2)).

So we have already covered a lot of ground, but, of course, there are many matters peculiar to companies which we have yet to look at.

What is a "company"? It is defined in the Taxes Act, s. 526[1] as meaning (except in certain contexts) "any body corporate or unincorporated association, but does not include a partnership, a local authority or a local authority association." (An authorised unit trust is deemed to be a company, but some special rules apply to it; see Taxes Act, s. 354.)

A non-resident company is not within the charge to corporation tax unless it carries on a trade in the United Kingdom through a branch or agency, in which case it is chargeable to corporation tax on trading income from the branch and on income from property held by the branch and on chargeable gains accruing from the disposal of assets within the United Kingdom in the same circumstances as would make an individual chargeable. In so far as it is not liable to corporation tax, a non-resident company is liable to income tax on the same footing as a non-resident individual.

Until 1965 companies in the United Kingdom were subject to income tax and profits tax. That regime was scrapped in 1965 and replaced by a system of corporation tax in what is called the "classical" form. Under that system a company paid corporation tax on all its profits. Then, if it made a distribution, e.g. paid a dividend, it deducted income tax at the then standard rate and paid over the tax to the Revenue. Thus distributed profits were fiscally discriminated against compared with undistributed profits. Indeed distributed profits were taxed twice; once in the hands of the company (corporation

---

[1] ss. 526–535 is a group of sections headed "Interpretation" and it is well worth looking at.

tax) and again in the hands of the shareholder (income tax). The company and its members (shareholders) were treated as separate entities. This is, of course, jurisprudentially correct, but it is generally considered to be commercially unrealistic.

By the Finance Act 1972 the "classical" form of corporation tax was replaced by the present system which is called the "imputation" system. It remains true that the company pays corporation tax on its profits and the shareholders pay income tax on the dividends, but the two taxes are linked by means of a "tax credit.' It is this link which explains the name "imputation" system. Part of the company's liability to corporation tax is "imputed" to the shareholder, that is, is treated as satisfying the basic rate income tax liability of the shareholder.[2]

It may be asked, why have a tax on company profits at all? Why not simply tax, in the hands of the shareholders, what emerges from the company in the form of distributions? The answer is that that would enable a company to be used as a kind of receptacle in which profits could be stored up tax-free; distribution (and hence income taxation) could be avoided by storing up the profits for years on end and then eventually selling the shares. This "receptacle problem" (a problem for the Revenue) is particularly acute in the case of narrowly-owned companies, such as one-man companies and family companies. Special rules have been devised to deal with such companies, called "close" companies, and we shall look at those in the next chapter but one.

The question whether a particular individual or partnership would gain (tax-wise) by forming a company is not easy to answer except in very general terms or alternatively in minutely particular terms with a full knowledge of all the circumstances of a particular case. In general terms the thing to do is to compare the corporation tax rate (normally, at present, 52 per cent.) with the individual's marginal rate of income tax. We shall shortly see that the corporation tax rate is less than 52 per cent. on capital gains and on income of a "small" company. If he does form a company, the individual trader will become a director and be taxable under Schedule E (and PAYE) (instead of Case I or II of Schedule D) and he will be subject to the rules about benefits from higher-paid employment. He will be better off as regards pension arrangements.

The change from Case I or Case II income tax to corporation tax is done by a discontinuance of the trade (see Taxes Act, s. 118); loss

---

[2] It is equally true to say that the shareholder's basic rate liability is imputed to the company.

relief (income tax) can be carried forward (Taxes Act, s. 172); and roll-over relief (capital gains tax) is available.

The decision whether to trade individually or by means of a company is not wholly, perhaps not primarily, a tax decision. There is one great advantage of incorporation, namely limited liability. Also it is easier for a company to arrange finance (either from inside or outside the business) for expansion. The disadvantage is more (and expensive) paperwork arising from the increasingly stringent requirements of the Companies Acts. And, of course, it must be borne in mind that some *professions* do not permit their practitioners to become incorporated.

HOW THE IMPUTATION SYSTEM WORKS

I want to conclude this introduction by giving a summary in numbered points of how the imputation system of corporation tax works.

(1) A company pays corporation tax on all its profits irrespective of whether or not they are distributed. Let us suppose that a company has an income of £100,000. For the sake of simplicity we will look at what happens in respect of each £100 of that income. The normal rate of corporation tax at present is 52 per cent. So the company's liability to corporation tax is £52.[3]

(2) If the company pays out a dividend (or other "qualifying distribution": see below) it is required to pay to the Revenue (virtually at the same time) advance corporation tax (ACT). This, at present, is at the rate of $^3/_7$, *i.e.* $^3/_7$ *of the dividend.* So if the company is minded to pay out the whole of the after-tax balance (namely £48) of the income, it will pay £48 in dividend to shareholders and $^3/_7$ of £48 in ACT to the Revenue. $^3/_7$ of £48 is £20.57.

(3) This amount of ACT (£20.57) is set as a credit against the company's corporation tax liability (namely £52) on its income. So what the company has to pay at the end of the year in corporation tax is £31.43, that is £52 less the £20.57 already paid. This set-off of ACT against the company's tax liability is only permitted against its liability on income as distinct from its liability on chargeable gains.

(4) An individual resident in the United Kingdom who receives a dividend receives along with it a "tax credit." This tax credit is the same in amount as the ACT; namely $^3/_7$ (in our example £20.57) of the dividend. The individual shareholder (let us call him Albert) is liable to income tax under Schedule F on the aggregate of the

---

[3] In this example we suppose that the company is not a "small" company and that it has no chargeable gains, and we put on one side the effect of capital allowances and stock appreciation relief.

dividend (£48) plus the tax credit (£20.57). That aggregate is £68.57. But the tax credit is, as its name implies, a credit against tax. So Albert, though liable to tax on the sum of £68.57, is credited as though he had already paid £20.57 in tax. If his marginal rate of income tax is say 50 per cent. his tax bill (on this item) is £13.71. This is made up of £68.57 at 50 per cent. (£34.28) minus £20.57 = £13.71. You will see that £13.71 is 20 per cent. of £68.57. And 20 per cent., of course, is the amount by which 50 per cent. (Albert's marginal rate of tax) exceeds 30 per cent. (the basic rate of income tax). So what has happened is that Albert has been credited with the basic rate of tax. That is the key to the whole operation; the tax credit, although it is expressed as a fraction of the dividend, is equal to the basic rate of income tax on the aggregate. Try it out on our example. $^3/_7$ of £48 (£20.57) is equal to 30 per cent. of £68.57. If a particular shareholder is only liable to basic rate tax he has no further tax to pay in respect of his dividend. If he is not liable even to basic rate tax, he can get a repayment from the Revenue. Every time there is an alteration in the basic rate of income tax, the Finance Act takes care to alter the rate of ACT (and hence the rate of tax credit) to keep them in step.

(5) The legislation makes a distinction between "qualifying distributions" of companies (of which a dividend is the prime example) and "non-qualifying distributions." We must now look to see what happens when a company makes a non-qualifying distribution. There are two kinds of non-qualifying distributions, namely bonus securities and bonus redeemable shares. The company making the distribution does not pay ACT. The individual shareholder does not get a tax credit. The distribution in the hands of the shareholder is not liable to basic rate income tax. But if the shareholder is within the threshold for higher rate tax and/or additional rate tax, he will be charged on the amount of the distribution. There will be no grossing-up because there is no tax credit. His bill for higher rate tax is reduced by an amount equal to basic rate tax. So if his marginal higher rate is 50 per cent. he pays tax at 50 minus 30 = 20 per cent. There is no reduction for additional rate tax; he pays that (if he is within the threshold) at 15 per cent. As was pointed out at page 50, above, whereas the higher rates are inclusive of basic rate, the additional rates are not; they are on top of basic rate.

(6) So far we have been talking about shareholders who are resident in the United Kingdom. A non-resident shareholder is not entitled to a tax credit unless he is (under section 27 of the Taxes Act: see p. 45, above) entitled to personal reliefs. But he is not liable to basic rate tax on the distribution and the distribution is not grossed-up. He may be liable for additional rate and for the balance of higher rate. This is so both for qualifying and non-qualifying distributions.

Of course, in any particular case the outcome may be affected by a double taxation relief arrangement.

(7) Now let us consider the situation where the recipient of the distribution is not an individual but a company. After all, a company may receive dividends from other companies in which it is a shareholder. A company which is resident in the United Kingdom and which receives a qualifying distribution is not chargeable to income tax or corporation tax in respect of it. But it has in effect suffered a kind of deduction in that the company making the distribution will have paid advance corporation tax in respect of the distribution. Because this is so, the receiving company is described as being in receipt of "franked investment income," and it gets a tax credit. It can set off this tax credit against its liability to ACT when it comes to make a qualifying distribution itself. This process can be spoken of as "franking."

(8) If a company resident in the United Kingdom receives a non-qualifying distribution, that does not amount to franked investment income. The distribution cannot be used by the recipient company to frank its own qualifying distributions, but it does not attract ACT if it is passed on by the recipient company to its own shareholders.

(9) A non-resident company making a distribution is not required to pay ACT, and the recipient does not get a tax credit.

(10) A non-resident company receiving a distribution does not get a tax credit.

CHAPTER 21

THE CORPORATION TAX

The corporation tax, along with many other taxes including income tax and capital gains tax, is under the care and management of the Commissioners of Inland Revenue, and the detailed provisions for administration set out in the Taxes Management Act 1970 apply to corporation tax.

The substantive law of corporation tax is to be found, for the most part, in Part XI (sections 238–303) of the Taxes Act, and Part V (sections 84–111) of the Finance Act 1972, plus Schedule 16. Part XI of the Taxes Act is a re-enactment of the sections of the Finance Act 1965 which set up corporation tax in the first place. Part V and Schedule 16 of the Finance Act 1972 was enacted to carry out the switch from the classical form of corporation tax to the imputation system. Both Part XI and Part V have been substantially amended by later Acts.

PERIODS

Corporation tax is levied by reference, not to "years of assessment," but to "financial years." A financial year begins on April 1 and ends of March 31. And each financial year is named by reference to only one calendar year and that is the year in which it begins, not the year in which it ends. So the financial year 1978 is the year from April 1, 1978, to March 31, 1979. Assessment is on a current year basis; there is no problem of a preceding year basis; the tax assessment for 1978 is based on the profits of 1978. But where a company's accounting period does not correspond to the financial year, the profits of the accounting period are apportioned into the appropriate financial years. This is important in that the rate of tax may differ in the two financial years. Corporation tax assessed for an accounting period shall be paid within nine months from the end of that period, or, if it is later, within 30 days of the issue of the notice of assessment; Taxes Act, s. 243 (4).

RATES

The rate of corporation tax for any particular financial year is set by Parliament in arrear. For example, section 2 (1) of the Finance Act 1979 set the rate, not for the financial year 1979, but for the financial year 1978; and it set it at 52 per cent. On the other hand, the rate of ACT (advance corporation tax) is set for the current year. Thus, the Finance (No. 2) Act 1979 set the rate of ACT (at $^3/_7$) for the financial year 1979. This is necessary in order to keep ACT in line with the basic rate of income tax.

Companies in effect pay tax at a lower rate on chargeable gains than they do on income.[1] This effect is achieved, not by setting a lower rate, but by decreeing that the chargeable gains are to be reduced *by* a named fraction. The present fraction, enacted by F.A. 1974, s. 10 (1) is $^{11}/_{26}$. So the tax rate (52 per cent.) is applied to $^{15}/_{26}$ of the chargeable gains. The point becomes clearer if one translates $^{15}/_{26}$ into $^{30}/_{32}$. 52 per cent. of $^{30}/_{52}$ of total chargeable gains is the same as 30 per cent. of total chargeable gains. For authorised unit trusts and investment trusts the fraction (enacted by F.A. 1978, s. 17) is $^{21}/_{26}$, which makes an effective rate of 10 per cent.

There is also a special lower rate of corporation tax on the income of companies whose profits do not exceed (per Finance (No. 2) Act 1979) £60,000. This lower rate is at present 42 per cent.: F.A. 1978, s. 17 (2). Apart from the financial limits and the rates (both of which are altered from time to time) the general scheme of the relief is set out in F.A. 1972, s. 95. The section is entitled "Mitigation of corporation tax liability of small companies." This phrase is rather misleading, because it is not the smallness of the company that matters; it is the smallness of the profits. And notice that though it is the size of the *profits* which determines eligibility for relief, relief is only given in respect of *income*. "Profits," of course, is a wider term than "income." Profits for this purpose are profits as reduced by charges on income but with the addition of franked investment income (on which see below). There are tapering provisions for a company which has profits of between £60,000 and £100,000. There are provisions to block the avoidance device of splitting a business into a number of companies in order to get the benefit of the lower rate.

COMPUTATION OF PROFITS

A company is charged to corporation tax on its total profits; that is, its income plus its chargeable gains. (Profits = income + chargeable gains.) It is declared in the Taxes Act, s. 250 that in general a company's income is to be computed on income tax principles, excluding income tax enactments which make special provision for individuals. This, however, does not mean that there are no differ-

---

[1] But the difference is almost eliminated if one takes into account the effect of imputation on distributed profits. See p. 219, below.

ences at all. One difference is that, whereas for income tax the major capital allowances (such as those in respect of machinery and plant) are given by way of *deductions from* profits, for corporation tax they come into the *computation of* profits, the amount of any such capital allowance being treated as a trading expense, and a balancing charge being treated as a trading receipt. (See p. 145 in Chapter 16, above.) But the differences are very minor compared with the broad principle which (I say again) is that a company's income is computed on income tax principles. If the law of income tax changes during the accounting period of a company, the law which applies for the computation is the law applying to the year of assessment in which the accounting period *ends*.

Similarly section 265 of the Taxes Act declares that the chargeable gains of a company are to be computed on the principles of capital gains tax.

The income of a company is allotted to the various Schedules and Cases just as is the income of an individual. So, for example, a company's trading income is assessed under Case I of Schedule D, its income from rents under Schedule A, and its receipts of interest under Case III of Schedule D. The rules for determining what expenses are deductible are as for income tax. Under Case I, directors' emoluments are on the same footing as salaries and wages of the company's employees; they are deductible to the extent that they are reasonable.

The several classes of income of a company together with the total of its chargeable gains constitute the total profits of the company.

DEDUCTIONS FROM TOTAL PROFITS

Having arrived at the total profits of the company the next thing to do is to consider what items are permitted to be deducted in order to determine the amount on which corporation tax is to be charged. There are four kinds of permitted deductions: (1) charges on income, (2) management expenses of an investment company, (3) minor capital allowances, (4) losses. We will deal with these in turn.

Charges on Income

It will be remembered from Chapter 7 ("The Taxation of Individuals") that, for income tax, certain payments out are called "charges on income" and are deductible in computing "total income." Those deductions are separate from the deductions which are expenses in earning the income under any particular Schedule or Case. The position is similar for corporation tax. Payments out which are expenses in earning the income under a particular Schedule or Case are deductible in computing the income of a company under that Schedule or Case. That still leaves some payments out which, although no deductible *in computing* income, are deductible *from* (or "against") the total profits of the company. Many payments are not deductible in either way. Those which are deductible against total profits are called "charges on income": see section 248 of the Taxes Act. Of course deductibility is only completely effective if the charges on income are less than the total profits. If the charges exceed the total profits in a particular accounting period, and the charges include payments made wholly and exclusively for the purposes of a trade carried on by the company, then up to the amount of that excess (or of those payments, if less) the charges are deductible as if they were trading expenses of the trade for the purpose of computing a trading loss: Taxes Act, s. 117 (8). (And see below at p. 215 under "Carry-forward of Losses.") Or, where a company is a member of a group of companies, it may in certain circumstances "surrender" its excess of charges on income to another company in the group: Taxes Act, s. 259 (6).

It is obviously very important to establish which kinds of payments count as charges on income and which do not.

Any payment which amounts to a distribution (whether qualifying or non-qualifying) cannot be a charge on income. This is obvious good sense; if it were otherwise corporation tax would be non-existent, because a company by distributing the whole of its income would escape tax. So the fact that a company has paid a dividend does not entitle it to deduct anything from its total profits. In this connection it is interesting to compare a preference dividend with loan stock interest. To the ordinary investor there might seem to be not much difference between a preference share and loan stock, but in law they are quite different animals, and particularly in tax law. A preference dividend (just as much as an ordinary dividend) is a distribution and so cannot be a charge on income. Loan stock interest (subject to certain conditions) *is* a charge on income. So it is advantageous to a company to raise money by borrowing rather than by issuing preference shares. For this reason in recent years many companies have (by agreement with their preference shareholders) converted their preference shares into loan stock.

"Charges on income" are defined in the Taxes Act, s. 248 (3) as being "(a) any yearly interest, annuity or other annual payment, and any such other payments as are mentioned in section 52 (2) of this Act but not including sums which are or, but for any exemption would be, chargeable under Schedule A, and (b) any other interest payable in the United Kingdom on an advance from a bank carrying on a bona fide banking business in the United Kingdom, or from a person who in the opinion of the Board is bona fide carrying on business as a member of a stock exchange in the United Kingdom or bona fide carrying on the business of a discount house in the United Kingdom." As an exception, the Taxes Act, s. 251 (3) provides that yearly interest payable to a bank in the United Kingdom may, instead of being deducted as a charge on income, be deducted in computing income from a trade.

Although section 248 (3) (above) refers to section 52 (2), that reference is only for the purpose of identifying certain payments, and it must be remembered that a payment by a company can never satisfy section 52 because that section is limited to payments which are made wholly out of profits or gains brought into charge to *income tax*. Thus the payments we are speaking of here fall within section 53 or section 54, and basic rate income tax must be deducted and accounted for to the Revenue by the paying company. (See Chapter 11, above at p. 106.)

But of course a company, as well as making payments under deduction of tax, may be the recipient of such payments. In that case the company is entitled to set off the amount which has been deducted from its receipts against its own liability to account for income tax deducted on the payments it has made. If this is not possible it may set off the income tax which has been deducted against its corporation tax liability. And if this is not possible because the income tax deducted is more than the corporation tax payable by the company then the company can get a repayment of the income tax deducted.

There are various conditions with which a payment must comply if it is to count as a charge on income. The conditions are set out in section 248. In summary, a payment is not to be treated as a charge on income in any of the following circumstances: if the payment is charged to capital; if the payment is not ultimately borne by the company[2]; if the payment is not made under a liability incurred for a valuable and sufficient consideration (except that a covenanted donation to charity *is* deductible); if (in the case of a non-resident company) the payment is incurred for the purposes of its overseas operations.

Where the payment takes the form of interest further rules apply. The payments will not be treated as a charge on income unless at least one of the following circumstances exist: the company making the payment exists wholly or mainly for the purpose of carrying on a

---

[2] Presumably this means if the payment is re-imbursed by some third party.

trade; or the payment is wholly and exclusively laid out for the purposes of the trade; or the company is an investment company; or the interest is on a loan for the purchase or improvement of land and would have been deductible if the payer had been an individual.

Certain further very stringent rules apply to payments made by companies to non-residents: see Taxes Act, ss. 248 (4) and 249.

Management Expenses of an Investment Company

Another possible deduction from total profits applies to an investment company. Such a company, if resident in the United Kingdom, is permitted to deduct its management expenses: Taxes Act, s. 304. The point of this provision is to make up for the fact that an investment company, unlike a trading company, has no opportunity of deducting expenses of management in the actual computation of profits. A similar, but more restricted, provision applies to insurance companies: section 305.

Minor Capital Allowances

Another possible deduction relates to what one might call the "minor" capital allowances. An example is the agricultural buildings allowance. The rules are complicated, but in certain circumstances such an allowance can be implemented by way of a deduction from total profits. (It has already been explained that what one might call the "major" capital allowances come into the actual computation of profits as though they were expenses: see p. 212, above.)

Losses

Losses of companies under corporation tax are dealt with in ways similar to losses of individuals under income tax. The reader is referred to Chapter 17, above.

Let me first make the general point that a loss in a trade is computed in the same way as trading income is computed. In other words, the computation process may lead to a plus answer or a minus answer.

There are three main ways in which a trading loss of a company may be relieved: see the Taxes Act, ss. 177–180.

Carry-forward

The company may claim to set off a trading loss of one accounting period against trading income from the same trade in succeeding accounting periods. For the purposes of this carry-forward relief, if a company in a particular accounting period has an excess of "charges on income" over profits and the charges on income include payments made wholly and exclusively for the purposes of a trade carried on by the company, then, up to the amount of that excess or of those payments, whichever is the less, the charges on income so paid shall in computing a loss be deductible as if they were trading expenses of the trade; Taxes Act, s. 177 (8). See page 213, above.

Set-off against general profits

The company may claim to set off a trading loss in any particular accounting period against profits of whatever description (including chargeable gains) of that accounting period. If the loss is not in this way completely absorbed, it can be set against the profits of preceding accounting periods, subject to the limitation that the loss can only be carried back for such period of time as equals the period of time in the accounting period in which the loss is incurred.[3] (There is a separate time limitation, namely three years, for the carrying-back of a loss which is attributable to the company not having disclaimed first-year capital allowances for machinery or plant. It may help on this point if the reader looks again at p. 146, above.) Set-off of a loss against general profits is not allowed unless either (a) the trade is being carried on in the exercise of functions conferred by an Act of Parliament or (b) the trade is being carried on on a commercial basis. It will be noticed that (b) above is parallel to a requirement for income tax (section 170) designed to exclude hobby-trading from the relief. And the special rules for hobby-farming (section 180) apply to corporation tax as well as to income tax. (Refer to p. 151, above).

Relief for terminal losses

A company can claim to set off a loss incurred in the last 12 months before it ceases to carry on a trade against trading income from the trade in the preceding three years. This is parallel to the relief given by section 174 for income tax: see page 153, above.

Case six

Apart from the above three modes of loss relief there is also a limited relief for Case VI losses. The company may claim to set off the loss against any other Case VI income for the same or any subsequent accounting period.

Company reconstructions

Where a company ceases to carry on a trade and another company begins to carry it on, the change of company is ignored if the funda-

---

[3] The point here is that a company sometimes alters the duration of its accounting period. If it has a loss in an eight-month period, the loss can only be carried back into the prior eight months, even though the prior accounting period was say 12 months.

mental ownership (*e.g.* by shareholding) is (to the extent of three-quarters or more) the same before and after the change of companies. So if Company A has accumulated losses, and its trade is transferred to Company B (and the common ownership test is satisfied) Company B can use the carry-forward provisions and set off the accumulated losses against profits of the transferred trade (but not against other profits).

Change of ownership

Sometimes the converse case arises; that is, the company carrying on the trade remains the same but the underlying ownership changes. There used to be a brisk business in the sale of companies which were bulging with unrelieved tax losses. This commerce was largely struck down by the Finance Act 1969 in a section which is now reproduced in the Taxes Act, s. 483. If in any period of three years there is both a change in the ownership of a company and a "major change in the nature or conduct of a trade carried on by the company" past trading losses will not be available for carry-forward relief. Nor is the relief available if "at any time after the scale of the activities in a trade carried on by a company has become small or negligible, and before any considerable revival of the trade, there is a change in the ownership of the company." The point of this latter provision is to strike at what was once a common practice; keeping a company in existence simply because it was big with losses.

Group relief

A company which is a member of a group of companies may "surrender" a loss to another company which is a member of the same group. This enables the transferee company to claim loss relief: Taxes Act, ss. 258 and 259 (1).

DISTRIBUTIONS

Some payments out made by a company are "distributions" and some are not. A dividend is a distribution; interest on loan stock is not. A distribution which is made by a company resident in the United Kingdom is chargeable to income tax on an individual recipient under Schedule F. A payment which is not a distribution is not subject to Schedule F, though it may be chargeable to tax under some other Schedule. For example, interest on loan stock is chargeable under Case III of Schedule D.

The concept of "distribution" is defined in the Taxes Act, ss. 233 to 237, as amended by Schedule 22 to the Finance Act 1972. The definition is widened where the paying company is a "close company": see Chapter 22, below. A distribution is never deductible from the total profits of the paying company, be it close or non-close.

The definition of "distribution" is involved, but putting the matter broadly it covers (amongst other things) dividends (including capital dividends) and anything else distributed in respect of shares in cash or otherwise out of the assets of the company (meaning that the cost falls on the company) and where the company does not receive any new consideration for that which it distributes. It follows that a bonus issue is not a distribution, because there is no cost falling on the company; and a rights issue is not a distribution, because there is new consideration.

The legislation draws a sharp distinction between distributions which are "qualifying distributions" and distributions which are non-qualifying distributions. The phrase "qualifying distribution" is not defined except by exclusion. The Finance Act 1972, s. 84 (4) declares that "qualifying distribution" means any distribution other than (a) bonus redeemable shares and bonus securities; and (b) any share capital or security which the company making the distribution has directly or indirectly received from another company in the form of bonus redeemable shares or securities. So there are only two kinds of non-qualifying distributions.

The importance of the distinction is this: if a distribution is a qualifying distribution advance corporation tax (ACT) becomes due from the company and the recipient gets a tax credit; if a distribution is a non-qualifying distribution no ACT is payable and there is no tax credit. The different effects of these two situations have been described above in Chapter 20 at page 207 *et seq*. under the heading "How the Imputation System Works." It is desirable to go over some of the ground again in more detail, dealing first with qualifying distributions and then with non-qualifying distributions.

Qualifying Distributions

The company making the qualifying distribution (*e.g.* a dividend) becomes liable to pay ACT to the Revenue at the rate (at present) of three-sevenths of the distribution (dividend). So for every £70 which a company pays to shareholders in dividends it must also pay £30 to the Revenue. The aggregate of the amount of the qualifying distribution and the amount of the ACT which is attracted to it is called "a franked payment": see F.A. 1972, s. 84 (3).

The amount of ACT paid by a company can be set off against its liability to "mainstream" corporation tax, but this set-off (or credit) can only be used against corporation tax on the income, as distinct from the chargeable gains, of the company. In other words, the imputation system only applies to distributions from the company's income and not to distributions from its chargeable gains. In this sense there is double taxation of chargeable gains, once on the company and again on the shareholder when he comes to dispose of the shares (which will have been enhanced in market value by the company's gains).

Let us take an example to see how these points work out. Suppose a company has income of £100 (and no chargeable gains). It decides not to retain any of it. It must provide for tax as well as paying a dividend. The sum goes like this:

		£
Dividend		48.00
ACT		20.57
Corporation Tax	£52.00	
Less set-off of ACT	£20.57	31.43
		100.00

Notice that the underlying rate of corporation tax on company income which is distributed is about 31.4 per cent. This compares with the underlying rate of 30 per cent. on chargeable gains.

"Excessive distribution"

It may happen that a company in a particular accounting period distributes more in dividend than it has got in as income in that period. There are various ways in which that situation might arise, but let us take as an example the case of a company which decides to pay a dividend financed partly from the income of an earlier period. In this situation there is a limitation on the extent to which ACT can be set off by the Company against its mainstream corporation tax. The maximum amount of ACT which can be set off is that amount of ACT which, with the distribution to which it relates, absorbs the whole of the company's income of the accounting period: F.A. 1972, s. 85 (2). Suppose a company in a particular accounting period has income of £50. It decides, in view of the very good income it had in recent earlier years, to pay a dividend of £48. ACT amounts to £20.57 (three-sevenths of £48). Not the whole of this £20.57 can be set off by the company against mainstream corporation tax. The maximum is £15.00, because a distribution of £35.00 together with related ACT of £15.00 ($^3/_7$ of £35.00) would have absorbed the whole of the £50 of company income. This rule boils down to the fact that the amount of ACT which can be set off is equal to the company's income multiplied by the basic rate of income tax: £50 × $^{30}/_{100}$ = £15.00.

(ACT is always equal to basic rate income tax.) Another way of putting it is to say that the set-off of ACT can never reduce the company's mainstream liability on its income to less than the difference between the rate of mainstream tax and the rate of ACT. Apply that to our example. The difference between mainstream rate and ACT rate is 22 per cent. (52 less 30 per cent.). The company's liability to mainstream tax cannot be reduced to less than 22 per cent. of £50, which is £11.00. Its mainstream liability (52 per cent. of £50) is £26.00. Its maximum set-off (see above) is £15.00. After that set-off its tax liability is £11.00.

A company in this situation is said to have surplus ACT; *i.e.* it has some ACT which has not been relieved by way of set-off. There are two main ways in which surplus ACT can be relieved. First, it can be carried back to the two preceding accounting periods and used as a credit in those periods. If that does not relieve it in full then, secondly, it can be carried forward into later accounting periods (indefinitely) and used as a credit in those periods. A third way of dealing with surplus ACT is open to a company which is a member of a group of companies; namely, it can surrender the surplus (so far as it relates to a dividend as distinct from other kinds of qualifying distributions) to its subsidiary company.

Section 101 of the Finance Act 1972 contains provisions to prevent a tax advantage arising from the sale of a company which is big with surplus ACT. The provisions are similar to those in section 483 of the Taxes Act dealing with tax losses: see page 217, above.

Tax credits

The recipient of a qualifying distribution gets a tax credit equal to the ACT attributable to the distribution. If the recipient is an individual resident in the United Kingdom he is chargeable to income tax under Schedule F on the aggregate of the distribution and the tax credit. The tax credit cancels out the basic rate tax applicable to the aggregate. For further details see paragraph (4) at page 207, above. If the recipient is a company resident in the United Kingdom that company is said to be in receipt of "franked investment income."

Franked investment income

A company which has received franked investment income gets thereby a tax credit. It can in certain circumstances get the amount of the credit paid to it by the Revenue.[4] But more usually it will make

---

[4] For example, an incorporated charity can "cash" its tax credit.

use of the credit by setting it off against ACT which it is liable to pay when itself making a qualifying distribution. Suppose a company in a particular accounting period has franked investment income amounting to £3,300, and that in the same period the company makes franked payments amounting to £5,000. Section 89 (2) of the Finance Act 1972 declares that where (as in this example) the amount of the franked payments exceeds the amount of franked investment income ACT shall be payable "on an amount which, when the advance corporation tax payable thereon is added to it is equal to the excess." Well, in our example the excess is £1,700. The amount which, when ACT is added to it, equals £1,700 is £1,190. So the amount of ACT payable is that which relates to £1,190. The amount of ACT payable is thus £510. The company, instead of having to pay the full amount of ACT relating to a franked payment of £5,000 (which would have been £1,500) receives against that sum a credit equal to the ACT (£990) related to its receipt (£3,300) of franked investment income. In other words, the amount of ACT now payable is £1,500 less £990, which is £510.

It is rather heretical to say this, but it may help if one suggests that in a sense the expression "distribution" is a kind of net expression, and the expressions "franked payments" and "franked investment income" are (kind of) gross expressions.

Now, it may happen that a company receives in a particular accounting period more in franked investment income than it pays out in franked payments. In this situation the company is said to have a surplus of franked investment income. How can it make use of it? First, the surplus can be carried forward indefinitely into succeeding accounting periods and treated as though it were franked investment income of those periods: F.A. 1972, s. 89 (3). Second, the surplus can, by virtue of section 254 of the Taxes Act (as amended), be treated as though it were a like amount of profits. Against the surplus the company can set off unrelieved current trading losses, charges on income, expenses of management (of investment companies and insurance companies) and minor capital allowances. Suppose a company has a surplus of franked investment income amounting in aggregate to £1,200. And suppose it has unrelieved losses of £400, a charge on income of £300, management expenses of £200, and capital allowances of £100. Those items together add up to £1,000. The tax credit on £1,000 is £300. The Revenue pays to the company £300. There is £200 left of the surplus of franked investment income. This £200 is carried forward under section 89 (3) of the Finance Act 1972. Similar provisions contained in section 255 of the Taxes Act deal with the set-off against the surplus of franked investment income of losses brought forward and terminal losses.

Groups of companies

Where a United Kingdom resident company pays a dividend (but not other qualifying distributions) to another United Kingdom resident company in the same group, an election can be made (by both companies) under section 256 of the Taxes Act to have the dividend treated as "group income," in which case the dividend is not a franked payment by the payer company and is not franked investment income of the payee company. Similar arrangements apply to payments which are within the phrase "charges on income." The payer company must either be (a) a 51 per cent. subsidiary of the other company or of a United Kingdom resident company of which the other is a 51 per cent. subsidiary or (b) a trading or holding company owned by a consortium the members of which include the payee company.

Non-Qualifying Distributions

Non-qualifying distributions are (see p. 218, above) bonus redeemable shares and bonus securities, or any share capital or securities which are (so to speak) the proceeds of such.

When a company makes a non-qualifying distribution it is not required to pay ACT and there is no tax credit. The reason is that bonus redeemable shares and bonus securities are not in themselves income, but rather the right to receive income in the future.

If the recipient of a non-qualifying distribution is an *individual*, he is not liable to basic rate income tax on it, but he is liable (if he comes within the threshold) to higher rate tax (less basic rate) and to additional rate tax. If the company subsequently makes a repayment of the share capital or of the principal of the security, that repayment is itself a distribution, but it is a qualifying distribution. The individual may be involved again in "excess liability," but he can deduct from it the amount of tax which he paid on the occasion of the non-qualifying distribution.

If the recipient of a non-qualifying distribution is a company resident in the United Kingdom it is not entitled to any tax credit and it cannot use the distribution to "frank" any of its own qualifying distributions. The non-qualifying distribution is not part of the recipient company's franked investment income. If the company passes on the distribution to its own shareholders, that event cannot be a qualifying distribution, and consequently it does not attract advance corporation tax.

TAILPIECE

We have seen that the nominal rate of corporation tax is 52 per cent. We have also seen that the underlying rate of tax on a company's distributed income (after set-off of ACT) is about 31.4 per cent., and that the rate on chargeable gains is 30 per cent.

In practice the amount of corporation tax paid by many companies is very small indeed and in many cases is nil.[5] The main reasons for this are: (1) that interest on loans to finance capital investment is deductible; (2) that capital allowances are deductible (notably 100 per cent. first year allowances on machinery and plant); (3) that there is a relief (which now appears to be permanent) for stock appreciation similar to that which applies for income tax (see p. 63, above).

---

[5] For further dramatic details see Kay and King, *The British Tax System* (mentioned at the end of Chap. 3 above) especially at p. 199.

CHAPTER 22

CLOSE COMPANIES

There is a considerable body of legislation creating a special code of rules for companies which are "close companies." We will be considering below the definition of that term. For the moment let us say that they are companies which are narrowly owned or narrowly controlled, notably one-man companies and family companies.

The background to the close company rules is that, if nothing were done about them, narrowly controlled companies would give tremendous scope for tax advantages to be reaped by their owners. These advantages could be gained along two lines: first, by taking benefits out of the company in tax advantageous ways; and, secondly, by *not* taking out benefits (such as dividends), but using the company as a storehouse[1] and then after many years selling the storehouse.

It was the latter mode of tax avoidance which first attracted the attention of the legislature. Soon after the First World War, in the early 1920's, measures were introduced to curb the storehouse use of narrowly owned companies. The legislation has changed a good deal over the years, but the basic idea has remained constant. Using modern terminology, the matter can be put broadly in this way: where a close company does not pay out in dividend all that it could reasonably be expected to pay out, the shareholders are subjected to tax *as though* they had been paid a dividend. This statutory process is called "apportionment of income of close companies"; the income of the company is "apportioned" to the shareholders for taxing purposes, even though it has not in fact been paid to them.

We must first consider a number of definitions in order to understand what constitutes a close company. When we have done that we will look in more detail at statutory apportionment of income. Finally we will look at the rules which deal with the taking of benefits from close companies.

The places in the legislation where matters relating to close companies are largely to be found are Chapter III of Part XI of the Taxes Act (as amended) and section 94 of and Schedule 16 to the Finance Act 1972.

---

[1] "Storehouse" is only one of the possible epithets for such companies. They have been called "receptacles," "money-box companies," and "incorporated pocket-books."

WHAT IS A CLOSE COMPANY?

Let us first clear the ground by noting that only a company resident in the United Kingdom can be a close company.

A close company is a company which passes either the "control" test *or* the "apportionment" test. The control test can be broken down into two alternatives. A company is a close company if it is under the "control" of five or fewer "participators" *or* if it is under the control of participators who are "directors" (however many directors there may be). Under the apportionment test a company is a close company if, on the assumption that it is a close company and that therefore its income could be subjected to apportionment, more than one half of that income could, on any of the permitted methods of apportionment, be apportioned among five or fewer participators, or among participators who are directors. Of course, a participator may itself be a company. Where that is so, the apportionment process provides for sub-apportionment, and so for the purposes of this apportionment test the persons who count are the persons among whom the income could be *finally* apportioned.

Definitions

In order to understand the above tests it is necessary to look a little more closely at some of the words used in the tests. What follows is only a summary of the very detailed and complex provisions contained in sections 302 and 303 of the Taxes Act (as amended).

"Control"

A person shall be taken to have control of a company if he exercises, or is able to exercise or is entitled to acquire, control (whether direct or indirect) over the company's affairs, and in particular (but without prejudice to the generality of the preceding words) if he possesses or is entitled to acquire:

(a) the greater part of the share capital or issued share capital of the company or of the voting power in the company; or

(b) such part of the issued share capital of the company as would, if the whole of the income of the company were in fact distributed among the participators (without regard to any rights which he or any other person has as a "loan creditor"), entitle him to receive the greater part of the amount so distributed; or

(c) such rights as would, in the event of the winding up of the company or in any other circumstances, entitle him to receive the greater part of the assets of the company which would then be available for distribution among the participators.

There may be attributed to any person all the rights and powers of an "associate" of his and/or all the rights and powers of any company of which he has control either alone or with his associates.

Where two or more persons satisfy any of the above conditions they shall be taken to have control of the company.

(It follows from all this that more than one person—or group of persons—may have control of the company at the same time.)

Summarising the control test, it comes to this: quite apart from director-controlled companies, a company is a close company if there can be found any five or fewer participators who, with their associates, have control in any of the senses set out above. Notice that a person can have control of a company without having a majority of the voting rights.

"Associate"

An associate means, in relation to a participator:

(i) any "relative" (which in turn means husband or wife, parent or remoter forbear, child or remoter issue, or brother or sister);

(ii) any partner;

(iii) the trustees of any settlement in relation to which the participator is, or any relative of his is or was, a settlor; and

(iv) (where the participator is interested in any shares or obligations of the company which are subject to any trust (with certain exceptions) or are part of the estate of a deceased person) any other person who has an interest in those shares or obligations. For this head to apply, the participator need not have a *beneficial* interest in the shares, etc. It is sufficient if his interest is as a trustee or executor. Thus a co-executor (for example) could be an associate of a participator.

"Participator"

A participator is a person having a share or interest in the capital or income of a company and (without prejudice to the generality of the preceding words) includes:

(a) any person who possesses, or is entitled to acquire, share capital or voting rights in the company,

(b) any "loan creditor" of the company,

(c) any person who possesses, or is entitled to acquire, a right to receive or participate in distributions of the company (construing "distributions" without regard to the extended meanings which relate to facilities and interest payments, on which see pp. 233, 234, below) or any amounts payable by the company (in cash or in kind) to "loan creditors" by way of premium on redemption, and

(d) any person who is entitled to secure that income or assets (whether present or future) of the company will be applied directly or indirectly for his benefit.

"Loan creditor"

A loan creditor means (i) a creditor in respect of any redeemable loan capital issued by the company or (ii) a creditor in respect of any debt incurred by the company:

(a) for any money borrowed or capital assets acquired by the company, or

(b) for any right to receive income created in favour of the company, or

(c) for consideration the value of which to the company was (at the time when the debt was incurred) substantially less than the amount of the debt (including any premium thereon).

Notice that a person can be a loan creditor without, in the narrow sense, lending money to the company. This is so, for example, of a person who sells an asset to the company and leaves the purchase price owing.

Bankers (or banks) are expressly stated not to become loan creditors merely by lending money in the ordinary course of their banking business.

"Director"

One might think that one knows what a director is without needing a definition, but there is a definition and it greatly extends the ordinary meaning. The term "director" includes:

(i) any person occupying the position of director by whatever name called;

(ii) any person in accordance with whose directions or instructions the directors are accustomed to act; and

(iii) any person who is concerned in the management of the company's trade or business and is, either alone or with associates, directly or indirectly able to control 20 per cent. or over of the company's ordinary share capital.

The reader may care to re-read, in the light of the above definitions, the passage at page 225, above, headed, "What is a Close Company?"

Companies which are not Close Companies

Certain kinds of companies are expressly stated not to be close companies even if according to the above definitions they might be. These are as follows.

(1) Non-resident companies

At first sight there may seem to be an easy way of escape here, but it must be borne in mind that section 482 of the Taxes Act makes it unlawful (except with the consent of the Treasury) for a company which is resident in the United Kingdom to cease to be so resident or to transfer the whole or part of its trade or business to a non-resident person.

(2) Quoted companies

One can describe these, in broad terms, as companies in which there is a substantial public interest. A company is not a close company if shares (other than any voting shares which are entitled to a fixed rate of dividend, with or without a further right to participate in profits) carrying not less than 35 per cent. of the voting power have been unconditionally allotted to, or acquired by, the public, remain beneficially held by the public, and have been dealt in and officially quoted on a recognised stock exchange within the preceding twelve months. There is no definition of "public," but certain holdings (*e.g.* holdings by a resident non-close company) are expressly stated to be public holdings, and certain other holdings (*e.g.* holdings by a director or his associate) are expressly stated not to be public holdings.

(3) Subsidiaries of non-close companies

A subsidiary controlled by one or more non-close companies is generally not a close company. Such a subsidiary is not a close company if it cannot be treated as a close company except by taking as one of the five or fewer participators requisite for it being so treated a company which is not a close company. One has to bear in mind in reference to this point the apportionment test, and it is possible to get a situation where a non-close company has a subsidiary which is a close company.

To stop up what would otherwise be an easy avoidance device, it is provided that a company controlled by a non-resident company is a close company if the non-resident company would be a close company under these rules if it were resident in the United Kingdom.

It is expressly provided that a company which would otherwise be a non-close company does not become a close company merely by taking a substantial loan from a close company thereby giving the lender what one might call "loan creditor control."

(4) Crown-controlled companies

A company controlled by the Crown and not otherwise a close company is a non-close company.

(5) Certain societies

A registered industrial and provident society is not a close company, nor is a building society.

STATUTORY APPORTIONMENT OF INCOME

If a close company could retain its income, instead of distributing it, its participators would thus avoid income tax, and this is the reason why the Revenue has been given power to counter that avoidance by directing, in effect, that the participators be taxed as if a dividend had in fact been paid.

This power to apportion income (now contained in section 94 of and Schedule 16 to the Finance Act 1972) can only be applied against close companies. Although the point is not entirely certain, it is probable that it can only be applied where a company has been a close company *throughout* the accounting period to which the apportionment relates.

Where the "relevant income" of a close company for an accounting period exceeds its distributions for that period, the excess may be apportioned by the Inspector of Taxes among the participators according to their respective interests in the company.

The sum apportioned to an individual counts as part of his total income, and as its top slice. The sum apportioned is in effect grossed up for this purpose by adding to the sum apportioned such proportion of that sum as *corresponds to* ACT. (ACT is not *in fact* payable, but there are special provisions to prevent a company from securing advantages by waiting for the Inspector to apportion income instead of making actual distributions.) The individual is treated as having paid basic rate tax; he is charged to tax at the appropriate higher rates and additional rate.

Where a participator is itself a company (and a close company) the sum apportioned is sub-apportioned to the participators of that company, and so on until everything has been apportioned to *individuals*.

Where an apportionment of income is followed by an actual distribution of that income, the amount already charged to tax is not charged again on the recipients.

In the case of a trading company or a company which is a member of a trading group no apportionment is made if the excess of relevant income over distributions is not more than £1,000.

An individual is not to be assessed by virtue of an apportionment unless the sum on which he is assessable amounts at least to £500 or 5 per cent. of the amount apportioned whichever is the less

In the case of a company which is not a trading company (*e.g.* an investment company) the Inspector may, if he sees reason for it, apportion the whole of the relevant income for an accounting period whether or not there is an excess of relevant income over distributions.

There are special provisions for the apportionment of certain *annual payments*. It will be remembered (from Chapter 14 , above) that in many circumstances an individual cannot escape "excess, liability" by making a covenant to an individual or to charity. The provisions under discussion here prevent an individual who is a participator in a close company from securing tax relief indirectly by getting the company to make the covenant for him. The covenanted amount is disallowed as a charge on income and it is treated as if it were income of the close company and it is apportionable. This apportionment is additional to the apportionment already described, and there need not be any excess of relevant income over distributions and the £1,000 limit does not apply. Payments made by the company wholly and exclusively for the purposes of the company's trade are not caught.

In certain limited circumstances a similar process applies to *interest payments* made by a non-trading company, if the interest would not have been eligible for relief if it had been paid by an individual.

Apart from the special cases just mentioned, the general principle is that apportionment operates on the excess of "relevant income" over distributions.

The "relevant income" of a company depends upon its "distributable income." The "distributable income" is the aggregate of:

(i) the amount on which the company has to pay corporation tax, less the amount of that tax, and exclusive of the amount attributable to chargeable gains; and

(ii) the amount equal to the qualifying distributions comprised in any franked investment income, other than franked investment income against which relief is given under sections 254 and 255 of the Taxes Act (set-off of losses); and

(iii) an amount equal to any group income.

Distributable income falls into one or other of two classes; it is either "distributable investment income" or it is "estate or trading income."

The "distributable investment income" of a company is the amount of the distributable income, exclusive of the part attributable to estate or trading income, less the smaller of (a) 10 per cent. of the estate or trading income, and (b) £1,000 (or, if the accounting period is of less than 12 months, a proportionately reduced amount).

The "estate or trading income" of a company means: (a) income which if the company were an individual would be earned income; and (b) income charged to tax under Schedule A or Schedule B, and income (other than interest) chargeable to tax under Schedule D and which arises from the ownership or occupation of land or from furnished lettings. As an exception, the income derived from investments of certain insurance, banking, moneylending and similar trades is treated as estate or trading income.

We are now in a position to consider the computation of relevant income. The rules differ according to the nature of the company and the nature of its income.

It is necessary to know what is a "trading company". It is a company which exists wholly or mainly for the purpose of carrying on a trade, and any other company whose income does not consist wholly or mainly of investment income.

In the case of a company which is a *trading company or is a member of a trading group* relevant income means so much of the company's distributable income for the accounting period as can be distributed without prejudice to the requirements of the company's business, meaning not only the current requirements of the business, but also such other requirements as may be necessary or advisable for the maintenance and development of that business, including the acquisition of a trade or of a controlling interest in a trading company or in a company which is a member of a trading group. (There are restrictions on acquisitions from associated companies.)

In the case of a *non-trading company* (or a company which is not a member of a trading group) *which has some estate or trading income* (*e.g.* a land-holding company which has some income from rents), the relevant income means (i) so much of the estate or trading income as can be distributed without prejudice to the requirements of the company's business so far as concerned with the activities or assets giving rise to estate or trading income, and (ii) its distributable income (if any) other than estate or trading income.

In the case of *any other company* (for example a pure investment company) the relevant income for an accounting period is the whole of its distributable income for that period.

For *all* companies there is a maximum limit as to what can be treated as relevant income. Subject to special provisions relating to cessations and liquidations (on which see below) the relevant income of a company shall in no case be taken to exceed the company's distributable investment income for the accounting period plus 50 per cent. of the estate or trading income for the period.

We can now state three general principles which can be seen through the fog of all these definitions: first, the relevant income of a company shall in no case be taken to exceed the company's distributable investment income plus 50 per cent. of the estate or trading income; second, a company can retain 50 per cent. of its estate or trading income without fear of any apportionment, and it can retain more than 50 per cent. if this can be justified by business requirements; third, above those thresholds an apportionment will be made.

Three special points, however, remain to be stated.

There is a *special reduction* available for trading companies. If the estate or trading income of such a company in an accounting period is less than £25,000 it is disregarded altogether. If it is between £25,000 and £75,000, the estate or trading income is treated as reduced by one-half of the amount required to make it up to £75,000. So this is a tapering relief. Let us take an example. Suppose a trading company has estate or trading income amounting to £35,000. This part of the company's income is treated as though it were £15,000, *i.e.* £35,000 less half of (£75,000–£35,000). If the point were left open a large company could come to qualify for this relief by dividing its business between associated companies. This avoidance device has been blocked by providing, in effect, that the reductions are to be applied to a group of companies as a whole.

There is a special rule relating to *cessations and liquidations*. The idea behind this special rule is that a company which ceases to carry on its main activity or which goes into liquidation does not need to retain income. So the relevant income of the company for the accounting period in which such an event occurs, or an accounting period which ends in or within 12 months ending with that event, is calculated on the whole instead of on only 50 per cent. of the estate or trading income (if any), and also no deduction is allowed in respect of the requirements of the business. But sums needed to meet the claims of certain creditors (not being participators and their associates, etc.) are not treated as available for distribution, and so are excluded from the apportionment.

It is possible for a close company (other than an investment company with no estate or trading income) to apply for a *"clearance."* Such a company may, after the general meeting at which its accounts are adopted, request the Inspector to intimate whether or not he proposes to make an apportionment in respect of the relevant accounting period. The request must be accompanied by a copy of the accounts, a copy of the directors' report (if any) and such further information as the company thinks fit. The Inspector can call on the company to give him further information. If the Inspector does not within three months intimate his intention to make an apportionment, no apportionment can be made unless the information given to the Inspector was incomplete or inaccurate or unless within twelve months of the accounting period in question the company ceases to carry on its main activity or goes into liquidation.

THE TAKING OF BENEFITS FROM CLOSE COMPANIES

At the beginning of this chapter we touched on the two possible kinds of advantage that might be reaped from a close company, namely by taking out benefits from the company and by *not* taking out benefits but rather using the company as a storehouse. We have seen how the latter kind of advantage has been restricted by the apportionment legislation. We must now consider the former possible kind of advantage, the taking of benefits out of the company.

The legislation dealing with such benefits falls under three heads, which we will look at in turn. The method adopted by the legislation for the first two heads is to extend, in the case of close companies, the definition of "distribution": the third head can be called a quasi-distribution.

Expenditure on Facilities for Participators and their Associates

Section 284 of the Taxes Act declares that where a close company incurs expense in connection with the provision for any participator or for his associate or for a participator in its controlling company of living accommodation or other accommodation, of entertainment, of domestic or other services, or of other benefits or facilities of whatever nature, the company shall be treated as making a distribution to him of an amount equal to so much of that expense as is not made good to the company by the participator or his associate. Two benefits are expressly excepted from the tax charge, namely (a) (for a person employed in director's or higher-paid employment) such benefits as are mentioned in sections 61–68 of the Finance Act 1976 (see p. 90, above, and (b) benefits on death or retirement for the participator (or associate) or his dependants.

Also there is no tax charge if the participator in the company is another close company and one is the subsidiary of the other or both are subsidiaries of a third company and the benefit arises on the transfer of assets or liabilities by or to the company, provided that all the companies are resident in the United Kingdom.

If two close companies have the bright idea that Company A should provide facilities for the participators of Company B and vice versa, well, the Revenue have thought of that; the facility is treated as coming from the company in which each person is a participator.

The expenditure is treated as a distribution. Consequently it cannot be deducted in computing profits nor counted as a charge on income. As it is not stated to be a non-qualifying distribution it must be a qualifying distribution. So ACT is payable.

Excess Interest Payments to Directors and their Associates

Section 285 of the Taxes Act declares certain payments of interest by close companies to be distributions, with the consequences stated in the preceding paragraph.

The section applies to interest paid to, or to an associate of, a person who (a) is a director of the paying company or of any company which controls or is controlled by the paying company and (b) has a material interest in the paying company or, where the paying company is controlled by another company, in that other company. A director has a material interest in a company if either alone or with associates he controls more than 5 per cent. of the ordinary share capital or if more than 5 per cent. of distributable income could be apportioned to him (or them). "Interest" includes any other consideration paid or given by the close company for the use of money advanced, or credit given, and references to interest "paid" are to be construed accordingly. So the section applies, for example, where a director sells an asset to the close company and the company pays interest on any part of the purchase price left unpaid.

It is only *excess* interest which counts as a distribution. How is that worked out? (1) One first calculates what is called the "overall limit," which is a sum equal to interest at 12[2] per cent. per annum on whichever is the less of (a) the average total over the accounting period of loans to directors and their associates and (b) the nominal amount of the issued share capital of the company plus the amount of its share premium account (if any), taking both amounts as at the beginning of the accounting period. (2) One apportions the "overall limit" between the recipients according to the amounts of interest paid to them respectively. (3) If the amount paid to any particular recipient exceeds the amount apportioned to him in (2) above, the excess is treated as a distribution made by the close company to that person.

The provision which blocks avoidance by means of reciprocal arrangements in respect of facilities, etc. applies to excess interest as well.

Notice that this section (285) dealing with excess interest is aimed at directors (and their associates) rather than at participators. The definition of "associate" (see p. 226, above) applies equally to an associate of a director as it does to an associate of a participator: Taxes Act s. 303 (3).

Loans to Participators and their Associates
Certain loans to participators and their associates are attacked by sections 286, 287 and 287A of the Taxes Act. Without some such provision a close company could make money available to its par-

---

[2] This figure can be varied by the Treasury by Order.

ticipators on very advantageous terms tax-wise. Under this head the method adopted by the legislation is not (as under the two previous heads) to make the transaction a distribution. These loans are not strictly distributions. When it makes such a loan the company is required to pay to the Revenue an amount *as if it were* an amount of corporation tax, and the amount is to be such as *corresponds to* the rate of advance corporation tax. So the amount which the company pays to the Revenue is not advance corporation tax; it is not even strictly corporation tax at all. It cannot be set off against the company's tax liability. On the other hand, if the loan is repaid the Revenue refunds tax to the company.

The loan is not treated as income of the borrower at the time it is made, but if the company releases the debt the borrower is treated as having then received income equal to the grossed-up equivalent of the amount released.

Loans taxable under section 451 of the Taxes Act (see p. 138, above) are excepted from the operation of these present sections.

These sections do not apply to a loan made by a close company in the ordinary course of a business which includes the lending of money. Nor do they apply to a loan to a director or employee of the close company or its associated company if the amount of the loan (with outstanding loans) to the borrower (or his spouse) does not exceed £15,000, provided the borrower works full-time for the close company or any of its associated companies and does not have a material interest in the close company or in any associated company.[3] There are provisions to catch the situation where the loan is channelled through a non-participator.

TAILPIECE

Another tax advantage that can be gained from a close company is that the owners can take out money in the form of directors' remuneration (which is earned income) instead of in the form of a dividend (which is unearned income and so liable to additional rate income tax). At one time this point was dealt with by special rules, but the rules were repealed by the Finance Act 1969. The matter is now left to the general rule that remuneration of directors (and of employees) can be disallowed as an expense of the company in so far as it is not reasonable. The Revenue issued a statement of practice on the point which is printed, for example, in [1973] B.T.R. at p. 423:

"Where directors' remuneration is disallowed for corporation tax

---

[3] Notice that this exception does not apply to participators who are not directors or employees.

1

purposes the disallowance will not rank as a distribution. Where such a disallowance has been negotiated with the Inspector of Taxes the Schedule E liability of the director will be reduced by the amount of that disallowance, provided that the amount disallowed is formally waived and refunded to the company by the director and a satisfactory settlement of the amount to be apportioned (if any) under Schedule 16 to the Finance Act 1972 for that accounting period is reached."

Part Five

CAPITAL TRANSFER TAX

CHAPTER 23

AN OUTLINE OF CAPITAL TRANSFER TAX

Capital transfer tax, if I may be pardoned by the shade of Lord Macnaghten for saying so,[1] is a tax on the transfer of capital. It is not in any way at all like income tax. It is more like an expenditure tax. It is like capital gains tax in that it operates when there is a transfer of capital, but unlike it in that it is measured by the whole amount of the capital transferred and not merely by the gain. It differs from a wealth tax in that (broadly speaking) it taxes capital only when it changes hands, and does not tax capital while it is standing still.

A witty commentator has said that the policy of the capital transfer tax is: "If it moves, tax it." That is a neat statement of the basic principle, but it is not wholly accurate. Sometimes, as we shall see, capital can move without being taxed and sometimes capital is taxed without moving.

Capital transfer tax was brought in by the Finance Act 1975, which received the royal assent on March 13, 1975. The more "routine" Finance Act of that year (August 1, 1975) is the Finance (No. 2) Act 1975, and that Act does not deal at all with capital transfer tax.

The tax was brought in rather hastily, and it was heavily amended by the Finance Act 1976 and to a lesser extent by the Finance Acts of 1977, 1978 and 1979 (No. 2).

The Revenue have from time to time issued Press Notices providing commentary on the enactments relating to the tax. For example, a comprehensive Press Notice was issued on April 8, 1975 which is printed in (for example) [1975] Simon's Tax Intelligence at p. 180 *et seq.* and in part in [1975] B.T.R. at pp. 415–434. The Revenue have also issued a very useful booklet called simply *Capital Transfer Tax*. It is commonly known by its number, "CTT1."

Capital transfer tax is a combination of two ideas; one old, one new. The old idea was estate duty, and in one of its aspects capital transfer tax is a replacement for estate duty (which was abolished, with transitional provisions, by the Finance Act 1975). The new idea is a gift tax, and in its other aspect this is what capital transfer tax is.

---

[1] See p. 8, above.

239

Let us look at these aspects in reverse order; first lifetime transfers, then transfers on death.

LIFETIME TRANSFERS

Section 19 (1) of the Finance Act 1975 declares: "A tax, to be known as capital transfer tax, shall be charged on the value transferred by a chargeable transfer." What, then, is a "chargeable transfer"? The answer is in section 20 (5): "A chargeable transfer is any transfer of value made by an individual after March 26, 1974[2] other than an exempt transfer."

So we need to know what is a transfer of value, what is the value transferred, what is an individual and what is an exempt transfer.

A *"transfer of value"* is defined by section 20 (2) as: "... any disposition made by a person ("the transferor") as a result of which the value of his estate immediately after the disposition is less than it would be but for the disposition; and the amount by which it is less is the *value transferred* by the transfer." Some transactions are expressly stated not to be transfers of value: see Chapter 24.

The word *"individual"* is not defined by the Act, but of course it is a word well-known in tax law; it does not include companies, nor trustees nor personal representatives. However, as we shall see later, certain dispositions made by trustees of settled property give rise to charges to tax as if they were chargeable transfers, and transfers of value made by companies which are close companies may also give rise to tax liability.

Transfers which are *"exempt transfers"* are dealt with in Chapter 24. They form a very important part of the law.

It is also as well to say here (and we shall look more closely at the matter later on) that some kinds of property are designated as *"excluded property."*

It is very important to appreciate that the *value transferred* by a transfer is measured by the diminution in value of the transferor's estate, and not by the increase in value of the transferee's estate. Of course, in many circumstances the result would be the same whichever measure one took. If Albert gives a motor car to his son Ben, Albert's estate is diminished and Ben's estate is increased by the same amount, namely the value of the car. But there are circumstances in which this is not so, and some of them are very important. For example, if Albert owns 51 per cent. of the shares in a company and Ben owns none, and then Albert transfers 2 per cent. of the

---

[2] March 26, 1974 was the date of the Budget speech in which the Chancellor of the Exchequer announced that the then newly installed Labour Government proposed to introduce a capital transfer tax.

shares to Ben the diminution in Albert's estate is much greater than is the increase in Ben's estate, because Albert has given up control of the company, and Ben has not obtained control.

One very important aspect of this diminution principle is that if the transferor pays the capital transfer tax the tax is itself taxable, because his estate is diminished not only by what he transfers to the transferee but also by what he has to pay to the Revenue. The payment of the tax forms part of the loss to the transferor's estate. So there is a grossing-up process. We will deal with this more fully later on.

It will be noticed that the definition of transfer of value includes the word "disposition." But it is provided by section 20 (7) (as amended) that this can be merely the omission to exercise a right. This provision prevents many possible avoidance devices. For example, but for this provision Albert could make a tax-free transfer to Ben (his son) by engaging him, for a lump sum paid in advance, to work for a specified time in his (Albert's) business and then standing by and omitting to sue for damages when Ben does not turn up.

It is stated in section 51 of the Finance Act 1975 (the definitions section, well worth looking at) that "disposition" includes "a disposition effected by *associated operations*" and "associated operations" are defined by section 44. They are

"(a) operations which affect the same property ... or
 (b) any two operations of which one is effected with reference to the other, or with a view to enabling the other to be effected or facilitating its being effected, and any further operation having a like relation to any of those two, and so on; whether those operations are effected by the same person or different persons, and whether or not they are simultaneous, and 'operation' includes an omission."

For example, if Albert transfers some property to his wife Zoë on condition that she shall transfer it to their son Ben, the transfer to Ben may be treated as if Albert were the transferor. The importance of this deeming is that it may greatly increase the tax payable. This depends on two factors that we shall be looking at later on; first, that transfers between spouses are exempt transfers and, second, that the amount of tax payable on a transfer varies according to the "tax history" of the particular transferor.

The word "*estate*" has cropped up several times already. It is defined in section 23 of the Finance Act 1975: "... a person's estate is the aggregate of all the property to which he is beneficially entitled, except that the estate of a person immediately before his death does not include excluded property." Pause to admire the sheer beauty of the last five words—"does not include excluded property." It is quite an important point really, and we shall be considering its significance later on. For the moment the point I want to emphasise about the word "estate" is that it is used in this legislation in reference to a living person as well as to a dead person.

The word "*property*" is stated in section 51 to include "rights and interests of any description." It thus includes (and the importance of this will be seen later) an interest under a settlement such as a life tenancy.

It has been said above that capital transfer tax is (in part) a "gift tax." That phrase is not used in the legislation, but it is made clear by the use of other words—"*gratuitous benefit*"—that the tax only bites on transfers which contain an element of gift. Sales at market value are not taxable because they do not involve any diminution in the value of the seller's estate. If Albert owns a car which is worth £800 and he sells it to Charles for £800 Albert's estate has the same value after the sale as it had before the sale; he has merely exchanged one asset (the car) for an equivalent asset (cash). But suppose Albert sells the car, not for £800, but for £500. That may occur either (1) because Albert wished to confer a benefit on Charles or (2) because he made a bad bargain. A gift (as in (1) is taxable; a bad bargain (as in (2)) is not taxable. This point is dealt with in section 20 (4) which declares:

"A disposition is not a transfer of value if it is shown that it was not intended, and was not made in a transaction intended, to confer any gratuitous benefit on any person and either—

(a) that it was made in a transaction at arm's length between persons not connected with each other, or

(b) that it was such as might be expected to be made in a transaction at arm's length between persons not connected with each other. . . ."

The subsection requires two conditions to be met; a subjective nondonative intent *and* the objective fact stated in (a) or the objective fact stated in (b).

Notice that section 20 (4) has the very desirable result that payment for services is not a transfer of value. If you pay a fee to a solicitor (for example) your estate has been diminished by the amount of the fee, but you are saved from tax by section 20 (4). You need only pay the solicitor, not the Revenue as well.

TRANSFERS ON DEATH

Section 22 (1) of the Finance Act 1975 declares that: "On the death of any person after the passing of this Act [March 13, 1975] tax shall be charged as if, immediately before his death, he had made a transfer of value and the value transferred by it had been equal to the value of his estate immediately before his death. . . ." It is this enactment which brings in capital transfer tax as a replacement of estate duty.

What is the point of deeming the transfer of value to have been made "immediately before" the death, not "on" the death? Presumably it is to knock out any argument that at the moment of death certain interests of the person dying cease to exist and therefore do not form part of his estate. This argument could have been put forward, for example, in relation to the interest of a joint tenant. Moving the deemed transfer from the moment of death to "immediately before" the death also makes it easier for the legislation to lay down its own code of rules, untrammelled by the general law, as to which assets are to be treated as forming part of the estate and which are not. Such a code is laid down in Schedule 10, paragraph 9.

It is important to know what is the tax position if two (or more) persons die (for example in a motor accident) virtually at the same instant. The law of succession to property in such a case is stated in section 184 of the Law of Property Act 1925, namely that the younger person is deemed to have survived the elder person. For tax purposes section 22 (9) provides that "where it cannot be known which of two or more persons who have died survived the other or others they shall be assumed to have died at the same instant." Suppose that the two persons are Albert and his son Ben. The effect is that the estate left by Albert to Ben is charged to tax on Albert's death but not also on Ben's death. Similarly, if Ben has left anything to Albert, that estate is charged on Ben's death but not also on Albert's death. Where the order of deaths *is* known (*e.g.* Albert dies five minutes before Ben) section 22 (9) does not apply, but there may be "Quick Succession Relief": see page 251, below.

RATES OF TAX

Because capital transfer tax is both a gift tax and an estate duty an important point of policy arose as to whether or not the rates of tax should be the same for transfers during life and transfers on death. The Bill as originally drafted provided for one common table of tax rates covering both events, but the Finance Act 1975 finally emerged with two separate tables set out in section 37. The line was not drawn precisely at the moment of death or "immediately before" death; it was drawn at three years before the death. A transfer made on or at any time within three years of the death of the transferor attracts tax (under the First Table) at what one might call the "death rates." Any other transfer attracts tax (under the Second Table) at what one might call the "lifetime rates." This general structure is still retained, but the actual rates of both tables were altered (reduced) by section 62 of the Finance Act 1978.

The fundamental point is that the lifetime rates are lower (except for the very rich) than the death rates. Up to £110,000 the lifetime rates are half the death rates. At that point the rates begin to converge, and at £310,000 and above they are the same in both tables.

The purpose of the difference is presumably to encourage people to distribute their property earlier rather than later, in life rather than on death. And certainly in general it is cheaper (tax-wise) to give property away without waiting for death. But is must be borne in mind that there is grossing-up on a lifetime transfer but not on a death transfer (a point which will be discussed more fully below) and also that a lifetime transfer will in many circumstances attract capital *gains* tax (as well as capital transfer tax) whereas a transfer on death does not attract capital gains tax.

It is very important to grasp that the tax is based on the principle of *"cumulation."* The rate of tax to be applied to any particular chargeable transfer is determined by the whole tax history of that particular transferor since March 26, 1974. When Albert's chargeable transfers since that date reach £25,000 he exhausts his nil rate,[3] and the next £5,000 worth of chargeable transfers will be taxed at 5 per cent., and the next £5,000 worth at 7.5 per cent. and so on. This principle of cumulation is carried over from life into death. If our friend Albert (whom God preserve) were to die having made chargeable transfers during his life amounting to £35,000, the tax payable on his death would begin at 20 per cent., that being the death rate next above £35,000.

SETTLED PROPERTY

It was pointed out earlier in this book that settlements and trusts present great difficulties for tax legislators and consequently for tax students. The difficulties are bad enough in income tax; they are worse in capital gains tax; worst of all in capital transfer tax.

We will deal with settled property in detail later on. For the moment I just want to point out the leading ideas.

The legislation draws a sharp distinction between settlements in which some person is beneficially entitled to an interest in possession and settlements in which no one has a beneficial interest in possession. One can call the former kind of settlement a "fixed interest" settlement; one can call the latter kind a "discretionary" settlement.

In a fixed interest settlement the person having the interest in possession (the life tenant) is treated as owning, not merely his interest, but the whole capital fund. So if there is a settlement of

---

[3] See Chap. 25, below.

Blackacre on A for life, with remainder to B, A is treated as owning Blackacre itself. As a concomitant of this very important idea, B (the remainderman) is treated as owning nothing. This is one context where the notion of "excluded property" (mentioned above at p. 240) comes into play. B's reversionary (or remainder) interest is excluded property. (All the other items of "excluded property" involve a foreign element.)

Discretionary settlements are subdivided according as they were created before or after the advent of capital transfer tax. Such settlements as were in existence before March 27, 1974 are taxed less heavily than those created on or after that date. The details are very complicated but the principle of the thing is that pre-existing trusts are taxed as though the trustees were an individual and as though the trust fund were that individual's estate. Trusts created on or after March 27, 1974 are taxed on the footing that the settlor is the chargeable person.

Another important distinction within discretionary settlements is that certain discretionary settlements, namely "accumulation and maintenance settlements," receive much more favourable tax treatment than do other discretionary settlements.

Let me end this section on settled property by emphasising that though there are special rules relating to property once it has *become* settled property, there are no special rules relating to transfers *into* settlement. Such transfers follow the ordinary rules for transfers in life or on death, as the case may be.

CHAPTER 24

EXEMPTIONS AND RELIEFS

The legislation gives relief from tax in various ways. Some kinds of property are declared to be excluded property. Some transactions are declared not to be transfers of value. Some transfers of value are declared to be exempt transfers, thus attracting no tax. Some transfers of value, though they are taxable, attract a reduced amount of tax.

No great benefit would accrue from expounding the exemptions and reliefs under separate heads corresponding to the four modes of relief mentioned above. The order in which the exemptions and reliefs are expounded in what follows is based largely (but not wholly) on the order in which they stand in the Finance Act 1975 and then on the order in which further reliefs have been added since. References in this Chapter are, unless otherwise stated, to the Finance Act 1975 (as amended).

First come a number of "exempt transfers" mentioned in section 29 and set out in detail in Schedule 6.

Transfers between spouses: Schedule 6, para. 1

Transfers between spouses are exempt transfers. This is true both of lifetime transfers and of transfers on death. This exemption is obviously of immense importance in family planning, by which I mean tax planning from the point of view of the family as a whole.

The exemption is stated (as amended) in Schedule 6 to the Finance Act 1975 at para. 1 (1): "... a transfer of value is an exempt transfer to the extent that the value transferred is attributable to property which becomes comprised in the estate of the transferor's spouse, or, so far as the value transferred is not so attributable, to the extent that that estate is increased." This is a rather curious phrase. The first part of it gives exemption to the straightforward case where one spouse transfers some item of cash or property to the other spouse. The second part of the phrase deals with less clear-cut cases. An example would be a case where one spouse forgives a debt owed to him (or her) by the other spouse. The forgiveness is a transfer of value, but it is an exempt transfer because, although no property becomes comprised in the estate of the forgiven spouse, that estate is increased by the amount of the debt.

The exemption does not apply if the disposition takes effect on the

246

termination *after the transfer of value* of any interest or period: Schedule 6, para. 15 (1). So if H (husband) leaves property to X (any third party) for life and then to W (H's wife) the exemption does not apply. Similarly if H leaves property to X for 10 years and then to W. Also, the exemption does not apply if the disposition depends on a condition which is not satisfied within 12 months. An example would be if H left property to W provided she survived him by 18 months. But the exemption is not excluded by reason only that the gift is conditional on one spouse surviving the other for a specified period. So a survivorship clause in a will does not knock out the exemption provided the survivorship period is not more than 12 months. In practice wills are commonly drawn with a survivorship period of 30 or 60 days.

As an anti-avoidance measure, the exemption does not apply if the spouse has purchased the reversionary interest in the property: see F.A. 1975, Sched. 6, paragraph 15 (4A).

There is no requirement that the spouses must be living together. But if the transferor spouse is domiciled in the United Kingdom and the transferee spouse is domiciled abroad, the exemption has a limit of £25,000 (calculated as a value on which no tax is payable, *i.e.* without grossing-up).

Values not exceeding £2,000: Schedule 6, para. 2

Transfers of value made by a transferor in any one year are exempt to the extent that the values transferred by them do not exceed £2,000. The values are to be calculated for this purpose as values on which no tax is payable; in other words, without grossing up. The year ends on April 5. Unused relief may be carried forward into the next year, but no further.

As husband and wife are separate chargeable individuals for the purposes of capital transfer tax, each can make gifts to (for example) their children up to £2,000 per year without either of them incurring any capital transfer tax.

This exemption only applies to lifetime transfers, not to transfers on death.

Small gifts to same person: Schedule 6, para. 4

Transfers of value made by a transferor in any one year to any one person are exempt to the extent that the values transferred by them (calculated as values on which no tax is chargeable) do not exceed £100. This exemption does not apply to transfers on death, and it only applies to lifetime transfers which are "outright gifts," as distinct from gifts in settlement.

Learned articles have been published arguing that the wording of the legislation is such that this "small gifts exemption" and the "£2,000 exemption" (and some other exemptions) are not wholly independent and that in some circumstances they are not cumulative.[1] The Revenue, however, in their Press Statement of April 8, 1975 at paragraph 13, and in CTT 1 at paragraph 53 have said that they *are* independent. Of course, that does not make it the law, but it is difficult to think of anyone (unless the Revenue changes its mind) who would have an interest in challenging the point in court. So I think one can say that a taxpayer (Albert perhaps) can give up to £100 to any number of different persons in a year and can also make £2,000 worth of gifts, all exempt from tax; *e.g.* £2,100 to B plus £100 to C plus £100 to D and so on through the alphabet (if his generosity extends so far).

Normal expenditure out of income; Schedule 6, para. 5

A transfer of value is an exempt transfer if, or to the extent that, it is shown (a) that it was made as part of normal expenditure of the transferor; and (b) that (taking one year with another) it was made out of his income; and (c) that, after allowing for all transfers of value forming part of his normal expenditure, the transferor was left with sufficient income to maintain his usual standard of living.

This exemption applies only to lifetime transfers, not to transfers on death. It would cover, for example, gifts made by a well-to-do (and generous) dad to his grown-up offspring. Notice that the exemption applies only to payments made out of the transferor's income, as distinct from his capital. For this purpose the capital element in a purchased life annuity (see p. 112, above) does not count as income. There is a special rule dealing with what are called "*back to back*" policies. That is the popular description for a situation where A buys an annuity and takes out an insurance policy on his own life and pays the premiums out of the annuity payments. If A gives the policy to X and continues to pay the premiums those payments are not regarded as part of his normal expenditure, unless it is shown that the purchase of the annuity and the making of the insurance were not associated operations. But it is the practice of the Revenue only to disallow the "normal expenditure" exemption if the purchase of the annuity enabled life cover to be obtained which would not otherwise have been available.

Gifts in consideration of marriage: Schedule 6, para. 6

A gift in consideration of marriage is not defined in the legislation.

---

[1] See particularly David Feldman in [1977] B.T.R. 164.

It has been established by case law that a gift is a gift in consideration of marriage if it fulfils three requisites: it is made on the occasion of a marriage; it is conditional on the marriage taking place; and it is made for the purpose of, or with a view to encouraging or facilitating, the particular marriage: see the Estate Duty case of *I.R.C.* v. *Lord Rennell* (1964) (H.L.).

Marriage is an immensely important occasion for tax planners (and for the happy couple), and it is worthwhile to look at the rules set out in Schedule 6, paragraph 6 in some detail.

Transfers of value made by gifts in consideration of marriage are exempt (if they are lifetime transfers, as distinct from transfers on death) to the extent that the values transferred by such transfers made by any one transferor in respect of any one marriage (calculated net) do not exceed:

(a) in the case of gifts satisfying the conditions set out below by a parent of a party to the marriage, £5,000;

(b) in the case of other gifts satisfying those conditions, £2,500; and

(c) in any other case, £1,000.

The conditions which have to be met to obtain the £5,000 or £2,500 exemption are:

(i) it is an outright gift to a child or remoter descendant of the transferor, or

(ii) the transferor is a parent or remoter ancestor of either party to the marriage, and either the gift is an outright gift to the other party to the marriage or the property comprised in the gift is settled by the gift, or

(iii) the transferor is a party to the marriage, and either the gift is an outright gift to the other party to the marriage or the property comprised in the gift is settled by the gift.

The total that can be bestowed tax-free on the happy couple is considerable, given the wherewithal. The four grandparents of each party to the marriage could chip-in £20,000 and the two parents of each party could contribute another £20,000, making £40,000 in all.

There are limits on who can benefit. To qualify for exemption an outright gift must be to a party to the marriage; and a settled gift can only include certain persons (notably the parties to the marriage and their issue) as beneficiaries or potential beneficiaries.

Gifts to charities: Schedule 6, para. 10

Transfers of value to charities are exempt transfers. There is no limit of amount except where the transfer is on death or within one year of the death of the transferor in either of which cases the limit is £100,000.

Gifts to political parties: Schedule 6, para. 11

There is a similar exemption for gifts to political parties.

Gifts for national purposes, etc. Schedule 6, para. 12

A transfer of value is an exempt transfer if it is made to certain bodies (sometimes referred to as "heritage bodies") being certain galleries, museums, libraries, national collections, universities, university colleges, local authorities, or any government department. The exemption applies to lifetime and death transfers, and there is no limit in amount. The reference to "any government department" makes it doubly sure that such museums as the Victoria and Albert Museum are within the exemption.

Gifts for public benefit: Schedule 6, para. 13

Transfers of value of certain types of property (sometimes referred to as "heritage property") are exempt transfers (in life or on death) if the property becomes the property of a body not established or conducted for profit and the Treasury so direct. The types of property include: (i) land of outstanding scenic or historic or scientific interest; (ii) a building (and land and objects associated with the building) for the preservation of which special steps should be taken by reason of its outstanding historic or architectural or aesthetic interest and the cost of preserving it; (iii) a picture, print, book, manuscript, work of art or scientific collection which the Treasury consider to be of national, scientific, historic or artistic interest; (iv) property given as a source of income for the upkeep of any of the above. The Treasury can require undertakings about preservation and reasonable public access.

Now come a number of "miscellaneous exemptions and reliefs" mentioned in section 29 and set out in detail in Schedule 7.

Death on active service, etc.: Schedule 7, para. 1

This exemption applies to death on active service against an enemy (or on other service of a warlike nature) and to death arising out of such service. The exemption operates by means of excluding section 22, the section which charges to tax a transfer on death.

Cash options under approved annuity schemes: Schedule 7, para. 2

Where, under an approved annuity scheme an annuity becomes payable on a person's death to the deceased's widow, widower or dependant and the scheme gave an option for the deceased to require that, instead, a sum of money should be paid to his personal representatives, that option will not involve that the deceased be treated as being beneficially entitled (under section 23) to that sum. In other words, that sum does not form part of his estate.

Government securities free of tax while in foreign ownership: Schedule 7, para. 3

Certain securities are issued by the Treasury subject to a condition for exemption from taxation so long as they are in the beneficial ownership of persons neither domiciled nor ordinarily resident in the United Kingdom. Such securities are exempt from capital transfer tax in the sense that they are treated as "excluded property." Some anti-avoidance measures were inserted into this enactment by the Finance Act 1978.

Overseas pensions: Schedule 7, para. 4

Certain overseas pensions relating to service in India, Pakistan and elsewhere are to be left out of account in determining the value of a person's estate immediately before his death. "Pension" includes a gratuity and any sum payable on death.

Savings by persons domiciled in the Channel Islands or Isle of Man: Schedule 7, para. 5

Certain national savings in the beneficial ownership of persons domiciled as above are treated as excluded property.

Visiting forces and staff of allied headquarters: Schedule 7, para. 6

This paragraph gives certain exemptions to pay and tangible movables of members of visiting forces (not being citizens of the United Kingdom and colonies) and personnel attached to any NATO military headquarters.

Double taxation relief: Schedule 7, paras. 7 and 8

These paragraphs provide for double taxation conventions and for unilateral relief by way of credit.

Relief for successive charges: section 30

This is generally called "quick succession" relief. The tax charge on a death is reduced if the death occurs within four years after some previous chargeable event relating to the same property. Section 30 (1) says this: "Where the value of a person's estate was increased by a chargeable transfer (in this section referred to as the previous transfer) made not more than four years before his death, the tax chargeable on his death ... shall ... be reduced by the following percentage of the tax charged on so much of the value transferred by the previous transfer as is attributable to the increase, that is to say—(a) by 80 per cent. if the period between the previous transfer and the death was one year or less; (b) by 60 per cent. if that period was more than one year but not more than two years; (c) by 40 per cent. if that period was more than two years but not more than three years; and (d) by 20 per cent. if that period was more than three years."

This is all quite straightforward except for the phrase "the tax charged on so much of the value transferred by the previous transfer as is attributable to the increase." That is a bit tricky, because the increase will always be less than the value transferred (by reason of the tax payable). It seems that what one has to do before applying the percentage reduction is to reduce the tax charged on the previous transfer by this fraction:

$$\frac{\text{increase in value of estate}}{\text{total value transferred}}$$

Let us take an example. Suppose X gives to Y £50,000 as a net gift. Grossed up this makes £52,794, on which the tax is £2,794. Then suppose that Y dies two and a half years later. The relevant percentage reduction is 40 per cent. This 40 per cent. reduction has to be applied, not to £2,794, but to £2,794 multiplied by £50,000 (increase in value of estate) "over" £52,794 (total value transferred). This works out at £2,646. So 40 per cent. of £2,646 (namely £1,058) is the amount of the relief or credit against the tax chargeable on Y's death. Suppose Y's total estate on his death is £50,000. Tax on that is £4,750. Take off the credit and the tax bill on Y's death becomes £3,692. This example, and this whole matter of quick succession relief, may be better understood when the next chapter (on computation) has been studied.

Changes in the value of the property comprised in the previous gift and prior to the subsequent death make no difference.

Notice that although the second chargeable event must be a death (not a lifetime transfer) the previous chargeable event may be of any kind. This can be seen from section 51 (2).

There is a similar (but, curiously enough, more generous) relief applying to settled property in which there is an interest in possession: see page 285, below. Where that relief applies this (section 30) relief cannot apply.

Conditional relief for works of art, historic buildings, etc.: Finance Act 1976 ss. 76–84

It is convenient here to speak of the "old regime" and the "new regime." The old regime (Finance Act 1975, ss. 31–34) provided an exemption for transfers of value of works of art, etc., and certain land and buildings. It only applied to transfers on death. It does not apply to any death after April 6, 1976, but it can apply (as amended) in certain circumstances to a sale or breach of undertaking on or after that date if the relevant death occurred on or before April 6, 1976.

The new regime is set out in sections 76–84 of the Finance Act 1976. The things to which the exemption relates are pictures, works of art, scientific collections, land and buildings which are of outstanding interest. Transfers of value after April 6, 1976 are exempt transfers whether *inter vivos* or on death. Similar provisions apply to property held in a discretionary trust. It is provided (no doubt as an anti-avoidance measure) that for relief to apply to a lifetime transfer the property must have been owned for six years or the transferor must have acquired the property on a death which was itself a "conditionally exempt transfer" (see below). To gain exemption the property has to be "designated" by the Treasury, and "undertakings" have to be given concerning preservation, access, etc. A transfer is then called a "conditionally exempt transfer." It is conditional because if the undertaking is not observed tax becomes payable. Also, tax becomes payable on a subsequent disposal of the property (including disposal on death). There are two exceptional cases where a subsequent disposal is not a chargeable event: (a) if a death or gift is itself a conditionally exempt transfer or the undertaking previously given is replaced by an undertaking given by such person as the Treasury think appropriate; (b) if within three years of the death the deceased's personal representatives (or, in the case of settled property, the trustees or the person next entitled) give the property or sell it by private treaty to one of the "heritage bodies" listed in F.A. 1975, Sched. 6, para. 12 (see p. 250, above) or transfer the property to the Revenue in satisfaction of tax.

The point of the exemption which has been discussed under this head,[2] as distinct from the heritage bodies exemption and the public benefit exemption discussed above (both at p. 250) is that an ancestral home (for example), or a Rembrandt in an ancestral home, can be kept in the family.

A maintenance fund can be set up under section 84 of the Finance Act 1976. It is possible for property to be settled on trusts to finance

---

[2] It is sometimes called the "national heritage exemption." So we have the "national heritage exemption" as well as "heritage bodies" and "heritage property."

the maintenance, repair or preservation of, or public access to, historic buildings or adjoining land without liability to capital transfer tax.

Mutual transfers: Finance Act 1976, ss. 86 and 87

This head of relief did not exist in the 1975 Act; it first appeared in the Finance Act 1976. Where the donee of a lifetime gift makes a gift back to the donor or his spouse during the donor's lifetime, or to the donor's widow or widower within two years of the donor's death, the donee's transfer will be an exempt transfer to the extent that the value transferred by it does not exceed the amount by which his estate was increased by the donor's gift. One could call this "donee's relief."

There is also a form of "donor's relief." The donor or his personal representatives or his widow or widower may claim that the donor's gift should be cancelled to the extent of the value restored by the donee's transfer. If the donee's transfer is not more than 12 months after the donor's transfer the amount to be treated as cancelled is the whole of the value restored; if the donee's transfer is more than 12 months thereafter the amount which is cancelled is the value restored reduced by 4 per cent. for every 12 months that have elapsed between the transfers. (It follows that there can be no relief at all if 25 years or more have elapsed.) Tax paid by the donor on the cancelled amount will be repaid, and also his cumulative total of values transferred will be reduced for the purpose of calculating the tax payable on his next chargeable transfer.

Voidable transfers: Finance Act 1976, s. 88

This relief was introduced in 1976, but it has retroactive effect to March 27, 1974. It refers to transfers set aside by law. An example would be a gift made within two years before bankruptcy, because such a gift could be set aside (under the Bankruptcy Act 1914, s. 42) by the transferor's trustee in bankruptcy. If a transfer is so set aside, tax is repaid (with—tax-free—interest) and also the transfer is wiped out from the transferor's cumulative total of values transferred.

Relief for business property: Finance Act 1976, s. 73 and Schedule 10

This relief was brought in in 1976 in response to claims that without some such relief many small businesses would face closure because of the tax on transfers, *e.g.* from father to son. The relief has been liberalised by subsequent amendments and now stands as follows for transfers of value made after October 26, 1977. Transfers of value in this context include not only lifetime transfers but also transfers on death and chargeable events in relation to settled property.

Where the whole or part of the value transferred by a transfer of value is attributable to the value of any relevant business property, the whole or that part of the value transferred shall be treated as reduced by the "appropriate" percentage. The value transferred is to be calculated as a value on which no tax is chargeable, *i.e.* without grossing up. Relevant business property means:

(i) a business or interest in a business;

(ii) shares in or securities of a company which gave the transferor control of the company;

(iii) minority shareholdings in a company whose shares are not quoted on a recognised stock exchange; and

(iv) any land or building, machinery or plant which was used wholly or mainly for the purposes of a business carried on by a company of which the transferor had control or by a partnership of which he was a partner.

Certain items are excluded from the definition of relevant business property, *e.g.* shares or securities of a company which is in process of liquidation.

And, putting it broadly, property is not relevant business property unless it has been owned by the transferor throughout the two years immediately preceding the transfer. But there are provisions adjusting this rule where there have been replacements of property or acquisitions of property on death.

The "appropriate" percentage reductions are: 50 per cent. for property falling within (i) or (ii) above; 20 per cent. for property within (iii) above; 30 per cent. for property within (iv) above. Notice that (iv) is directed to a case where an individual owns the item of property which is used by the company or partnership. It quite commonly happens in practice. The relief on such an item is only a 30 per cent. reduction, whereas if the item had been owned by the company it would (indirectly) have enjoyed a 50 per cent. reduction. And for (iv) to apply at all the transferor's interest in the business or company must itself be relevant business property.

Business property relief is not available on so much of the value of any property as receives agricultural property relief (see below).

Relief for agricultural property: Finance Act 1975, s. 35 and Schedule 8

This relief applies to lifetime transfers and transfers on death, and it applies to transfers into settlement as well as to "outright" transfers.

Hobby farmers and deathbed purchasers of farms are excluded from the relief; for the relief to apply, both the transferor and the land must fulfil certain conditions. The transferor must have been a working farmer in not less than five of the seven years ending with April 5, immediately preceding the transfer; that is, he must have been wholly or mainly engaged in farming as a trader (alone or in partnership) or as an employee or director of a farming company, or as a full-time student. A person who inherits a farm from his or her spouse, provided the spouse fulfilled the above condition, can transfer the farm with benefit of the relief.

For the land to qualify it must be agricultural property in the United Kingdom, and it must be occupied by the transferor or by a company controlled by him for the purposes of agriculture at the time of the transfer and throughout the two years immediately preceding the transfer. If one farm has been replaced by another, it is sufficient if occupation of the farms viewed together lasted for at least two out of the five years immediately preceding the transfer. If a "qualified" farmer retires from farming and allows a member of his family to occupy and farm the property, agricultural relief is available on the farmer's death.

The relief, where it is available, takes the form of reducing by one-half the "agricultural value of the agricultural property" (which is described as the "part eligible for relief"). "Agricultural property" means "agricultural land or pasture and includes woodland if occupied with agricultural land or pasture and the occupation is ancillary to that of the agricultural land or pasture; and also includes such cottages, farm buildings and farm-houses, together with the land occupied with them, as are of a character appropriate to the property": Schedule 8, paragraph 7. "The agricultural value" is "the value which would be the value of the property if the property were subject to a perpetual covenant prohibiting its use otherwise than as agricultural property": Schedule 8, paragraph 8.

Let us take an example. Suppose A at his death owns 500 acres of farming land, with an open market value of £700 per acre, but an agricultural value of only £560 per acre (a matter for valuers). The open market value of the land will be £700 × 500 = £350,000. The agricultural value will be £560 × 500 = £280,000. £280,000 reduced by half gives £140,000. The chargeable value of the land will be:

£70,000 (the part not eligible for relief)
plus £140,000 (the part eligible for relief, after the reduction)

= £210,000

There is a maximum limit on the amount of relief which can be obtained. The limit is whichever of the following alternatives is more beneficial to the taxpayer:

(a) the "part eligible for relief" does not exceed £250,000;
(b) the area of the agricultural property does not exceed 1,000 acres.
(In the example given above full relief could be obtained, because, although the (a) limit was exceeded, the (b) limit was not.)

The limits are cumulative for each transferor; that is, account is taken of all his previous chargeable transfers in respect of which the relief has been given.

Transfers of shares or debentures in a farming company controlled by the transferor can qualify for agricultural property relief.

Although, as we said above at page 255, a farmer cannot have business property relief and agricultural property relief on the same part of any property, a farmer can have business property relief (if he qualifies for it) to the extent that agricultural property relief is not available, *e.g.* because the maximum limit has been passed.

Relief for woodlands: Finance Act 1975, s. 36 and Schedule 9

Relief is available where any part of the value of a person's estate immediately before his death is attributable to the value of land in the United Kingdom on which trees or underwood are growing but which is not agricultural property. Deathbed purchases of woodland as a tax avoidance ploy will not work. For the relief to apply the deceased must have been beneficially entitled to the land throughout the five years immediately before his death or have become beneficially entitled to it otherwise than for a consideration in money or money's worth.

The relief takes the form of leaving out of account, in determining the value transferred on death, the value of the trees or underwood. Notice that the relief does not apply to a lifetime transfer and also that it is only the value of the timber which is relieved, not the value of the land on which it is growing.

The relief is not absolute; a subsequent disposal of the timber can give rise to a retrospective charge to tax. This will be so if the disposal occurs otherwise than on a subsequent death. Tax will be charged on the sale proceeds if the disposal is for full consideration; otherwise on the then net value of the timber. Business property relief (see above at p. 254) is available (at 50 per cent.) if the timber would have qualified for that relief at the time of the death. If the disposal following the death is itself a chargeable transfer, there will be a tax charge on that disposal as well as the retrospective tax charge relating to the death, but the value transferred by the disposal will be calculated as if the value of the trees or underwood had been reduced by the amount of tax charged in respect of the death.

If another death occurs, and there has been no disposal between the first death and the second death, the second death wipes out any possibility of a tax charge arising in respect of the first death.

Dispositions for maintenance of family: Finance Act 1975, s. 46

The official Revenue view is that section 46 only applies to lifetime transfers, and not to transfers on death. The point has never been tested in the courts, but the Revenue view is almost certainly correct, for one or other (or both) of two reasons: (1) The section uses the word "disposition." It is noticeable that the section relating to death (section 22) nowhere uses the word "disposition." It would seem to be a fair inference that wherever in the capital transfer tax legislation the word "disposition" occurs the enactment is referring only to lifetime transfers. (2) The section uses the phrase "not a transfer of value," and it may well be (as some commentators assume) that wherever the legislation gives an exemption by saying that such-and-such shall "not be a transfer of value" that exemption is confined to lifetime transfers and does not cover transfers on death. Points (1) and (2) come to much the same thing in practice, because a "not a transfer of value" section almost always includes the word "disposition" and where it does not include that word then either other words in the section or sheer physical facts exclude transfers on death.

Section 46 (1) declares that a disposition is not a transfer of value if it is made by one party to a marriage in favour of the other party or of a child of either party and is:

(a) for the maintenance of the other party, or

(b) for the maintenance, education or training of the child for a period ending not later than the year in which he attains the age of 18 or, after attaining that age, ceases to undergo full-time education or training.

"Child" includes a step-child and an adopted child. A similar disposition in favour of an illegitimate child is exempt, but in this case only if the child is the child of the disponer (not of the other party to the marriage). A similar disposition in favour of a child who is someone else's child is exempt if the child is not in the care of a parent of his. But in this case, if the disposition is made after the child attains 18 years of age, it is only exempt if the child has for substantial periods before attaining that age been in the care of the disponer.

Also, a disposition is not a transfer of value if it is made in favour of a dependent relative of the disponer and is a reasonable provision for his care or maintenance. Here there is an explicit reference to reasonableness (of amount), whereas in the case of a disposition to a spouse or child there is no explicit mention of reasonableness. However, such a limit seems to be implicit, because it is stated that, where a disposition satisfies the conditions to a limited extent only, so much of it as satisfies them and so much of it as does not satisfy them shall be treated as separate dispositions.

The section gives exemption to a disposition made on the occasion of a decree of divorce or nullity. But it equally applies to a disposition made during an on-going marriage. It is true that so far as a disposition to a spouse is concerned section 46 is not needed because a transfer to a spouse is exempt anyway, but so far as a child is concerned section 46 is very useful as it exempts a payment made by a parent to assist (for example) a child who is a student if the payment is outside the "normal expenditure out of income" exemption (see p. 248, above).

The section is made to apply to a disposition on the occasion of the dissolution or annulment of a marriage (and to a disposition varying a disposition so made) by subsection (6) which provides that in relation to those events "marriage" (see subsection (1)) includes a former marriage. In *G.* v. *G.* (1975) a High Court judge held that the court has power to defer a decree absolute in order to prevent capital transfer tax arising. But one wonders whether such deferment is really necessary. Would not a transfer ordered by a divorce court, shortly after decree absolute, be *on the occasion* of the dissolution? Moreover, in a Practice Note issued on August 20, 1975 it was stated with the agreement of the Revenue that transfers on the order of a court in relation to divorce would normally be exempt from capital transfer tax on another ground, namely as not being intended to confer any gratuitous benfit within the meaning of section 20 (4).

Alteration of dispositions taking effect on death, etc.: Finance Act 1975, s. 47 and Finance Act 1978, s. 68

This topic was originally dealt with by section 47 of the Finance Act 1975. That enactment has to a great extent been replaced by section 68 of the Finance Act 1978, but some parts of section 47 (as amended) remain in force. So one needs to look at both Acts.

The scheme of the sections is this: certain re-arrangements of the deceased's estate shall not be treated as transfers of value and tax shall be charged on the death as if the deceased had left his property in accordance with the re-arrangements. The main provisions can be stated in five numbered points.

(1) By the Finance Act 1978, s. 68, where within two years after a person's death any beneficiary makes (after April 10, 1978) an instrument in writing which effects a variation or disclaimer of any of the dispositions (whether effected by will or under the law relating to intestacy or otherwise) of the property comprised in the deceased's estate immediately before his death, the variation or disclaimer shall not be a transfer of value and tax shall be charged as if the variation

had been effected by the deceased or (as the case may be) the disclaimed benefit had never been conferred. In the case of a variation, written notice of election must be given to the Revenue within six months after the date of the instrument by the parties thereto and also, where the variation results in additonal tax being payable, by the deceased's personal representatives. But the personal representatives can only decline to join in an election if insufficient assets are held by them for discharging the additional tax. Additional tax could become payable, for example, if some item of property which had been left by the deceased to his widow is now, by family agreement, to go to his daughter. The section does not apply to a variation or disclaimer which is made for any consideration in money or money's worth other than consideration consisting of the making of another variation or disclaimer relating to the same estate. For the purpose of this section the deceased's estate includes excluded property but not settled property in which he had an interest in possession. It does not matter whether or not the administration of the estate is complete, and it does not matter that a benefit has been received under the original dispositions, and there is no objection to the variations extending beyond the deceased's family or beyond the original beneficiaries. Where a variation results in property being held in trust for a person for a period which ends not more than two years after the death the disposition at the end of the period is treated as though it had had effect from the beginning of the period.

(2) By the Finance Act 1975, s. 47 (1A), where by his will a settlor creates a settlement in which there is no interest in possession, but within two years of death the settled capital is paid to a beneficiary, or a person acquires a beneficial interest in possession, or the settlement becomes an accumulation and maintenance settlement then the event in question will not be a capital distribution (though it will be a distribution payment)[3] and tax will be charged on the death as though the event in question had been provided for by the will.

(3) Section 47 (1B) deals with the case where assets are left to a legatee with a request (which is not legally binding) that the legatee should distribute them in accordance with the testator's wishes. If within two years after the death the legatee does so distribute the assets, the transfers by the legatee are not transfers of value and tax shall be charged in relation to the death as if the property had been bequeathed by the will to the transferees. (Such a provision in a will is called a precatory trust; it is quite common, particularly in respect of household effects, etc.)

---

[3] The significance of this will become clearer to the reader when he has read Chap. 27, below.

(4) Section 47 (3) deals with the case where a surviving spouse elects, under section 47A of the Administration of Estates Act 1925, to redeem for a capital sum his or her life interest which arises under the intestacy rules. Where such an election is made, the election does not count as a transfer of value and tax is charged in relation to the death on the footing that the surviving spouse had from the outset been entitled to the capital sum.

(5) By section 47 (4) where a person becomes entitled (on death or otherwise) to an interest in settled property but disclaims the interest, then, if the disclaimer is not made for a consideration in money or money's worth, the capital transfer tax provisions shall apply as if he had not become entitled to the interest.

Family provision orders: Finance Act 1976, s. 122

A court has power, under the Inheritance (Provision for Family and Dependants) Act 1975 to order that provision be made for the family and dependants of a deceased person out of his estate, and for this purpose to change the destination of property. Section 122 of the Finance Act 1976 enacts that when a court makes an order of this kind the property shall be treated for the purposes of capital transfer tax as if it had on the deceased's death devolved in accordance with the order.

Dispositions allowable for income tax: Finance Act 1976, s. 89 (1)

A disposition made by any person is not a transfer of value if it is allowable in computing that person's profits or gains for the purposes of income tax or corporation tax. This provision in F.A. 1976, s. 89 (1) replaces paragraph 9 of Schedule 6 to F.A. 1975, which is repealed. It is difficult to think of a disposition which is allowable for income tax (or corporation tax) and yet which would need this section to protect it from capital transfer tax; most commonly such a disposition would be a disposition for value and would consequently be excluded from capital transfer tax by section 20 (4) of F.A. 1975 (no gratuitous intent). Perhaps certain kinds of business gifts would "fit the bill."

Dispositions conferring retirement benefits: Finance Act 1976, s. 89 (2)

Contributions to approved retirement benefit schemes for employees and also dispositions to provide in some other way comparable benefits on or after retirement for an employee not connected with the disponer, or, after the death of the employee, for his widow or dependants, are not transfers of value.

Dispositions by close company on trust for benefit of employees: Finance Act 1976, s. 90

A disposition of property made to trustees by a close company whereby the property is to be held on trust for the employees is not a transfer of value. The conditions of exemption are very strict (despite some relaxation by F.A. 1978) and it seems likely that not much use will be made of this provision.

Employee trusts set up by an individual: Finance Act 1978, s. 67

This topic used to be dealt with in section 90 of the Finance Act 1976. It is now separately dealt with by section 67 of F.A. 1978. The relief is similar to that relating to close companies (see preceding paragraph).

Waiver of remuneration: Finance Act 1976, s. 91

Sometimes an employee, or more commonly a director, waives (or repays) his remuneration for a period to his employer (company). If nothing were done about it, such waiver or repayment would be a chargeable transfer by the employee or director. Section 91 declares that the waiver or repayment shall not be a transfer of value provided that it is brought into charge in computing the profits or gains of the employer for income tax or corporation tax.

Waiver of dividends: Finance Act 1976, s. 92

A person who waives any dividend on shares of a company within 12 months *before* any right to the dividend has accrued does not by reason of the waiver make a transfer of value.

TAILPIECE

After such a long chapter on Exemptions and Reliefs, the reader may be thinking that there is not much left of the tax. But the reality is that, though the exemptions and reliefs take a long time in the telling, there is plenty indeed for the tax to bite on.

In the next chapter we shall look to see the strength of the bite.

CHAPTER 25

COMPUTATION[1]

Capital transfer tax is charged on any lifetime transfer of value which is a chargeable transfer, and also on the quasi-transfer of value deemed to be made by a deceased person immediately before his death. In the case of a lifetime transfer the charge is on the value transferred. In the case of a deemed transfer on death the charge is on the value of the deceased's estate. Section 20 (4) declares that: "... a transfer of value is any disposition made by a person ("the transferor") as a result of which the value of his estate is less than it would be but for the disposition; and the amount by which it is less is the value transferred by the transfer." So for a lifetime transfer, one has to compare the value of the transferor's estate (remember that "estate" can refer to a living person's wealth, as well as to a dead person's) before the transfer with its value after the transfer. For a death transfer this comparison does not arise. (The tax charges relating to settled property are discussed in Chapter 27.)

RATES OF TAX

The tax is charged at rates which are laid down in tables in section 37 of the Finance Act 1975 (as amended). It is very much a progressive tax, each slice of value transferred being taxed at a higher rate. There are two tables, called simply "First Table" and "Second Table." The First Table is "the appropriate Table for a transfer made on or at any time within three years of the death of the transferor," and the Second Table is "the appropriate Table for any other transfer." Naturally, a transferor does not (usually, anyway) know in advance that he is going to die within three years after making a transfer, so in the first instance a living transferor calculates the tax on the Second Table. If he does come to die within three years the Revenue makes a retrospective re-calculation of tax: see below.

The Tables are as follows:

---

[1] Reference in this Chapter, unless otherwise stated, are to the Finance Act 1975.

FIRST TABLE

| Portion of value | | Rate of tax |
Lower limit £	Upper limit £/*50,000*	Per cent.
0	25,000	Nil
25,000	30,000	10
30,000	35,000	15
35,000	40,000	20
40,000	50,000	25
50,000	60,000	30
60,000	70,000	35
70,000	90,000	40
90,000	110,000	45
110,000	130,000	50
130,000	160,000	55
160,000	510,000	60
510,000	1,010,000	65
1,010,000	2,010,000	70
2,010,000	—	75

SECOND TABLE

| Portion of value | | Rate of tax |
Lower limit £	Upper limit £	Per cent.
0	25,000	Nil
25,000	30,000	5
30,000	35,000	$7\frac{1}{2}$
35,000	40,000	10
40,000	50,000	$12\frac{1}{2}$
50,000	60,000	15
60,000	70,000	$17\frac{1}{2}$
70,000	90,000	20
90,000	110,000	$22\frac{1}{2}$
110,000	130,000	$27\frac{1}{2}$
130,000	160,000	35
160,000	210,000	$42\frac{1}{2}$
210,000	260,000	50
260,000	310,000	55
310,000	510,000	60
510,000	1,010,000	65
1,010,000	2,010,000	70
2,010,000	—	75

It will be seen that the lifetime rates are lower than the death rates (as was pointed out at p. 244, above). Up to £110,000 the lifetime rates are half the death rates. At that point the rates begin to converge, and at £310,000 they are the same in both tables. So, except for very large transfers, there is an inducement to transferors to make their gifts, etc. in life rather than waiting for death. On the other hand, a lifetime transfer may have to be grossed up (see below) whereas a death transfer is not grossed up, and also a lifetime transfer may well attract capital *gains* tax whereas a transfer on death does not attract that tax.

The portion of value between 0 and £25,000 enjoys what is called a "nil rate." This is sometimes loosely described as an exemption, but that is not correct, and I suggest that a great deal of confusion will be avoided if one makes a resolution never to refer to it as an exemption but always as a nil rate of tax.

Capital transfer tax is not only a tax on "the rich." After all, quite a modest house is worth more than £25,000 nowadays. *Now/50 -ow*

THE CUMULATIVE PRINCIPLE

There are half a dozen or so *leading ideas* in capital transfer tax, and one of them is that the tax is applied on a cumulative basis to all the chargeable transfers made by any one particular individual. This point was made at p. 244, above, but it deserves to be mentioned again. It would be nice and neat if one could say that cumulation applies to all the transfers made by an individual throughout his life, from the cradle to the grave. But that is only strictly true of an individual who was born after March 26, 1974. For those of us who arrived in the cradle before that date, one has to say that cumulation applies to all *chargeable* transfers, which is another way of saying (see section 20 (5)) all transfers of value (other than exempt transfers) made after March 26, 1974. The cumulation principle carries over from life into death. If an individual makes chargeable transfers in his lifetime amounting in aggregate to £50,000, tax on his death (see First Table) begins at 30 per cent.

Death within three years after transfer

If a transferor makes a chargeable transfer and fails to survive for the next three years extra tax becomes payable because the transfer now falls within the First Table, not the Second. Liability for the extra tax falls on the transferee (not on the transferor's executors). Cumulation is not affected and (on the other hand) there is no question of "de-grossing." Take an example. Suppose X has already made chargeable transfers of £50,000 (gross), so that his next gift on the lifetime Table will be charged at 15 per cent. He wants to make a gift to Y of £10,000 (gross). He pays to the Revenue £1,500 tax, and he pays to Y £8,500. Two years later X dies. The Revenue now claim extra tax from Y. The £10,000 moves over from the Second Table, where it attracted tax (at 15 per cent.) amounting to £1,500, to the First Table where the tax (at 30 per cent.) amounts to £3,000. Y has to pay to the Revenue £1,500 to make up the difference. There are provisions in the Finance Act 1976 (section 99 and Schedule 12) dealing with the situation where additional tax becomes payable but the gift has fallen in value between the time of the gift and the subsequent death. The additional tax payable cannot exceed the difference between the tax already paid and the tax (at death rates) on the value of the gift at the time of death. If the property has been sold before the death, then the extra tax is limited to the difference between the tax already paid and tax (at death rates) on the sale proceeds. This relief does not apply if the property in question is movable plant or machinery or if it is tangible movable property that is a wasting asset, such as motor cars and most household goods.

Transfers of more than one property

It is provided by section 43 (1) that where the value transferred by a chargeable transfer is determined by reference to the values of more than one property the tax chargeable on the value transferred shall be attributed to the respective values in the proportions which they bear to their aggregate, but subject to any provision reducing the amount of tax attributable to the value of any particular property. The "but subject" part of the subsection means that if, for example, on death X leaves a farm to Y and shares in Unilever Limited to Z, Z does not enjoy any part of the agricultural property relief. The main part of the subsection means that, for example, if A leaves property worth £60,000 to B and property worth £40,000 to C, the tax is spread evenly over the whole value transferred. The gift to B bears 60 per cent. of the tax bill and the gift to C bears 40 per cent.

Transfers on the same day

Transfers on the same day by the same transferor present some difficulty. The basic principle is stated in section 43 (2): where the value transferred by more than one chargeable transfer made by the same person on the same day depends on the order in which the transfers are made, they shall be treated as made in the order which results in the lowest value chargeable. For example, if on the same day A makes a gift to B (A paying the tax) and a separate gift to C (C paying the tax), the gift to B will have to be grossed-up, whereas the gift to C will not. So it is "cheaper" in tax to count the gift to B before the gift to C, because the grossing-up will come at a point lower down the scale. The legislation permits that. Then, the order of the gifts having been established, section 43 (3) declares that there shall be an "effective rate," namely the tax which would have been charged if the transfers had been a single transfer. So A pays tax on the gift to B and C pays tax on the gift to himself, both at the same rate.

Transfers reported late

This is dealt with by section 114 of the Finance Act 1976. Where an earlier transfer is not notified to the Revenue until after the tax has been paid on a later transfer, the earlier transfer is to be treated as made on the date on which it was discovered or, if the later transfer was on death, immediately before the death transfer. (But if the *rate* of tax has altered between the actual date of the earlier transfer and its discovery, it is the old rate which applies to it: F.A. 1978, s. 62 (8).)

LIABILITIES

In considering this topic it is necessary to distinguish between liabilities resulting from a chargeable transfer and other liabilities. The matter is dealt with in Schedule 10.

Liabilities Resulting from a Chargeable Transfer

One has to remember that the value transferred is the amount by which the transferor's estate immediately after the disposition is less than it would be if the disposition had not been made.

A chargeable transfer may give rise to capital transfer tax and also to several other taxes—capital gains tax, development land tax, stamp duty. Also there may be incidental costs of the transfer, such as conveyancing fees. All these items, if paid by the transferor, will diminish the value of his estate immediately after the transfer. So, in the absence of any provision to the contrary, they would all increase the amount of the "value transferred" and so increase the amount of tax payable. Schedule 10 does make provisions to the contrary, to some extent. Paragraph 1 (2) provides that in determining the value of the transferor's estate immediately after the transfer, his liability to capital transfer tax on the value transferred shall be taken into account, but not his liability for any other tax or duty. And by paragraph 6 (*a*) the incidental expenses (if borne by the transferor) shall be left out of account.

The great point to grasp is that when one is considering liabilities immediately *after* the transfer, the effect of taking a liability into account is to increase the diminution in value of the transferor's estate and so increase the value transferred and so increase the capital transfer tax. Conversely, the effect of leaving a liability out of account is that that liability (*e.g.* liability to capital gains tax or liability to pay conveyancing fees to one's solicitor) does not increase the capital transfer tax.

And if the capital gains tax is borne by the transferee, that is treated (for capital transfer tax) as actually reducing the value transferred: Schedule 10, paragraph 4 (1). And the same is true of the incidental expenses of making a transfer, if these are borne by the transferee: paragraph 6 (*b*).

Grossing up

The principle of grossing up a lifetime gift is embedded in Schedule 10, paragraph 1 (2) (above). If the transferor is to pay the capital transfer tax, his liability to the tax is to be taken into account in calculating the diminution in his estate caused by the transfer. If A makes a gift to B of £x in cash or of property worth £x (tax free) A's estate is diminished by £x plus the relevant capital transfer tax. So £x must be grossed up to find what sum must be paid by A to the Revenue to put £x into the hands of B free from any liability to the tax. If one calls that sum £y, A must pay £x to B and £y to the Revenue.

If A makes a gift to B, stipulating that B must pay the capital transfer tax on it, no grossing up arises. This is because A's estate is not diminished by capital transfer tax, since he is not going to pay any of it.

In a general sense there is no grossing up in the case of a transfer on death. This is because grossing up is, in effect, built into the situation since it is only the sums net of tax which will reach the beneficiaries. However, where a specific gift is left by will "tax-free" a kind of grossing up has to take place to determine the entitlements of other beneficiaries: see in Chapter 28 below under the heading Incidence.

With regard to the actual process of grossing up, in principle it is just like grossing up for income tax. If A wants to put into the hands of B £40,000, one has to work out what sum, after deduction of tax, will leave £40,000 clear. But in practice it is often very much more complicated than is the income tax process. This is because (a) the tax on any particular transfer has to take account of the transferor's previous tax history under the principle of cumulation and (b) the particular gift itself may cross several "slice lines."

The legislation itself does not contain any grossing up tables, but the Revenue have issued various very useful tables. Some are set out in their booklet "CTT 1."

Here is a basic grossing up table[2] which enables one to find the amount of capital transfer tax which is payable on a given net cumulative total.

GROSSING-UP TABLE

Net cumulative total		Capital transfer tax payable		
£	£	£ £		£
25,000 –	29,750	NIL + $\frac{1}{19}$ for each £ over		25,000
29,750 –	34,375	250 + $\frac{3}{37}$,, ,, ,, ,,		29,750
34,375 –	38,875	625 + $\frac{1}{9}$,, ,, ,, ,,		34,375
38,875 –	47,625	1,125 + $\frac{1}{7}$,, ,, ,, ,,		38,875
47,625 –	56,125	2,375 + $\frac{3}{17}$,, ,, ,, ,,		47,625
56,125 –	64,375	3,875 + $\frac{7}{33}$,, ,, ,, ,,		56,125
64,375 –	80,375	5,625 + $\frac{1}{4}$,, ,, ,, ,,		64,375
80,375 –	95,875	9,625 + $\frac{9}{31}$,, ,, ,, ,,		80,375
95,875 –	110,375	14,125 + $\frac{11}{29}$,, ,, ,, ,,		95,875
110,375 –	129,875	19,625 + $\frac{7}{13}$,, ,, ,, ,,		110,375
129,875 –	158,625	30,125 + $\frac{17}{23}$,, ,, ,, ,,		129,875
158,625 –	183,625	51,375 + 1 ,, ,, ,, ,,		158,625
183,625 –	206,125	76,375 + $\frac{11}{9}$,, ,, ,, ,,		183,625
206,125 –	286,125	103,875 + $\frac{3}{2}$,, ,, ,, ,,		206,125
286,125 –	461,125	223,875 + $\frac{13}{7}$,, ,, ,, ,,		286,125
461,125 –	761,125	548,875 + $\frac{7}{3}$,, ,, ,, ,,		461,125
over 761,125		1,248,875 + 3 ,, ,, ,, ,,		761,125

To see how the table works, let us take the example mentioned a moment ago, namely the situation where A wants to put £40,000 tax-free into the hands of B. Let us suppose that A has already made gross chargeable transfers amounting to £30,000. The tax on those transfers would have been £250 (£25,000 at nil rate; £5,000 at 5 per cent.). So his net cumulative total was £29,750. His present gift is to be £40,000 (net). So his cumulative net total will be, after this gift, £69,750. Now look at the grossing-up table. Take the "slice" on the left-hand side of the table which embraces £69,750; that is the slice £64,375–£80,375. Read off what is written in the right-hand half of the table: "£5,625 + ¼ (£) for each £ over £64,375." So the tax payable is £5,625 plus ¼ × (£69,750 − £64,375). The answer to this sum is £6,968. This is the amount of tax on the new net cumulative total. The amount of tax on the old net cumulative total was £250. So the tax on this present transfer must be £6,968 minus £250 = £6,718.

---

[2] Reproduced from "CTT 1" with the permission of the Controller of Her Majesty's Stationery Office.

(The new gross cumulative total to be carried forward for the future will be £69,750 plus £6,968 = £76,718.)

If you want to avoid all this arithmetic you can buy from law book shops detailed Tables which will do it all for you.

In any case, let us take a much simpler example to try and see how the process works (although it is perfectly possible to use the Revenue tables or the detailed shop tables without understanding how they work). Let us suppose that X wishes to give to Y £25,100 tax free, and that X has made no previous chargeable transfers. Looking at the grossing-up table (p. 269, above), it can be seen that the tax will be "nil plus $\frac{1}{19}$ (£) of each £ over £25,000." So the tax is $\frac{1}{19}$ of £100. That works out at £5.263. One can check this with the statutory table on page 264, above (Second Table, lifetime). X is giving £25,100 to Y and £5.263 to the Revenue making a gross total of £25,105.263. £25,000 is in the nil band, so in the 5 per cent. band there is £105.263. 5 per cent. of £105.263 is £5.263. So net £25,100 = gross £25,105.263. It may help if one translates "net" into "tax exclusive," and "gross" into "tax inclusive," and also if one remembers that the statutory table is "gross" ("tax inclusive").

Now let us look to see why the grossing-up table directed us that the tax would be $\frac{1}{19}$ of each £ over £25,000. Why $\frac{1}{19}$? The clue to the understanding of this is that tax has to be paid not only on the net gift but also on the related tax. It is a case of tax on tax.

In our example of X giving £25,100 to Y, X has a nil rate up to £25,000 and then above that he has to pay tax as follows:

	tax (at 5 per cent.) on (£)	100		= (£)5.00	
+ tax (	,,	) on	5.00	=	0.25	
+ tax (	,,	) on	0.25	=	0.0125	
+ tax (	,,	) on	0.0125	=	0.000625	

This could go on for ever, but as we have now got down to less than 1p let us stop and add up the tax items. The total is £5.263125. Let us call it £5.263. £5.263 is $\frac{1}{19}$ of £100. It is also (of course) 5.263 per cent. Some commentators have produced tables in percentages rather than in fractions.

Another way of approaching the matter is this. X is making a transfer of £25,100 *plus* such sum as after tax will leave £25,100. £25,000 is at the nil rate, so only £100 of the net sum is taxable. But it is not simply a question of applying 5 per cent. to £100. If it were so, the tax would be £5. But it is more than £5. It is

$$£5 \times \frac{100}{100 - 5}.$$

That is the same as
$$£5 \times \frac{100}{95.}$$

That works out at £5.263.

We came to look at grossing-up as an aspect of "liabilities resulting from a chargeable transfer." We now turn to look at "other liabilities."

Other Liabilities

What we are talking about here is liabilities other than those which result from a chargeable transfer. The importance of the topic is that it is clearly relevant to the comparison which has to be made in the case of lifetime transfers between the value of a person's estate before and after the transfer (its relevance is to the "before" part) and it is clearly relevant to the valuation of a person's estate on death.

A liability is not taken into account unless it is a liability imposed by law or it was incurred by the transferor for a consideration in money or money's worth: Schedule 10, paragraph 1 (3). So, for example, if A covenants to pay to B £100 a year for seven years (without consideration) A cannot claim that before the first annual payment his estate was worth £x minus £700 and that after the first payment his estate was worth £x minus £600 (and minus the £100 paid under the covenant). If A could so claim he would eliminate tax on the covenant payment. Suppose his estate was, before the first payment, £1,000 minus £700 = £300; after the first payment it would be £1,000 minus £600 (liability on the covenant for the future) and minus the £100 paid = £300; therefore no diminution and hence no tax. This sub-paragraph prevents such a result.

Where a liability falls to be discharged after the time at which it is to be taken into account it shall be valued as at the time at which it is to be taken into account: Schedule 10, paragraph 1 (4). In other words its value has to be discounted. This rule does not apply to liability for capital transfer tax itself.

A liability in respect of which there is a right to reimbursement shall be taken into account only to the extent (if any) that reimbursement cannot reasonably be expected to be obtained: paragraph 1 (5). So if A owes £100 to B but for some reason C is liable to reimburse A, A cannot have his liability taken into account if there is no reason to suppose that C will not pay up.

Before we leave liabilities, notice this general point about them: if it is a question of valuing an estate *before* a transfer (or immediately before death) it is advantageous to the taxpayer if a liability can be taken into account: if it is a question of valuing an estate *after* a transfer it is disadvantageous if a liability is to be taken into account.

VALUATION

Open market value

The basic principle of valuation is stated in section 38 (1). Except as otherwise provided the value at any time of any property shall be the price which the property might reasonably be expected to fetch if sold in the open market at that time. This is generally called "open market value."

The subsection then goes on to say (perhaps rather inconsistently) that the price shall not be assumed to be reduced on the ground that the whole property is to be placed on the market at one and the same time. So if A owns 100,000 shares in XYZ Ltd. the shares are valued (in the absence of an actual sale) without any reduction for the fact that if such a parcel of shares were put on the market at one time the price would be depressed.

Section 38 (2) then refers us to more detailed rules set out in Schedule 10.

Restriction on freedom to dispose: Schedule 10, para. 5

This is quite a difficult point, which is best understood if we take one particular kind of restriction on freedom to dispose, namely an option. Suppose A grants to B an option to purchase a house. If the option price is the same as the then market price, say £50,000, there is no transfer of value. If the option price, say £35,000, is less than the then market price there is a transfer of value unless B pays for the option a sum (£15,000) equal to the difference between the prices. If, later, B exercises his option and buys the house for £35,000 when it is worth £60,000, the amount of the "value transferred" depends on how much consideration B gave for the option. If B gave no consideration, the "value transferred" by the sale is £25,000 (the gratuitous element). If B gave £15,000 for the option, the "value transferred" by the sale (assuming B pays the tax) is £45,000 (£60,000 − £15,000) less £35,000 = £10,000.

Valuation of related property: para. 7

The concept of "related property" is an important one. Property is related to the property comprised in a person's estate if (a) it is in the estate of his spouse, or (b) it is included in a discretionary settlement made by him or his spouse before March 27, 1974, or (c) it is (or has been within the preceding five years) the property of a charity etc. and became so on an exempt transfer made after April 15, 1976 by him or his spouse.

Where the value of any property *would be* less than the appropriate portion of the value of the aggregate of that and any related property, it *shall be* the appropriate portion of the value of that aggregate. That is the rather obscure wording of paragraph 7 (1). I have italicised "would be" and "shall be" in the hope of making it a bit clearer. But it needs an example. The background is that the enactment is intended to stop up a tax-avoidance device. Suppose A owns 70 of the 100 issued shares in XYZ Ltd. Mrs. A owns none. A transfers 30 shares to his wife. Controlling shares are worth say £10 each; non-controlling shares are worth say £6 each. The transfer to Mrs. A is exempt. The legislation ensures that after the transfer A's holding is valued (*e.g.* on his subsequent death) as being worth not merely 40 × £6 (*i.e.* £240), but $^{40}/_{70}$ of the value of the combined (controlling) holding. The combined value is £700, so A's holding is valued at £400. And Mrs. A's holding is valued at £300.

A relief is provided (by paragraph 9A) where property was valued on death on the related property basis and is subsequently (within three years of the death) sold for a lesser amount.

Value of lessor's interest: para. 8

We saw at p. 244 above that in a settlement the life tenant is treated as owning the whole settled property and the holder of the reversionary interest is treated as owning nothing, because his interest is "excluded property." We now need to know that a lease for life, if the lease was not granted for full consideration, is treated (see Schedule 5, paragraph 1 (3)) as a settlement, but with the modification that the lessor's interest is not excluded property. This present paragraph (paragraph 8 of Schedule 10) provides that the value of the lessor's interest in the property shall be taken to be such part of the value of the property as bears to it the same proportion as the value of the consideration, at the time the lease was granted, bore to what would then have been the value of a full consideration. So, if L grants a lease for life to T at 75 per cent. of full consideration, L's interest in the property is taken to be 75 per cent. of the value of the property. (And T's interest is taken by Schedule 5, paragraph 3 (6) to be 25 per cent. of that value.)

Value of life policies, etc.: para. 11

This paragraph provides that the value of certain life policies and contracts for deferred annuities shall be treated as not less than the total of premiums paid (minus any surrender value paid, *e.g.* on a partial surrender). This was intended to be an anti-avoidance measure, but in fact it was turned into a pro-avoidance measure by a "diabolically clever scheme." The paragraph was amended by the Finance Act 1978 so as to knock out this scheme.[3]

---

[3] For the whole story, see an article by Barry McCutcheon in [1978] B.T.R. at p. 174, from which I have taken the quoted words.

Value transferred on death: para. 9

Capital transfer tax is charged on the death of a person as if, immediately before his death, he had made a transfer of value and the value transferred by it had been equal to the value of his estate immediately before his death: section 22. His estate does not include "excluded property": section 23 (1). It does include property over which he had a general power to appoint or dispose, and it does include settled property in which he had a life interest (except, in certain circumstances, where the property reverts on the death to the settlor or the settlor's spouse). And it does include his share in a joint tenancy.

Paragraph 9 of Schedule 10 lays down some detailed rules, as follows.

An allowance shall be made for reasonable funeral expenses.

Certain changes (whether increases or decreases) in the value of the estate which occur *by reason of* the death are treated as having occurred before the death. An example of an increase would be the proceeds of a life insurance policy; these proceeds count as part of the estate. An example of a decrease would occur if a restaurant business lost value through the death of its successful proprietor; this fact is to be taken into account in valuing the business as part of the deceased's estate.

Part II of Schedule 10 provides some relief where "qualifying investments" (notably quoted shares and holdings in an authorised unit trust) are sold within the 12 months following the death for less than the value at the date of death.

Part III of Schedule 10 provides a similar relief where land (which may include buildings) is sold within three years of the death for less than the value at death.

CHAPTER 26

"OTHER CHARGES"

This rather curious chapter title is taken from the Finance Act 1975 where "Other Charges" is the cross-heading to sections 39–42. They are probably grouped together in that Act as being, broadly speaking, anti-avoidance measures.

CLOSE COMPANIES

In general capital transfer tax is not charged on companies because they are not "individuals." But, by section 39, where a company which is a close company makes a transfer of value a tax charge may arise. Tax is charged as if each participator had made a transfer of value proportionate to his interest in the company. But against this can be set the amount (if any) by which the value of his estate is increased. So (for example) a reduction of capital would be a gratuitous transfer by the company, but no tax would be payable because each member's estate would be increased by the amount received. His estate (for this purpose) does not include any rights or interests in the company. The section is aimed at various avoidance devices, and consequently it provides that a "close company" includes not only a company which is a close company for purposes of corporation tax[1] but also a company which would be such a close company if it were resident in the United Kingdom. Foreign-based companies are important units in many avoidance schemes.

FUTURE PAYMENTS

This matter is dealt with (in rather obscure language) by section 40. Where a transfer of value takes the form of a disposition for which payments are made (or assets are transferred) more than a year after the disposition, each payment is taxed separately when it is made, the tax being based on a proportionate part of the value transferred. For example, if A buys a property for more than its market value, that is, on the general principles of the tax, a transfer of value by A of the amount by which the price exceeds the market value—the gratuitous element. The effect of this present section is that if A agrees to pay by instalments, each instalment counts as a separate transfer of value.

---

[1] See p. 225, above.

(The rule does not apply to a disposition for no consideration at all, such as an ordinary seven-year covenant.) The point of the section is (presumably) to spread the amount of value transferred. This may effect the amount of tax payable overall, because the transferor's cumulative total may go up between one instalment and the next by his making other transfers. Also, it may have the effect that one or more of the instalments falls within three years before A's death, thus attracting the death rate. Also the tax rates may be changed between one instalment and the next by a Finance Act.

FREE LOANS, ETC.

This matter was originally dealt with by section 41 (of F.A. 1975) but it was replaced by F.A. 1976, s. 115.

Where an individual allows another person the use of money or other property in any year the lender is treated as making a disposition as a result of which the value of his estate is reduced by the amount (if any) by which any consideration for the use falls short of the cost to him of allowing it.

Notice that the section only applies where the lender is an individual (as distinct from a company or the trustees of a settlement).

There are a number of express exceptions. One exception is where the use of the property (including money) is allowed for a period specified in advance. The reason for this exception is that a loan for a specified period at less than a commercial rate is caught for tax on the ordinary principle of section 20 (2) of F.A. 1975, because the value of the lender's estate is diminished by the loan. For example, if A lends a house to B rent-free for a five-year period the value of his estate is diminished because a house of which A cannot have possession for the next five years is worth less than a house which he has the immediate right to possess. Indeed the whole point of this section (F.A. 1976, s. 115) is to deal with loans which are not for a fixed period but are at will. Without this section such a loan would not be caught for tax; the lender's estate is not diminished, because he can repossess the property at any time he wishes. The section produces, in effect, a deemed transfer of value.

As well as the built-in exceptions, the general exemptions in Schedule 6 of the Finance Act 1975 can apply: see the first nine headings in Chapter 24 above. It is not stated, and is not clear, whether certain other exemptions can apply or not. For example, it is possible but by no means certain that the exemption offered by F.A. 1975, s. 46 (disposition for maintenance of family) could apply where a parent makes an indefinite loan of a flat (rent-free) to his student daughter.

ANNUITY PURCHASED IN CONJUNCTION WITH LIFE POLICY

We had occasion to mention these "back-to-back" policies, as they are called, in Chapter 24 at page 248, above in connection with the exemption for normal expenditure out of income. Section 42 imposes a charge to tax where the purchase of an annuity is an associated operation with the issue of a life policy on the life of the annuitant and the policy is vested in someone other than the purchaser of the annuity. The purchaser is treated as making a transfer of value at the time the life policy becomes vested in that other person. The amount of the transfer of value is whichever is the less of the following: (a) the sum paid for the annuity plus premiums paid under the policy up to the time of the transfer; (b) the greatest benefit capable of being conferred at any time by the policy.

It seems that this special charge to tax is additional to the charge which may arise (if no exemption applies) from the transferor's keeping the policy on foot by paying the premiums, each premium payment being a transfer of value.

The reason why the Revenue are so concerned about back-to-back policies is that a linked contract for life assurance and an annuity with the same company can be obtained on very favourable terms, because if the company loses on the assurance policy it will gain on the annuity contract. Because of this background, it seems that the Revenue will be prepared to treat the arrangements as not being associated operations (and hence not taxable) if the life policy has been issued on no different terms from those which would have been obtainable without the annuity link.

CHAPTER 27

SETTLED PROPERTY

GENERAL INTRODUCTION

Section 21 of the Finance Act 1975 announces somewhat bleakly: "Schedule 5 to this Act shall have effect with respect to settled property." References in this chapter are, unless otherwise stated, to Schedule 5, for that is where the meat is.

"Settled property" is not separately defined; it is simply property comprised in a settlement.

What, then, is a settlement for the purposes of the Act? It is a disposition whereby property is for the time being:

(1) held in trust for persons in succession; or

(2) held in trust for any person subject to a contingency; or

(3) held on discretionary trusts; or

(4) held on trust to accumulate the income; or

(5) charged (otherwise than for full consideration)[1] to pay an annuity; or

(6) subject to a lease for life if the lease was not granted for full consideration.[2]

Property subject to provisions equivalent to heads (1) to (5) above under the law of a foreign country can constitute a "settlement."

The legislation makes no distinction between a trust for sale and a strict settlement.

Neither a tenancy in common nor a joint tenancy is *ipso facto* a settlement, but either of them will be a settlement if it falls under any of the heads enumerated above.

There is nothing special about putting property into settlement. That occurrence is a disposition, and is taxed on ordinary principles in just the same way as (for example) an absolute gift.

What we are concerned with in this chapter is the kind of charges to tax which may arise *after* the property has become settled property.[3]

For this purpose the Act makes a sharp distinction between (1)

---

[1] An annuity not charged on property (*e.g.* an annuity purchased from an insurance company) is not a settlement. Even an annuity which is charged on property is not a settlement if it is granted for full consideration. Hence (probably) an annuity granted by continuing partners for a former partner or his dependants is not a settlement.

[2] Presumably the point of this is to prevent a person from seeking to avoid the rules relating to settled property by granting a lease for life instead of a life tenancy.

[3] Survivorship clauses (see p. 247, above) are in effect relieved from any settled property tax charges by para. 22A.

settled property which is held on fixed interest trusts, that is to say, where some person is beneficially entitled to an interest in possession (*e.g.* where there is a life tenant) and (2) settled property in which no one has a beneficial interest in possession (*e.g.* where the property is held on discretionary trusts). The underlying practical point is that fixed interest trusts are more favourably treated for tax purposes than are discretionary trusts.

There are also (3) some special kinds of settlement which are subject to special rules. We will deal with these three categories in turn, but the reader should bear in mind that some of the property in a settlement may fall within one of these categories and some within another, and that even the same property may change its category from time to time.

WHERE THERE IS A BENEFICIAL INTEREST IN POSSESSION

The basic point to grasp here is that the person holding the beneficial interest in possession is treated "as beneficially entitled to the property in which the interest subsists": paragraph 3 (1). So if A is entitled to a life interest in Blackacre he is treated for the purposes of the tax as though he were the owner of Blackacre itself. And if B is entitled to a life interest in a settled fund worth £50,000 he is treated as though he were the owner of £50,000. But if a life tenant is entitled to part only of the income of settled property his interest is taken to subsist in only a proportionate part of the capital. So, if B were entitled to, say, half the income of the settled fund he would be treated as the owner of £25,000.

"Beneficial interest in possession" is not defined in the Act; one has to apply the general principles of property law.

The main point is that a reversionary interest is not an interest in possession. A reversionary interest is defined in section 51 (1) of the Finance Act 1975 as "a future interest under a settlement, whether it is vested or contingent. . . ." A future interest cannot be an interest in possession because it is not "*in possession*." An interest in possession means an immediate entitlement; a present right of present enjoyment. There is a distinction in the general law between a reversionary interest and a remainder interest, but the definition quoted above makes no distinction of this kind—both are reversionary interests. So, if property is held on trust for A for life with remainder to B absolutely, A has an interest in possession and B has a reversionary interest.

It was pointed out above that in this situation A is treated as though he were the owner of the settled property itself. If B is also to be treated as owning something there will be some degree of double taxation. So the legislation treats B as owning nothing. This is achieved by declaring a reversionary interest to be "excluded property": F.A. 1975, s. 24. The effect of this is most clearly seen in relation to a death. Section 23 provides that "the estate of a person immediately before his death does not include excluded property." So, if property is settled on trust for A for life with remainder to B, and B dies while A is still alive, B's reversionary interest is not taxed on B's death.

There are three (perfectly reasonable) exceptions to this principle. A reversionary interest is not excluded property if (1) it has at any time been acquired for consideration, or (2) it is one to which either the settlor or his spouse is beneficially entitled, or (3) it is the interest expectant on the determination of a lease for life which is treated as a settlement.

Another kind of interest which is not an interest in possession is a contingent interest. This again is because a contingent interest does not carry an immediate entitlement and so is not "in possession." If property is held on trust for A if he attains the age of 25 years, A's interest in the capital of the trust is contingent upon his attaining that age. Until he is 25, he does not have an interest in possession in the capital. But a very important point arises here. He may well become entitled (by statute[4] or otherwise) to the *income* of the trust on attaining his majority, namely 18 years of age. Where that is so, his interest in income vests in possession at 18. And his interest in income is sufficient to make him a person "beneficially entitled to an interest in possession." In other words, a contingent gift of capital which carries what is generally called "the intermediate income" confers an interest in possession.

During the time that the estate of a deceased person is being administered, a person who will be entitled to an interest in possession when the administration is completed is treated as having the interest from immediately after the death: paragraph 22. Of course, this only matters if the beneficiary dies or disposes of his interest during the administration period.

There is one interest which is an interest in possession under the Act, though under the general law it would not be an interest in settled property at all. This is the interest of the lessee where the lease is treated as a settlement because it was granted for life and for less than full consideration. That the lessee's interest is an interest in possession emerges, by implication, from paragraph 3 (6).

---

[4] See the Trustee Act 1925, s. 31, as amended.

The Revenue issued a Press Notice on February 12, 1976[5] setting out their understanding of the term "interest in possession," and dealing particularly with the situation where an interest in settled property is subject to a discretion or power to accumulate the income of the property. In *Pearson* v. *I.R.C.* (1979) the Revenue's view of this matter was rejected by Fox, J. The learned judge held: (1) that the expression "interest in possession" has the same meaning in the general law of trusts *and* in the law of estate duty *and* in the law of capital transfer tax; (2) that the point of the expression is to distinguish present interests, with rights to present enjoyment, from interests in reversion; and (3) that a discretion or power residing in trustees to accumulate income (and so withhold it from the beneficiaries) does not prevent the beneficiaries from having interests in possession. This decision was affirmed by the Court of Appeal.

The Charging Provisions

We must now look at the circumstances in which a charge to tax arises in respect of settled property where there is a beneficial interest in possession, or (to put it in more popular terms) where there is a "fixed interest settlement," as distinct from a "discretionary settlement."

Death of the beneficial owner

Let us again take the simple case of a settlement by which property is settled on A for life with remainder to B. A, the life tenant, dies. A's life interest is part of his estate (section 23 (1)) and is taxed under section 22 (1), just as is his unsettled property. The only special point that arises (and it is one that has already been made) is that (under Schedule 5, paragraph 3 (1)) A is treated as owning the settled property itself. So, if the subject-matter of the trust is Blackacre, what falls to be valued on A's death is Blackacre itself, and not merely A's life interest in Blackacre. Apart from this (very important) valuation point, there is no difference on the occasion of death between a life interest and any other kind of property (except that the tax is normally payable by the trustees out of the settled property).

We now turn to look at the two circumstances in which tax may arise during the lifetime of the life tenant.

Termination of an interest in possession

This circumstance is dealt with in paragraph 4 (2) as follows: "Where at any time during the life of a person beneficially entitled to

---

[5] The Press Notice is printed (as Appendix IV) in "CTT 1" and also (*e.g.*) in [1976] B.T.R. at p. 418.

an interest in possession in any property comprised in a settlement his interest comes to an end, tax shall be charged . . . as if at that time he had made a transfer of value and the value transferred had been equal to the value of the property in which his interest subsisted." Notice the valuation point cropping up again in the last few words: what has to be valued is the property itself, not the value of the interest merely. There is no grossing up.

An example of an interest coming to an end during lifetime would be where property is held on trust for X until she shall re-marry. Another example would be where property is held on trust for Y for life with remainder to Z, and Y surrenders his life interest to Z.

Disposal of an interest in possession

This depends on paragraph 4 (1). Where a person beneficially entitled to an interest in possession in any property comprised in a settlement disposes of his interest, the disposal is not a transfer of value but is treated as the coming to an end of his interest. So if a paragraph 4 (1) situation arises, it is equated with a paragraph 4 (2) situation; that is to say, disposing of the interest is treated as a coming to an end of the interest. So, if A gives away to X his life interest in Blackacre, a tax charge arises just as if his interest had come to an end. Consequently the charge (without grossing up) is on the whole value of Blackacre.

It is interesting to follow up what happens if A does give away (or, for that matter, sell) his life interest in, say, Blackacre to X. There then arises what is called an "interest *pur autre vie*." This describes the interest which X acquires. He has an interest in Blackacre "for another's life"; that is, his interest lasts only as long as A lives. When A dies, X's interest comes to an end, and a tax charge arises (under paragraph 4 (2)). If X were to die while A was still alive, X's interest (the interest *pur autre vie*) would pass by his will or on intestacy to, say, Y. The interest would be part of X's estate and tax would be charged (under section 22 (1)) on X's death. Y would then hold the interest, and if A were then to die, Y's interest would end, and a tax charge would arise under paragraph 4 (2). There might be quick succession relief: see p. 285, below.

Notice the phrase "as if" in paragraph 4 (2) (which also, because of the linking between the sub-paragraphs, applies to paragraph 4 (1)). There is not an actual transfer of value, only a deemed transfer of value. One effect of this is that four exemptions which might otherwise apply are knocked out. These are the exemptions for: £2,000 gifts, small gifts to the same person, normal expenditure gifts, and marriage gifts. These exemptions only apply to actual transfers of value, not to deemed ones. This result is achieved by a combination of section 51 (2) and Schedule 6, paragraph 8.

Extension of the termination and disposal rules

If the point were not dealt with in the legislation it would be very easy to minimise the tax by depreciating the value of settled property by various transactions between the trustees and persons connected with the settlement. The point is dealt with by paragraph 4 (9). If such a transaction takes place there is a deemed partial termination of the interest and so a tax charge arises. Thus, for example, if the trustees let a house rent-free to a beneficiary on a lease a tax charge will arise. A depreciatory transaction by an individual is taxable on the ordinary principle that it diminishes his estate. But trustees do not have an estate. That is why it is necessary to have this express rule.

Qualifications to the termination and disposal rules

We now have to look at a number of qualifications to the disposal and termination rules.

NEW ENTITLEMENT. If A's life interest terminates but he becomes on the same occasion entitled to the property or to another interest in possession in the property, there is no charge to tax unless the later interest is of less value than the former, in which case there is a deemed transfer of value equal to the difference: paragraph 4 (3) and 4 (10) (*b*). This exception is a logical consequence of the principle that the holder of an interest in possession is treated as the owner of the property. If property is settled on trust to pay the income thereof to A for eight years and thereafter to A absolutely, there is no tax charge when the eight years are up and A takes the property absolutely; he was already treated for tax-purposes as the absolute owner of the property. But if the trust was to pay the income to A for eight years and then to divide the property three-quarters to A and one-quarter to B, there would be a tax charge on that division. There is a notional loss to A of one-quarter of the settled property. Mind you, it may not be a real loss, because what A has after the eight-year period may well be (and probably will be) more valuable than what he had before. But it is a notional loss (and so taxable) because during the eight-year period he was treated as though he were the owner of the whole trust property, whereas after the division he is the owner of only three-quarters of it. The same point applies to an agreed "partition" between a life tenant and a remainderman, which is quite a common occurrence in practice. The proportion of the property which is partitioned to the remainderman is caught for tax as being property in which the interest of the life tenant comes to an end.

DISPOSAL FOR A CONSIDERATION. If the life tenant disposes of his interest for a consideration (that is, sells it as distinct from giving it away) the value transferred is reduced by the amount of the consideration: paragraph 4 (4). So, if A, the life tenant of settled property worth £70,000, sells his life tenancy for £20,000, tax is chargeable not on the whole £70,000 but on £50,000. One might think that this provision would mean that no tax at all would arise if a life tenant were to sell his interest for its full market value. This is not really so because in practice a life interest (except in very rare circumstances) is always worth less than the property itself in which the interest subsists. The full market price of a life interest in Blackacre is almost certain to be less than the value of Blackacre itself. So if the life tenant sells his interest in Blackacre even for the full market price of the interest there will still be some tax to pay on the disposal.

A reversionary interest in the property does not count in this connection as consideration. So in a partition (discussed under the previous heading) the fact that the life tenant gets in return for his life tenancy part of the remainderman's reversionary interest does not reduce the amount of tax chargeable on the partition.

REVERTER TO SETTLOR. The word "reverter" is lawyers' old-fashioned jargon for reversion. So what we are talking about here is the situation where S settles property on X with a provision that on a certain event the property is to revert to S. It is provided by paragraph 4 (5) (as amended) that if the interest comes to an end during the settlor's life and on the same occasion the property reverts to the settlor tax shall not be chargeable. The reason for this exception from charge is that it is considered desirable that a person should be able to provide a life interest (or other interest) for his dependants without a charge to tax when the property reverts to him. An example might occur on a divorce; a husband might want to transfer the matrimonial home to his former wife until the children of the marriage reach (say) school leaving age, with a provision that the house should then revert to him. Paragraph 4 (5) ensures that when the reversion takes place no tax charge arises. Paragraph 4 (5) is dealing with the situation where the interest comes to an end during the life of the beneficiary—in our example during the life of the former wife. Parallel provision is made by section 22 (2) for the case where the "reverter to settlor" occurs on the occasion of the death of the beneficiary. An example would be where a man gives a life interest in a house to his widowed mother.

The relief does not apply if the settlor or his spouse had acquired the reversionary interest for consideration. The point of this rule is to stop an avoidance device. Suppose a settlor (S) were to settle £50,000 on X for life, remainder to Y. If it were not for this rule, S could, when

X was old and about to die, buy Y's reversionary interest for £50,000. In this way he could pass the £50,000 to Y without any tax arising.[6]

REVERTER TO SETTLOR'S SPOUSE. A similar exception applies where the property reverts not to the settlor but to the settlor's spouse, provided the spouse is domiciled in the United Kingdom at the time the reversion occurs: paragraph 4 (6).

TRUSTEE'S REMUNERATION. Sometimes a trustee is remunerated for his service as a trustee by being given an interest in possession in the settled property (or in some part of it). Paragraph 19A declares that provided the interest does not represent more than reasonable remuneration, no tax charge shall arise on the termination of the interest.

Relief for successive charges

There is "quick succession" relief for successive charges on interests in possession: paragraph 5. The relief applies if an interest in possession comes to an end within four years of a previous chargeable transfer of the property. The value chargeable is reduced by a percentage. If the period since the last chargeable transfer is one year or less the reduction is 80 per cent.; if the period is not more than two years the reduction is 60 per cent.; if the period is not more than three years the reduction is 40 per cent.; if the period is not more than four years the reduction is 20 per cent.

Where relief is given under this paragraph relief under section 30 (see p. 251, above) is not available. Notice the differences between the two reliefs. First, this (para. 5) relief is a reduction in the chargeable value of the property, whereas that under section 30 is a reduction in the tax chargeable. So this (para. 5) relief is much more generous, but then it needs to be because of the principle that the life tenant owns the whole property. Second, for section 30 relief the second chargeable event must be a death; for paragraph 5 relief it need not be. (And, by the way, for paragraph 5 relief, the previous chargeable event may be the putting of the property into settlement.)

Close companies

We have seen (see p. 275, above) that by section 39 a transfer of value by a close company can be apportioned to the participators. That provision relates to unsettled property. A close company may be involved in settled property in various ways.

Where a participator in a close company is a trustee of settled property in which there is an interest in possession a transfer of value by the company can be apportioned to the interest holder. This is

---

[6] See Barry McCutcheon's article in [1978] B.T.R. at p. 170.

effected by deeming there to be a partial termination of his interest: see paragraph 24.

Where a close company is itself entitled to an interest in settled property the participators are treated as being the persons beneficially entitled to that interest according to their respective rights and interests in the company: paragraph 24 (5).

WHERE THERE IS NO BENEFICIAL INTEREST IN POSSESSION

We now turn to look at the totally different regime of tax charges which applies to settled property where for the time being there is no beneficial interest in possession. The charging provisions themselves speak only of there being no "interest in possession," but the notion of *beneficial* interest is imported into the situation by the definition in paragraph 11 (10), which is also adopted by paragraphs 12 (7) and 15 (6).

Paragraph 11 (10) declares that:

" 'Interest in possession' means an interest in possession to which an individual is beneficially entitled or, if the following conditions are satisfied, an interest in possession to which a company is beneficially entitled, the conditions being:

  (a) that the business of the company consists wholly or mainly in the acquisition of interests in settled property; and

  (b) that the company has acquired the interest for full consideration in money or money's worth from an individual who was beneficially entitled to the interest."

One also has to bear in mind paragraph 24 (5) which (as mentioned above) provides that where a *close* company is entitled to an interest in possession the participators shall be treated as the persons beneficially entitled to that interest.

Let us try to summarise the above points, using the broad phrase "discretionary trusts" to describe the present category, as distinct from the "fixed interest trusts" which we looked at previously. The regime for discretionary trusts will apply unless there is in existence an interest in possession which interest is (1) beneficially held, and (2) held by an individual *or*, in certain circumstances, by a company. My understanding of the provisions about companies is this. Where a *close* company holds an interest in possession, the rules for fixed interest trusts always apply and the rules for discretionary trusts never apply. Where a *non-close* company holds an interest in possession the rules for fixed interest trusts apply if the two conditions set out at (a) and (b) in paragraph 11 (10) are fulfilled, and the rules for discretionary trusts apply if those conditions are not fulfilled. It is logical that where a company is in the business of buying life interests and similar interests from hard-up beneficiaries the rules for fixed interest trusts should apply.

Taxable Events

No question can arise in a discretionary trust of a life tenant dying or disposing of his interest or having his interest terminated, for the simple reason that, by definition, there is no life tenant. So the legislation has set up other events on which to charge tax. The charge to tax is always at the lifetime (not the death) rates.

The taxable events are as follows:

(1) the making of a capital distribution (paragraph 6 (4));

(2) the coming into existence of an interest in possession in the whole or any part of the settled property (paragraph 6 (2));

(3) the expiry of a period of years which triggers off what is called the "periodic charge" (paragraph 12 (1));

(4) the coming into existence of an "accumulation and mainte-nance settlement" (paragraph 15 (3)).

Event number (1) above is an *actual* capital distribution. Events (2), (3) and (4) are brought into the tax net by providing that a capital distribution shall be "treated as" (being) made.

There are provisions about depreciatory transactions and about apportionment to trustee-participators similar to the provisions which apply to fixed interest trusts: see pages 283 and 285, above.

It is now necessary to look at the meaning of "capital distribution." That phrase is closely linked to, but is distinct from, a very similar phrase used in the legislation, namely "distribution payment."

A *"distribution payment"* is a payment (which can include the transfer of assets other than money) which is not income of the recipient for income tax purposes and is not a payment in respect of costs or expenses: paragraph 11 (7). So a distribution payment is essentially a capital payment.

A *"capital distribution"* is, in effect, defined by paragraph 6 (1), which says this: "Where a distribution payment is made out of property comprised in a settlement and at the time the payment is made no interest in possession subsists in the property or in the part of it out of which the payment is made, the payment is in this Schedule referred to as a capital distribution."

Now, at first sight it might seem from the above that there can never be a capital distribution which is not also a distribution pay-ment. But this is not completely so. On the occasion of a periodic charge (see below) a capital distribution is treated as made, but a distribution payment is not treated as made. All the other deemed capital distributions (but not the periodic charge) are covered by paragraph 11 (8) which declares that "the amount of any capital distribution treated as made ... shall also be deemed to be a distribution payment."

The importance of the point is this. A capital distribution is an event which gives rise to a charge to tax; a distribution payment is an event which affects cumulation. The occasion of a periodic charge is the only circumstance in the whole legislation where there is a capital distribution (actual or deemed) without there being a distribution payment (actual or deemed). On the other hand there are several occasions where there is a distribution payment (actual or deemed) without there being a capital distribution (actual or deemed). And of course there are many occasions where there is both a capital distribution and a distribution payment.[7]

Let us now look in turn at the four taxable events listed on page 287, above.

The making of a capital distribution

Here we are talking about actual capital distributions such as the absolute appointment to a beneficiary of part of the capital fund or an advancement of capital or the supplementation out of capital of the income of a beneficiary. In each case capital actually leaves the discretionary settlement. See paragraph 6 (1).

The distribution has to be grossed-up unless the tax is payable by the recipient: see paragraph 6 (4).

A payment of capital made to the settlor or his spouse, provided that the recipient is domiciled in the United Kingdom, is not a capital distribution, though it is a distribution payment. So it is not taxable, but it does count for cumulation. "Spouse" includes a widow or widower if the payment is made less than two years after the settlor's death. See paragraph 6 (6). To combat certain avoidance devices the exemption does not apply if the recipient or certain linked persons had acquired an interest under the settlement for a consideration: paragraph 6 (6B).

Payments of capital to a charity or a political party or for national purposes or for public benefit (provided the payments meet the requirements discussed in Chapter 24 above) are not capital distributions nor are they distribution payments; consequently they are not taxable and do not affect cumulation. See Schedule 6 (not Schedule

---

[7] There is a curious uncertainty in the legislation as to whether the *amount* which cumulates is always the same as the *amount* on which tax is charged. See an article by B. McCutcheon at [1978] B.T.R.. p. 223.

5) at paragraphs 10, 11, 12, 13 and 15. There is an anti-avoidance provision at paragraph 15 (4B).

The coming into existence of an interest in possession

Paragraph 6 (2) provides that: "Where a person becomes entitled to an interest in possession in the whole or any part of the property comprised in a settlement at a time when no such interest subsists in the property or that part, a capital distribution shall be treated as being made out of the property or that part of the property...." What is envisaged here is, for example, a discretionary beneficiary becoming entitled to a life interest (a fixed interest trust). There is grossing-up unless the tax is payable out of the property in which the interest in possession arises, in which latter case there is no grossing-up: paragraph 6 (5). By paragraph 11 (8) there is a deemed distribution payment (and hence cumulation), but if later there is an actual distribution payment the amount of this deemed distribution is normally treated as reducing the actual payment.

The provisions about spouses and about charities, etc., are as under the previous heading.

In 1978 a new paragraph 6 (2A) was inserted to stop up a tax avoidance device which had been developed from the provision in paragraph 11 (10) that many non-close companies (as explained at pp. 286, 287, above) cannot have an "interest in possession" as defined for capital transfer tax, and so cannot fall within paragraph 6 (2) above. Paragraph 6 (2A) closes the gap.

The periodic charge: paragraphs 12 and 13

This charge, called the "periodic charge," is designed to prevent the trustees of a discretionary settlement getting a tax-free ride by not making any distribution payments and simply accumulating the income. The Act prevents this by imposing a periodic charge to tax at every ten-year interval in the case of a United Kingdom settlement, and every year in the case of a non-resident settlement.

UNITED KINGDOM SETTLEMENTS. Where, at a relevant anniversary, no interest in possession subsists, there is a charge on the settled property. A "relevant anniversary" occurs every tenth year from (broadly speaking) the creation of the settlement, provided that it is an anniversary falling on or after April 1, 1982.

The charge is on the value of the property. There is no grossing up. The rate of tax is 30 per cent. of the rate which would have been chargeable if an actual capital distribution had been made. The charge is reduced if some of the property has not been held on discretionary trusts during the previous ten years. There is a deemed capital distribution but not a deemed distribution payment, so there is no cumulation. The effective rate[8] at which tax is charged goes to reduce the rate at which tax is charged on all capital distributions (other than a periodic charge) which take place within the next 20 years, but the reductions are not to exceed the amount of the tax charged on the periodic charge.

OVERSEAS SETTLEMENTS. Where the majority of the trustees are not resident in the United Kingdom an annual charge at the rate of 3 per cent. of the full rate is made. A credit is then given against the 30 per cent. charge due at the end of each 10-year period.

The coming into existence of an "accumulation and maintenance settlement"

An "accumulation and maintenance settlement" is a settlement for the benefit of young people which fulfils certain conditions (discussed below at p. 293). Such settlements receive very favourable treatment (comparatively) for capital transfer tax purposes. Consequently it is not surprising that a tax charge arises when settled property in which there is no interest in possession passes into an accumulation and maintenance settlement: paragraph 15 (3). This happens, for example, when the trustees of a discretionary settlement exercise a power of appointment to appoint the trust property (or some of it) to certain beneficiaries contingently upon attaining the age of 25 years.

A capital distribution is treated as being made out of the settled property equal to the value of the property concerned. There is grossing up unless the tax is payable out of that property, in which latter case there is no grossing-up: paragraph 6 (5). By paragraph 11 (8) there is a deemed distribution payment (and hence cumulation) but if later there is an actual distribution payment the amount of the deemed distribution payment is normally treated as reducing the actual payment.

The Rates of Charge

As regards the rates of charge the legislation draws a sharp distinction between those discretionary settlements which were created before the advent of capital transfer tax and those which were created after.[9] Such settlements as were in existence before March 27, 1974 are taxed less heavily than those created on or after that date. The principle is that "pre-existing" settlements are taxed as though the trustees were an individual and as though the trust fund were that

---

[8] The effective rate is the actual tax charged (after the 30 per cent. and other reductions) as a percentage of the value of the property.

[9] This is putting it somewhat broadly; for full details see para. 11 (2).

individual's estate, whereas "post-created" settlements are taxed as though the settlor were the chargeable person. One can say that the tax on pre-existing trusts is "trust-based" and the tax on post-created trusts is "settlor-based." In either case tax is charged on the lifetime rates, not the death rates.

Settlements made before March 27, 1974

These settlements are governed by paragraph 8. The rate of tax to be applied to any given capital distribution[10] (sometimes grossed up, sometimes not—as discussed above) is found by aggregating it with previous distribution payments[11] out of the same settlement since March 26, 1974 *and with nothing else.* What I mean by the phrase "and with nothing else" is that the tax history of the settlor does not come into the matter at all. Suppose S makes a settlement of £100,000 in 1973. (No tax was payable on that transfer—and it is not cumulated—because the tax did not then exist.) The trustees make a first capital distribution of £30,000 in 1975. They are entitled to the nil rate up to £25,000, so tax is payable on £5,000. Tax is £270.25 if grossing-up applies, £250 if it does not. If the trustees subsequently make a second capital distribution the tax rate on that will take into account the first one—and so on for later capital distributions.

The tax on pre-existing trusts was heavily criticised as being unfairly retrospective, and to meet this criticism paragraph 14 provided for substantially reduced rates on capital distributions made up to March 31, 1980. The Finance (No. 2) Act 1979 extended this relief to March 31, 1982. This gives time for trustees to wind-up these settlements (or convert them into fixed settlements) on very favourable tax terms. The relief only applies if the recipient is an individual domiciled in the United Kingdom. There will be no relief after the end of March 1982.

Settlements made after March 26, 1974

These settlements are governed by paragraph 7, which is pretty complex. The position appears to be as follows. Capital distributions (actual or deemed) which do not in total exceed the "initial value" of the settled property are charged at what one might call a "basic rate" which takes account of the chargeable transfers made by the settlor up to and including the making of the settlement. This "basic rate" is the rate at which tax would have been charged when the settlement was made if the amount (tax inclusive) of the chargeable transfer then

---

[10] Or deemed capital distribution.
[11] Or deemed distribution payments.

made had been equal to the value of the property originally comprised in the settlement (other than excluded property) and any related settlement. The basic rate will often differ from the rate which was in fact charged on the chargeable transfer which constituted the making of the settlement because the basic rate depends on the net value of the property originally comprised in the settlement and not on the gross amount before tax, and also because the basic rate ignores any exemptions available to the settlor.

Let us take an example. S has already made taxable gifts totalling £30,000. He then makes a discretionary settlement, transferring £42,000 to the trustees. The trustees pay the tax. S's annual £2,000 exemption is available. Tax is paid on the balance, £40,000. The tax amounts to £5,375. So the trustees are left with £36,625. The next step is to work out what tax would have been paid if the settlor (S) had transferred £36,625 (tax inclusive), ignoring the £2,000 exemption, but remembering that he has already made transfers totalling £30,000. This works out at £4,784 tax. The basic rate is then found by calculating what percentage 4,784 is of 36,625. The answer is 13.06 per cent. So the basic rate is 13.06 per cent. Another way to describe this basic rate is to call it the "flat rate." This is a good expression, because it is this same rate which applies to all capital distributions out of the settled fund until their aggregated total reaches the figure of the "initial value," which in our example is £36,625.

Once the figure of the initial value has been reached, further capital distributions fall into higher rate bands just as further gifts by the settlor would have done. In other words, a process of cumulation for the settlement begins. The rate to be applied to any given capital distribution is determined by adding the amount of the distribution to the sum of chargeable transfers made by the settlor before the making of the settlement and the amount of distributions already made out of the settlement. Let us go on with our example. Suppose the trustees make a capital distribution of £30,000. That is taxed at the basic rate (or flat rate) of 13.06 per cent. Then suppose the assets in the trust fund appreciate (whether by inflation or otherwise) so that the value of the fund (even after paying out the £30,000) stands at say £20,000. The trustees decide to make a capital distribution of this whole £20,000. The first £6,625 (of this £20,000) is taxed at 13.06 per cent. The tax is £865. At that point the figure of the initial value is reach (£36,625). The balance of the £20,000, which is £13,375, is charged as if it were a tax-inclusive lifetime transfer by an individual who had already made chargeable transfers of £30,000 plus £36,625 = £66,625. The rate of tax between £60,000 and £70,000 is 17.5 per cent., and the rate between £70,000 and £80,000 is 20 per cent. So on this £13,375 the tax is £2,591. The total tax payable on the whole £20,000 capital distribution is £865 plus £2,591 = £3,456.

SPECIAL KINDS OF SETTLEMENT

We must now look at some special kinds of settlement all of which to a greater or less extent receive favoured treatment under the capital transfer tax legislation.

Accumulation and Maintenance Settlements

One can think of these settlements as being settlements for the benefit of young people.

Where a discretionary trust comes within the definition of an accumulation and maintenance settlement it is relieved from the normal tax charges relating to discretionary settlements.

The matter is dealt with in paragraph 15. Paragraph 15 applies to any settlement where:

(1) one or more persons ("beneficiaries") will become entitled to the settled property or to an interest in possession in it at some specified age not exceeding 25;

(2) there is no interest in possession in the settled property[12];

(3) any application of the income must be for the maintenance, education or benefit of a beneficiary;

(4) to the extent that it is not so applied, the income must be accumulated; and

(5) not more than 25 years have elapsed since the latest time when conditions (1) to (4) above became satisfied, except that this rule does not apply if all the persons who are or have been beneficiaries are or were (putting it broadly) grandchildren of a common grandparent.

There are three tax advantages applying to settlements which meet the above requirements. First, a payment to a beneficiary is not a capital distribution. Second, there is no deemed capital distribution when a beneficiary becomes entitled to an interest in the property. Third, there is no periodic charge. So these settlements are an important feature in tax planning.

Protective Trusts

The point of a protective trust is, as its name perhaps implies, to protect someone from his own financial folly. For example, there

---

[12] It should be borne in mind that in many cases a beneficiary will become entitled at 18 to the income (*e.g.* under the Trustee Act 1925, s. 31). As we have seen, that is enough to constitute an interest in possession. So this requirement would cease at that time to be fulfilled.

could be a settlement under which X (the "principal beneficiary") is given a life interest (a fixed interest trust) *until he is declared bankrupt*, in which event his life interest terminates and a *discretionary trust* arises in favour of X and his family. See the Trustee Act 1925, s. 33.

For purposes of capital transfer tax the matter is dealt with by paragraph 18. As originally enacted that paragraph gave some scope for tax avoidance, and so it was substantially amended in 1978. As it now stands the change (on, *e.g.* bankruptcy) from a fixed interest trust to a discretionary trust is for the purposes of capital transfer tax disregarded and the "principal beneficiary" is treated as still being beneficially entitled to an interest in possession. So the discretionary trust rules do not apply and the fixed interest trust rules do apply.

Charitable Trusts

If settled property is held for charitable purposes only none of the charges on capital distributions (actual or deemed) apply, nor does the periodic charge: paragraph 20.

Other Favoured Trusts

There are some other kinds of trust which to some extent receive favoured treatment in regard to capital transfer tax. We will not discuss the details. Here is a list of the trusts concerned: superannuation schemes (paragraph 16); trusts for benefit of employees, etc. (paragraph 17); newspaper trusts (paragraph 17A)[13]; trusts for the benefit of mentally disabled persons (paragraph 19); compensation funds (paragraph 21); settlements concerned with works of art and historic houses and land (see F.A. 1976, ss. 76–84).

THE PURCHASE OF A REVERSIONARY INTEREST

We have seen (notably at pp. 279 and 280 above) that except in certain circumstances a reversionary interest in settled property in the United Kingdom is excluded property, thus giving effect to the principle that the life tenant owns the whole settled fund and the reversioner owns nothing.

There are a number of special provisions in the legislation, some of which are designed to prevent over-charging in respect of reversionary interests and some of which are designed to prevent tax avoidance.

---

[13] Paragraph 17A was enacted in 1976 to give relief to the Scott Trust which holds shares in *The Guardian* newspaper. It was said in Parliament that "that trust ensures that no benefit can come out to a private individual" and that without this provision the trust would have been "affected by" the discretionary trust rules.

We will only deal here with the main avoidance possibility, and how the legislation has stopped it up.

Suppose that property having a value of £200,000 is settled on A for life with remainder to B. And suppose further that A has free estate (*i.e.* unsettled property) worth £100,000. If A were to die his estate would have a value of £300,000. If A (before dying) were to buy from B the reversionary interest for its full actuarial value (say £80,000) he could do so without any tax charge, because although A's life interest terminates he becomes on the same occasion absolutely entitled to the property: see Schedule 5, paragraph 4 (3). The reversion merges with the life interest and the property ceases to be settled property. If A were now to die, his estate would have a value of only £220,000, made up of £200,000 (the former settled property) plus £20,000 (his free estate, previously £100,000 but diminished by the £80,000 which he has paid to B). In this way tax would be saved. The "trick" lies in having brought into his estate something which in reality increases his wealth, but which (for the purposes of the tax) he already owned, and in having depleted, by that transaction, his taxable estate.

The legislation meets this avoidance device by treating A as having made a gift to B of £80,000, and so as having made a chargeable transfer of that amount. This is done by means of section 20 (4) and section 23 (3) of the Finance Act 1975. Section 20 (4) is the section which declares that a disposition is not a transfer of value if it is made without donative intent, etc. It contains these words: "but this sub-section does not apply to a disposition by which a reversionary interest is acquired in the circumstances mentioned in section 23 (3). . . ." And section 23 (3) says this: ". . . where a person entitled to an interest (whether in possession or not) in any settled property acquires a reversionary interest expectant (whether immediately or not) on the interest, the reversionary interest is not part of his estate. . . ." Thus, although A gives full value to B for the reversionary interest, and although there is no donative intent, he is treated as having paid £80,000 for nothing, and so as having made a transfer of value amounting to £80,000.

CHAPTER 28

LIABILITY AND INCIDENCE

In this Chapter we deal with two matters which are separate but related, namely liability and incidence.

Liability is concerned with who is to pay the tax to the Revenue. The previous legislation, dealing with Estate Duty, described this duty to pay the tax as "accountability." That was somewhat confusing, because there is also a separate duty to deliver to the Revenue an account. The capital transfer tax legislation describes the duty to pay the tax as "liability," which is much clearer.

Incidence is concerned with who is ultimately to bear the burden of the tax. So, for example, an executor may be under a duty to pay the tax to the Revenue. He then looks to the rules of incidence to see against what beneficial interests under the will he is to charge it.

LIABILITY

The following persons may, in various circumstances, be liable to pay the tax: transferor, transferee, trustee, beneficiary, settlor, personal representative.

The details are set out mainly in section 25 of F.A. 1975.

For *lifetime transfers of unsettled property* the persons liable are: (a) the transferor and the transferee; and (b) so far as the tax is attributable to the value of any particular property, any person in whom the property is vested (whether beneficially or otherwise) at any time after the transfer or who at any such time is beneficially entitled to an interest in possession in the property; and (c) where by the chargeable transfer any property becomes comprised in a settlement, any person for whose benefit any of the property or income from it is applied.

For *transfers of settled property* the persons liable are: (a) the trustees of the settlement; and (b) any person entitled (whether beneficially or not) to an interest in possession in the settled property; and (c) any person for whose benefit any of the settled property or income from it is applied; and (d) where the chargeable transfer is made during the life of the settlor and the trustees are not for the time being resident in the United Kingdom, the settlor.

For *transfers on death* the persons liable are: (a) in respect of unsettled property and in respect of settled property being land in the United Kingdom which devolves upon them, the deceased's personal

296

representatives; and (b) in respect of settled property, the trustees; and (c) so far as the tax is attributable to the value of any particular property, any person in whom the property is vested (whether beneficially or otherwise) at any time after the death or who at any such time is beneficially entitled to an interest in possession in the property; and (d) so far as the tax is attributable to the value of any property which, immediately before the death, was comprised in a settlement, any person for whose benefit any of the property or income from it is applied after the death.

In any circumstances where two or more persons are liable for the same tax, each is liable to the Revenue for the whole of it. But, of course, the Revenue cannot get more tax than is due.

References in the above contexts to any property include references to any property directly or indirectly representing it. So one does not escape the tax charge merely by selling the original property and investing the proceeds in some other property. (For the tax position of the purchaser, see below on this page.)

Where a person dies within three years of having made a chargeable transfer so that extra tax becomes payable in respect of that transfer it is the transferee who is liable for the extra tax and not the transferor's estate.

Transfers between spouses

Where a transferor is liable for any tax and by another transfer of value made by him any property becomes the property of a person who at the time of both transfers was his spouse, that person is liable for so much of the tax as does not exceed the value of the property at the time of the other transfer: see F.A. 1975, s. 25 (8) and F.A. 1976, s. 119. These provisions are designed to stop up a rather crude avoidance device—namely, make a transfer of value to someone overseas and make also an exempt transfer of the rest of one's estate to one's spouse, and leave the Revenue to whistle for their money.

Exception of purchaser from liability

A purchaser of property is not liable for tax attributable to the value of the property purchased, unless the property is subject to an Inland Revenue charge (on which see p. 303, below) F.A. 1975, s. 26 (1).

Limitations of liability

There are limitations on the extent to which a person is liable for the tax. For instance, a personal representative is liable only to the extent of the assets he has received or might have received but for his own neglect or default. Somewhat similar limitations apply to trustees, beneficiaries and transferees. See section 27.

Primary and secondary liability

For a lifetime transfer of unsettled property the transferor is primarily liable, and for settled property the trustees are primarily liable. In either case, other persons are only secondarily liable, that is, they are liable only if the tax remains unpaid after it ought to have been paid. In a case where any part of the value transferred is attributable to the tax on it, a person secondarily liable shall be liable to no greater extent than he would have been had the value transferred been reduced by the tax remaining unpaid: see section 27 (6). Suppose A (who has made no previous chargeable transfers) makes a gross transfer of £50,000 to B. The tax is £2,375. If A pays no tax at all, B becomes liable to pay tax on £47,625 (which is the net equivalent of £50,000 gross) for which the tax works out at £2,078. If A pays (say) £1,000 tax, B becomes liable to pay tax on £48,625 (*i.e.* on £50,000 less £1,375 tax remaining unpaid) with credit for the £1,000 tax already paid by A. So B has to pay £1,203 in tax.

INCIDENCE

We now come to the question of who is to bear the ultimate burden of the tax, bearing in mind that the person who pays the tax may not be the person on whom the burden should fall.

Problems of incidence are most acute in relation to tax arising on death.

Prima facie, each item of property comprised in a person's estate at death carries its own burden of tax.

But this prima facie rule can be displaced by provisions in the will. Thus if T (testator) leaves certain property to D (donee) "free of capital transfer tax" and gives to R (residuary beneficiary) the residue of his estate, that provision throws the burden of tax which would otherwise fall on the property given to D on to the residue, so that the tax burden is borne by R.

Specific rules are laid down by Part III (paragraphs 16 to 23) of Schedule 6 to the Finance Act 1975, as amended by the Finance Act 1976. The problems are, as mentioned above, most acute on the occasion of a death, and especially where a person dies leaving legacies and residue partially taxable and partially exempt.

The following explanation is based[1] on a Press Notice issued by the

---

[1] With the permission of the Controller of Her Majesty's Stationery Office.

Inland Revenue on April 15, 1976, and printed (for example) in [1976] B.T.R. at p. 414. But I have up-dated the tax rates.

The main problem is the determining of the chargeable amount of the specific gifts which do not bear their own tax and hence the amount of the residue. Suppose T dies, leaving an estate of £200,000. He leaves a legacy of £40,000 to his son and one of £10,000 to his nephew, providing in each case that the tax is to be borne out of residue. He leaves the residue to his widow and daughter equally. So there are two tax-free specific gifts and a residue partially exempt (part to widow) and partially taxable (part to daughter). Let us suppose that T has made no previous chargeable transfers. The chargeable amount of the "tax-free" specific gifts is determined by going through the following stages.

(1) The gifts (£50,000 tax free) are grossed up at the rate of tax which would be appropriate if they alone comprised the transfer in question. The legacies when grossed up come to £56,786, on which the tax would be £6,786.

(2) By reference to the gross figure so obtained, the exempt and chargeable parts of the transfer are calculated. On that basis the residue would be £143,214. Half of this (£71,607) would be exempt, so that for the purpose of this stage the chargeable part would be £200,000 minus £71,607 = £128,393.

(3) The gifts (at their original net value) are grossed up again by reference to the chargeable part of the transfer ascertained at (2). The tax on £128,393 would be £37,447. That produces a rate of 29.17 per cent. At this rate of tax £50,000 grossed up comes to £70,591.

(4) The exempt and chargeable parts of the transfer are finally recalculated by reference to the gross figure ascertained at (3). On that basis the residue is £129,409 (i.e. £200,000 less £70,591). Half of this (£64,704) would be exempt, so that the chargeable part would be £200,000 minus £64,704 = £135,296. Tax on this sum is £41,163.

This is where the Revenue's Press Notice stops. But one still has to make some further calculations in order to attribute the tax to the legacies and to the daughter's share of residue.

What rate of tax does (4) throw up? The rate is

$$\frac{41,163}{135,296} \times 100 = 30.42 \text{ per cent.}$$

One next has to apply this rate to the gross figure found for the legacies in (3). £70,591 at 30.42 per cent. = £21,473. So the residue is £128,527 (i.e. £200,00 minus the legacies (£50,000) and minus the tax attributable to them (£21,473). The widow's half of the residue (£64,264) is exempt. Take the daughter's half as being £64,263. To

calculate the daughter's net share one has to apply the tax rate of
30.42 per cent., not to £64,263, but to the *notional* figure found in
(4), namely £64,704. Applying 30.42 per cent. to £64,704 produces
£19,682. So what the daughter actually gets is £44,581, being
£64,263 minus £19,682.

In summary what everybody gets is this:

Son	£40,000
Nephew	£10,000
Daughter	£44,581
Widow	£64,264
Revenue	£41,155
	£200,000

The Revenue's share is made up of £21,473 attributable to the
legacies and £19,682 attributable to the daughter's share (non-
exempt) of the residue.

The outcome of the whole exercise is that the legatees (as directed
by the will) bear none of the tax burden. But the tax attributable to
the legacies has got to come from somewhere, and the only fund it can
come from is the residue. Putting it more strictly, the residue is what is
left after paying the legacies and their related tax. The widow is
entitled to half the residue as so computed. In a world without tax the
widow would have got £75,000. In fact she gets £64,264. So she has
borne a tax burden of £10,736. That is half the tax attributable to the
legacies (*i.e.* half of £21,473 to the nearest pound). The daughter
bears the burden of half the tax related to the legacies and the whole
of the tax related to the non-exempt part of the residue. In a no-tax
world the daughter would have got £75,000. In fact she gets £44,581.
She has borne a tax burden of £30,419. This is made up of half the tax
related to the legacies (*i.e.* £10,737 to the nearest pound) plus the
whole of the tax related to the non-exempt part of the residue (*i.e.*
£19,682).

If in the above example the daughter had been left out of the will
and the whole of the residue had been exempt by being left to the
widow, only stage (1) of the four stages stated above would have been
needed. The son would have got £40,000 and the nephew £10,000
and the tax would have been £6,786. The widow would have got what
was left, namely £143,214.

CHAPTER 29

ADMINISTRATION AND COLLECTION

Paragraph 1 of Schedule 4 to the Finance Act 1975 announces that capital transfer tax "shall be under the care and management of the Board" (*i.e.* the Commissioners of Inland Revenue). The rest of Schedule 4 provides detailed rules concerning the administration and collection of the tax.

DELIVERY OF AN ACCOUNT: PARA. 2

The personal representatives of a deceased person are under a duty to deliver an account to the Revenue specifying to the best of their knowledge and belief all relevant property and its value. And a similar duty rests on a transferor and a trustee of a settlement concerning a life-time transfer.

Personal representatives must deliver their account within 12 months from the end of the month in which the death occurs or within three months of the time when they first acted (if this period expires later).

Any other person must deliver his account within 12 months from the end of the month in which the transfer took place, or (if it expires later) the period of three months from the date on which he first became liable for tax. (There are special rules about conditionally exempt works of art, etc., and about timber.)

Personal representatives cannot get probate until they have paid the tax, and they cannot sell any of the estate assets (so as to get cash with which to pay the tax) until they have got probate. That looks like a vicious circle. But the problem can be overcome. The personal representatives can submit a provisional account and pay tax on that, then get probate, then sell off some of the estate assets, then submit a corrective or supplementary account and pay tax on that.

RETURNS BY CERTAIN PERSONS ACTING FOR SETTLORS: PARA. 4

There is a special provision concerning overseas settlements. Where any person, in the course of a trade or profession (other than the profession of a barrister) has been concerned with the making, after March 26, 1974, of a settlement and knows or has reason to believe that the settlor was domiciled in the United Kingdom and that the

301

trustees of the settlement are not or will not be resident in the United Kingdom, he must within three months of the making of the settlement make a return to the Board stating the names and addresses of the settlor and of the trustees of the settlement. This requirement does not apply to a settlement made by will nor to any other settlement if such a return has already been made by another person or if an account has been delivered in relation to it. The provision applies to (amongst others) solicitors and accountants. The point of the provision will become clearer to the reader when he has studied Chapter 30, below.

POWER TO REQUIRE INFORMATION AND INSPECT PROPERTY: PARA. 5 AND PARA. 11

The Board may by notice in writing require any person to furnish them within such time, not being less than 30 days, as may be specified in the notice with such information as the Board may require for the purposes of capital transfer tax. The notice may be combined with a notice relating to income tax. Legal professional privilege is protected except that a solicitor (not a barrister) can be required to disclose the name and address of his client and (in certain circumstances relating to an overseas client) the names and addresses of his client's clients in the United Kingdom.

If the Board authorise any person to inspect any property for the purpose of ascertaining its value for the purposes of capital transfer tax the person having the custody or possession of that property shall permit him to inspect it at such reasonable times as the Board may consider necessary.

ASSESSMENT AND APPEALS: PARAS. 6 TO 10

Instead of the word "assessment" which is the technical term applying to income tax, capital gains tax and corporation tax, the term used in relation to capital transfer tax is "determination." The Board make a determination and then serve a notice of determination.

Appeals (which must be made within 30 days of service of notice of determination) go to the Special Commissioners except in two cases as follows. (1) Where it is so agreed between the appellant and the Board, or where the High Court (on an application made by the appellant) is satisfied that the matters to be decided are likely to be substantially confined to questions of law and gives leave, the appeal goes to the High Court direct, thus cutting out the Special Commissioner stage. (2) Any question as to the value of land in the United Kingdom must be determined by the appropriate Lands Tribunal.

The procedure before the Special Commissioners is similar to that in relation to other taxes.

Appeal lies from the Special Commissioners to the High Court on a point of law only. The appeal is by way of Case Stated, which must be applied for by written request to the Special Commissioners within 30 days of their determination.[1]

PAYMENT OF TAX: PARA. 12 ET SEQ.

In general capital transfer tax becomes due six months after the end of the month in which the chargeable transfer was made, or, in the case of a transfer made after April 5 and before October 1 in any year otherwise than on death, at the end of April in the next year. So in many instances tax is due before the account is due.

Tax which is due and unpaid attracts interest at 6 per cent. on death transfers and at 9 per cent. in other cases, and there is no income tax relief for the interest payments. Where there has been an overpayment of tax the repayment by the Revenue carries interest (at the same rates as above) from the date on which the overpayment was made, and this interest is not subject to income tax.

In certain circumstances the tax can be paid by instalments. This facility applies only where the tax is attributable to certain kinds of property: land, controlling shares or securities; other shares or securities which are unquoted and in respect of which certain detailed conditions are satisfied; a business or an interest in a business to the extent of its net value (as defined).[2]

The instalment provisions apply to transfers on death. They also apply, with certain modifications, to lifetime transfers but only if either (a) the tax is borne by the person benefiting from the transfer or (b) the property is settled property and remains in the settlement after the transfer.

In general interest is payable on instalments from the date on which the first instalment is due. But in some cases (detailed in paragraph 16 of Schedule 4) there can be interest-free instalments, with a ceiling of £250,000 placed on the total value on which instalments may be interest-free.

INLAND REVENUE CHARGE FOR UNPAID TAX: PARAS. 20 AND 21

The word "charge" in this context is being used in the same sense in which a mortgage is a charge. Paragraph 20 automatically imposes an

---

[1] There is no mention of having to express dissatisfaction! (See p. 30, above.)

[2] Rather special instalment provisions apply to timber in certain circumstances.

Inland Revenue charge on all property included in a chargeable transfer and, in the case of settled property, on any property included in the settlement. The holder of the property can thus be liable for the tax. On a transfer on death the charge does not apply to personal or movable property in the United Kingdom. Personal property here includes leaseholds and undivided shares in land held on trust for sale (whether statutory or not). A bona fide purchaser without notice is not subject to the charge; where this is the case the charge attaches to the proceeds of sale.

CHAPTER 30

FOREIGN ASPECTS

The basic approach of the capital transfer tax legislation to what one might call "the foreign problem" is by means of the concept of "excluded property."

We have seen in Chapter 23 and in Chapter 27 that the legislation has used that concept in dealing with the reversionary interest problem.

Now we meet the concept again, but this time in connection with foreignness. The effect of declaring any property to be excluded property is that the property is exempt from the tax.

Unsettled property situated outside the United Kingdom is excluded property if the person beneficially entitled to it is an individual domiciled outside the United Kingdom: F.A. 1975, s. 24 (2).

Where property comprised in a settlement is situated outside the United Kingdom, the property (but not a reversionary interest in the property) is excluded property unless the settlor was domiciled in the United Kingdom at the time the settlement was made: F.A. 1975, Sched. 5, para. 2 (1).

A reversionary interest in settled property situated outside the United Kingdom is excluded property if the person beneficially entitled to it is an individual domiciled outside the United Kingdom: F.A. 1975, Sched. 5, para. 2, applying section 24 (2).

It will be seen that a reversionary interest is subject to the same rule as is unsettled property, and that in both these cases exclusion depends on *the individual who is beneficially entitled* having a foreign domicile. In sharp contrast is the rule for settled property, in which case exclusion depends on *the settlor* having a foreign domicile at the time of the making of the settlement.

As well as these general rules, there are three special instances of property with a foreign element being designated as excluded property as we saw in Chapter 24, "Exemptions and Reliefs." These relate to certain Government securities while in foreign ownership, certain savings by persons domiciled in the Channel Islands or Isle of Man, and visiting forces, etc.

Meaning of "Domicile"

The ordinary legal meaning of "domicile" was discussed at p. 160, above. For capital transfer tax purposes that ordinary meaning applies but also, by F.A. 1975, s. 45, certain persons who are not (within the ordinary meaning) domiciled in the United Kingdom are treated as domiciled in the United Kingdom at any time (referred to in the section as "the relevant time").[1] This rule applies to a person in any of the following circumstances:

(1) that he was domiciled in the United Kingdom on or after December 10, 1974 and within the three years immediately preceding the relevant time;

(2) that he was resident in the United Kingdom on or after December 10, 1974 and in not less than 17 of the 20 years of assessment ending with the year of assessment in which the relevant time falls;

(3) that he has, since December 10. 1974, become and has remained domiciled in the Islands (the Channel Islands and the Isle of Man) and, immediately before becoming domiciled there, he was domiciled in the United Kingdom.

Point (3) above is modified somewhat by F.A. 1977, s. 49, in respect of earned income from employment or (with exceptions) from self-employment. Subject to those modifications a United Kingdom–domiciled person can *never* escape (fiscally speaking) to the Islands. Points (1) and (2) above do permit escape elsewhere, but have the effect of imposing a three-year waiting period.

Section 45 applies generally throughout the legislation, but there are three circumstances where it is left out of account: in determining whether property comprised in a settlement which became so comprised *before December 10, 1974* is excluded property (per F.A. 1975, Sched. 5, para. 2 (2)); in determining foreign ownership of free-of-tax Government securities (Sched. 7, para. 3); and in determining domicile in respect of savings by persons domiciled in the Islands (Sched. 7, para. 5).

Double taxation relief

Provision is made in F.A. 1975, Sched. 7 for double taxation conventions (paragraph 7) and for unilateral relief against double taxation by way of credit (paragraph 8).

Other foreign aspects

Three points require to be mentioned here.

In regard to liabilities (see Chapter 25, above) there are special rules about debts due to foreign residents: F.A. 1975, Sched. 10, para. 3.

---

[1] Meaning the date in relation to which the question of domicile arises; *e.g.* the date of a transfer.

In determining the value transferred on a death an allowance is made, not exceeding 5 per cent. of the value, for the extra expense of administering or realising foreign property: F.A. 1975, Sched. 10, para. 9 (1) (*d*).

There is a limit of £25,000 on the spouse exemption where the transferor spouse is domiciled in the United Kingdom and the recipient spouse is domiciled abroad: F.A. 1975, Sched. 6, para. 1 (2). (See p. 247, above.)

Part Six

DEVELOPMENT LAND TAX

CHAPTER 31

DEVELOPMENT LAND TAX

INTRODUCTION

It is a view widely, but not universally, held that justice requires that gains which accrue to a person from the development value of land should be passed to the community.

Since 1947 (and before) various attempts have been made by governments to put this idea into legislative and practicable form. We have had "development charge," "betterment levy," "development gains tax." Now we have Development Land Tax. This tax was brought in by the Development Land Tax Act 1976. This Act was intended by the Labour Government as a companion to the Community Land Act 1975, but that Act (1975) was marked down for repeal by the following Conservative Government.

The Labour Government's White Paper entitled *Land* (Cmnd. 5730, September 1974) stated two objectives: (a) to establish a permanent means to enable the community to control the development of land in accordance with its needs and priorities, and (b) to establish a permanent means to restore to the community the increase in land values arising from its efforts. The Community Land Act 1975 was concerned with the first of those objectives. The Development Land Tax Act 1976 was concerned with the second objective.

In this chapter Development Land Tax will be called DLT, and all references, except where otherwise stated, are to the Development Land Tax Act 1976 (D.L.T.A.).

The basic principle of DLT is that it is a tax on the "realised development value" which accrues as a consequence of the grant of planning permission.

Development value may be realised either by an actual disposal or by a deemed disposal, that is, the commencement of a "project of material development."

In either of those circumstances (so the thinking goes) the owner of the land gets a kind of windfall.

Putting it very broadly, the realised development value is the amount by which the net proceeds of the disposal exceed the current use value.

The first £50,000 of realised development value accruing to any

311

person in a financial year is exempt from the tax. The rate of the tax is 60 per cent.

DLT interacts to some extent with other taxes—income tax, capital gains tax, corporation tax and capital transfer tax. There are elaborate provisions in the D.L.T.A. which, broadly speaking, are aimed at separating that part of a transaction which concerns realised development value and taxing that part under DLT and leaving the other aspects of the transaction to be taxed by the other taxes.

DLT does, of course, have some resemblances to capital gains tax, and it uses some of the same devices, including the notion of "disposal and immediate re-acquisition." But one must be on one's guard, because as well as the resemblances there are many subtle differences in the mechanics of the two taxes.

OCCASIONS OF CHARGE

The tax charge depends on there being a disposal of an interest in land in the United Kingdom irrespective of whether the disponer is or is not resident in the United Kingdom. A disposal may be either an actual disposal or a deemed disposal.

Actual disposal

The term "disposal" is not defined. The simplest case of all would be the sale of land. A gift of land is not a chargeable event, not because a gift is not a disposal but because the tax is levied on the realised development value which accrues to a person on a disposal, and on a gift there is no realisation. (Notice that we have immediately come up against a very strong difference from capital gains tax.)

"Interest in land" is defined in section 46 to mean "any estate or interest in land, any right in or over land or affecting the use or disposition of land, and any right to obtain such an estate, interest or right from another which is conditional on the other's ability to grant the estate, interest or right in question." So it would include (amongst other things) a fee simple, a lease, a sub-lease, an agreement for a lease, an easement, and a restrictive covenant. It does not include the interest of a mortgagee.

"Disposal" includes a part disposal. There are two kinds of part disposal. First a part disposal may be the grant of an interest less than the owner's interest, such as the grant by the fee simple owner of a lease of the whole of his land. Secondly, a part disposal may be the grant of an interest equal in status to the owner's interest, but in part only of his land, such as the sale, by the owner of fields X and Y, of field X.

Deemed disposal

Section 2 (1) says this: "Immediately before a project of material development is begun on any land, every major interest then subsisting in that land shall be deemed for the purposes of this Act to be disposed of for a consideration equal to its market value at that time and to be immediately reacquired at that value."

One can see at a glance the basic point of this. If one starts building, with planning permission, on a plot of unbuilt-on land, one is, in effect, realising the development value of the land. But in order to understand the point more fully, we need to know what is "material development," when does a project "begin," and what is a "major interest."

"Material development" (see section 7 (7)) means any development other than that for which planning permission is granted under a Town and Country Planning general development order and other than development which is excluded from being material by Part II of Schedule 4 of the D.L.T.A. To give one example, the enlargement of a building by not more than one-tenth of its cubic content is not material development.

The answer to the question "When does a project begin?" is to be found in Schedule 1 to the D.L.T.A. It shall be taken to be begun at the time when any specified operation in the project is begun. So, for example, the time at which the digging of a trench which is to contain the foundations of a building is begun marks the beginning of a project.

A "major interest" is any interest in land except (a) a reversion on a lease with an unexpired term of more than 35 years and without a rent review clause, and (b) any interest which has a market value of less than £5,000 and which does not confer a right to possession. An example would be an easement.

COMPUTATION

The tax is charged on the realised development value. The realised development value, in the case of an actual disposal, is the amount by which the proceeds of the disposal (net of the incidental costs of the disposal) exceed the relevant base value. In the case of a deemed disposal, the realised development value is the amount by which the market value of the interest in the land exceeds the relevant base value. See section 4.

There are three alternative base values, called base A, base B and base C. The relevant base value in any particular case is whichever of the three alternatives is the highest: section 5. This provision is, of course, favourable to the taxpayer, because the higher the base value the lower the excess and the lower the tax.

Base A is the cost of acquisition *plus* expenditure (if any) on relevant improvements and *plus* the increase in current use value from the date of acquisition or from April 6, 1965 (if that is later). A *"special addition"* is included in the calculation of Base A in the following circumstances: see section 6. If the acquisition was before September 13, 1974, the special addition is 15 per cent. of the acquisition cost for each year of ownership subject to a maximum of four years. If the acquisition was before May 1, 1977 the special addition is 10 per cent. for each year of ownership, subject to the same maximum (four years). A *"further addition"* is also included in base A provided that, in any particular case, the calculation of base A has included both expenditure on relevant improvements and the special addition. The further addition is arrived at by the formula

$$RI \times \frac{A}{C}$$

RI is the expenditure on relevant improvements; A is the special addition; C is the acquisition cost.

Base B is 110 per cent. of current use value *plus* 110 per cent. of any expenditure on relevant improvements.

Base C is 110 per cent. of the acquisition cost *plus* 110 per cent. of any expenditure on improvements.

Notice that there is a distinction between "improvements" and "relevant improvements." Improvements are relevant improvements only to the extent that they increase the development value (as distinct from the current use value).

Devolution on death

Devolution on death is not a disposal: section 9. The *acquisition* by the deceased and his *expenditure* is treated as being that of the personal representatives. A charge to DLT, calculated on that footing, arises if the personal representatives sell the land in the course of administering the estate. If, on the other hand, the personal representatives vest the land in a legatee, that vesting is treated as an acquisition (by the legatee) by gift (on which see the next heading below).

Acquisition by gift

The acquisition of an interest in land by way of gift is not a chargeable event (see p. 312, above). When the donee comes to sell the land, the charge to DLT is computed on the basis of the donor's acquisition cost and expenditure. See section 10.

EXEMPTIONS AND DEFERMENTS

There are a number of exemptions and deferments, as follows.

Public bodies

Bodies such as local authorities, police authorities and fire authorities are completely exempt from DLT: section 11. Statutory undertakers are entitled to a deferment of DLT until they come to dispose of their interest in land: section 23. The Housing Corporation and certain Housing Associations are entitled to a measure of exemption or deferment: for details see section 26.

Private residences

By section 14 realised development value accruing to an individual on the disposal of his private residence is exempt from DLT if the residence is that individual's only or main residence. The individual must have owned it for six months or more, and it must have been his only or main residence during at least one year out of the last two years before the disposal or (if his ownership has been for less than two years) during at least half the period of his ownership. The exemption also applies to disposals by personal representatives within two years of the death of a person who would have satisfied the conditions of exemption (except that he need not have satisfied the requirement of a minimum six months' occupation).

Houses built for owner-occupation

The building of a dwelling-house for owner-occupation is not a deemed disposal subject to the following conditions: section 15. The person building the house must have owned the land on September 12, 1974, and the house must be intended for occupation by himself or a dependent relative or an adult member of his family. The exemption can cover two such houses provided that one of them is built on land within the curtilage of a dwelling-house which was owned and occupied by the owner on September 12, 1974.

Land held as stock in trade

If land was held on September 12, 1974, by an individual or a company as stock in trade there is an exemption from DLT on the disposal of the land. The exemption extends only to the realised development value which is attributable to planning permission which existed at that time. If a more profitable planning permission has been granted since that date the realised development value attributable to that permission is not exempt. The benefit of the exemption passes on death or on gift to the recipient. See section 16.

Minerals

On a deemed disposal, any material development which includes the winning or working of minerals for which planning permission exists is exempt from DLT: section 17.

Projects begun within three years of acquisition

There is an exemption from DLT on a deemed disposal if the project of material development is begun within three years of the acquisition of the land and no significant amount of realised development value would have accrued had the project been begun immediately after the acquisition: section 18.

Development for industrial use

There is no immediate charge to DLT on a deemed disposal at the beginning of a project of material development if the project relates to a building or other land to be used for the industrial purposes of a person's trade. There is a deferment of the charge until either the land is actually disposed of or the industrial purposes cease: section 19.

Companies

Companies are, of course, subject to DLT. There are special arrangements (exemptions, in effect) where one company in a group of companies makes a disposal to another member of the group or where a disposal takes place in the course of company amalgamations or reconstructions: sections 20 and 22. Section 21 deals with the situation which arises when a company ceases to be a member of a group.

Charities

There is exemption from DLT in respect of a disposal by a charity if the land in question was held by it (or by another charity) on September 12, 1974, but there is a deferred charge to the tax which bites if the body ceases to be a charity. As regards land acquired by a charity after September 12, 1974, a disposal will normally be a chargeable event. But on a deemed disposal arising from the development of the land for the charity's use there is no immediate charge to DLT; the liability is deferred until the land is actually disposed of or until the land ceases to be used for charitable purposes. See sections 24 and 25.

TRUSTS, SETTLED PROPERTY, PARTNERSHIPS, MORTGAGEES AND LIQUIDATORS

This heading is the cross-heading in the D.L.T.A. to sections 28 to 33.

Bare trusts and settled property

A bare trust exists where an interest in land is held on trust for a person absolutely entitled as against the trustee or for a person who would be so entitled but for being an infant or other person under disability. Where there is a bare trust the acts of the trustees are treated as being the acts of the person so entitled. Two or more persons may be so entitled as joint tenants, tenants in common or coparceners. The most likely occasion for the coming into existence of a bare trust is when a person becomes absolutely entitled to an interest in land which was previously settled property. When such a person disposes of his interest it is he who is liable to DLT (if, of course, there is a realisation of development value).

An interest in land held on trust other than a bare trust is settled property. The trustees (and not the beneficiaries) are the chargeable persons and they are treated as a single and continuing body of persons. By virtue of the Interpretation Act 1978[1] they are treated as *a* person. This is important in relation to the £50,000 exemption (section 12: see p. 311, above). Where the land is "settled land" within the meaning of the Settled Land Act 1925, the "single and continuing body" of persons comprises the trustees of the settlement *and* the tenant for life or statutory owner for the time being.

Partnerships

Partnership dealings are treated as dealings by the partners and not by the firm as such and DLT is charged on them separately: section 31. But this does not apply for the purpose of the £50,000 exemption; for this purpose the firm is treated as a single person.

Mortgagees, liquidators, etc.

Special rules apply to mortgagees and other creditors, and to liquidators and trustees in bankruptcy, etc.

DEDUCTION, ADMINISTRATION AND COLLECTION

Section 39 provides that where an interest in land is disposed of to an exempt body (such as a local authority) that body must on paying any amount by way of consideration for the disposal make a deduction on account of DLT, and the chargeable person is treated as having paid an amount of DLT equal to the deduction. Details are in Schedule 7.

Section 40 provides that a person who buys development land (as defined) for £50,000 or more from a non-resident must make a deduction of one-half the consideration and remit the amount deducted to the Revenue. In addition to section 40, there is a statutory instrument dealing with this matter; DLT (Disposals by Non-Residents) Regulations 1976 (S.I. 1976 No. 1190). There is a procedure whereby a non-resident vendor can get a clearance certificate

---

[1] In Schedule 1 to the Interpretation Act 1978 "Person" is defined to include "a body of persons corporate or unincorporate."

from the Revenue (*e.g.* if he has a high base value) directing that some lesser deduction (or no deduction at all) shall be made by the purchaser.

DLT is under the care and management of the Board (the Commissioners of Inland Revenue). Details are in Schedule 8, which, amongst other things, amends the Taxes Management Act 1970, so as to accommodate DLT. Appeals go to the Special Commissioners except that matters of valuation go to the Lands Tribunal, and matters relating to exemptions for private residences and for houses built for owner-occupation go to the General Commissioners. The normal time-limit (subject to fraud, wilful default or neglect) for making assessments is six years from the end of the financial year in which the disposal occurred. Not surprisingly, chargeable persons are required to give notice of a disposal to the Revenue. Notice of an actual disposal must be given within one year, and notice of a deemed disposal must be given not earlier than 60 days before the date of the beginning of a project of material development and not later than 30 days after that date.

Payment of DLT is due on the "reckonable date" (which is three months after the disposal) or, if later, 30 days after the issue of a notice of assessment.

In some circumstances there is a right to pay the tax by instalments; either eight yearly instalments or 16 half-yearly instalments. This right exists in the case of (a) a deemed (as distinct from an actual) disposal, and (b) a part-disposal by way of the grant of a lease at a rent not exceeding the commercial rent, and (c) the triggering (otherwise than by disposal) of a deferred liability. In these cases interest only runs from the date when each instalment becomes due. Besides the three special cases mentioned above, the Revenue may allow payment of tax by instalments where the consideration for a disposal is payable by instalments and the chargeable person satisfies the Board that he would otherwise suffer undue hardship. In this case, unlike the other three cases mentioned above, interest runs on the total consideration from the reckonable date. Where a person transfers his business to a company and as part of that transfer he disposes of an interest in land, he may postpone payment of DLT for up to eight years.

Apart from the special cases of instalment payments mentioned above, the general rule for interest on DLT is that it runs from the reckonable date until payment of the tax. The rate of interest is 6 per cent. The Revenue issued a sad little Press Notice on September 7, 1978[2] saying: "The DLT legislation provides for interest to be at the

---

[2] Printed in, for example, [1978] B.T.R. at p. 439.

'prescribed' rate. The Board are advised that for DLT purposes this rate is 6 per cent. (not, as was intended, the rate currently applying for other taxes). Consequently a 6 per cent. rate will be applied for the time being." (The rate for other taxes is currently 9 per cent.).

INTERACTION OF DLT WITH OTHER TAXES

Section 34 and Schedule 6 lay down detailed rules concerning the interaction of DLT with other taxes. This matter was touched on at page 312, above. There are two basic principles. First, that part of a transaction which throws up realised development value and so attracts DLT is not to be charged also to other taxes. Second, if other taxes have been paid in the preceding 12 years, then, to the extent that those other taxes were in respect of development value, the amounts of those other taxes are credited against DLT. Where the other taxes were income tax, corporation tax and capital gains tax, a proportion of the tax paid may be set off against the subsequent DLT liability. Where the other tax concerned was capital transfer tax, a proportion of that tax may be deducted from the chargeable realised development value accruing on a subsequent DLT disposal.

PART SEVEN

STAMP DUTIES

CHAPTER 32

STAMP DUTIES

GENERAL SURVEY

The law relating to stamp duties was consolidated by two Acts passed in 1891: the Stamp Duties Management Act 1891 and the Stamp Act 1891.[1] Those Acts have been amended and supplemented by subsequent Finance Acts.

The Stamp Duties Management Act 1891 deals, not surprisingly, with the administration of stamp duties. Section 1 places stamp duties under the care and management of the Commissioners of Inland Revenue. The day-to-day administration is delegated to the Controller of Stamps.

The Stamp Act 1891 is in three parts. Part I contains the charging section (section 1) which charges duty on the instruments set forth in the First Schedule to the Act. Part I also contains the provisions applicable to the stamping of instruments generally. Part II explains and amplifies some of the particular heads of charge in the First Schedule. Part III contains miscellaneous supplemental provisions. "Instrument" is not (in a strict sense) defined, but section 122 declares that: "The expression 'instrument' includes every written document." In the First Schedule one finds a great number of particular instruments set out in alphabetical order, and against each is stated the duty or duties to be charged on it. These are the "Heads of Charge."

Each instrument is charged either to *fixed duty* or to *ad valorem duty* (meaning "according to the value"). A fixed duty does not vary according to the amount stated in the instrument; an *ad valorem* duty does so vary. Fixed duties tend to be "sweeping-up" duties. For example, a "deed of any kind whatsoever, not described in this schedule" is charged to a fixed duty of 50p.

An instrument which is liable to duty has to be taken (or posted) to a Stamp Office, where a stamp is *impressed* upon it by means of a die (usually red). There is one exceptional instrument, namely a contract note,[2] which may be stamped otherwise than by an impressed stamp: it may instead be stamped with an adhesive stamp, but it must be an

---

[1] *Cf.* the two Acts consolidating the enactments relating to income tax etc. passed in 1970: see p. 21, above.

[2] This is a note sent by a stockbroker advising his client that a sale or purchase has been made.

"appropriated" stamp. An "appropriated" stamp is one which bears words on its face which limits its use to a particular description of instrument. So ordinary postage stamps are not (now) valid for any stamp duty purpose.

In many circumstances it is necessary or desirable to get a *denoting stamp*. When the duty on an instrument depends in any manner on the duty paid on another instrument, then on production of both instruments to the Stamp Office the fact of payment of duty on the latter instrument will be denoted on the former instrument by a blue impressed stamp. There are two kinds of denoting stamp.

The first kind is a *duplicate denoting stamp*. The duplicate or counterpart of an instrument is not duly stamped unless either it is stamped as an original or it is denoted. There is one exception to this: the counterpart of a lease does not need to be denoted if it is not executed by the lessor. As well as the denoting stamp, a duplicate or counterpart must bear a fixed stamp of 50p (or, if the stamp on the original is less than 50p, then the same stamp as on the original).

The second kind is a *duty paid denoting stamp*. This is used (a) on a conveyance, if ad valorem duty has already been paid on the agreement for sale, and (b) on a lease, if ad valorem duty has already been paid on the agreement for the lease. In the case of a conveyance ((a) above) an alternative procedure is for the Stamp Office to transfer the *ad valorem* duty to the conveyance.[3]

There are a number of basic principles, or leading ideas, in stamp duty law, and the most basic principle of all is that the duty is charged on *instruments* (documents). If there is no document there is no duty. If a transaction can be carried out by spoken words or by conduct, there need be no document and consequently no duty. To take an absolutely straightforward example, the sale or gift of a chattel can be made entirely validly by delivery of the chattel to the transferee.

Other basic principles are as follows.

Duty is charged in accordance with the substance of an instrument, not its mere form.

If more than one instrument is written on the same paper (or other material) each must be separately stamped.

If one instrument contains (or relates to) "several distinct matters" it is to be stamped as if it were a separate instrument in respect of each of the matters. But it has been established by case law that "all that is required is that the instrument should be stamped for its leading and principal object, and that this stamp covers everything accessory to this object": (*Limmer Asphalte Paving Co.* v. *I.R.C.* (1872)). For

---

[3] This paragraph will become clearer when the reader has studied "Contracts for sale" and "Leases," below.

example, the stamp on a lease covers an option to purchase the reversion, but it does not cover an option to purchase *other* property.

If one transaction is effected by more than one instrument, only one *ad valorem* duty is charged. This is helpful in relation to the formation of a settlement, which is often effected in practice by two instruments.

If an instrument falls under more than one head of charge in the First Schedule, the Revenue can choose whichever head involves the most duty.

Ad valorem duty is payable on whatever sum may be calculable at the date of the instrument as the maximum consideration which *may* arise. This is called the "contingency principle." In *Coventry City Council* v. *I.R.C.* (1978) the corporation undertook to pay a yearly rent of £17,500 plus 8.142 per cent. of total development expenditure up to a maximum expenditure of £1,300,000. It was held that the Revenue had been correct in assessing the *ad valorem* duty on the basis that the rent *could* be £123,346, *i.e.* £17,500 plus 8.142 per cent. of £1,300,000.

Sanctions for the payment of duty

Payment of stamp duties is enforced (primarily) by an indirect means. The legislation makes unstamped instruments useless to the parties. Section 14 (4) of the Stamp Act 1891 provides that "an instrument executed in any part of the United Kingdom, or relating, wheresoever executed, to any property situate, or to any matter or thing done or to be done, in any part of the United Kingdom, shall not, except in criminal proceedings, be given in evidence, or be available for any purpose whatever, unless it is duly stamped...." This rule indirectly compels the stamping of, for example, conveyancing instruments. Because an unstamped instrument would be inadmissible as evidence of title a purchaser can insist that every instrument which forms a link in the vendor's title be duly stamped. And as regards registered land, the registrar will refuse to complete the transaction by registration if instruments are unstamped.

This basic idea is backed up in three ways. First, there are penalties for stamping out of time. Second, there are fines for some offences relating to stamp duty. For example, a company secretary can be fined if he registers a share transfer which is not properly stamped. Third, there are a few particular heads of charge under which the Revenue may sue for the duty in the High Court. An example is "capital duty": see page 332, below.

Adjudication

Stamping is not in itself conclusive that the instrument is *duly* stamped. But the Commissioners can be required to express their opinion whether an executed instrument is chargeable with any duty and, if so, with what amount it is chargeable. If the Commissioners are of opinion that the instrument is not chargeable with duty, it will be stamped "Adjudged not chargeable with any duty." If the Commissioners are of opinion that the instrument is chargeable, they will *assess* the duty. The instrument will then be stamped in accordance with the assessment, and an adjudication stamp will be added bearing the words "adjudged duly stamped." An appeal can be made to the High Court against an assessment, by way of case stated. The appeal is heard by a judge of the Chancery Division.

In the case of some instruments, adjudication is compulsory in the sense that without adjudication the instrument is not duly stamped. An important example is a voluntary disposition: see below at page 328.

And there are a few instruments which, even if they have been adjudicated, are not duly stamped unless they are produced to the Commissioners and stamped with "a stamp denoting that the instrument has been so produced": F.A. 1931, s. 28. This is called a "produced stamp" or a "particulars delivered" stamp. The latter name derives from the fact that the Second Schedule to F.A. 1931 provides that a person producing to the Commissioners an instrument transferring land must produce with it a document giving certain particulars, including the consideration.[4] The point is to give the authorities information about land values. The rule applies to any transfer on sale of the fee simple of land; the grant of any lease of land for a term of seven or more years; and any transfer on sale of any such lease. (A similar rule applies to "bearer instruments," *e.g.* such stocks and shares as are transferable by delivery: F.A. 1963, s. 60.)

General exemptions

There are a number of instruments which are exempt from all stamp duties. The following are some of the more important examples: transfers of government stocks; transfers of ships; wills; instruments of apprenticeship; articles of clerkship to a solicitor; charterparties; contracts of employment; transfers of loan capital.[5]

Foreign element

The territorial limits of the Stamp Act 1891 are in effect laid down

---

[4] The Stamp Office has a form on which the particulars are to be set out. This is called the "LVA form" or the "PD form" or, more formally, "Stamps L(A) 451."

[5] "Loan capital" is defined in F.A. 1976, s. 126 (5). It comprises (a) capital raised by a U.K. company, "being capital which is borrowed, or has the character of borrowed money," and (b) stock or marketable securities issued by a Commonwealth government.

by section 14 (4). That subsection was cited on page 325, above. The effect is that stamp duty is charged (1) on instruments executed in the United Kingdom whatever they relate to, and (2) on instruments executed abroad which relate to "any property situate, or any matter or thing done or to be done" in the United Kingdom.

PARTICULAR INSTRUMENTS

We now turn to look separately at some of the more important heads of charge.

Conveyance or Transfer

This head of charge really contains two heads. Head (1) deals with "conveyance or transfer on sale of any property"; head (2) deals with "conveyance or transfer of any kind not hereinbefore described." Head (1) carries *ad valorem* duty whereas head (2) carries a fixed duty of 50p, so the distinction is of great practical importance. Also, head (1) links up with a number of other heads, notably a voluntary disposition, a contract for sale, and a transfer in contemplation of a sale (see below).

Conveyance or transfer on sale

This is head (1). It relates to any kind of property; personal property as well as real property; things in action as well as things in possession; shares as well as land.

But there must be a sale. So there must be consensus, a price in money[6] and a transfer of property (or, as in the case of a declaration of trust, a vesting of property).

A word must be said about the formation and dissolution of a partnership. A partnership agreement is chargeable to conveyance on sale duty in respect of any price paid by an incoming partner for his share, but not in respect of assets brought in by him as capital of the business. A dissolution agreement incurs conveyance on sale duty in respect of any price paid to the outgoing partner for his share of the business by the continuing partners. But this duty is not incurred if the sums paid to the outgoing partner come out of the assets of the business. This would be a "partition" and under that head of charge the duty would be a fixed duty of 50p.

Where conveyance on sale duty does apply the full rate of *ad valorem* duty is £1 for every £50 (or part thereof) of the amount or

---

[6] This has a wide meaning and includes the transfer of stock and the discharge of a debt. But an exchange or a partition is not a sale and is normally subject only to a fixed duty of 50p. In an exchange or partition of *real* property, if "equality" money exceeding £100 is paid, then *ad valorem* duty is payable on that: see Stamp Act 1891, s. 73.

value of the consideration. There are reduced rates where the consideration does not exceed £30,000, provided that the instrument has a "certificate of value" worded as follows: "It is hereby certified that the transaction hereby effected does not form part of a larger transaction or of a series of transactions in respect of which the amount or value or the aggregate amount or value of the consideration exceeds [£15,000 or £20,000 or £25,000 or £30,000 as the case may be]." The scale of reduced rates is this:

	Rate per £50 (or part thereof) of the consideration
Consideration £15,000 or under	nil
„ £20,000 or under	25p
„ £25,000 or under	50p
„ £30,000 or under	75p

None of these reduced rates apply to instruments which transfer stock or marketable securities.

There are some circumstances where the certificates of value and/ or the calculation of the consideration presents problems. An example is the common transaction whereby a person buys land under an arrangement that the purchaser will erect a building on the land or that the vendor will erect a building at the expense of the purchaser. In the former case (purchaser to build) the contract of sale and the building contract are not parts of a series of transactions (for the purposes of the certificate of value) unless they are so interlinked that, if the purchaser defaults on the building contract, he cannot enforce the contract for the sale of the land. In the latter case (vendor to build) the amount of the consideration (for the purposes of the certificate and the duty) depends on the state of the building at the date of the contract or conveyance. If the building has not been started the building price is not part of the consideration. If the building has been finished the whole cost is part of the consideration. If the building has been started but not finished the proportion of the building price attributable to the building as it stands should be included in the consideration. For further details see a statement issued by the Revenue in August 1957.[7]

Voluntary dispositions

After the introduction of estate duty by the Finance Act 1894 it became common to make voluntary dispositions of property as a

---

[7] See *Law Society's Gazette* (1957), pp. 450–1.

means of avoiding estate duty. "Voluntary" here means without consideration, so what we are talking about is gifts. Under the Stamp Act 1891 a voluntary disposition did not attract *ad valorem* duty, only a fixed duty of 10 shillings.

In 1910 this avoidance of stamp duty was stopped. The Finance (1909–10) Act 1910 provided, in section 74 (1), that "Any conveyance or transfer operating as a voluntary disposition *inter vivos* shall be chargeable with the like stamp duty as if it were a conveyance or transfer on sale, with the substitution in each case of the value of the property conveyed or transferred for the amount or value of the consideration for the sale. . . ." And section 74 (5) deals with the case where there is *some* consideration but it is inadequate. If A transfers to B for £15,000 property which is worth £25,000 the instrument will be treated as a voluntary disposition transferring property of the value of £25,000. The Revenue do not need to prove that a gift was *intended*; so a "bad bargain" suffices.

At one time the *ad valorem* duty could be avoided by including in the instrument a power of revocation. This device was stopped by F.A. 1965, s. 90 (5) which requires the property transferred to be valued without regard to any power of revocation. But if revocation in fact takes place within two years, the Commissioners will repay the appropriate amount of duty.

There are several exemptions from the voluntary disposition charge, of which perhaps the most important is a conveyance or transfer in consideration of marriage.

Contracts for sale

Section 59 of the Stamp Act 1891 deals with another possible avoidance device. In many circumstances a purchaser could be content with the vendor's contract *to sell* property to him without going on to take an actual conveyance or transfer. This would, if it were not for section 59, avoid conveyance on sale duty. The section was aimed particularly at the sale of a business. It provides that any contract or agreement for the sale of certain kinds of property shall be charged with *ad valorem* duty as if it were an actual conveyance on sale. The kinds of property caught by the section are as follows:

(1) any equitable estate or interest in any property whatsoever; or
(2) any (legal) estate or interest in any property *except*
    (a) land;
    (b) property locally situate out of the United Kingdom;
    (c) goods, wares or merchandise;
    (d) stocks and shares;
    (e) marketable securities;
    (f) ships or shares of ships.

Items of property which are caught by the section and are likely to be involved in the sale of a business are: goodwill, book debts, cash on deposit, patents, copyrights, "know-how," the benefit of pending contracts, tenant's fixtures, trade fixtures.[8]

There is still, however, considerable scope for saving duty on the sale of a business. For example, book debts need not be transferred. There can instead be a provision that the purchaser is to collect the book debts as the vendor's agent and apply the proceeds in discharging the vendor's liabilities. And where an unincorporated business is sold to a limited company it seems that duty may be avoided by first selling the business for cash by an oral contract and then using the cash to subscribe for shares: see *Spargo's case* (1873). But presumably if the transferor took that course he would not be entitled to roll-over relief for capital gains tax under the Capital Gains Tax Act 1979, s. 123; see p. 176, above.

Transfer in contemplation of sale

An avoidance device emerged in the 1960's of transferring property, *e.g.* shares, without a sale, but in contemplation of a sale in the future. This manoeuvre avoided conveyance on sale duty. The gap was stopped up by the Finance Act 1965, s. 90 (1): "... any instrument whereby property is conveyed or transferred to any person in contemplation of a sale of that property shall be treated ... as a conveyance or transfer on sale of that property for a consideration equal to the value of that property."

Exemptions from conveyance on sale duty

There are several exemptions of which the most important in practice are as follows.

RECONSTRUCTIONS OR AMALGAMATIONS OF COMPANIES. If, in connection with reconstruction or amalgamation, a company is formed or has its capital increased for the purpose of acquiring the whole or part of the undertaking of another company or of acquiring not less than 90 per cent. of the issued share capital of another company, then any instrument made in connection with the transfer of the undertaking or of the shares is exempt from conveyance on sale duty: F.A. 1927, s. 55 (as amended). The conditions for the exemption are very strict.

TRANSFERS BETWEEN ASSOCIATED COMPANIES. Exemption from conveyance on sale duty is given by F.A. 1930, s. 42 (as amended,

---

[8] The Stamp Office has a form which is designed to sort out the chargeable and non-chargeable items. The form is "Stamps/No. 22" and it is headed "Apportionment of Consideration under Agreement for Sale."

and as supplemented by F.A. 1967, s. 27) in respect of transfers between associated companies. The exemption is subject to strict conditions. Either one of the companies must own beneficially 90 per cent. or more of the issued share capital of the other, or another company must own beneficially 90 per cent. or more of the issued share capital of the transferor company and of the transferee company. Also, there must be no arrangement whereby the consideration for the transfer is to be provided or received by any person other than a company which is associated (in the sense set out above). And there must be no arrangement for the transferor and transferee companies to cease to be associated (in the above sense).

Reliefs from conveyance on sale duty

There are reduced rates of conveyance on sale duty (as distinct from complete exemption) for transfers to charities, and for transfers of stock or marketable securities to certain non-residents.

Conveyance of any other kind (Head (2))

We must now turn to look at Head (2) of "Conveyance or Transfer." This covers a "conveyance or transfer of any kind not hereinbefore described." It does not carry *ad valorem* duty, but only a fixed duty of 50p. To be within Head (2) the conveyance or transfer must be outside any other head of charge. So it must be a conveyance or transfer which is not "on sale," and not a voluntary disposition, and not a contract for sale, and not a transfer in contemplation of a sale.

If you look on the back of a stock (or share) transfer form, you will find nine examples of transfers coming within Head (2). One example is a transfer to a nominee; another example is a transfer by trustees to a beneficiary; another is a transfer to a legatee under a will.

Leases

Leases of land are charged to stamp duty under the heading in the First Schedule "Lease or Tack." (Tack is the Scottish equivalent of lease.) This head of charge applies only to leases of land; it does not apply to (for example) the hiring of chattels in consideration of periodical payments. Land, of course, includes buildings.

In general leases are charged to *ad valorem* duty. One important exception is a lease for a definite term less than a year of a furnished dwelling where the rent exceeds £250; in this instance there is a fixed duty of £1. (If the rent does not exceed £250 there is a nil rate: see at foot of Table, below.)

For other leases there is a charge on the premium (if any) *and* a charge on the rent.

The duty on the premium is *ad valorem* and is the same as conveyance on sale duty for the same amount, except that where the average rent does not exceed £150 per annum (and a certificate of value is included in the lease) reduced rates apply.

The duty on the rent is *ad valorem* and the main features are as follows:

Term	Rate per £50 (or part thereof) of the average rent per annum
(a) Not exceeding 7 years, *or indefinite*	50p
(b) Exceeding 7 years but not 35 years	£1
(c) Exceeding 35 years but not 100 years	£6
(d) Exceeding 100 years	£12

If the rent does not exceed £250 there is a nil rate for (a) and reduced rates for (b), (c) and (d).

Section 75 (1) of the Stamp Act 1891 provides that an *agreement for a lease* for any term not exceeding 35 years, or for any indefinite term, is to be charged with the same duty as if it were an actual lease. Notice that this rule does not apply to an agreement for a lease for a definite term exceeding 35 years. Such an agreement would attract only a 50p stamp under the head of "Deed" (if it were made by deed).

CAPITAL DUTY

"Capital duty" (as it is commonly called) was brought in (in place of some previously existing stamp duties) by the Finance Act 1973 (ss. 47 to 49 and Sched. 19). The purpose was to bring the United Kingdom into line with the requirements of European Community Law.

Capital duty is a stamp duty, and it is charged *ad valorem* at the rate of £1 for every £100 (or part of £100) of the amount on which duty is chargeable. That amount is, generally speaking, the actual value of the assets contributed by the members less the liabilities assumed by the company; except that if the nominal value of the shares is more, that nominal value is the chargeable amount.

The duty is levied on the occurrence of any "chargeable transaction" in relation to a "capital company" if that company falls within either of the two following conditions: (a) the place of effective management of the company is in Great Britain; or (b) the registered office of the company is in Great Britain but the place of its effective management is outside the member States (that is, the member States of the European Communities).

A "capital company" is one which falls within any of the following heads:

(1) a limited liability company or a limited partnership incorporated or formed in the United Kingdom;

(2) a company incorporated according to the law of another member State;

(3) any other corporation or body of persons whose shares can be dealt in on a stock exchange in a member state;

(4) any other corporation or body of persons operating for profit, whose members have the right to dispose of their shares to third parties without prior authorisation and whose liability is limited to the extent of their shares.

The *chargeable transactions* are as follows:

(1) The formation of a capital company. If the formation consists of the conversion into a capital company of a corporation or body of persons which was not previously a capital company the duty is charged on the actual value of the assets of any kind belonging to the capital company immediately after the conversion, less its liabilities at that time. (*Cf.* the general statement at p. 332, above.)

(2) An increase in (issued) capital by the contribution of assets of any kind.

(3) The conversion of an unlimited company into a limited company.

(4) The transfer to Great Britain of the registered office or the place of effective management of certain companies or bodies of persons.

There are two *exemptions* from capital duty (F.A. 1973, Sched. 19). Paragraph 9 of Schedule 19 exempts from the duty an increase in the issued capital of a capital company if it follows within four years of a reduction in nominal capital, provided that the reduction was "as a result of losses sustained." Paragraph 10 of Schedule 19 gives an exemption, subject to strict conditions, for a transaction whereby a capital company (a) acquires 75 per cent. of the issued share capital of another capital company or (b) acquires the whole or any part of the undertaking of another capital company. One could call this a "take-over" exemption.

Relation of capital duty with conveyance on sale duty

When a capital company is formed (or increases its capital) it will often be the case that a person makes a transfer of assets to the company in consideration of an issue of shares in the company. If it is a case of "take-over" of a capital company by another capital company, the "take-over" exemption from capital duty mentioned above may apply; if that exemption does not apply capital duty will be payable. It is very likely that conveyance on sale duty will also arise. There are two possibilities of exemption from conveyance on sale duty. First, there is the exemption contained in F.A. 1927, s. 55: see page 330, above. Second, there is an exemption in F.A. 1973, Sched. 19, para. 13. The section 55 exemption is a "take-over" exemption with very restricted operation. The paragraph 13 exemption, though not limited to "take-over" situations (and therefore available, for example, when an *individual* transfers assets to a capital company) is limited to certain types of property. The exemption does not apply if the assets transferred to the company are (a) stocks or securities, or (b) the whole or any part of an undertaking, or (c) any estate or interest in land.

So, where a capital company is formed (or increases its capital) there may well be a double charge to stamp duty—a charge to capital duty and a charge to conveyance on sale duty.

agency workers & dues 56

INDEX

335